Praise for

"*Burn It Down* is a Howard Bea... going to take this anymore' mani... ladies of show business, complet... redemption. . . . [Ryan] is a dogged and dedicated journalist."
—*New York Times*

"Essential reading for all viewers of TV and film. . . . Ryan's writing is passionate and personal, and I found *Burn It Down* to be a life-changing read." —NPR's Best Books of 2023

"Fascinating. Devastating. Important."
—Kerry Washington, actor, director, producer, and author of *Thicker Than Water: A Memoir*

"Dishy behind-the-scenes dispatches about popular TV series including *Lost, Saturday Night Live,* and *Sleepy Hollow* give the deeply reported book its fire, but Ryan tempers that flame with a call to improve the system—and some solid suggestions as to how that might be achieved."
—*Daily Beast*

"[A] breathless compendium of malfeasance, which provides a valuable service in giving voice to those who have long gone unheard."
—*Los Angeles Times*

"Film and television journalist and critic Ryan has written the kind of book the phrase 'searing indictment' was invented for: a straight-shooting, rigorously researched and documented exposé of Holly-wood's culture of abuse. . . . This powerful, angry, shocking, and important work should grip all readers interested in the truth about the entertainment industry." —*Booklist*

"Galvanizing. . . . She's had enough, and now she's lighting a match. . . . Ryan is more akin to Michaela Coel, the creator and star of 'I May Destroy You': personal, indignant, and unimpressed by 'big-swinging-dick' behavior. Ryan is also . . . hopeful."
—*The New Yorker*

"Ryan savvily presents Hollywood and the entertainment industry not just as the wellspring of your favorite movies and TV shows, but as a *workplace*—with all the workplace problems that are familiar across corporate America."

—*Fortune*

"Maureen Ryan is a dogged, clear-eyed reporter, legendary for her miles-deep exposés of Hollywood abuse, toxicity, and bullying. In *Burn It Down,* she makes a powerful case for a less romanticized view of the entertainment industry, one that rejects the ugly traditions of the past, holds bad bosses accountable, and marks a path to a better future."

—Emily Nussbaum, Pulitzer Prize–winning critic and author of
I Like to Watch: Arguing My Way Through the TV Revolution

"*Burn It Down* does the heavy lifting in helping to uncover not just the ugliness of the behavior of high-profile individuals but the mundane abuses common in the broader television and movie landscape. There's a reason a lot of network personnel with a lot they're trying to keep in the dark hate nothing more than to see Maureen Ryan coming with a flashlight and a pen."

—Linda Holmes, *New York Times* bestselling author of
Evvie Drake Starts Over and host of NPR's
Pop Culture Happy Hour podcast

"As a journalist, Mo Ryan saw the need for #MeToo coming years before it went viral. There are unfortunately many more painful truths about show business that have to be dug up. And there are also more skeletons in closets that need to be dragged out into the light. Mo is fierce, funny, unbossed, and unafraid."

—W. Kamau Bell, director of
We Need to Talk About Cosby and
New York Times bestselling coauthor of
Do the Work: An Antiracist Activity Book

BURN IT DOWN

IT

DOWN

Power, Complicity, and a
Call for Change in Hollywood

MAUREEN RYAN

MARINER BOOKS
New York   Boston

For Dave

HarperCollins books may be purchased for educational, business,
or sales promotional use. For information, please email the
Special Markets Department at SPsales@harpercollins.com.

A hardcover edition of this book was published in 2023 by Mariner Books.

FIRST MARINER BOOKS PAPERBACK EDITION PUBLISHED 2024.

Designed by Renata DiBiase

Library of Congress Cataloging-in-Publication Data has been applied for.

Library of Congress Control Number: 2023934670

ISBN 978-0-06-326931-6

24 25 26 27 28 LBC 5 4 3 2 1

We have rigorously established our delusion, and it will likewise take some effort to disassemble it.

—ELIZABETH MATTIS NAMGYEL,
Editor's Preface, *Light Comes Through*

Contents

PART TWO

Author's Note

Much of *Burn It Down* is based on hundreds of hours of conversations that took place, mostly in 2021 and 2022, with more than one hundred people at all levels of the entertainment industry. Interview subjects typically work for companies based in the United States and Canada, though a subset of people have worked in other nations' entertainment industries. Some interviewees spoke with me on condition of anonymity, so that they could share their experiences freely while also protecting their mental health, physical safety, or career. In this book, when you see someone referred to by a first name only, it is an alias for an anonymous source. It is not that person's real first name. Additionally, I do not identify the race, gender, sexuality, or disability of a source unless the source brings it up or it is pertinent to their account. That said, more than half of the people I interviewed come from communities that have been historically excluded by Hollywood. Some hold multiple marginalized identities. I do not always reveal all of a source's identities, as doing so may make them identifiable.

PART
ONE

1

The Myth of Sufficient Progress

We've conflated abuse with artistry.
—*Liz Hsiao Lan Alper*

We were lost.

It was early 2007, and I was driving down a dusty road in rural Texas. It had been a while since we'd seen any signs of civilization. I'm sure more than one Hollywood publicist has thought about leaving a journalist in a ditch. Was this the time one would finally do it?

I took heart from the presence of my husband in the passenger seat. It'd be harder to leave two of us behind. But where were we going? The pair of publicists in the car ahead of us were supposedly leading us to a remote field where NBC's *Friday Night Lights* was filming a first-season episode. We had long since left the outskirts of Austin, and the few abandoned-looking houses we'd seen along the way were a memory.

Then we saw the cranes. Not birds; the kind of enormous cranes used to give grand scope to something being filmed. What we witnessed on an improvised football field far outside Austin was certainly epic. We'd arrived in time to see the show shoot scenes for "Mud Bowl," a grime-filled, grass-stained, heart-stirring episode that became a fan favorite and helped establish the show as one of the best on network television.

Within a few months of *Friday Night Lights*'s debut, it was increasingly clear that the show was not just good but *magical*. It brought extraordinary intimacy and specificity to the fictional Texas town of Dillon, and its ensemble cast of established actors and promising newcomers impressed me more and more each week. The relationships and characters were gripping, funny, and bittersweet—often all at once. The immediacy of its aesthetic style and the acute emotional perception of the writing and acting made it not just unique but unmissable. I knew that if I did not see how these people did this magic trick, I would explode.

So deep into the heart of Texas I went, and I had one of the best experiences of my professional life.

The slideshow of memories is exquisite and precious. Not long after we turned up, a helmeted man arrived on a motorcycle. Tucked inside the man's leather jacket was the most adorable Jack Russell terrier of all time. The dog jumped out of the jacket, off the bike, and skittered away. Kyle Chandler then removed his helmet and said hello. That evening, Taylor Kitsch reclined in a director's chair and roasted the low-budget projects he'd appeared in, making Jesse Plemons and me laugh. On the football field, rain machines pelted the actors with water over and over. Lots of people got soaked. It was glorious.

Earlier in the day, my husband and I sat in folding chairs on the edge of the field, absorbing the vibe. Between takes, actors tossed around a football in the golden Texas light. Someone from the production handed me a heavier jacket than the one I had on. "You might be in the shot," we were cheerfully told.

Because the drama's highly mobile camera teams roved everywhere, everything and just about everyone was fair game for the show's directors. I donned the borrowed jacket so I looked like I was enduring a chilly fall football game. Months later, we shrieked when we saw my husband in the background of a "Mud Bowl" shot, wearing his own yellow coat. It remains a deep source of joy and wonder in our household that my spouse and the NBC drama share that bond, however tiny. We are forever linked to a show we love. What a gift.

And that's the point, right? Not just of *Friday Night Lights,* not just of Hollywood, but of storytelling. It's supposed to connect us. When the connection is strong, it's easy to believe that connection is not just a fluke but a universal aspiration. That kindness, vulnerability, artistic excellence, and healthy cooperation are always the core goals.

The generosity, openness, and undeniable creativity I witnessed on the *Friday Night Lights* set *is* how the Hollywood machine works sometimes. Of course, the show hewed to high standards on a lot of fronts. It was famously a set where actors were free to improvise lines and other performance elements, though I would be remiss if I did not note that it had a talented writing staff. The arcs, lines, and architecture the writers provided blended with the actors' efforts to produce scenes that were perceptive, amusing, and often tremendously moving. I choose not to dwell on certain unfortunate Season 2 plot developments; what affects me more to this day was watching Connie Britton and Plemons film a gripping Season 1 scene in a nondescript high school office, shifting the dialogue in each take in order to inhabit their characters more fully and empathically. I was not just inside that room with those actors and that crew, I was inside the characters' emotions too. I'll never forget it.

I wanted to believe that the feeling on the *Friday Night Lights* set— undergirded by a sense of community and sustained by the hard work of the actors, producers, writers, and crew—was a vibe all workplaces at least *attempted* to achieve. How I could think that, when my first experiences with a TV production included more troubling dynamics, is a question I continue to ask myself.

The first show I ever got to visit in person was *The X-Files,* back when it was filming in Vancouver in the '90s. My feelings as I arrived on the set that day are the same feelings I still get when I visit an active production now, thirty years into my career. I'm always a little nervous and usually very excited—driving onto the lot, showing my pass, seeing crew members chatting or carrying equipment around. Once I'm there, I drink everything in—who does what, how line readings change with each take, off-camera conversations that are funny, arcane, or filled with hot gossip. There are mundane moments too, and a lot of waiting around, but in the main, it's thrilling—hundreds of professionals coming together to capture lightning in a bottle, if they can. What astonishes me is how often they do. How often this punishing, cruel, amazing industry supplies entertainment that illuminates, provides escape, or delivers fun; how regularly it transmits moments that are beautiful, shattering, or unforgettable (or all three).

It's not *all* wonderful, of course. The Canadian crew of *The X-Files,* plus most staffers working out of cramped trailers and offices on the Fox lot in Los Angeles, were great. *Really* great. But two people who had power at the show were mean in ways that knocked the breath out of me. On different occasions and in very different settings, they each managed to deeply humiliate me in front of others, and one person's ongoing bullying tactics gave me literal nightmares. Beyond my experiences, I could see how certain behaviors created cliques on and off set, and isolation for the unchosen few. Most crucially, I saw firsthand that people with less power in the industry often take their cues about how to treat others from those with more power. It doesn't take much to set a troubling tone or establish a destructive pattern that can be dreadfully hard to combat, let alone break.

Lots of unfortunate shit from Hollywood's past has come out in recent years, which is both necessary and infuriating. The industry trained so many of us to think that creative people are "temperamental," and that that word—along with "passionate," "driven," and "difficult"—automatically encompasses some terrible things. The not-so-subtle subtext is that those damaging "norms" and processes are the price of creating memorable art. I muse a lot about how I defined the words "creative" and "genius" ten or twenty years ago. My mid-'90s—or even mid-aughts—definitions of those terms probably involved giving a pass to behaviors and attitudes I now recognize as abhorrent and gross.

I'm not the only one who's had to reprogram my brain. "We've always talked about the abusive artist like, 'Yeah, they threw a chair at someone, but by God, they were brilliant,'" said Liz Hsiao Lan Alper, a writer/creator and industry activist. "We've conflated abuse with artistry. And that created the conditions so that the worst of us are able to get the furthest."

No lies detected. But because it was convenient, because it was tempting, because it was easier, because it was what most other people did, I chose to believe that healthy, respectful, creative, and equitable workplaces were, more or less, the industry norm. I . . . don't think that anymore.

Wherever you land on the status of industry reform, know this: it is not in any Hollywood employee's interest to tell the world about the difficulties, unprofessional conduct, biases, toxicity, or abuses they've endured. There's often no upside in it, and tons of potential downsides. Unless a creative person feels they can risk rejection from an industry that is already brutal on its best day, what is the motivation to expose awful workplaces or powerful people by name? For a hundred years, the Hollywood machinery has been programmed to minimize, if not outright crush, people who step out of line or bring unwanted attention to individual, institutional, or systemic problems.

For years, I've done a lot of what I call "journalism triage"—talking to folks confidentially to help them decide if they want to work with members of the press. In these conversations, I explain how responsible journalism works and what a reporter needs if someone wants to tell their story in a public forum. Many times, the people I talk to decide they are not quite ready to go public. I get it, truly. I'm fully aware that telling an excruciating story even off the record can be terrifying. And as an assault survivor myself, I understand the need to slow down, process, and figure out what the least-bad survival strategies might be. I say without judgment that in the wake of many, many off-the-record conversations over the years, a sizable chunk of the worst stuff I know about the industry remains inside my brain, unpublished. (Yes, I am in therapy.)

That said, things are shifting, to a degree. The courage of those who find themselves able to speak out publicly has awed me, many times. Hollywood executives and powerbrokers are being pushed by whistleblowers, social media, the court of public opinion, and journalists like me to deal with accusations of harm, exploitation, and abuse in ways they've never had to before.

But the process is not without migraine-inducing setbacks. I recall a conversation I had a few years ago, in my role as a reporter and the chief television critic for the Hollywood trade publication *Variety*. As had become my unsettling new normal, I was investigating a story about abuse of power in the realm of television. Again.

The conversation I'm thinking of was with a PR person for a large entertainment conglomerate. It is memorable because it helped illuminate why the industry has been so resistant to change. I'd dealt with this person before, when I was slogging my way through a series of stories about nightmare bosses at that company. After this individual confirmed some information, we talked more broadly about the issues facing Hollywood. My phone and inbox were still jam-packed with tales of misery from those who feared their chance to be honest about their experiences was about to evaporate because the industry would do what it always does: wait for the storm to blow over and carry on as usual. More than a year after #MeToo broke wide open, it felt like things were getting worse, not better. The Hollywood ending I'd been trained to expect—the catharsis and change I'd been programmed to think were possible—that was nowhere in sight.

My weariness and wariness were amplified by the positive spin this PR person tried to put on the demoralizing quagmires I'd been excavating at that firm. When I mentioned the wreckage and pain we'd been wading through for months, this person brightly offered a statement along these lines: Remember how long it took for that other person at our company who was accused of abusive behavior to be fired? You have to admit, this time it took our company less time to fire this different unprofessional, toxic person you're calling about!

This was *progress?*

I've thought, many times, of what I could have said in that moment. Sometimes I wish I had launched into a big, ranty speech. But any time I did that—usually to sympathetic industry friends and loved ones—it just tired me out. I knew a spirited tirade would be no match for a see-no-evil type who thought a tiny step toward accountability was in fact a giant leap for all Hollywood-kind. This person wasn't alone. Every single time I dealt with a high-level loyalist from this conglomerate, they'd conveyed a similar attitude: now that they'd gotten rid of this month's Bad Person, everything was fine. *Sigh.*

Even though I spent a lot of that time in a haze of exhaustion and fear, certain communications from lawyers, spin doctors, or somebody's "team" still managed to rile me. One day I will publish a compendium of the willfully stupid reframings of toxicity as misunderstood genius that I have heard. One alarmingly awful person is convinced his emails to me—which contain false and repugnant innuendoes about a certain key source—will persuade me that I simply misunderstood him. If you need another example, here's an exchange I had not long ago with one powerful man's high-priced lawyer:

Me: I have dozens of sources who say that the work environment he created was abusive, unprofessional, and damaging.

Lawyer: Well, he's worked with hundreds of people over the years, so if you think about it, that's only a small percentage of them. Pretty good ratio, don't you think?

This attitude is all too common: *Nothing to see here! Move along.*

And that was the attitude I got from that PR person. Many reporters, a huge array of sources, not to mention dozens of brave editors and publications, had risked so much to illuminate the industry's most grotesque behaviors, patterns, and practices, and that denial-soaked conclusion was the takeaway? Many Bothans died for . . . *this?*

I didn't have a response then. I do now. It's this book.

I've gotten paid to watch, assess, think about, investigate, and write about popular culture and the people who make it all my adult life. Over the years, I've written for dozens of outlets, including the *New York Times, Huffington Post, GQ,* Salon, *Vulture, Variety, Entertainment Weekly,* and *The Hollywood Reporter.* These days, I'm a contributing editor at *Vanity Fair.* As I've matured as a writer, reporter, and critic, it's been impossible to ignore the patterns, beliefs, and assumptions—the myths, really—that are so foundational to the industry that many people (including me) overlook them at first.

Myths and archetypes are among the building blocks of storytelling, and there's nothing wrong with that. But when we use hazy, convenient fictions and magical thinking to shield ourselves from the truth—worse yet, when the powerful employ them as shovels to bury dangerous realities that create ongoing harm for large numbers of human beings—myths are no longer useful. A lot of beliefs and norms still enshrouding Hollywood are in dire need of reboots. Several of them come together in an incident from David Thomson's 2021 book *A Light in the Dark: A History of Movie Directors.*

He mentions the Telluride Film Festival premiere of *The Assistant,* a film by Kitty Green in which a low-level employee is introduced to the toxic culture that permeates the offices of her horrific entertainment industry boss. At that festival, "*The Assistant* faced some resistance from movie people, good friends." Thomson writes of the men around him, "Yes, they said, the film was well done, but they wanted more, including the revelation of monstrousness in this company being spelled out *and vanquished.* Perhaps they foresaw a Weinstein figure emerging from the shadowy, withdrawn way he was framed out of sight. They wanted a woman to pull the rotten castle down? These were guys, and movie men are raised to get wins."

When they are displeased, the gods want a better myth, one that doesn't make them look like the villains of the piece. They are the heroes, aren't they? *Aren't they?* Well, what if they aren't? Even if they're not the good guys, even if they're in denial about that, they want the goddess—or rather a powerless, freshly minted tree sprite—to pull down the temple. All while remaining chaste and pure and not talking about the monsters who hurt her kind.

The kind of attitudes Thomson describes embody many of the worst, most self-serving myths Hollywood believes about itself. But they're far from the only ones that slow down or stop the industry from making meaningful, sustainable progress. In these pages, I explore more myths about the entertainment industry, ones that workers and reporters alike have been trying to explode for years (before and after #MeToo and other reckonings). Here are just a few of them: people get ahead (more or less) based on talent and initiative; those without power are not routinely harmed or exploited; there must be something fundamentally good about people who are able to tell good stories on screens; the pursuit of putting comedy and drama on screens involves healthy liberation for all; and the kinds of biases in the civilian world don't also permeate the workplaces that construct the stories of who we are (and who we could be). And of course, there's also the granddaddy of them all, the myth from which so much terribleness flows: it's normal and natural—necessary, even—for human beings to be harmed in order for creativity to be tapped and for pieces of commercial entertainment to get made.

Long ago, these myths morphed into weapons. Many people must come together to pull down what remains of the rottenest temples of belief in Hollywood. Burning it all down and creating something better—permanently, reliably better? Now *that* would be something.

"In this industry, the stakes are high. The costs are high, so there was always a priority put on bringing something in that was good—and that was on budget," John Landgraf, chairman of FX Content and FX Productions, told me. "That's a very hard thing to do in television and film—to be both good and on budget. But I think society as a whole has become distinctly aware that there's a revolution going on right now in terms of what people will or will not tolerate for the privilege of working."

In Hollywood, he noted, "there was almost no attention paid to that question of, 'What are the working conditions like?'" He's not wrong.

I've also encountered safe, helpful, and professional working conditions, and not just on the *Friday Night Lights* set. Part of the reason I can opine on what it's like to be a Hollywood creative is because I am one. I sold a TV project to FX in 2018 and developed it for three years. It's not going to get made, but it's okay. I learned a lot, I have no regrets, and my dream not ending up on screen means I've had an experience just about every other industry writer has had.

Now I also know what it's like to be exposed—your soul just fully exposed—on the page, and I have more respect than ever for people who create TV shows and films. That shit isn't easy! And I say that as someone who was treated with respect and kindness every step of the way. But that is one more weapon in my arsenal of truths about creativity: I know firsthand that it does not need to involve toxicity, abuse, bias, mismanagement, repulsive behavior, or other unprofessional and damaging bullshit. Of course, I had all sorts of insulations and privileges protecting me. Still, now I know even more deeply the answer to this question: If the process could be challenging even when every person within it acted appropriately and respectfully, *what on Earth* is it like when those who have power over a creative process are monsters, assholes, or toxic in any way?

Well, *bad*. Real, real bad.

By now, you might be saying or thinking the thing that occasionally causes steam to come out of my ears. When I talk about endemic and horrendous problems in the entertainment industry, I often get the response that "it's like that in [insert name of industry] too." Of course it needs to be fixed there also. Exploitative, unacceptable, and biased behaviors have to be eradicated everywhere they exist. But I write about *this* industry, where the power dynamics are especially skewed. In Hollywood workplaces, you'll find people worth millions working twelve to eighteen hours a day beside people who are living on ramen and barely able to pay their bills. It's a setup that very much invites exploitation of all kinds.

Another big and extremely consequential difference: Hollywood tells us who we are—and who we can be. It may not be America's biggest industry, but it's surely one of the most influential. If abusers, clinical narcissists, and other awful or monstrous people control the stories that are told, that comes out in the work. Whether they're good or bad, thoughtful or not, these stories reach billions of people all over the planet. What the industry churns out influences norms, cultures, and events that occur in reality *all the time*. And this goes way beyond millions of people adopting the haircuts, catchphrases, or styles of their favorite on-screen personalities. Just one example: Hollywood's long

history of promulgating offensive stereotypes about Muslims was amplified by the pulse-pounding Fox drama *24*.

"In real life the time bomb situation rarely manifests and torture
doesn't produce reliable results," James Poniewozik writes in his 2019
book *Audience of One: Donald Trump, Television, and the Fracturing of
America*. But during and after the run of *24*, which featured Jack Bauer
hunting down and torturing vast numbers of (typically nonwhite) bad
guys, "military officers had to deal with soldiers who now believed,
because of *24*—whose DVDs were passed around in Iraq—that torture
worked."

Another real-world fiasco: Donald Trump ending up in the White
House. In any number of ways, the American media and entertainment industries propped up the false image of Trump as a successful businessman, then NBC came along in 2004 to supersize that
lie with *The Apprentice*. Around the same time, TV was saturating
the pop-culture landscape with an array of norm-breaking, violent,
bullying men. Trump's "character was, essentially, an antihero: the
blunt, impolite apex predator who knew how to get things done,"
Poniewozik writes.

After all, Tony Soprano, perhaps the most famous television character of all time, was both "an indictment of male aggression and entitlement. But he was also a fantasy of it," Poniewozik notes. Thanks
to Jeff Zucker, the former NBC executive who later supersized CNN's
coverage of Trump, the aspiring despot was able to give the people—
the people who voted for him, anyway—much of what they wanted.
And who had trained them to want a take-charge male rule breaker?
Could it be the industry that has long celebrated destructive men, on-
and off-screen?

The people who make the major decisions in the industry "don't
care. They can make a big show over how they're oh-so-forgiving or
know the 'real' Mel Gibson or prize the work over the man, but the
end result is the same: a total lack of empathy and a willingness to perpetuate bigotry through empowering the bullies," writes critic Kayleigh
Donaldson in a piece about Gibson—who has been violent and used
racist and anti-Semitic slurs—continuing to get work. "Besides, isn't
the industry full of people who have said or done things just as bad
as Gibson? Roman Polanski's still making films and winning awards.
Woody Allen's got a whole army of defenders despite 30 or so years of

the allegations made by his daughter being public knowledge. Bryan Singer isn't in jail."

Donaldson goes on to outline a mindset I have run into endlessly: "I'm convinced that far too many people decided that [Harvey] Weinstein's punishment was proof enough that they'd fixed the problem. Not only that but it became the new benchmark for abuse. I've lost count of the number of times I've seen abusive male celebrities be discussed with the dismissive insistence that what they did 'wasn't as bad as Weinstein' so it's okay, somehow. Unless you're a serial predator with three or more decades of violence under your belt, it's fine."

All these mentalities and dynamics came together in an ouroboros of monstrousness in early 2016, when alleged serial abuser and predator Leslie Moonves, then chairman of CBS, said of the presidential campaign of alleged serial assaulter Donald Trump, "It may not be good for America, but it's damn good for CBS." This idea—that breaking the world matters less than making a buck from that destruction—is far from uncommon in the highest tiers of various entertainment megacorporations and the tech companies that now own many of them.

And that matters, because, like I said, what happens in the real world is influenced by what Hollywood churns out. The rise of dangerous people—in the entertainment industry and beyond—was not a preordained inevitability. The insulation and protection of Moonves (who has denied all allegations of misconduct) and men like him has not been an inevitability either. These events are the results of *choices* that specific people, institutions, and organizations have made, again and again. I'm one of the people who made questionable decisions, by the way: I don't regret praising the good performances, the better seasons, and the aesthetic innovations of *24*, but I could have written a lot more about its most damaging themes and their real-world implications.

We can all make different choices. And if we want a better world, we must.

It's not that the industry has made zero progress. It's made some. But we're just at the start of this process. In screenwriting terms, we're not even at the end of Act 1.

My hourlong conversation with David Nevins in the summer of 2022 was realistic, thus not migraine-inducing. Nevins is a longtime industry executive who, at the end of that year, departed his role as chairman and CEO of Paramount Premium Group (which includes Showtime) and chief creative officer of scripted series at Paramount+. He and I talked about the systemic and institutional reforms that he and his colleagues made and refined over time. When the press was policing these companies, back when #MeToo broke open the industry, executives were in pure reaction mode, observed Nevins. "You're not making good decisions" when "you're playing whack-a-mole," he remarked. Having gotten past the reactive phase, there has been "a clear laying out of expectations—articulations of what is expected and what is acceptable behavior and what is not acceptable behavior," Nevins said. "That line has moved. And it's moved because of internal pressure, employee pressure, and press pressure. Of course, it needed to move."

Is the whole industry fixed? Nope. But David Slack, an established writer/producer in the TV drama realm, took a CBS HR seminar in 2022. He told me it was not the perfunctory clown show that most industry people have come to expect. "It was very thoughtful," he said. "It was grounded and real world, and you know—it didn't feel naive. It was honest and really thorough and talked about things beyond sexual harassment."

Slack continued with his typical frankness: "There have been some improvements, but in the industry as a whole at this time, there are no meaningful financial consequences for a company for running workplaces that are physically, mentally, emotionally, and professionally disastrous for the people who work in them."

More fodder for that argument came in late 2022 from New York Attorney General Letitia James, whose office announced a $30.5 million settlement in relation to a series of #MeToo-related cover-ups emanating from the highest levels of CBS. After being tipped off by a Los Angeles Police Department captain about sexual assault allegations filed against then-CEO Leslie Moonves, the network's executives, including Moonves, worked in 2017 and 2018 "to prevent the complaint from becoming public," the AG's office noted. This is infuriatingly ironic, given that CBS made a fortune from crime procedurals that tended to condemn, if not vilify, anyone who broke the law. But we've all seen enough to know that the rule of law and the imperatives of common-sense decency are frequently disregarded when it comes to powerful industry figures.

"CBS and its senior leadership knew about multiple allegations of sexual assault made against Mr. Moonves and intentionally concealed those allegations from regulators, shareholders, and the public for months," James said in a statement, adding that "CBS and Leslie Moonves' attempts to silence victims, lie to the public, and mislead investors can only be described as reprehensible." According to the settlement agreement, at an industry event in November 2017—the day Matt Lauer was fired from NBC, in fact—Moonves declared, "There's a lot we didn't know." I thought I detected a note of lawyerly fury in the next sentences of the legal document James's office made public November 2, 2022: "That statement was misleading as it implied that Moonves and CBS were just learning of problems with workplace harassment at CBS, when, in truth, Moonves and other top CBS executives were actively seeking to conceal and suppress allegations" about Moonves himself.

So . . . yeah. There is indeed a lot we—the public and even the press—didn't know. In some ways, we're no longer as lost as we were, but we are really and truly not there yet.

You will hear, in these pages, from people who, in low and high and middle places in the entertainment industry, have treated their colleagues with kindness and consideration and lived to tell the tale. You will hear from established artists such as Harold Perrineau, Orlando Jones, and Evan Rachel Wood, from high-level executives and assistants, and all sorts of folks in between. You will hear from people who know that accountability, respect, and professionalism can coexist with creativity and inspiration—and in fact are necessary to nurture the latter entities. You will hear from those who know change is possible because they've helped bring it about.

The day before I interviewed Wood, I had lunch with two established writer/producers. Both are people of color. As we consumed an impressive number of coffees, one of them observed that the industry was notably different than it had been in the '90s, when he started out. "True," I answered. "But back then, the bar was set in hell."

Neither disagreed.

Speaking of hell, let's talk about Scott Rudin.

2

Scott Rudin and the Myth of Necessary Monsters

The rationale was this: "We need to shut you up."
—*Samuel Laskey*

When you spend a long time covering the entertainment industry, you encounter a lot of food on little sticks.

I live in the Midwest, but I regularly head to Los Angeles or New York to do interviews, see friends, and connect with professional contacts. I occasionally attend industry parties, where the vibe ranges from awkward mandatory work event to classy networking shindig with free booze. Sometimes there's a sit-down meal, but more often, what you find is mini burgers on platters, vegetable concoctions on trays, and teriyaki chicken on tiny wooden skewers.

I've met some of the most engaging people in Hollywood in settings like these. I've often found myself sipping wine and grabbing canapés while talking to people who may be famous, or fame-adjacent. But usually they're not, which is fine by me. Less well-known but connected people tend to know—and be willing to share—things that reporters may want to dig into later. Besides, at gatherings like these, the more famous someone is, the more likely they are to have a lot of people in their face. There are events where the very well known are not cornered like escaped zoo animals and actually appear to be having a good time, but in my experience, those functions are the exceptions to the rule.

In any case, the industry parties I go to tend to be dominated by people like Kevin Graham-Caso—folks who are curious, thoughtful, irreverent, and have names you will probably never know. I've met a thousand Kevins over the years. They don't all look like him or have his background—handsome, intelligent, driven, and a former UCLA fraternity president—but we often share a similar set of interests. It's fun to hang out with people like Kevin, fellow Hollywood trivia nerds who devoured the VideoHound movie guides, thick volumes that list tons of film facts and information nuggets. According to his identical twin brother, David, Kevin pored over those reference volumes to the point where he could find not just six degrees of separation between Kevin Bacon and other actors but between any two people mentioned within those pages.

Like so many eager, motivated young people who love pop culture, Kevin wanted to break into the film business.

"He always loved movies," David recalled. "Our mom was diagnosed with breast cancer when we were ten, and she passed away when we were fifteen. During her chemo, we'd pop a bag of popcorn, put it in a big ziplock bag and hide it in her purse, and go to a movie." If I had met Kevin, I absolutely would have grilled him about attending early-ish incarnations of San Diego Comic-Con. The Graham-Casos grew up in that city and got to hang out at the event before it became a gigantic, overwhelming behemoth. When conversation lags at industry parties, grabbing another chicken skewer and sharing Comic-Con stories has been an effective go-to move for many a partygoer, including me.

With his sights set on Hollywood, Kevin, in his brother's telling, wasn't averse to getting an education in political maneuvering, inside and outside the classroom. When they were both attending UCLA, Kevin came up with a scheme that allowed the two of them to "dictate Greek policy for the school for the entire year, absolutely infuriating the faculty advisor." Later, a script Kevin wrote made it to the quarter-final round of the respected Nicholl Fellowships screenplay competition. Kevin cared about what was happening in the world as well. "He would sometimes joke about wanting to be more open about supporting Bernie Sanders," David reflected, but "white, bearded thirtysomethings on the internet ruined it for the rest of us by being toxic assholes."

That sentence kind of says it all. Kevin wanted to take up space and exert his own taste but not at the expense of others. He was driven but self-aware, and he wanted to help all kinds of artists tell stories. Kevin's natural industry savvy, education, and knowledge of Hollywood history surely positioned him well among newbies in the industry. All the qualities he brought to the table probably would have, over time, helped get him into rooms with the right people, and quite possibly achieve notable success in his chosen field.

But we'll never know. Kevin died by suicide in 2020. The sentences above, about Kevin's college years and Bernie Sanders affinity, are from David's eulogy for his brother.

All deaths leave unanswered questions. David knows there are several surrounding his brother's passing, and that some of those mysteries will linger forever. But David is also aware of specific situations that put Kevin on a very difficult path. David told me that he believes one of the key turning points was the eight-month period, beginning in the fall of 2008, that Kevin spent working for film, television, and theater producer Scott Rudin. Rudin's treatment of Kevin, David said, "was abusive, it was bullying, it was horrific."

Building up a well-rounded, entertainment-focused résumé during college and right after graduation was all part of Kevin's systematic pursuit of his ambitions. After gigs as an assistant to writer/director Jody Hill and at the powerhouse talent agency Creative Artists Agency (CAA), moving from California to New York to work as an executive assistant to Scott Rudin was a big step on the path Kevin was traveling. It did not take long for friends and roommates to notice changes in Kevin: he lost weight, he threw up a lot, his hair fell out, and he was frequently afflicted by painful kidney stones. David noticed changes in his brother when they talked and texted. He was worried, and that worry continually deepened.

Part of Kevin's job, David learned, involved acting as a shock absorber for those who were even more vulnerable than he was. "Kevin would say, 'Rudin's horrible to me. But it's better me than the next person down the rung, because he's worse the further down you go,'" David told me.

So why didn't Kevin just quit?

That's a reasonable question, but it ignores a dynamic thoroughly baked into the entertainment industry. Jobs such as the one Kevin had can and often do lead to bigger and better things. "Those jobs are incredibly valuable," a veteran writer/producer named Taura told me. "You are the least protected and you make the least amount of money, but you're getting to be with the power players. In a lot of parts of the industry, you can't get to your ultimate goal without going through the torture of being an assistant on a desk. So you put up with it, because what is the alternative?"

Writer and producer Samuel Laskey is among many I've spoken to over the years who have witnessed or experienced this exact scenario. He started a job as an intern at Scott Rudin Productions in 2008. He went into the office two days a week, without pay (aside from a $10 daily lunch stipend). Later, Laskey worked as a reader providing "coverage," or summaries of novels Rudin was interested in. For that, he got $70 per book. Given that most novels he read were around 400 pages, Laskey's compensation was, as he told me, "not even minimum wage."

Around the same time that Laskey started, film, television, and theater producer Eli Bush began working there. Bush stuck it out in Rudin's employ and ended up with his name in the credits of acclaimed films like *Lady Bird* and *Fences*. Bush's years with Rudin clearly paid off, career-wise; he ended up with the kind of stature and credits people like Kevin dream of acquiring.

"He was something of a friend. I liked him," Laskey said of his relationship with Bush. "Personally, I don't see how you can work for Rudin for that long and not be morally compromised. I think for monsters like Scott Rudin to exist, it requires a network of people who consider themselves to be genuinely decent and good who, for reasons of power and ambition, look the other way. But the thing is, it would have been extremely easy for me to have gone along with it all and worked for somebody that I knew was a monster. I like to think of myself as a good person. I like to think of myself as somebody who would not participate in awful behavior that hurts people. But when I was twenty-one, the only reason I didn't continue [after a few years working for Rudin] was because I was burned out. There but for the grace of God go I, you know?"

People in low-level jobs also put up with awful things because of the consequences of pushing back. "Assistants are the easiest people to blackball," Taura said. When a high-status person sets out to ruin another individual's career—even if all the powerful person has are lies, innuendos, and false stories—it often works. Even if it doesn't work permanently, a campaign to destroy someone's professional (and even personal) reputation can do massive, lasting damage—mentally, physically, and financially. It's not uncommon for me to come across people who haven't worked for years or who left the industry because they were punished for standing up for themselves in a bad work situation—or for simply making a powerful person feel angry or embarrassed. False stories about the "offender" generally circulate through the informal backchannels that are the hallmark of many Hollywood relationships; the hiring ecosystem revolves around personal networks and word-of-mouth referrals. As a result, those rumors can profoundly disrupt a career—or a life.

Some of the revelations about what Kevin—and many others—endured from Rudin came to light in a series of stories that were published in the spring of 2021. *Vulture, The Hollywood Reporter,* and the *New York Times* published long, detailed exposés of decades of Rudin's horrific behavior. His reputation was not an industry secret. But the sheer tonnage of horrifying stories was sobering, to say the very least.

According to the allegations in those articles, Rudin smashed a computer monitor on one assistant's hand, sending that man to the hospital. He screamed at people and became enraged so often that it wasn't unusual for employees to hide from him. Many former Rudin employees—and thanks to the high turnover at the producer's company during the past few decades, they are legion—talked about living with major mental and physical aftereffects from the towering stress their boss created every day.

At one point, after a Rudin tantrum involving a shattered glass bowl, an HR staffer had a panic attack and left the office in an ambulance. She never returned. Multiple sources described the incident in which Kevin was forced by Rudin to exit a car that was in motion. (Kevin told his brother the car was "not all the way pulled over or stopped.") Taken as a whole, the Rudin stories paint a picture of a workplace that was, for decades, severely abusive and traumatizing for nearly every employee who came through the door.

Over the years, Rudin profiles hadn't shied away from describing his despicable behavior, but they often put a frame around it that lent it a certain glamour, if not necessity. These pieces made him sound like an effective tough guy who knew how to get things done. A semi-admiring 2005 *Wall Street Journal* profile, for example, bore the headline "Boss-Zilla!"

In a Rudin feature published by *The Hollywood Reporter* in 2010, the writer notes that Rudin could be "angry" and hard on employees, but overall, the piece paints a picture of a serious man who can be "utterly, almost dazzlingly charming." In that profile, Rudin indicates that he is calmer and more centered than he was in previous years, and that assertion goes largely unchallenged. The writer notes that in the '90s, Rudin called him "'a pathological liar' while not quite telling the truth himself," and does not meaningfully push back against what appears to be the producer's preferred story line, which amounted to the following: *if* Rudin did bad things, that was in the past. The piece, like most others, does not meaningfully excavate what it was really like to work for Rudin but points out how valuable he was as a purveyor of high-minded films and plays, many of which were based on well-regarded literary works.

The overall vibe of that *Hollywood Reporter* piece recalls a story that appeared a decade earlier in the *Observer*. The verbal abuse, the constant firings, the throwing of objects—every box on the Rudin profile checklist was ticked, but within the confines of a droll piece that characterized his management style as containing "explosive verve." The wry, knowing flavor of that 2001 story could be summed up as "we're all adults here, let's just recognize that Rudin is the kind of abrasive guy who naturally rises in this dog-eat-dog industry." Rudin apparently relished the reputation these kinds of pieces promoted: One *Vulture* source noted that he was "proud" of the "Boss-Zilla!" profile. Rudin "*produced* that article," a former assistant said.

The blend of cynicism and credulous condescension on display in these profiles is disappointing. Even more dispiriting are the quotes from former Rudin assistants who gladly describe how they themselves had gone on to become abusive bosses. Then again, the cycle of bullying and unprofessional conduct is not that surprising, given the ways in which Rudin-style workplace horror shows have long been normalized and rewarded by Hollywood.

Defenders of Rudin and those indifferent to his approach like to point out that Rudin has not been accused of putting his hands on anyone, so what's really the problem? They believe that abusive, cruel, vindictive behavior is beyond the pale only if it involves some form of physical contact, and if you can't handle a "tough" work environment, you shouldn't be in the business. It's worth noting that this attitude has trickled down, generation after generation, from the biggest, most influential powerbrokers in Hollywood; they're the one who set these "rules." Even if people with power in the industry *right now* don't personally hew to this code, they came up when this was emphatically how it often worked.

"The mindset is, unfortunately, 'Why are you raking this guy over the coals?'" said Laskey. "Because anything short of stabbing someone or assaulting someone or raping someone—it's like, 'That doesn't count.'"

Laskey remembers a lot about the day he started working as an intern for Rudin. The office manager made Laskey sign various documents, including an NDA, or nondisclosure agreement. She said the NDA was necessary because reporters were always trying to figure out what Rudin was working on. That may well have been a concern, but Laskey now sees the NDA in a different light: "Looking back on it now, the point of signing the NDA that first day—the first moments I was in the office—I think the rationale was this: 'We need to shut you up.' It was to stop me from talking about whatever happened in that office."

The office manager also offered a list of tips to Laskey and other new employees: Don't make eye contact with Rudin. Whenever he comes in, look like you're working. Do whatever you can to be seen and not heard. "All the 'rules' amounted to, 'Don't make yourself a target of his wrath,'" Laskey said.

It sounded like the office manager was trying to normalize a culture of abuse, I pointed out.

"Yes, 100 percent," Laskey replied. "What's weird about it is, I have extremely fond memories of this person, because it felt like she was the bulwark against the bad things happening to interns. It felt like she was protecting us. But at the same time, she was permitting an environment that was hugely abusive to everybody in it."

Laskey didn't know any better, and that may have been the point. Most people working for Rudin during Laskey's time at the company were under twenty-five. "This was a lot of people's first job," he observed. Laskey and others were young, enthusiastic about movies, and naive. All these attributes are not just utilized by many industry bosses—they're weaponized against employees. "You assume that the way you're treated in your first job is the way you're supposed to be treated, because you don't know any differently," he said.

Of course Rudin, like most industry abusers, could be winning at times: "I never met a more charming man when he wants to be," Laskey recalled. But those engaging moments did not change the basic dynamics of the office, where living in fear and hair-trigger changes in the boss's mood were the norm. "He would break somebody. He would ruin somebody's day," Laskey said. "And then Meryl Streep would walk into the office, and he would flip a switch. 'It's so wonderful to see you,' and a kiss on each cheek."

According to Laskey, he regularly saw coworkers sobbing in the break room, and he remembers with particular fondness—and regret—a female coworker whom he calls "one of the sweetest, nicest, most generous human beings I've ever met." She left the entertainment industry after her experiences with Rudin, as far as Laskey knows. "I repeatedly saw her crying because she was so broken by the way he treated her," Laskey recalled. "And this was someone he'd given a pashmina—a gift worth thousands of dollars."

In 1994, George Huang wrote and directed a film called *Swimming with Sharks*, which centered on a monstrous film-industry type not unlike Rudin. Huang had worked for the famously abrasive producer Joel Silver, and in the decades after the movie came out, there's been a lot of speculation about who served as the inspiration for *Swimming with Sharks*'s central character, a film executive who terrorizes a young assistant, who then snaps and turns on the exec. Over the years, industry people have generally agreed that the character could be a blend of Silver, Rudin, and any number of other industry moguls.

Certainly, many bold-faced names (past and present) would more than qualify as inspirations for the character. A former assistant for an Oscar-winning film and television producer told me that, years ago, the man asked him to locate a French magazine called *Cuir* (pronounced "queer"). The assistant assumed it was a specialist magazine, perhaps catering to an LGBTQ+ audience. After many hours in bookstores, he came back empty-handed, expecting an outburst; the producer greeted success "with anger—failure got totally undiluted rage," the former assistant told me. There was no *Cuir*; the whole thing had been a prank.

Veterans of the industry and reporters covering it have too many similar confirmations of its toxic folkways in our memory banks. A 2018 piece by *Chicago Tribune* critic Nina Metz quotes since-deleted tweets from writer/producer Angelina Burnett, who'd written that when she was coming up, *Swimming with Sharks* was "required viewing" for those starting out in Hollywood: "Veteran assistants recommended it as a way to emotionally prepare for what was coming. It was near guaranteed you were gonna get screamed at, and it was a badge of honor to be able to take it."

Huang talked to Metz about realizing that Hollywood insiders had gone in a completely unexpected direction with their response to the movie. "It does sort of frighten me that people see the film as a primer," Huang said. "It isn't proscriptive. I was merely holding a mirror up to the way it works. It was supposed to be a cautionary tale, not a how-to—but I still had agents and managers and producers calling me and saying, 'Hey, can I get a copy of the film? We want to show it to our trainees.'"

"As assistants, we were treated like machines," writer/producer Liz Hsiao Lan Alper told me. "It's *The Hunger Games*—everyone jokes about that, and that joking normalizes it. It all is treated as if it has comedic value—it's *The Devil Wears Prada*. All these norms and movies are basically saying to you, 'This is what you have to do, what you have to commit to, if you want to succeed. And if you don't, you're the problem.'" And if those climbing the ladder don't go along with that, according to writer/producer Wendy Mericle, who started out as an assistant, "You'd get told, 'You're just not cut out for this.'"

Perhaps the pervasiveness of this mindset explains what occurred in the spring of 2021, after the Rudin stories came out and the response was, for the most part . . . silence. Four years after #MeToo, four years of many reporters and sources trying to expose all kinds of horrendous "norms" for what they were, and what had any of it accomplished?

It was hard not to wonder, because only a dozen or so even moderately well-known industry people spoke out against Rudin and his conduct around the time the *Vulture*, *The Hollywood Reporter*, and *New York Times* stories came out. Those who did speak up included Sutton Foster and Hugh Jackman (the leads of Broadway's *Music Man* revival, which Rudin had been set to produce before "stepping away"), writer and producer Michael Chabon, and actors Karen Olivo, Anthony Rapp, and Tavi Gevinson. Also on that short list was producer Megan Ellison, who said on social media that *The Hollywood Reporter* story barely scratched "the surface of Scott Rudin's abusive, racist, sexist behavior."

In an April 2021 piece, Chabon writes about his complicity in having collaborated with Rudin for twenty years on various projects. He didn't know everything, but, Chabon notes, "I knew enough. I regularly, even routinely, heard him treat his staff, from the new kid doing the coffee run to the guy just under Scott on the SRP [Scott Rudin Productions] organizational chart, with what I would call a careful, even surgical contempt, like a torturer trained to cause injuries that leave no visible marks." Chabon apologizes, adding that he knows that apology isn't enough: "I'm ashamed. I regret, and I want to apologize for my part in enabling Scott Rudin's abuse, simply by standing by, saying nothing, looking the other way. I regret most of all that Kevin Graham-Caso is not here for me to tell him personally how sorry I am."

"For me to act like I can't afford to support those coming forward would be to act out of careerism and call it powerlessness," Gevinson writes in an essay that came out the same month. Chabon and Gevinson—both established but far from the most powerful people in Rudin's orbit—started a conversation about complicity, enabling, and toxic norms. It ended quickly. Because from the dozens of A-listers and major companies Rudin had long worked with . . . nothing. A vast, echoing nothing.

Joel and Ethan Coen, Jennifer Lawrence, Denzel Washington, Wes Anderson, Noah Baumbach, Greta Gerwig, Aaron Sorkin, producer Amy Pascal: none of them would comment on Rudin to the *New York Times*. I wasn't the only one stunned by the wall of "no comments" from studios and dozens of "A-list names that Rudin has helped propel to more than 150 Oscar nominations and 17 Tonys," as one 2021 story about the "crickets" from the industry noted. "It's not exactly controversial to say that abuse shouldn't be tolerated," actor Anthony Rapp said in that Associated Press piece. "That's the least someone can do, and that almost no one has done it is sad and infuriating to me."

There was one tiny blip in the A-list radio silence: According to a *Vulture* piece published in June of that year, Rudin once verbally abused a female assistant in front of Frances McDormand and Joel Coen, who have worked with Rudin a number of times. In that story, both denied (through their representatives) witnessing the incident, and they otherwise made no comments on Rudin until that fall, when they began promoting an awards-bait film that the producer had been attached to until his name was removed from it.

In their first comments on Rudin, McDormand and Joel Coen both repeatedly made the point that they had never seen unprofessional behavior by Rudin. They went out of their way to note that, over the years, their own workplace behavior has been impeccable, as if that explained years of working with Rudin despite the negative stories they confirmed they'd heard about him. McDormand ended her brief remarks on Rudin by saying, "I think that's enough. And so I'm really interested, this article . . . is it about the film?"

Wow.

To hear such dismissive, tone-deaf sentiments from anyone is disappointing. But to see that level of callous deflection from a woman who'd championed greater inclusion in the industry while carving out a brilliant career as an artist, well, it was both infuriating and an enormous blow to the spirit.

Around that time, Aaron Sorkin, in his first public comments on Rudin, noted that he was glad that the producer was no longer associated with Sorkin's Broadway show, *To Kill a Mockingbird,* and pointed out that Rudin had faced other professional consequences (though Rudin would, Sorkin mentioned, still make money from the play). But Sorkin, who worked on multiple projects with Rudin over the years, echoed the see-no-evil mentality that remains prevalent in the industry. "The stories that I had heard over the last 12 years were the kinds of things that—they could have been scenes from *The Devil Wears Prada.* There was no violence," Sorkin said. "There's nothing physical at all in the stories that I heard."

Sorkin probably does not wake up in the morning with the intention of giving me rage migraines, but he's spectacularly good at it. As actor Josh Charles (the star of Sorkin's *Sports Night*) put it that week on Twitter when referring to the "cringeworthy" interview, "I don't hate the man [Sorkin], and actually feel kinda bad for him as being the most insecure and egotistical must be really hard."

In any event, given his long-term association with Rudin and how many press accounts have mentioned unacceptable behaviors spanning many years, Sorkin's assertion that he had *no* awareness of unprofessional or abusive incidents is difficult to believe. But even if we take him at his word, in that interview, Sorkin reaffirmed those truly noxious— and widespread—entertainment industry mentalities. Once again, a powerful industry person indicated that it was okay for a peer to create a bullying, vindictive, traumatic work culture, as long as it stopped short of certain kinds of physical violence.

Sorkin, not quite done putting both feet in his mouth, added that he didn't comment to the *New York Times* or other publications in the spring of 2021 because Rudin was "flat on the mat." He said, "I couldn't think of anyone who would benefit from my saying something but me." What about Rudin's employees, past and present? What about the legions of assistants, support staff, crews—on Broadway, in TV, and in film—who have been subjected to all kinds of abuse from Rudin and people like him for decades? The irony of Sorkin trying to drum up business for a play about moral choices by repeatedly abdicating his own is almost hilariously depressing. And yet it is so on brand when it comes to many in the industry's elite echelons. Sorkin may be a pompous, oblivious blowhard who has written some decent things now and then, but he's also a blowhard whose attitudes indicate what many in the top ranks of the industry think and are too savvy to say in interviews.

Even if his assertions were myopic and harmful, at least Sorkin said something, making a change from the silence about Rudin, which *still* reverberates through the industry. Producer Megan Ellison said online that she understood the silence, although she didn't endorse it: "Too many are afraid to speak out. I support and applaud those who did. There's good reason to be afraid because he's vindictive and has no qualms about lying."

Even so, all the "no comments" made quite a contrast to late 2017 and 2018, when dozens of high-profile industry people put out statements condemning Weinstein and other men accused of harassment and assault. The many allegations going back decades about Rudin do not involve sexual violence, and perhaps this partly explained the reticence after the Rudin stories emerged. His conduct might be at one end of the Hollywood abuse spectrum, but given the toleration—no, the *veneration*—of *Swimming with Sharks* behavior, the things he did were tacitly condoned. Especially if those actions were directed, as Laskey pointed out, at "nobodies."

"The fame of Weinstein's victims helped drive the campaign to take him down," Laskey told me. "I mean, it sounds like Scott yelled at writers or directors or actors at certain points. But I think the reason Scott was not immediately, roundly condemned by all the talent in Hollywood is because this was kind of viewed as par for the course. You can't attack celebrities and get away with it forever. You can abuse the twenty-one-year-old assistant who left the industry and nobody ever heard from again."

It's not hard to come to the conclusion that Kevin Graham-Caso knew this.

"I think the quote was, 'You quit on me—you're dead to me. You'll never work again.' It wasn't subtle," David recalled of Kevin's stint with Rudin. "It was very clear that once you started working for him, if you left on anybody's terms but his, you were giving up on your career."

For Kevin, working under these abjectly awful conditions was compounded by the stress of repeatedly getting "soft" fired by Rudin—i.e., let go but expected to return to work as if nothing had happened. Or when Kevin was told he was "nothing." Or when he had to duck the objects Rudin threw at him.

After his time working for Rudin, Kevin lived with depression, anxiety, and PTSD. Years after finally leaving the producer's employ, Kevin sent his brother a link to a trade publication article containing accounts of the industry's routinely disrespectful treatment of assistants. The stories from support staffers had been compiled by Pay Up Hollywood, a grassroots group that advocates for better pay and treatment of entry-level workers. "It was still very much affecting him a decade later," David told me. "He said he had thrown up reading this article. It induced a panic attack."

"It's hazing," said Kyle, a screenwriter who has worked as an assistant for renowned producers and actors. Even though he has generally liked his employers (despite a weird incident in which a famous actor pressured him to eat cupcakes because the actor could not do so), he said that the job of an assistant in Hollywood is "100 percent exploitative. I truly think the way the industry has structured it makes it so."

And so we arrive at the costs that do not appear on any industry balance sheet: the value, the profit, and the art that would have been added to our world had so many not been driven out by bias, abuse, toxicity, and norms that are not remotely normal at all.

Erika Herzog was a rarity at Scott Rudin Productions, in that she was approaching thirty when she worked there in the late '90s. She'd come East after getting a film degree at the University of Michigan and working in the industry as a production assistant and a script supervisor. The fact that she had Hollywood credentials and experience were *not* points in her favor, she told me. Rudin didn't hire her—his business manager did—and in the office's "bullpen" and on the literary acquisitions team, he often surrounded himself with attractive men "fresh out of the Ivy League," Herzog noted. "I was none of those things." It was not pleasant to be an "outlier," she said. The eight months at Rudin's company were so stressful that she developed a severe anxiety disorder, and after she left, she went to work for an investment bank, where "people were throwing balls at my head and stuff." She reflected, "It was so much better to go work in a bullpen at an investment bank in New York City than it was to work at Scott Rudin's."

Years later, Herzog got a job at a well-known television network in New York, but she found the industry no more welcoming than it had been earlier. "It was an environment of fear," said Herzog. "In meetings, I was told not to speak up, not to ask any questions. I was told to just shut up and do what I was told. Really, they just wanted fresh meat just graduated from college that they could pay some completely unlivable salary like $22,000 a year."

After repeated attempts to contribute to it, she's given up on the entertainment industry and now works a corporate job in another field. One small blessing is that these days, she's able to watch movies; for years after working for Rudin, the former film studies major couldn't bring herself to do so. The atmosphere Rudin created made her turn her back on her biggest artistic love. "The team before mine was subjected to much worse conditions in the realm of physical and mental abuse. . . . And the team when I was there was absolutely terrorized," she said.

Though they didn't work there at the same time, the atmosphere Herzog described was on a continuum with what Laskey endured and what was depicted in the 2021 stories. Most people in Rudin's office were young, and they existed in various states of extreme dread and fear due to their boss's "explosive rage," in the words of Herzog, who remembers a male assistant's hands shaking as he rolled calls and forced himself to speak in a smooth, calm voice.

The assistants, who were generally a little older than the interns, tried very hard to protect the interns from abuse, Laskey told me. "It was kids protecting kids," Laskey said. "You don't know any better. And for the longest time, I thought this was what the industry was."

It doesn't have to be like that. And it was encouraging for David to read the 2021 essay by Chabon, with whom he later had a "gracious" DM conversation. "I let him know that it really mattered and how much we appreciated him saying something," David said. "As the brother of somebody who killed himself after this abuse, to hear somebody say that and to acknowledge that meant the world." But while Chabon's effort to be accountable brought with it a measure of healing, in some ways, the attention paid to his brother's story was excruciating for David.

"The idea that his memory would cause some sort of change or dent in the world, even after his death, that made me feel good," David noted. "And then it made me feel absolutely crushed, because I wanted nothing more than to call him and say, 'Look at all these people who love you; look at all these people who care and who are willing to say something on your behalf.' And he's not here."

What is still here are the norms, the dynamics, and the routine mistreatment and exploitation that allow men like Rudin to flourish. The industry's many intake valves too often function as machinery meant to keep out—or wear down or break down—people like Kevin. I often compare the industry to a series of linked sifting devices. Frequently, when it comes to positions of leadership, influence, wealth, and power, the industry machinery has sifted in favor of assholes, sociopaths, toxic jerks, nightmare narcissists, well-connected incompetents, and garden-variety abusers. Those at the highest tiers of the industry generally don't want to talk about why that's so. In the spring of 2021, the well-regarded studio A24, which worked with Rudin many times, ended its relationship with him. A year later, I asked an A24 PR person if executives there would talk about the firm's involvement with Rudin and whether they'd ever work with him again. The A24 representative said they declined to comment.

Once again Hollywood—which I sometimes call the Forgetting Machine—waited for something to blow over, so that business as usual could resume. It typically works. And that pattern generally allows the worst usual suspects to take cover and regroup.

What's strange is that, as writer/producer Hannah told me, for all the industry's reputation as a place of swagger and overconfidence, it's very easy to come across executives who "don't stand by their own taste" and aren't willing to be decisive. "You're not rewarded for bold choices," she said. "You're not rewarded for taking a risk. No one gets fired for saying no."

Holding on to their current job and getting a better job—"Those are priority one and priority two," Hannah said. And we both understand that mentality, up to a point. The industry is precarious on its best days, and the last few years of corporate churn and upheaval, not to mention a worldwide pandemic, have been anything but ideal. So I get the caution.

What can get tiring for creatives, Hannah said, is talking to executives whose "job feels like figuring out the opinion of their boss and parroting that." She recalled talking to a Broadway friend about how "Scott Rudin was a monster, but he also felt like the only person that people with money would listen to, one of the only people who could push something of quality forward." She and her friend certainly weren't endorsing that dynamic or Rudin's abusive ways, however they were very familiar with the relatively common viewpoint that "it takes a tyrant, someone like Rudin, to get anything off the ground."

It is indeed horribly difficult to get *anything* off the ground; covering this industry makes me well aware of the daunting odds in every corner of it. If you think anything I've written in this chapter means I'll never watch a Greta Gerwig or Denzel Washington project again—or that I'll never check out the work of any people who worked with industry monsters in the past—you are wrong. I watched the latest Wes Anderson film during the terrible year I've dwelled on here, and it was fine. What's more relevant to me is that he has made seven movies with Rudin. That number, seven . . . it makes my soul ache.

I have often said that the best thing and the worst thing about Hollywood is that it is made up of storytellers. All too often, the story-spinning abilities that produce great art are transferred in unhealthy ways to reality, so that people can prevent themselves from seeing or recognizing what is right in front of them. I want all artists to be able to make good work, and I know that the machinery is often rigged against that outcome. I also wonder what would have happened if people at the top tiers of the industry had, long ago, banded together to make the industry unwelcoming to dangerous, damaging individuals. Not just Rudin but so many others like him. It's hard not to wonder if both the workplaces *and the work* would have been better.

No matter its causes and origins, I get to be sad about the silence. And the aversion to addressing the Rudin situation from so many segments of the industry became, in the end, its own statement. "This is why I think there is so much reluctance to do the work of repentance and accountability. It is deeply, deeply threatening to structures of power, full stop," Rabbi Danya Ruttenberg, author of the book *On Repentance and Repair*, told me.

Doing the real work to make the industry meaningfully and fundamentally better—healthy, even—would also require lifting up different kinds of people. The nonmonsters, the folks who already do so much of the industry's day-to-day work without hurting other people—or while helping them. It would involve elevating and emulating the irreverent, thoughtful, intelligent people who eat dry chicken skewers and drink barely passable wine at industry events. The ones who don't want anyone—including themselves—to go through hell to put on a play, to make a costume, to write a sketch, to put a show or a film or a documentary in front of people. We could elevate and sift in favor of those people.

Or we could all dejectedly wait for the thing that seems, if not inevitable, then probable.

As Laskey put it, "They all think Rudin is coming back."

3

The Myth of Value

This is a different kind of desperation.
—*Emily Silver*

Against all odds, for a long time, I had a fair bit of fondness for awards shows.

Some part of my lizard brain liked them, despite the protestations of my rational brain. Throughout my career, I have been paid to assess the good and bad of many awards shows, and despite the cogent arguments against the bigger, flashier ones—*How can you quantify art and declare a winner? Don't these nominations and ceremonies often reinforce exclusionary patterns? Shouldn't someone somewhere be penalized for forcing presenters to recite cringe-inducing banter?*—I have found myself watching and enjoying aspects of them from time to time. It's like telling me candy is bad for me. I'm still going to eat Kit Kats now and then.

If nothing else, the prospect of rich, famous people dressing up in exquisite, uncomfortable clothes so that I, a person in sweatpants, can judge them is pleasing to me. Let me see the famous people's couture and jewels and fashion disasters and who they're dating. I don't care how familiar their acceptance monologues sound. Let me hear those speeches, which they have probably rehearsed in front of a mirror since age five. Chances are their orations will be spontaneous and heartfelt, or at least sound that way.

On top of all that, why shouldn't creative people get to attend splashy events where the fruits of their labor are celebrated? After all, a reasonable amount of the time, the winners did good work. And every now and then, you get wonderful, life-giving moments. When writer/director Bong Joon-ho low-key dragged Hollywood in his acceptance speeches and strolled off stage with statue after statue for the masterful *Parasite,* casually mentioning how drunk he was about to get? I *loved* it.

Yes, sometimes these ceremonies are dopey and ridiculous, but so is life a decent amount of the time. At least awards shows let me look at fabulous dresses while pretty people espouse lovely ideals to audiences of millions.

And that's the deeper thread that draws me in: the commercial entertainment industries are very good at marketing not just hairstyles and haute couture but the idea that human dignity matters to them. These ceremonies are one of the primary ways in which Hollywood loudly tells us that it is working hard to excavate, celebrate, and illuminate what matters most about being a person in the world.

In clips, speeches, and ill-advised dance numbers, the industry reminds us of the themes of the works being celebrated. Whatever the story, whatever the execution or genre or tone, it's usually about how much love and compassion and pain and bittersweet hope people can display, even in the darkest and most challenging moments. "How could anyone imagine human dignity doesn't matter to us," the subtext of these events proclaims, "when here we are, as an industry, doing nothing but celebrating its complexity, endurance, and worth?"

There's another layer subtly tucked under that (occasionally true) humblebrag. As they hand out hardware, industry people lend their credibility and image-making skills to another one of the commercial entertainment world's biggest projects: convincing us the industry is full of people who may have their differences now and then but who are part of a massive endeavor that is overall *good and safe* for the people creating all that content. As the gowns and tuxes flit by, as people extend gratitude in every possible direction, a benign, glamorous spin on industry norms is deftly woven together.

"Everybody's basically doing okay here; we practice the values that we preach." That's the message a lot of the shiny image management sends. For a long time, I was somewhat taken in by this crafty pitch. As I observed the attractive, driven, articulate people picking up statues, I kind of, sort of bought that there was a baseline of respect extended to the vast majority of human beings working inside the machine.

Until I didn't. The post-Rudin silence broke something in me. I know, I know—by that point, I had already done a lot of tough reporting on the industry on multiple fronts. I didn't think I had many illusions left to break. But I've spent even more time in the last few years talking to workers in a large number of Hollywood trenches. The conversations I've had in the past half decade, plus the post-Rudin letdown—they've been especially eye-opening, to say the least.

A 2020 Pay Up Hollywood study noted that half of the respondents were experiencing job burnout—and between June 2019 and December 2020, the period of time covered by the report, 77 percent of those surveyed, who came from the ranks of support staff and entry-level workers, said the pace of their work left them unable to address mental health concerns, despite the pandemic raging for half that time. "It's a given that people are expected to be harshly mistreated, particularly at talent agencies," said Nick, an industry executive (and former assistant). "It's essentially seen as a boot camp that filters out those who can't handle the stress and aggression."

The formerly common job-listing phrase "must have a thick skin" ("a tell that the boss is abusive," Nick said) may be infrequently seen these days. But these days, technology makes low-level workers reachable at all times and all places, which often leads to its own form of hell. "You *have* to answer," even if it's late at night or a weekend, said Kyle, the former assistant turned screenwriter. For some, the pandemic made things worse. It's not unusual, said writer/producer Taura, for assistants to be "expected to work 24/7, when they are working from home and seen as completely comfortable."

"I do feel like seeing Scott Rudin get taken down caused some abusive bosses to realize there were consequences for their actions," Nick added. "But I suspect that the smarter abusive monsters simply find ways to do it that are less publicly visible. They either are too oblivious to understand how bad their behavior is or they simply don't care—and can't imagine there will ever be consequences."

Those impressions align with what I've been told over the years by hundreds of sources, who describe an industry in which those on the first few rungs of the ladder are taught to expect mistreatment or even to be put in mental or physical danger. One woman of color who worked on a reality show recalled a line producer getting angry at a group of production assistants because they "wouldn't jump up and down in a massive dumpster filled with broken wood and nails so he wouldn't have to pay to empty it." PAs were also expected to help build sets, she told me; it was a task they had no qualifications for and certainly weren't paid extra for.

"Every assistant I know has had something thrown at them. I had a football thrown at my head," Taura said. "The workplace feels unsafe," one young woman told me for a story *Variety* published in November 2017 on Andrew Kreisberg, who was then an executive producer on a number of CW shows and who was accused of a pattern of harassment and inappropriate actions. (Kreisberg has consistently denied any inappropriate behavior of any kind.) After being let go, he got a check for nearly $10 million from Warner Bros. Even three years after his departure, the studio would not publicly state what the money was for. People who'd worked for him found that payout infuriating, especially as many had their own careers knocked off course by awful events that transpired when they worked for him.

"They didn't care what he did," Aral, a writer of color, told me in 2020. "If a show's doing well, who cares? If he's 'hard on the staff,' who cares? The toxic way he acted wasn't viewed as abnormal, let alone a fireable offense."

Hannah, a writer/producer, is now out of the assistant trenches, but hers are among the most harrowing tales I have heard. Harassment from her well-connected boss was part of an extremely punitive work culture, where staying at the office nights, weekends, and holidays was expected. "There was a view that if I wasn't willing to stay at the office all night, I was lazy," Hannah said. The disrespect continues in other forms now. During negotiations over a new project she'd created, she asked for the compensation a man of her acquaintance with less experience had gotten five years earlier. She didn't get it. "Every time I asked a question that poked a hole in the party line," she recalled, "it was just like, 'This is how it's always been done.'"

Kyle said he was generally treated decently by his employers—and once in a while, by the stars his A-list bosses were meeting with. "One time I spilled hot coffee all over myself in front of Renée Zellweger," and not only did she help clean up the mess, "she came back looking for me after her meeting to check on me."

But Kyle, like many other low-level workers, went into major debt over the years. It was frequently impossible to live on the minuscule pay endemic to the lower rungs of Hollywood. The bad behavior from bosses, the pressure, the mental and physical dangers, the inability to complain, the low pay—whatever hazards a person is navigating, and there are usually a number of them, they take a toll.

The myth that the industry values the people who make its content goes beyond matters of routine exploitation at the lower (and often middle) levels. It also affects people's ability to claw their way into any kind of financial stability and stay there.

"There are a lot of profits in what we're making, but somehow we are not doing as well financially," Meredith Stiehm, president of the Writers Guild of America West, told me. "I believe that's because of the change to streaming." The streaming revolution has made the professional lives of those in the industry even more unstable than they were before. In the past few years, I've talked to a lot of industry professionals—some in or just past entry-level jobs but also many whose careers are (or were) firmly established—who are barely able to pay their bills. Some have left California or are contemplating moving out of Los Angeles, where the only appropriate word to describe housing prices is "batshit." But the problem goes beyond one city or even one country, as writer/ producer Liz Hsiao Lan Alper noted.

"People from all over, whether it's New York or Atlanta or Chicago or Los Angeles, or even Vancouver—everyone is seeing and feeling this shift, because everywhere you go in this country, it is hard to pay rent," Alper said. Industry workers "are not asking to be millionaires. They are asking for a roof over their head, for money in the bank for when they get sick, and to not have to work themselves to death in order to have a career." But that's harder than ever because gigs are shorter than ever. When Alper was an assistant on *House*, her weekly pay was low and she was pretty broke—but she got that paycheck for well over forty weeks of the year. During the two-and-a-half-year period that ended in the middle of 2022, she worked thirty weeks *total*.

Hollywood workers have, for the most part, been freelancers—gig workers, if you will. Many people are used to salting away money to draw on during dry spells. But now some need to search for additional work "to supplement their sixty- to eighty-hour-a-week entertainment industry job," Alper said. "You need to take on a second job to afford to work in Hollywood a lot of times now. And the only people who don't have to do that are already at the top of the ladder."

One driver of the current wave of financial hardship—at least in television—is shorter seasons. Fifteen years ago, most American shows were ordered in thirteen- or twenty-two-episode batches, which meant people working on those shows were employed for half or most of a year. Seasons of twenty-five or even thirty episodes of hit shows weren't that rare back in the day. But in recent years, the rise of shorter seasons—a trend driven by but not limited to big streaming platforms—means that number has gone down significantly. According to *The Ringer*, "in 2005, the median length of the most popular U.S. TV seasons was close to 21 episodes; [in 2022] it's a bit above eight." Though for decades many industry fortunes were built on the backs of programs that ran for several seasons of twenty episodes or more, a show that runs for one hundred (or even forty) episodes is, in most cases, a thing of the past. As one streaming showrunner told me in 2020, "Four seasons seems like a miracle. They might let you go longer if the show gets awards or is made by their in-house studio. But in general, they want to kill you at three seasons." Or less.

Adding to that angst are the recent rounds of consolidation and cutbacks among big media companies and waves upon waves of pandemic-related uncertainty. But even before COVID-19 hit, I'd heard from many people that streamers in particular are not averse to lowballing writers, actors, and others. The result is that many people have had to pull together more gigs at a tough time—all to end up making *less* than they made a few years ago.

"Quotes aren't being respected," said Emily Silver, who created the MTV show *Finding Carter* and was coshowrunner of TNT's *Claws*, among many other credits. I've known Silver for some time, and she climbed the ladder the way you are supposed to—working hard, being a giving and respectful colleague, and honing the skills she'd need to be a good leader. And then, in an echo of similar stories I've heard in recent years, the ladder she'd climbed so diligently collapsed under her. She described being hired to work on an eight-episode streaming season of television, but when everything shook out, the compensation she brought home was closer to what she'd have gotten a few years ago for working on five episodes. "If you had told me ten years ago that I'd be a showrunner who was struggling to pay bills, I would have laughed."

Silver talked about having more than a half-dozen projects in some stage of development at one time—a state of affairs that is, anecdotally speaking, quite common. Of course, it's never been unusual for creatives to juggle more than one potential project, but these days, many are working on *a lot* more than ever before. "I'm hearing from producers, 'Don't dilute your brand by taking out so many projects—people aren't going to want to see your face so often when you're selling things,'" Silver said. "I'm like, 'That's nice for you to say—you have a paycheck. I have no idea which iron on which fire is going to get even a little bit hot—and my paycheck only comes when I sell something.'" That's the wild part many non-industry people don't know: an enormous amount of work done to develop new projects is done without compensation.

Another growing trend: writers being asked to participate in "bake-offs," in which they'll offer ideas for a project, usually for existing intellectual property, or IP. Coming up with those concepts takes time and effort, as does working up an engaging pitch, which often requires more razzle-dazzle than ever. "I have not only figured out all the characters, what the pilot is, I've figured out Season 1 and Season 2 in detail," Taura said. "And not only do you need to do all that, you have to have a really dynamic visual presentation. This is all for free. We're doing months and years of development for no pay—how are we supposed to feed our families?" Writer/producer David Slack noted, "When I ask about paid development, I get told, 'We don't have the money for that.' And I'm like, 'Well, you're getting paid to have this conversation with me.'"

Another huge problem many creatives are facing is that pay from residuals "has fallen off a cliff," as Slack put it. When he worked on *Law & Order,* he would not only get a script fee for his episode, but he'd get two-thirds of that amount every time NBC aired the episode again (those *Law & Order* marathons on basic cable helped pay many a mortgage over the years). But the financial models prevalent now have generally reduced residual pay, which helped a lot of industry folks ride out rough patches in the past.

"The longer you had a career, the more residuals you would get paid," noted Slack, who observed that Marc Cherry wrote the pilot for the ABC hit *Desperate Housewives* on spec, while living off residuals. "You'd have a stable income and it was kind of a consistent thing. So it wasn't such a big deal to be doing development stuff that you weren't getting paid for immediately. As streaming orders have shrunk, it's harder and harder to sustain a career in this industry as a writer, as a director, as an actor," Slack continued. "By the way, the studio's still making money off the thing you created, the thing they themselves are incapable of creating without you."

Some folks are making out like bandits, you'll be glad to hear. In 2021, the total compensation for David Zaslav, head of the newly combined Warner Bros. Discovery, was just shy of $247 million. The next year, the wild-eyed socialists at *Fortune* magazine determined that he was the second most overpaid CEO in the Fortune 500.

"That's the frustrating thing," Taura said. "There is money. They just don't want to spend it on creative people—especially lower-level staff."

And climbing the ladder to the top—or just the middle—has gotten harder in other ways too. Short seasons ended up destroying a lot of the apprenticeship pathways that existed under older industry models. For a long time, when creative people were coming up, they got to spend time on sets and learn about the day-to-day realities of production. Not everyone got to do this, but a significant number—including many of the most acclaimed creators in the game—picked up many necessary skills that way.

As they rose through the ranks, they sat in editing bays and in pre- and post-production meetings, and they learned how to wrangle actors and Teamsters and studio notes. But these days, many shows are written for a few months, then the writing staff is dispersed. The showrunner has to shoulder the rest of the many jobs that are left when the program films episodes (if that person is kept around during production, that is). The result is that many aspiring creators have worked on projects without ever having spent a minute on those projects' sets. For those rising now, "no one is giving them the tools they need to have," Taura said.

On top of that, Slack observed, those trying to rise in the industry are "facing profound, downward pressure from the studios on their wages. They face enormous pressure to keep repeating [the low-level job of] staff writer as many times as the studio can get them to do it, especially women and people of color. I talked to one writer who had been a staff writer eight times—good God! [The studios] try really hard not to promote."

All in all, "I feel like the chance of sustainability is more and more remote," Silver said. "This is my passion. This is what I've wanted to do since I was twelve years old." But the dream of coming up with stories that she gets adequately compensated for—and getting to tell those stories within a respectful, safe environment—seems more remote than when she started.

Though she cares about creating good workplaces and it clearly pained her to say this, she observed that "issues of bullying and toxicity are falling by the wayside now. Right now the scramble is not even about how unhealthy your workplace is—it's about getting a workplace at all. This is a different kind of desperation than I think existed before."

Even for those who are established, their careers are typically in the hands of people whose assessment of their value is often arbitrary yet portrayed as business-driven—and within that sphere of compensation, certain questionable patterns recur. This might be one of the most relatable things about Hollywood: people's financial and professional fates are frequently controlled by those who'd rather folks stay in the dark about what their peers make. In any event, executives whose names you may never know decide who is valued within the industry. And then, when a person who is less valued wants to increase their paycheck, or their "quote," all too often, executives for those companies, most of whom publicly proclaim they're committed to industry equality, deputize business-affairs employees or other underlings to say something like, "We just can't do that, and by the way, we're agreeing to this other person's much higher quote because in the past, they've done [insert name of project] and they received a paycheck in a much higher ballpark then."

Thus you arrive at situations like the one Gillian Anderson found herself in when *The X-Files* was in the process of returning in 2015, and she was offered half of costar David Duchovny's pay. Anderson, who was also paid less than her costar during the first several seasons of the Fox show, was taken aback: "It was shocking to me, given all the work that I had done in the past to get us to be paid fairly," she said. Anderson got equal pay for the reboot, but the fact that this wrangle occurred two decades into her career is illuminating.

As awkward as it can be to broach these topics, people in the industry at all levels appear to be talking to each other more about compensation, publicly and privately. At one point, participants in a Time's Up meeting discussed the fact that *Black-ish* star Tracee Ellis Ross was bringing home "significantly less" money than costar Anthony Anderson, a fact that emerged in the press in 2018. That pay situation was resolved, but examples of unequal pay abound: Natalie Portman made a third of what Ashton Kutcher did for 2011's *No Strings Attached*; in 2021, it emerged that Jennifer Lawrence made $5 million less than Leonardo DiCaprio for *Don't Look Up*; Mark Wahlberg made $5 million for *All the Money in the World* and his costar Michelle Williams made *one-eighth* of that amount: $625,000. When there were reshoots for that film, Williams got $1,000, Wahlberg $1.5 million.

According to Ohio State University's Timothy A. Judge, who examines career success and how it's achieved, research shows that "when we evaluate others, we have biases that carry a lot of history that we don't consciously process or recognize. So what you often see is this neurotic tendency to profess one set of values—fairness—but when you look at their decisions, there's this discrepancy." A 2014 study Judge coauthored, *Age, Gender, and Compensation: A Study of Hollywood Movie Stars*, stated that "the average earnings per film of female movie stars increases until the age of thirty-four but decreases rapidly thereafter. Male movie stars' average earnings per film reaches the maximum at age fifty-one and remains stable after that." You might wonder about the statistics for actors of color, but Judge could not provide those numbers because at that time, "there weren't enough actors of color in starring roles to qualify for the study."

Indeed, as is the case in so many other professional arenas, for women of color, fair or equal compensation is all too often a pipe dream. "If Caucasian women are getting 50 percent of what men are getting paid, we're not even getting a quarter of what white women are getting paid," Viola Davis said in 2018. Taraji P. Henson wanted $500,000 for her work in *The Curious Case of Benjamin Button*; she was offered a fifth of that and ended up getting $150,000. Jessica Chastain helped Octavia Spencer get five times more than she was supposed to get on one project, and, in 2019, Spencer said LeBron James intervened to help get her a better deal for her work on a project he was producing. Among them, Spencer, Henson, and Davis have (as of this writing) eight Oscar nominations and two wins. Imani M. Cheers, author of *The Evolution of Black Women in Television: Mammies, Matriarchs and Mistresses*, told the *Chicago Tribune*'s Nina Metz, "The fact that these women have reached the highest accolade in their field and still don't have pay equality; there's a problem there." She went on to say, "That's a reality, unfortunately, because studio executives and others don't hold them in the same regard despite their achievements."

These patterns play out far from the spotlight too. A two-year study funded by IATSE Local 871, a guild for crew members, noted "a history of gender segregation," stereotyping, and sexual harassment, and the 2018 survey found that when it came to four female-dominated jobs, women were paid "hundreds or even thousands of dollars per week less" than male peers in comparable positions. A man of color at a senior creative level told me recently that he did not get the deal he felt he deserved from a major industry company. That company gave a white woman associated with the project—who is talented but less experienced than him—an even better deal than he'd asked for. "They don't see that as being anything racial at all. You know, they just see that as a business decision," he said.

The lack of regard or valuation can play out in all sorts of ways. In the run-up to the third season of *American Gods*, Orlando Jones told me his option was not picked up, meaning his work on the show was effectively over. But he wasn't given that information until eight days before he was scheduled to begin work on the new season, and he wasn't paid or officially released from his *Gods* contract—making him unable to pursue other acting work—until he went to the Screen Actors Guild to file a complaint. Powerful entities in the industry, Jones observed, regularly "create an environment of instability among actors, and they like it that way, because that means they can control you."

It's one thing to call out specific monsters and debilitating norms within the industry. But it's also worth noting that a general attitude of callous indifference—one that I've heard about and seen in action for years on a number of fronts—can manifest in very serious ways. We should talk about the ultimate cost of these attitudes more.

In 2021, cinematographer Halyna Hutchins died after a gun was fired by Alec Baldwin on the set of the film *Rust*. Actors Jon-Erik Hexum and Brandon Lee both died in gun-related incidents in 1984 and 1993, respectively. Extra Antonio Velasco Gutierrez was accidentally shot twice on the set of the movie *Revenge of the Scorpion* in 2003; he died shortly after his arrival at a hospital. My-ca Dinh Le was seven and Renee Shin-Ye Chen was six when they, along with fellow actor Vic Morrow, died in a helicopter incident on the set of the 1983 movie *The Twilight Zone*.

Camera assistant Sarah Jones was killed and several other crew members were injured on the set of the film *Midnight Rider* in 2014. The next year, during the making of *Resident Evil: The Final Chapter*, a stuntwoman was injured in one on-set accident—among other consequences, her arm had to be amputated—and a crew member died in another (he was crushed by a prop car). Also in 2015, two pilots died and another was badly hurt on the set of the Tom Cruise film *American Made*. Actor Dylan O'Brien has talked about how a 2016 accident on the set of *Maze Runner: The Death Cure* left him "a mess" and "so f—king broken." The same year, actor Brendan Fletcher was hospitalized after being injured by a gun on the set of the Canadian series *Cardinal*. In 2017, a stuntman working on *The Walking Dead* died from injuries suffered in an on-set fall, an event that resulted in a fine from the Occupational Safety and Health Administration. Also that year, a stuntwoman working on *Deadpool 2* died after a motorcycle scene went awry. In 2019, a crew member was injured by an explosion that "tore the roof and the walls off the 007 Stage" during production of the James Bond movie *No Time to Die*.

In 2020, a worker on the set of the CW's *Batwoman* sustained serious spinal injuries, including "burst vertebrae," when equipment was mistakenly lowered onto her head. Though Warner Bros. disputes Ruby Rose's account, in 2021 the former star of *Batwoman* alleged their departure from that program was driven in part by injuries they endured on set. In 2021, production on *America's Got Talent: Extreme* paused when a performer attempted "to escape from a straitjacket while hoisted 70 feet in the air and suspended between two swaying cars." The stunt went so wrong that some people "initially thought he was dead," one news report said.

In 2022, two actors working for a Netflix show died when a van they and others were riding in went off the road and crashed. "Some Mexican observers have raised questions about Netflix and Redrum, the production outlet behind the TV series [*The Chosen One*], suggesting the film crew was overworked and operating in unsafe working conditions as the companies cut corners to save money," according to a news story about the tragedy.

It wasn't until 2022 that actor Kristin Chenoweth felt she could share the truth of an injury she sustained on the set of *The Good Wife* in 2012. She was knocked into a curb by equipment in an incident that left her with cracked ribs, a broken nose, a skull fracture, and nerve, tissue, and muscle damage, causing her "head-to-toe pain on a daily basis." She was advised not to take action because if she were "to hold CBS accountable" and sue a major network, it would mean she'd "never work again." Chenoweth noted that the network's current regime is different, but she also stated plainly that back then, "they knew I was hurt really badly, but they exploited the power they held over a person like me."

This is by no means a comprehensive list of every major injury or fatality on a TV or film set in Hollywood history. Far from it. But one thing worth noting about serious accidents and deaths: there appear to be a lot more of them in recent years. This increase correlates to an increase in programming. In 2009, there were 210 scripted series available to Americans; in 2022, it was 599. There have been many gems among those programs, but the uptick in production, much of it driven by the arrival of deep-pocketed streamers, has taken a human toll. As a 2015 pair of stories by the *Los Angeles Times* noted, reality TV programming can be particularly dangerous because "producers need dramatic footage to compete for viewers"; the newspaper provided a "breakdown of 205 production accidents from 1990 through 2014 involving 251 catastrophic injuries and 44 deaths."

Not surprisingly, the working people who make the entertainment you see are, in many cases, fed up.

"We're in a moment where there's a lot of hopelessness out there, but the thing that's giving me hope is the growth of the labor movement, or even the rebirth of the labor movement in this country," said Slack, who has served on the board of the WGA West. Grassroots alliances are springing up as well. In 2019, Liz Hsiao Lan Alper cofounded Pay Up Hollywood, which began as a hashtag and became a force for change in the industry. A lot of formal and informal organizing is helping to combat the attitudes that some have internalized for years—that workers are just, as Alper put it, "widgets, they don't matter."

"I think from its inception, Hollywood benefited from being an industry that exploited workers," said Alper, who served on the WGA West board. "The entire foundation is built on exploitation. It was never okay. We were just gaslit into thinking it was. We've so often been divided and conquered and isolated. Everybody is tired of it, what we were told is 'normal,' and through social media, we're now getting to connect with one another in a more meaningful way. That allows us to see the issues we're facing are not just individual—they're systemic."

One example Alper provided: assistants reported to Pay Up Hollywood that when a number of productions went over budget on spending for coffee or food, *the studios took those funds from the paychecks of assistants,* most of whom are barely making ends meet. (They have been known to trade information about where to sell plasma for money.) In a Facebook group Alper was in, some veterans couldn't believe it. More accurately, they *wouldn't* believe it. "It was like the five stages of grief," Alper observed. One producer, Alper said, asked her assistant about this practice—and that producer and others discovered that not only was this happening, the assistants had been too scared to tell anyone.

It's those kinds of stories that have led to, among other developments, union growth—the Directors Guild of America (DGA) has gone from 16,000 members in 2015 to 19,000 members in 2022. (The DGA comprises several different kinds of workers; about 11,000 are directors.) To the shock of many in Hollywood, where a number of unions have spent long periods not rocking the boat, nearly 99 percent of International Alliance of Theatrical Stage Employees (IATSE) voters authorized a strike in 2021.

That action by the membership of IATSE—which many crew members and other workers belong to—was part of a larger national revival of the labor movement, as Kim Kelly discusses in her 2022 labor history *Fight Like Hell.* "Pro-union sentiment rose to 68 percent in September 2021, the highest that mark has been since 1965," Kelly writes. In October of 2021—or "Striketober," as organizers dubbed it—Chris Smalls and other organizers filed for a National Labor Relations Board election; months later, workers at a Staten Island warehouse voted "by a wide margin" to be represented by the fledgling Amazon Labor Union. Also that month, "more than one thousand Nabisco workers and fourteen hundred Kellogg's workers [walked] out for higher wages and weekends off, just before ten thousand John Deere workers hit the picket lines over a discriminatory two-tiered employment system, while at the same time, sixty thousand IATSE members in Hollywood were threatening to strike."

The IATSE strike didn't happen, in large part because the strike authorization got everyone's attention—studios included. It's not that the gains IATSE achieved were massive—they were generally modest, a guild insider told me—but the sky-high number of yes votes was a reflection of industry workers' desperation to be heard. That year, in part due to the longer and more challenging workdays brought about by the COVID-19 pandemic, many casts, crews, and creatives were at the end of their tethers, as evidenced by the horror stories shared on the Instagram account @ia_stories. "We had a dept head die of a massive heart attack a few weeks ago and we just kept shooting," one contributor wrote. "Then they added more days, more hours, and more weekend work. They brought in a grief counselor the next day but didn't even break for lunch so no one could visit them."

"Why do studios insist on working 16–18 hour days?" Salvador Perez, then president of the Costume Designers Guild, asked in a news story on IATSE demands for meal breaks and meaningful rest on weekends. "We are expected to do it for months, there is no logical reason to work the crews to death."

All the narratives—they are really one narrative.

The litany of names of the injured and the dead; the roster of abuse exposés in the press; the Rudin stories, the Cosby stories, the Weinstein stories; the half decade's worth of #MeToo coverage, the chronicles of exploited creatives and crew members on social media and elsewhere: they're all, in the end, the same story.

As that overarching story permeated more and more of my work, it led me to this unfortunate conclusion: *it is not the inclination nor the habit of the most important entities in the commercial entertainment industry to value the people who make their products—at all.*

The American entertainment industry has not only normalized abuse, mistreatment, and exploitation, it has too often relied on these things to function. Hollywood employs its considerable public relations and image management strategies—awards shows among them—to minimize and obfuscate these truths. You might say, "Well, lots of industries use PR to make themselves look good." Sure, but it doesn't necessarily work all the time, because the industries are not that glamorous or the spin jobs aren't as convincing. (Find me one person who routinely believes every press release the oil industry puts out.)

When it comes to Hollywood, however, many of us have been conditioned to believe the words of the most sincere actors and creators on sparkly awards show stages. Hollywood is *good* at this stuff, and it's disarmingly easy to accept that the most powerful entities in the industry share the values of the most decent people within it. That is sadly not the case.

For some folks, the statements I've made in this section may be unsettling and unwelcome. They fly in the face of so many of the things that people say on awards podiums, in magazine features, and in press releases. Despite all the time I've spent talking to people in all kinds of industry trenches, it took me a long time to decipher all this myself, let alone accept it.

Before I go further, let me be clear about one thing: I am not promoting the idea that the commercial entertainment industry creates nothing of value. I've spent much of my adult life celebrating the many things it does well. And I'm not asserting that no one in the industry cares about anyone else. Far from it. There are some heroes in Hollywood: many have put their livelihoods at risk to help me and other reporters expose the terrible choices made by some of the most powerful people and companies in this industry.

But an important distinction must be made: While certain *people* care about their colleagues and collaborators, the most powerful entities (and that word encompasses companies and some individuals) typically *do not*. And to those very powerful entities, the fact that many employees are constantly broken, crushed, demoralized, or driven out may well be a feature of the system, not a bug. As one tired industry woman told me recently, "They'll give anyone a contract for twenty weeks and make them think they have a career."

I don't watch awards shows anymore. If you do, and you enjoy them, I'm happy for you—truly. As for me, I'm no longer interested in the words spoken on those stages. If I have bandwidth available, I use that time to do things I enjoy, things that help me survive knowing something I'll admit is pretty grim: workers brought inside the Hollywood machine have routinely been told, in a million different ways, that they should regard experiencing patterns of abuse, trauma, exploitation, or dangerous treatment as *a net good*. People are pressured to believe that unacceptable, grueling, unprofessional, biased, or unsafe conditions— common among employees at all levels but especially on the lower rungs of every industry ladder—will "toughen them up" and "give them a thick skin."

"That's how people are weeded out," production coordinator Katie Sponseller said in a story on burned-out IATSE workers. "We're asking who can mentally put themselves through a certain amount of torture for however long." In 2018, 64 percent of female writers who responded to a WGA West survey said they'd been sexually harassed at work (11 percent of men reported harassment). Open letters published by Latinx and Black creatives in 2020 denoted any number of indignities—including low pay, racist treatment, and biased hiring dynamics—they've been asked to bear silently.

It has crushed me, at various points in my reporting career, to see how much effort is expended to get people to accept many varieties of abuse as not just normal but helpful. As *necessary*. All too often, a key feature of entry-level jobs involves ensuring that young people not only put up with abusive behaviors but think of them as something else entirely—*good*, useful, beneficial to their futures. Training whole generations of workers to think that way was and is wrong.

It's not happening everywhere, but it still happens a lot. And it has been going on for way too long, as evidenced by the number of times *Swimming with Sharks* has been treated as a training tool. Many young people, many newcomers, many well-intentioned people of all kinds have been told—in actions, if not words—that *their ability to endure abuse, toxicity, and all manner of potential and actual injury* is crucial to determining whether they would be allowed to stay in the industry at all.

Fuuuck that.

4

Some Myths of Freedom and Nonconformity

I promised to be quiet and not say anything.
—*Shernold Edwards*

It's worth taking a closer look at Hollywood's spine-removal industry. Not everyone undergoes the procedure, of course. I'd never try to sell the narrative that you have to be gutless or spineless to make it. But it's not hard to see why some folks begin to regard their (metaphorical) spines as unnecessary encumbrances, and either ignore them or excise them entirely.

Executives, storytellers, directors, artisans, assistants, and other people working in various trenches undoubtedly *do* take chances, in their creative pursuits and as part of efforts to make the industry better. But what many of those folks are put through, just for trying to do the right thing or the brave thing, occasionally sends me sliding into a pit of despair. There's a big chunk of cognitive dissonance with me in that pit; when I think about the ways the industry tries to crush the good folks, it doesn't compute sometimes. Given Hollywood's penchant for telling stories about plucky characters exhibiting brash derring-do against incredible odds, maybe we should all be forgiven for assuming (or hoping) that inspired risk-taking is not just rewarded but baked into every one of its interactions and productions.

It's not. It's really not. And there are practical reasons behind some of the industry's reliance on standardization, rote processes, and streamlining.

If a production does not regularly "make its days"—i.e., complete the number of scenes that the production had planned for that day—heads are likely to roll. Money and time are not infinite, unless you are making the later seasons of *The Sopranos* or you are the star of a certain tentpole series (the headline on a story about the making of an Ethan Hunt espionage movie: "The Real Mission Impossible: Saying 'No' to Tom Cruise").

For most of the industry, though, the parameters people work within are well defined: terms in scripts must have shared meanings, so that crews know what to do. People need to have a clear understanding of what specific jobs entail and what creative leaders want, so that the right people are hired, usable sets are built, appropriate costumes are created, and, in general, everyone knows what they're supposed to be doing at specific times and locations.

But artists and artisans should also be allowed to try new things, to take chances and see what works. Every commercial artistic endeavor is an attempt to balance profit-seeking with aesthetic coherence and ambition, and with ambition comes the occasional failure, miscalculation, or mistake. Those missteps and mistakes are often a necessary aspect of learning and evolution.

Even David Chase, creator of *The Sopranos*, regretted slightly altering the show's lauded "College" episode, in which Tony kills a mob snitch while on a college tour with his daughter. Chris Albrecht and other HBO executives were afraid the audience might lose interest in a lead character who could do something so brutal. After much debate, the murder stayed in, but Chase inserted a scene that showed the snitch dealing drugs and attempting to order a hit on Tony and his daughter. The 1999 episode, which won a writing Emmy, is seen as a landmark moment in TV history that helped launch TV's antihero-focused Golden Age, but the alteration never sat right with Chase. "I don't think it was a terrible compromise, but it was a compromise," Chase said in an interview for the book *Difficult Men: Behind the Scenes of a Creative Revolution*. "I wish we hadn't done it."

When is a compromise too much to ask and when is listening to others' input the right move? The *Lost* creative team, for example, initially wanted to kill lead character Jack Shephard in the drama's pilot, but according to the TV history *The Revolution Was Televised*, executive input made them reconsider. But that question—one most people in the industry regularly wrestle with—is unresolvable. The dual mandates that underlie most projects—make it within the time frame and budget allocated and make it really *good* (or just pretty good)—are often in tension with each other. Trying things and making mistakes can cost time and money and can lead to long days and short tempers. Those pressures can in turn fuel a lot of coverage of the industry and possibly do reputational damage. There are countless ways the attempts to balance a project's many competing personalities and agendas can go awry, and I haven't just written my share of How It All Went Wrong play-by-plays; I've read thousands of books and stories that follow a similar template.

But beyond issues of workplace conduct and conflict, a theme has emerged from my travels in Hollywood: people in the industry are *not* routinely rewarded for stepping outside the frequently narrow confines that still often define what most people are allowed to do, say, or be. Stepping up or speaking out, publicly or privately, frequently comes at a cost for many people below the level of a David Chase or a Tom Cruise. "I say to people all the time, it doesn't matter if a person worked at the network on Thursday, if they work at the studio on Friday, the way they approach you is going to be different," Orlando Jones said. "Because they're a part of the agenda of the whatever company they now work for. No matter what they say, they have to play by the rules of that agenda, or they cannot move up the ladder."

Jones has worked on everything from *Abbott Elementary* to *Sleepy Hollow* to *MADtv*, and these days, he acts, produces, writes, and does stand-up comedy. He's also owned an entertainment company for more than twenty-five years and is active in fan communities and on the convention circuit, all of which gives him insight into the industry on a number of fronts. There's also the wisdom he absorbed while watching power players in their natural habitat early in his career. Back in the '90s, he wrote and acted on *A Different World* and wrote for *Roc*, among other credits, but he told me his real education came from being around producers, agents, executives, and creatives such as Susan Fales-Hill (a writer and producer on *A Different World, Suddenly Susan,* and *Twenties*) and Debbie Allen (a longtime actor with many credits as a producer and director), along with their friends and associates.

"I was this twenty-year-old Black kid from the Deep South—who the fuck was I? I was no one, so these people were entirely themselves around me," Jones said with a laugh. He's learned a lot in three decades in the industry, but in our conversations, he frequently returned to this general idea: "The punishment is severe for those who step outside the rules."

He recalled a fraught moment (one of many) from his time on *American Gods,* which went through an enormous amount of up-heaval behind the scenes and which displayed a notable deterioration in quality after its atmospheric debut season. At the first Season 2 table read, in the presence of the creative team (including *American Gods* executive producer Neil Gaiman, who wrote the book the show was based on), the actors read through the script. When it was over, a white cast member spoke first. "I love this guy," Jones said. "He pro-ceeded to let them know that this was not the fare he had signed up for. He had signed up for something with depth and meaning, and this was not that."

Jones did not disagree with anything his castmate had said (nor did many of his colleagues, he added). But that doesn't mean Jones believed he would have been allowed to say it: "I'm telling you right now, Mo, if I ever spoke like this white man spoke in that meeting, they would have carried me out in handcuffs."

It was especially weird to learn about how regimented life at *Saturday Night Live* could be. I'd grown up reading about the wild antics of the original cast and many who came after them, and the word "disci-plined" did not frequently come up. But when I talked to insiders at the show, I quickly learned how many rules, strictly delineated processes, and schedules they have to follow—and again, some of that is under-standable. Putting on a ninety-minute sketch show every week means almost everyone must be able to work quickly and efficiently. But an-other truth also emerged from those conversations: in many ways that matter, *SNL* is not a freewheeling, collective endeavor. It is, for all prac-tical purposes, a fiefdom presided over by one all-powerful person.

Executive producer Lorne Michaels "is God," Ben told me. "If you were in his presence, you were either lucky or you had done something wrong."

Ben, now a writer/producer, grew up idolizing not just *SNL* but Adam Sandler's work in particular. Most weeks, there is a standby line for *SNL* tickets, and Ben camped out to get tickets "four or five times—just to have experienced it live," he told me.

When he got a job on the show less than a decade ago, he was de-termined to prove himself—to work as hard as possible to impress his colleagues. And it didn't take him long to realize that if things went his way and he began climbing the *SNL* ladder, he'd probably have more job security than most in the industry. People in the crew and in other jobs in and around *SNL*'s Studio 8H tended to stay in those positions for years, if not decades.

"It was like, 'Wow, so many people here have been doing this for as long as I've been alive,'" Ben recalled. "A thing they did really well was to make you feel part of the institution." This meant that when one department received an Emmy, everyone in the department got a certificate commemorating the win. Other shows do that too, but most don't have *SNL*'s storied history, and the romance of *SNL* as a long-running institution was something that drew Ben into its orbit and still makes him understandably nostalgic for the good aspects of the job. When Tracy Morgan came back to host after his serious car accident, he was especially kind to Ben, and an *SNL* photo of Morgan graces Ben's wall.

But there was a dark side to *SNL*, one that eventually drove Ben away from it. It wasn't just other employees regaling him with tales of when interns were unpaid—a situation that was *better*, in their opinion, because then they were "free" to work as many hours as they wanted to. He came to see that, despite the enjoyable or exciting times, the workplace was often infused with "such a warped way of thinking."

Ben told me he felt "constant fear" and was regularly assigned tasks that felt questionable, if not wrong. Though he was never asked to do so, he was aware that other low-level employees obtained illegal drugs for *SNL* cast members. He did regularly buy alcohol for an employee of the show, which made him very nervous, given that Ben was underage and using a fake ID. But he quickly absorbed the ethos of the show: don't complain and do what you're told—or else. At one point, Ben had a back injury, which he said he was grateful happened during a week that the show was off. If he'd called out sick, he felt sure he would have been replaced. (Several PR people for NBC, *SNL*, and Michaels were sent an extensive list of questions about the allegations in this book. A representative for the network sent a one-sentence reply: "We appreciate you reaching out, however NBC is declining participation.")

"They really made you feel like you were a part of the team until you stepped too far, and then you were reminded of your place," said Ben. That said, being male protected him, to some degree. He has heard horror stories—involving allegations of harassment and assault—from women he worked with at *SNL*. He did not feel it was appropriate to tell me the details of those stories because they did not happen to him. But a *Business Insider* story from 2022 outlined what could be a perilous environment at the show.

"For the young women who worked on the show—the interns and NBC pages who had fought for their coveted positions—this environment could be treacherous," the story notes. "Several former staffers said male members of the cast and staff would hook up with female college-age interns at post-show parties. The young staffer said that when she interned on the 1999–2000 season before being hired full time, the cast member Horatio Sanz followed her into a bedroom at a party and asked to touch her breasts. Another former intern said that at a different party at about this time, a high-profile cast member asked her to sit on his lap and licked one of her cheeks. At the *SNL* offices, it often felt as if there were no rules, with the young staffer saying a colleague showed her a nude photo of himself without her consent."

One ex-staffer told the publication it "would be difficult to imagine more than two women who 'had a great experience or felt valued'" while working at *SNL* during the early 2000s, the time frame covered by the story. "It was an incredibly sexist environment."

Ben worked there more than a decade later, but the overall culture hadn't changed much, by his account. Over time, he learned to keep his mouth shut and absorbed the unspoken lesson that "people who looked the other way" would thrive at *SNL*. This was brought home to him after an incident that, in a healthier environment, might not have been such a big deal. One day, Ben asked a supervisor to not pair him with a coworker who was being particularly disrespectful and verbally combative.

Not only was his request denied, Ben was sent home. Feeling devastated, he abjectly apologized to his boss for making the request, but their working relationship was never the same. After talking to Ben, I described the outlines of this situation to Grant, whose time at *SNL* did not overlap with Ben's. Grant said that it was possible that Ben's boss was just a bad manager. Or, a possible counterargument is that Ben's manager had absorbed the core rule of *SNL:* the only thing that matters is getting the sketches on the air once a week.

Grant, who spent several years at *SNL*, has retained a high opinion of Michaels. "Watch what happens when he dies. They'll have to rent out Madison Square Garden for his funeral," he observed. "Everyone who has worked for him will want to be there—including me." But he also conceded that the longtime producer's power is absolute. "Lorne is so powerful and so revered, and the show is in New York, far away from the LA executives and everything else," Grant remarked. "He runs his own kingdom out there and as the years go on, it only becomes more like he's the Godfather."

Over time, the unhappy side effects of how that power was used caused Ben to remove his "rose-colored glasses." "The thing about *SNL* is, it's a job," Ben said. "A lot of what we did was thankless, boring work." But whether someone was holding cue cards for an A-lister or completing unglamorous minion tasks, the atmosphere those people operated in, Ben said, had one overriding philosophy: don't rock the boat.

Seamus was asked to stop coming to casting sessions.

The request, which came midway through pre-production on an episode of a hit broadcast network drama he cowrote more than a decade ago, surprised him; he could not think of anything distracting or unprofessional he'd done. Given the kinds of ridiculous and abusive conduct he'd seen and experienced in the industry, he'd always tried to avoid being an asshole, but maybe he'd slipped up. He asked what he'd done wrong.

Turns out, during a casting session, he'd brought up a previous film by an actor who'd come in to read for a role. Seamus told her he liked her performance. A day or two after that, the well-known casting director of the show asked him not to attend any other sessions. Seamus could only infer that his comment to the actor got him banned. It never occurred to him that showing enthusiasm, or simply treating an actor like a human being, would be frowned upon. Later, when he ran into a higher-ranking colleague and excitedly recounted a chance meeting with a different actor, he said the coworker "chewed me out for it." Gushing to actors was not just gauche, his colleague indicated, it might give them false ideas about their importance. "She was like, 'The actors are chess pieces that we move around the table,'" Seamus recalled.

Seamus's more senior colleague was generally helpful and kind, but he said that conversation "really changed the way I looked at the business. I remember going home that night thinking, 'What the hell are we doing? There are so many easier ways to make a living. If this isn't supposed to be fun, what's the point?'"

The point, for some, is to amass as much power as they can—and the ability to wield it however they want. They shut down the enthusiasm, the joy, the contributions, and the imaginations of others. It's very strange to realize that the industry, despite many proclamations and poses indicating otherwise, is a series of autocracies and dictatorships. But that's often what it is—in executive suites, on sets, in production offices, anywhere. Some who keep encountering the industry's most punishing, brutal attitudes and gatekeepers end up facing a choice: they become spineless (temporarily or permanently) or they leave whatever gig they're in. Some quit the industry entirely.

Seamus thought he'd never have to face a choice like that, especially when the critically acclaimed show he worked on was riding high and winning awards. It wasn't shot in Los Angeles, so the actors weren't around the writers much. And that was fine. By that point in his career, Seamus was already familiar with the standard ritual of actor-writer interactions in the television world. Much of that dance revolves around the table read, which is a chance for everyone to assess what is and isn't working in the script.

Seamus gave me the rundown of what usually happens: "At the table read, everybody claps and there's applause, and the actors say it's fantastic, they *love* it. The writers go back to the writers' room. And one by one, the actors will show up and say, 'My God, I laughed. I cried. You just keep getting better. It's incredible. And also—I thought maybe my character might have a little bit more to do here. What do you think?'"

Those kinds of gentle suggestions are generally seen as okay. But if an actor offers anything more substantial in the way of feedback, it can have disastrous consequences. One of the actors from the show happened to be in LA at one point, and he came by to make suggestions about his character to the writing staff. Not long after that, his character was killed off. "If you'd like to get your character written off, show up in the writers' room and tell them how to write the show," Seamus said with a wry laugh.

Most Hollywood veterans reading this passage will understand—as Seamus certainly does—why key creatives sometime bristle at suggestions from actors or from anyone else who's not sweating blood to conceive story lines, create memorable visuals, or polish scripts. Those in crucial creative roles on a film or TV show often know its goals and the themes more intimately than anyone else. Having expended a lot of effort to get the damn thing made, they don't necessarily want an actor to throw a wrench into the gears, especially once production is underway.

Of course, it's easy to see these situations from the actor's side too. They're artists who have the challenging task of bringing what's on the page to life, and their collaborators don't always know how to effectively help them do that. These kinds of collisions and differences of opinion are common, and handled thoughtfully, they can lead to better work. But ultimately, there isn't a singular best practice in these situations—aside from "Don't be a horrifying jerk about it"—because every project's needs, evolution, and goals are different.

"It's riddled with paradoxes and contradictions," Shernold Edwards said of the collaboration-versus-command part of the creative process. Edwards has been a writer, a producer, and a television executive, and she understandably believes that "you need somebody in charge to make the decisions, or else you're not going to get anywhere." That view reflects the general opinion of many industry people I've talked to over the years, which could be summarized as follows: department heads, showrunners, directors, executives—whoever is in charge of a given situation—need to be able to set an agenda.

But before (and sometimes, if appropriate, after) some decisions are made, in a healthy workplace, there can be "a bunch of opinions," as Edwards put it. A good leader allows the kind of helpful or even challenging input and feedback that may improve a project; that leader lets people feel meaningfully heard, and then, in Edwards' words, "says yea or nay" to what's been suggested.

Because so many people without proper training, support, or supervision are put into positions they're not ready for, all too often, they respond to the many pressures of leadership by going the petty-dictator or screaming-asshole route, shutting down most or all well-intentioned input. They become so fixated on protecting their territory or their vision that they become paranoid, cruel, or abusive, all while guarding their turf in an overly zealous fashion. In situations like that, as I and others have so often reported, the people around the dictatorial personality are routinely dismissed, damaged, or destroyed in the face of the autocrat's implacable, defensive, and toxic will.

David O. Russell—the director who verbally abused Lily Tomlin in a video clip that went viral years ago—was so awful to Amy Adams on the set of *American Hustle* that it came up in emails uncovered in the 2014 hack of the Sony studio. ("His abuse and lunatic behaviour are extreme even by Hollywood standards," journalist Jonathan Alter wrote in an email to his brother-in-law, Sony's then CEO Michael Lynton.) Later, she told one publication "he was hard on me, that's for sure. It was a lot . . . I was really just devastated on set." According to a 2022 *Washington Post* excavation of the director's history, Russell headbutted and grabbed the throat of George Clooney (who told an interviewer in 2000 that Russell also assaulted an extra during the fraught production of *Three Kings*). At another point, according to the *Washington Post* story, Russell put director Christopher Nolan in a headlock. Russell is still working, despite an investigation into an incident in which he touched his nineteen-year-old niece's breasts—an interaction he confirmed while describing his niece as "very provocative and seductive" to police. (The case was closed without charges being filed.) Nobody seems to care about the long list of terrible behaviors openly ascribed to Russell. And if that's how A-listers like Clooney, Adams, and Nolan are treated, what do you think happens to people without any power?

Well, they encounter abuse and bullying regularly, if my conversations and email inbox are any indication.

I get how hard it is to be a leader, by the way: there are sometimes disruptive or distracting worker bees whose input isn't helpful and who can, from whatever perch they occupy, derail or even poison a creative environment. Sometimes those employees have to be guided into better workplace habits, reprimanded, or even fired. But in my experience—and in the experience of many, many Hollywood veterans I've talked to—most people in the industry are aware that their job involves helping execute someone else's vision. People sign on to do exactly that; they know the deal. Of course, folks want to bring their own contributions to any creative endeavor, but when they're not in charge, they're generally quite mindful of that (and if they aren't, the likelihood of someone overtly or covertly reminding them is not small).

Seamus told me about a writer he thought was very talented but who "just shut down" after being treated badly in a hit show's writers' room. The showrunner perpetuated an environment that everyone had to pretend involved "joking" and "teasing" but was actually cruel, draining, and toxic. One day, the writer Seamus admired was being bullied with a particular relentlessness. Finally, the showrunner got everyone to ease up and asked that writer to share the suggestions he'd wanted to make. "It took a whole lot of doing to get him to open up about the idea he was going to pitch," Seamus recalled. "But he was never the same" after the hazing he endured that day. "He left the show shortly thereafter. He was beaten down to the point of, 'I don't want to even open my mouth anymore, because it's not worth it.'"

Anyone who routinely shuts down, fires, or threatens others for offering good-faith efforts to make something better is not just propagating a shitty, fear-driven work atmosphere. They're depriving themselves of potentially valuable input from people who are literally *on their team*. Still, if I had a dollar for every time I heard about a Hollywood leader who refused to delegate and enforced total conformity from the increasingly beaten-down people trying to help them, I'd be writing this book in a chateau in France.

The showrunner Seamus worked for is a perfect example of this syndrome: no one questioned his right to be in control, but his "leadership" evolved into a quest for total domination and obedience. "He went down the wrong path," Seamus said. "He engineered a scenario where he'd have to do everything because he didn't let anybody else do anything. It's like Sisyphus looking for more rocks to carry up that mountain." And those Sisyphean martyrs usually don't let anyone forget who has the power to not just fire them but potentially end their careers.

Writer/producer Taura recalled her time working for such a leader: "The stress of not knowing, 'What's his mood going to be today? Is he going to be in a bad mood? Is he gonna be angry at me for no reason—is he going to lash out? Is he going to throw something?'" She observed, "You're at this high level of anxiety and stress all the time because you never know and there's nothing you can do. Everyone's like, 'Yeah, that's just how he is. Either deal with it or get a new job.' Because if you get fired, good luck getting work anywhere else."

Not every leader is like this, but the truth is, these kinds of stories are everywhere. Too many people I know have dozens of them.

When writing for the Fox drama *Sleepy Hollow,* on set and in the writers' room, Shernold Edwards told me her input was routinely discounted. It is (or at least it used to be) fairly standard for the writer of an episode to be kept in the loop as that installment of the show progresses toward completion. But the only way Edwards got to sit in on post-production sessions for an episode she wrote was to make a vow in advance to her superiors: "I promised to be quiet and not say anything." So much for Hollywood as a place of risk-taking, artistic debate, and unfettered creativity.

Seamus learned this lesson too. His mistake is the same one I made for a long time—assuming an admirable film or show or song *must* have been made by admirable people. It is human to want to ascribe positive qualities to people whose stories or art have left us moved, changed, challenged, and feeling seen. And there were some good times at that high-profile show. Seamus remembers traversing the studio lot and feeling blissful about where he was in life, despite pulling in the grand salary of just over $500 per week.

"Everybody else in the room was a millionaire except for me, but I remember riding my bike going, 'I'm so happy. I can't believe that I'm finally here.' I ate so much shit to get to an environment where not only could I be around unbelievably talented people, but I could get the charge of creating a story, the best story we could possibly tell—and the show was well received," he recalled. "All I wanted to do was spend my career doing exactly that—tell great stories with great people."

But on that job, he also witnessed casual cruelty, sexism, and stupidity. He realized that "making it" meant repressing his enthusiasm, all to sustain a power dynamic he found bizarre and inhumane but that people in the business considered appropriate—or worse, necessary.

In some places—not enough, but some—dynamics like these are slowly starting to change. But a problem remains: not only are the skills involved in exercising healthy leadership generally not taught, but having power *at all* can be unsettling for some, according to Silas Howard, who has acted in, produced, and directed feature films and television.

"Some people are expected to have power and they wear it like loose clothing. They're comfortable in their power," said Howard. "For those of us that have not been raised to have power, it's very uncomfortable."

When Howard and I met up midway through 2022, we had half an hour to talk. Right after our interview, he headed to a virtual meeting with the editor of his latest film. Given our time constraints, I tried not to spend much of the interview fangirling over *Dickinson,* the Apple

TV+ program on which Howard was an executive producer and director. Few shows in recent memory have taken more tonal and stylistic chances than *Dickinson,* which had a distinctive and astute take on the life and art of poet Emily Dickinson. The show took a lot of big swings: every so often, Emily (played by Hailee Steinfeld) conversed with a giant bee; she and her sister time-traveled to meet Sylvia Plath; she was not averse to the occasional opium party; and she frequently boarded a gorgeous carriage drawn by ghostly horses. It belonged to Death, who was played by Wiz Khalifa.

Emily and Death debated the meaning of life, death, love, art, and poetry in conversations that were earnest but never plodding; the show combined the soulful, the silly, and the sublime in a host of memorable and meaningful ways.

Dickinson, which was created by writer and producer Alena Smith, used irreverence, bangin' music, surreal tableaux, and irony to make serious points about what it can cost an artist to not just make her art but be her authentic self in a world full of oblivious or controlling gatekeepers. The scene in which a male editor who plans to publish Emily's work against her will steals her poems, and then, as he's making his getaway, shouts "I'm a feminist!"—now *that* is relatable content.

Unlike that charming, manipulative character, Howard's methods don't involve shady or dictatorial tendencies. He told me he seeks out the input of actors: on every job, he makes an effort to call them as soon as he can. Making contact in advance can help establish a collaborative and trusting atmosphere on set, he has found. And even if, in that first phone call, Howard and the actors don't get around to talking about the work, at least they've broken the ice.

"The ones that don't [call back]—I take no offense," Howard said. Part of his motivation in seeking input is practical, since once production has begun, he noted, there's "no time at all." He arrives on set prepared but not ferociously locked in to what he has planned. Imposing his will unilaterally on others isn't his goal, he told me, even though he knows sometimes "we conflate confidence with competence." But being "the withholding dad" who knows all and commands the set in a top-down fashion doesn't appeal to him; he'd rather "create trust," as he put it.

"Leadership is, for me, about reading a room, making people feel seen, making them feel they're in a safe environment—enough to try something that doesn't work," Howard said. There are a lot of pressures on TV and film sets—time pressures, money pressures, when-is-lunch pressures. He knows that if he makes the "wrong" choices, "a blame game" that he might lose can ensue. But he wants to encourage experimentation and risk-taking, despite knowing how much is on the line. It surely informs Howard's approach that he was an indie musician and filmmaker for years, not reaching anything approaching economic security until he was around forty. He told me the fear of slipping back into poverty is always with him. And yet, he also knows that he wouldn't be where he is now if he had avoided creative risks and never *gone for it*. "I often say, I want permission for bad ideas. I want it to feel okay to suggest bad ideas, because then I just feel comfortable. I feel relaxed," Howard said. "Especially if you're doing comedy, if you don't have the kind of trust that allows you to make a fool of yourself, you're not going to really do good comedy."

But part of the problem is that trying to create an environment that encourages freedom *and* ensures the day's work is completed on time isn't easy to do; what's more, nobody teaches you how to do it. It's been like this from the beginning. While leaving most leaders (and potential leaders) to fend for themselves, the industry also places entire groups of people inside a series of interlocking and claustrophobic limitations.

In the 1920s, film star Clara Bow was one of the most famous women in the world, but by around 1930, the industry had decided she was a liability, in part due to a legal case involving a former personal secretary. It emerged that Bow liked playing poker, bought men jewelry, and had large amounts of liquor delivered to her home. Bow had also gained weight, and all of that just *would not do*. How Bow lived was not unusual then (or now), but as Anne Helen Petersen writes in her book *Scandals of Classic Hollywood*, between "the weight gain and the gambling, it was easy to frame Bow as an unruly woman, with appetites quickly spiraling out of control."

It was worse for women of color, who were pigeonholed on-screen as temptresses, comic relief, or domestic servants. Actor and producer Rita Moreno, who was born in Puerto Rico, has talked about being restricted for years to "dusky maiden" roles and having her skin darkened in the first film adaptation of *West Side Story*. For her Hollywood employers, African American actor Louise Beavers's body was also a problem—it was the wrong shape. For decades, especially in the 1930s and '40s, Beavers played the maid roles that were usually the only ones offered to Black women, as Donald Bogle writes in *Toms, Coons, Mulattoes, Mammies, and Bucks: An Interpretive History of Blacks in American Films*. The women she played were, as Bogle notes, "always happy, always kind, always intricately involved in the private lives of her employers, so much so that she usually completely lacked a private life of her own." But before she could take on those roles, the Cincinnati-born Beavers had to learn to speak with a Southern dialect, which she was required to deploy in her work. An even bigger "problem" in the eyes of her potential employers was the fact that Beavers "was heavy and hearty, but not heavy and hearty enough," Bogle observes. She'd force herself to eat to keep her weight up, but when she was making a film, it wasn't unusual for her to lose weight, and according to Bogle, she sometimes "had to be padded to look more like a full-bosomed domestic who was capable of carrying the world on her shoulders."

That impulse to control, change, and corral the unruly—or eject them if they won't submit—has never really gone away. Power in the industry is still too often channeled into corrosive impulses and mindsets. "I've seen what power does. It can create a lot of division," Howard observed. "For a lot of people, myself included, who've not had power much, there's more conflict [about being in charge]. I'll work on a show with a straight white guy who's got his issues. He's had stuff he's had to work on, but he's comfortable with having power. He's been raised to have power. It's something that is not odd. . . . As a trans guy, when I transitioned, I did this job for an ad agency and I was like this unintentional gender spy."

Howard's experience revealed not just that, in his words, "misogyny is *so* alive and kicking" but that his male collaborators banded together to increase the power that *all* of them got to wield. He found that revelatory. By contrast, those from historically excluded groups are often trained to view one another as the competition. "We were left with 'divide and conquer,'" Howard noted.

Of course, Howard doesn't play that zero-sum game, but he—like so many people interviewed for this book—does worry that the financial security he finally gained after two decades of scratching and scrambling could go away. "I still think I could be out in the street, you know?" Howard observed.

That view was echoed by Christopher, a writer/producer who has worked on many mainstream dramas, a number of them in the broadcast-TV realm. The kind of precariousness Howard and many others fear is something Christopher thinks about all the time, especially given the shorter seasons and smaller paychecks now common in the industry. He's working hard to earn less than he did a decade ago, and the lessons he absorbed when rising through the ranks have stayed with him.

"Every showrunner has a different process. And as I have learned over the years, some are not so great. But when you come up in the era that I did, it was kind of like, 'Shut up and do the job, because it's not your show,'" Christopher said. "You have to get through it because you want the next job." In some ways, he and Howard are no different from Beavers and Bow. "You're a contract player, and you're always thinking, 'I don't know where my next paycheck's coming from. I could get bounced at any time,'" Christopher observed. "You are in constant fear of not being able to provide for the people you love."

Not every workplace is like the worst ones Shernold Edwards, Christopher, and Seamus encountered. But a lot are—and I'm not just talking about film sets and TV shows; a number of production companies, networks, and studio workplaces fall into the "run by repressive dictators" category. Every person I know in the industry has worked in a fear-driven workplace at least once, if not repeatedly. Thus almost everyone has had to acquire armor—the kind of thick, ungainly shield you need when you, with good cause, fear being attacked, berated, humiliated, fired, and defamed just for doing your job.

After leaving the hit show that became toxic, Seamus had a good experience with a veteran from that program who ran a different series with "grace and kindness." But he's out of the industry now, more or less. He simply got to a point where maintaining a cowering pose wasn't worth the stress it created. When that part of his life comes up in conversation, he's often asked, "Knowing what you know now, would you do it all over again?"

"I'm at that point where you start to take stock of the life you have lived and the one you've got left. I don't have to wonder, what if I'd given it a shot? I did. I gave it my absolute best shot, as hard as I could for twenty years, and I have no regrets. I got further than I ever thought or hoped I would," Seamus responded. "But if I'm honest, it's no. I wouldn't, because it's just too hard."

—

One big industry reckoning that still needs to happen on a much larger scale involves the treatment of children. There are hundreds, if not thousands, of kid-centered screen stories that celebrate childhood as a time of rebellion, exploration, creativity, and even liberation. Young people breaking the rules and having fun while learning life lessons is an enormous subcategory of the vast array of films and shows Hollywood has churned out over the years.

Many of those stories feature a wise adult who is a source of knowledge and help for the kids. If only all child performers had reliable access to that kind of protection.

Of course, the American entertainment industry has attempted to tackle the issues surrounding underage performers in the past. Laws have been passed that regulate, among other things, how many hours kids can work and what should be done with their income. But here's just one indication of how profoundly broken this part of the system can be: a 2012 California law designed to protect industry children from predators was, for years, disregarded, by both the industry and the criminal justice system.

The law requires that publicists, managers, acting coaches, and photographers who work with minors get fingerprinted and pass an FBI background check in order to receive a Child Performers Services Permit. The trade site *Deadline* reported in 2018 that "not a single Hollywood publicist who represents child actors has obtained a permit," yet no one had ever been charged under the law, which arose partly to prevent publicist, manager, and convicted child abuser Robert Villard and other dangerous people from continuing to work in the industry under assumed names. The law, the piece notes, has been "largely ignored and unenforced since it was enacted." Why did so few industry folks required to have this permit actually get it? "One, people are lazy," a manager who acquired the permit told *Deadline*. "And two, nobody assumed anybody would follow through, and nobody has. They figure that if there are no consequences, what does it matter?"

Consequences have certainly been a long time coming for kid-centric TV network Nickelodeon and everyone who enabled its culture of silence, complicity, and abuse.

In her 2022 memoir *I'm Glad My Mom Died,* actor Jennette McCurdy shared disturbing details of what it was like to work on the Nickelodeon shows *iCarly* and *Sam & Cat.* She got the *iCarly* job when she was fourteen. In a book excerpt published in *Vanity Fair*, McCurdy says that during her time working on those programs, she developed an eating disorder, and "The Creator" gave her massages and pressured her to drink alcohol, all while she was still underage. When *Sam & Cat*, one of many Nickelodeon programs created by Dan Schneider, was canceled, she was offered $300,000. Her representatives at the time tried to make the payout sound like a gift, but the present came with strings. She could never talk about her experiences "specifically related to The Creator." McCurdy turned down the "hush money."

Within weeks of publication of McCurdy's book, Alexa Nikolas, a former star of *Zoey 101* (also created by Schneider), led a protest outside Nickelodeon's animation studio in Burbank, California. She and her fellow actors were "not safe" when they worked for the network, she told the *Los Angeles Times*, adding that she "did not feel protected at Nickelodeon as a child." She called Schneider "the creator of childhood trauma." For her part, McCurdy noted that the powerful writer/producer could be "over-the-top complimentary" in one moment and "mean-spirited, controlling and terrifying" the next, frequently making "grown men and women cry with his insults and degradation." Thanks in part to the toll the psychological manipulation took, McCurdy stopped acting around 2018. That year, after an investigation, Nickelodeon ended its relationship with Schneider, who had been the most powerful writer/producer at the network for a long time. He took with him the $7 million still owed on his contract.

A trade story at the time noted his "temper issues" and "complaints of abusive behavior," not to mention the "raised eyebrows" regarding his practice of sharing photos of the toes of young female stars on social media. In a 2021 interview, Schneider denied acting inappropriately around the children who worked at the network. But a *Business Insider* article on his Nickelodeon reign—published the same month that McCurdy's book ignited a new conversation around these topics—paints a picture that conforms to the dark portrayal in *I'm Glad My Mom Died*. Children were sexualized and pitted against one another, and their parents' desire to stay in Schneider's good graces led to an atmosphere of "desperation," former Nickelodeon actor Raquel Lee told *Insider*. "Out of desperation, people will do a lot of things," Lee said.

Some former Nickelodeon performers still kept in touch with Schneider, according to the article, but overall, "Schneider created an uncomfortable, bizarre environment that he ruled over like a fiefdom. . . . One longtime writer said it took years before he understood what he now describes as the 'maddening, disgusting, controlling little bubble' that Schneider created. 'It's why people stayed for so long and never said anything' publicly, the writer said. 'It was very effective.'"

It takes an enormous array of willing participants—executives, accountants, business affairs employees, managers, and agents—to smoothly, and I'll bet routinely, offer young people shut-the-fuck-up money and make it seem like a gift. (How many other desperate parents would have grabbed a six-figure "gift" and told their kids to keep quiet?) It's also worth noting that according to a 2018 story in BuzzFeed, Nickelodeon creator John Kricfalusi (the man behind *The Ren & Stimpy Show*) was accused of grooming an underage woman and of sexual harassment by teens who worked for him. In addition, Nickelodeon workers Ezel Ethan Channel and Jason Michael Handy, both of whom used their jobs to gain the trust of children, were convicted of sexual crimes. The case of Handy, a Nickelodeon production assistant who wrote in his journal that he was a "pedophile, full blown," was "among at least a dozen child molestation and child pornography prosecutions since 2000 involving actors, managers, production assistants and others in the industry," according to a 2012 *Los Angeles Times* investigation.

Not all children in the industry encounter predators, but the "normal" things they endure can be plenty terrible. "I never appeared in anything more revealing than a knee-length sundress," former child actor Mara Wilson, who appeared in *Mrs. Doubtfire* among other roles, writes in a 2021 article for the *New York Times*. "This was all intentional. My parents thought I would be safer that way. But it didn't work. People had been asking me, 'Do you have a boyfriend?' in interviews since I was 6. . . . It was cute when 10-year-olds sent me letters saying they were in love with me. It was not when 50-year-old men did. Before I even turned 12, there were images of me on foot fetish websites and photoshopped into child pornography."

Producer, actor, and director Alex Winter—who appeared in the *Bill & Ted* movies and helmed *Showbiz Kids*, a documentary on what it's like to be a child performer—said in a 2020 interview he thinks the industry may be changing on this front. But he also indicated that there needs to be a bigger acknowledgment of the inherent challenges that working in Hollywood adds to a child's life. "If you put your kid in the business or you allow your kid to enter the business, you have to understand that there will 100 percent be consequences," said Winter, who has spoken of enduring "prolonged" sexual abuse as a twelve-year-old appearing in *The King & I* on Broadway. "Those could be incredibly severe; they could be fatal; they could be minor. But absolutely there will be consequences."

"I imagine this stuff can take years to work through, mentally and emotionally," observes Stephanie in a perceptive essay the site Lainey Gossip published after McCurdy's book came out. "How do you negotiate such a heavy and ongoing experience, especially one that happens in one of the most defining stages of your life?" Those are the kinds of murky, knotty questions many former child actors are still working through—not because they want to, but because they have to in order to survive.

One thing was crystal clear to Evan Rachel Wood when she was a child actor: the ironclad rule she absorbed on set—and on red carpets and at photo shoots—was that she *must* obey the adults in charge.

Another important dictum: never slow down production for any reason. "There's this intense pressure not to hold anything up, not to cost anybody money," Wood told me. "And there's this intense fear that if you slow things down, then you're labeled a troublemaker. No one's going to want to work with you." As a child and teen, Wood's artistry and her abilities were recognized and encouraged, of course. But what the industry really wanted from her was "compliance," she said

When she was coming up, many Hollywood interactions and dynamics "normalized abuse and mistreatment." Wood added, "That was something that took me a long time to realize and reflect on. Growing up as a child in the industry, your boundaries are just—there are none. You are not taught boundaries. You are actually rewarded for having no boundaries, and that was something I had to reprogram in myself, and I'm still working on that. I was rewarded for never saying no and for never putting up a fight and never questioning anything. And the more compliant I was, the more people wanted to work with me."

The rules extended to how she appeared—when she was a teen, some articles casually mentioned her weight—and how she was allowed to dress; suits with trousers were definitely out. "On photo shoots, I did not want to show my legs. I did not want to wear dresses," Wood recalled. "I did not want to be sexualized. I did not want to dress older than I was. And it was made very clear to me and my mother that if we did not do this, then we would not be supported. We would be told flat out, 'Well, we're just not going to take the picture,' or 'We're not going to run the story.' Maybe the story dies, or maybe it's awards season and the studio won't put any money behind you. You are low-key threatened, essentially."

Wood also absorbed the idea that if she allowed herself to be depicted and sexualized in very specific ways—ways that often troubled her—it would help her career. "The more adult you were, the more serious of an actor you were. That's how the reward systems functioned, from what I could tell—you'd be taken more seriously if you were pushing the boundaries more and more," she said. Moving up in her craft, leveling up in the industry—these things involved "doing things that are out of your age range and are more adult and more sexual. I was rewarded a lot for engaging in behaviors that I was uncomfortable with, but, when I listened to how people talked about those kinds of performances and roles, it felt as though the message was, 'That's being a serious actor,'" Wood added. "It wasn't like they said it exactly like this, but the idea was, 'This is how you're going to be rewarded or loved—if you push these boundaries.'"

For Wood, using her body on camera in ways that could feel weird and confusing—beginning at a very young age—led to success and greater opportunities. "I did the film *Thirteen* when I was fourteen. I had my first sex scene when I was sixteen years old, with Edward Norton. Not only was there no intimacy coordinator, but I was also a minor and there was still nobody there. This is the only industry where you are allowed to film minors in a sexual manner and it's legal." As a young teen, Wood often heard—or saw in the media—comments that revolved around the idea that she was "wise beyond her years." That may well have been true, but she noted, "those are usually the kids that get picked. The 'precocious' ones. Mature enough to get the job done but young enough to take advantage of."

Wood did have teachers on set, but she eventually realized some were better than others when it came to prioritizing not just her education but her overall well-being. "There are certain hours that a child can work, a certain amount of time they need in school," Wood said. "But what I didn't notice [until later] was that there are good set teachers and set teachers that are going to be a little more relaxed about certain things, because they want to get hired again. They know that they'll get hired if they bend the rules. And unfortunately, the children are the ones that take the hit."

Once she was sixteen, Wood no longer needed a teacher or guardian on set, because she was done with high school. She had been raised by an industry that told her that being "professional" meant acting older than her age. She was rewarded by an industry that told her to be sexual, but only in the ways that it deemed acceptable. She had spent years absorbing the message that the way to be an artist, a professional, a truly creative person, involved never saying no to those with more power, influence, resources, and connections.

When she was eighteen, she met Brian Warner, a.k.a. Marilyn Manson.

As an expert on how sets function, Wood knew that when an actor is doing a scene in which they appear nude, there is always someone standing by to hand them a robe. They're there after every take. That's just how things are done.

That is not how it was done on the set of Marilyn Manson's music video *Heart-Shaped Glasses*, according to Wood. Nothing went right. There was no robe for her at the end of most takes. She told me she was pressured into consuming alcohol and drugs. She had not agreed to any nudity, let alone any sex acts. No one protected her. Wood told me—and said in *Phoenix Rising*, an HBO documentary about her experiences with Manson and her domestic violence activism—that, in that video, she was "essentially raped on-camera." (Manson's lawyer told *Rolling Stone* there was no sex on the set of *Heart-Shaped Glasses* and that "Evan was not only fully coherent and engaged during the three-day shoot but also heavily involved in weeks of pre-production planning and days of post-production editing of the final cut.")

According to Wood, there were two crews on that set—a group of people hired and controlled by Manson, and an "old-school" crew that was hired in part because those folks could wrangle some then-new technology that was important to the video. The latter crew was largely made up, Wood said, of veteran guys, some of whom had worked with *Titanic* director James Cameron (an MTV story at the time referenced the video's use of "3-D technology developed by" the director).

When Wood used the term "old-school" to describe a sizable contingent of the crew, I rolled my eyes. Because, not to paint with too broad a brush, a lot of crew guys of a certain age have absorbed and sometimes enabled questionable "norms" about what big-name actors and directors should be allowed to do. Not all crew members are alike, of course, and the majority don't want to work in punishing environments for terrible people. But some partly or fully accept the thinking that horrible behavior connotes "passion" and "creativity."

During the video shoot, however, the old-school crew did something surprising: they walked off the set, according to Wood. They saw how she was being treated, and they weren't okay with it. And they definitely weren't okay with filming alleged sex acts involving someone still in her teens. In 2022, two members of the crew spoke to *Rolling Stone* not long after the release of *Phoenix Rising*. "The crew was very uncomfortable," one said. After one or two takes, according to *Rolling Stone*, "the shoot was shut down over the sex scenes as arguments between Manson and producers and crew members escalated." Everyone "in the cast and crew was all alienated. So that's why it became somewhat uncomfortable for all of us around," another crew member said.

Wood told me that executives from Interscope, Manson's record label at the time, were at the shoot. "I don't have their names, but they witnessed me being given absinthe," despite the fact that the nineteen-year-old Wood was under the legal drinking age. "No one wanted to make waves," she recalled. "Brian created an environment of fear and nobody did anything. I was an impaired teenager, and I was scared and had no voice." The situation was not just tragic but ironic, given that Manson—whose dictatorial whims and terrible acts were enabled by dozens of industry people and companies for years—had portrayed himself as some kind of rebel.

Years after their relationship ended, Wood actually rebelled by calling out the grooming and sexual abuse she says she endured, and in early 2021, she and several other women publicly named Manson as their abuser. (Manson has denied misconduct of any kind with Wood or anyone else. In March 2022, Manson sued Wood and another woman, Ashley "Illma" Gore, citing defamation, among other accusations. In 2023, a judge dismissed some legal claims but others are still pending.)

Though many good things have come from her journey into activism for survivors of domestic abuse, Wood told me that the path she has traveled has also led to some people in the industry avoiding her, being unwilling to hire her, or just generally treating her as "the abuse police."

"There's a whole person in here," she said as we sat under the pergola in her sunny yard. "I'm not unhinged. If you say good morning to me and touch my shoulder, I'm not going to run to HR." At least these days, there is an HR to go to. And in 2021, Wood began working with an intimacy coordinator for the first time, on the HBO drama *Westworld*. "I tear up every time they're on set," Wood said. "And I thank them every time they show up, because it's shocking to me that there was a time when somebody wasn't looking out for your body and your well-being and your emotional state when you're doing intimate scenes, or exposing yourself and becoming very vulnerable."

Wood and the creative team at *Westworld*, where she said she has always felt valued as an artist and a human being, are among those pushing industry change forward. She and other activists also changed the law in California regarding the statute of limitations in domestic violence cases. "I think if more people knew how to navigate that process or how to advocate for change or knew how powerful they actually were, then more would happen," she observed. "But there's also a million systems in place to disempower people and to make them afraid and to make them feel like they can't do anything. And the same goes for the entertainment industry."

Many actors are only now just beginning to talk about the kinds of intense pressures and autocratic environments they've encountered in their careers. The pressure is great to accept long hours, to take whatever roles—and whatever kinds of treatment—are dished out. When you work long hours on a set, "that's your world," Wood noted. "You're constantly busy problem-solving, so you don't have time to ask questions or to go, 'Hang on a minute.' Because you're just trying to get it done." And if you step out of line and say something that challenges those with more power—Wood finished my sentence—"You're out of the group."

"This business is brutal," Winona Ryder told *Harper's Bazaar* in 2022. "You're working constantly, but if you want to take a break, they tell you, 'If you slow down, it's going to stop.'"

"At 19, [Christina Ricci] had breast reduction surgery because she couldn't stand the way people talked about her body. A few years before that, she had developed an eating disorder. Anxiety became a constant companion in her life," Thessaly La Force writes in a 2022 profile of Ricci, who made her feature film debut when she was a child. "Uncomfortable with the attention, she began to act out with the news media . . . [and this] confrontational attitude, she believes, probably cost her roles." To deal with all the intense and contradictory pressures, Ricci "used to tell herself none of it—this world, this set, this part—was real."

"I used repeat to myself over and over again, 'You don't exist,'" she said.

I have looked into the eyes of people who have been encouraged to believe—or have accepted—that they don't exist. Sometimes that look is intentionally created for a performance, but sometimes it's the result of a person, in real life, finally giving in. Allowing themselves, at last, to be worn down by an industry that keeps telling them, in so many ways, that they don't matter, that they didn't see what they saw, that they shouldn't tell the truth about what they'd been through, that they're expendable. I've also heard it in too many people's voices—the fading desire to fight destructive mindsets that can be as subtle and pervasive as smoke. You can't grab smoke, you can't contain it, you can't break it, so at some point, after exhaustion arrives, you just lie down and breathe it in.

I saw that empty, defeated look in the first season of *The Vow*.

In 2020, I reviewed the HBO series for the *New York Times*. I liked it more than some other critics; I thought it used its running time—seven (occasionally baggy) installments—to lay out the story of the cult known as Nxivm in skillful ways. It used those hours, at times, to nurture a vibe; it attempted to atmospherically convey what it might feel like to have one's values slowly but inexorably altered by the repetitious, initially attractive propaganda of a manipulative narcissist and his acolytes. Sometimes people call Nxivm a "sex cult," and I understand why that phrase gets people to click on stories. What's less easy to summarize in a headline are the many similarities between cults such as Nxivm and Hollywood.

I still think about a moment I mentioned in my review: the first meeting between Allison Mack, who began acting at age four, and the cult's leader, Keith Raniere. There was something haunted in her eyes, and it felt as though you could see a spark of relief flare as he began to spin his web of superficially clever bullshit, much of it revolving around the purpose of art. A decent chunk of what Nxivm was selling sounded plausible, at least at first. Things got darker and far more terrible, obviously.

Knowing what I know now about the industry, I find it increasingly difficult to join in any genuinely cruel schadenfreude party that involves mocking and belittling Hollywood people who have been snared by cults and the gaslighters and bullshitters who run them. I have questions about these artists' decisions, naturally—how can some people be so smart on creative fronts and yet taken in so completely by some of these ridiculous and even dangerous organizations? But it happens. And it might be because, to some degree, Hollywood trains them to do exactly that.

A lot of the worst cult or cult-adjacent exploiters don't seem all that different from the most predatory creators, executives, managers, agents, lawyers, and directors in the industry. There are some genuinely good people in those jobs, of course. But how is a cult that keeps people running around for fourteen or eighteen hours a day all that different from a set (or a workplace) that keeps people running around for fourteen or eighteen hours a day? By now, we're more aware than ever that many Hollywood companies and film and TV sets were—or are—controlled by narcissistic abusers who do not care about anything but what they can extract or compel from the relatively powerless people around them. Even if they don't deliver, cults at least promise some kind of existential deliverance or higher consciousness in return.

Alexander, a writer/creator who has worked in the industry for decades, recalled an instance of a very high-level executive "go[ing] shrill and childlike in the hallway, outside of [former CBS executive] Les Moonves's office." He said, "I remember the total helplessness he had in the face of unrealistic deadlines and things like that. It's like the curtain went up, and I saw a six-year-old version of this guy, who was stuck in a cycle of abuse and just trying to prevent more abuse from coming his way." And that's to say nothing of the assault, brute intimidation, and other heinous offenses outlined by Ronan Farrow and other journalists in their coverage of Moonves and other titans such as Harvey Weinstein.

These kinds of industry players—from the powerful bigwigs to the everyday hustlers—don't make people wear colored scarves, but some of them don't sound tremendously different from Nxivm's Keith Raniere or those who did his bidding. Nxivm told women they were not submissive enough and not thin enough; only a few people at the very top had any power, and everyone else was subject to the whims of those powerful, secretive leaders. Rocking the boat could very easily get you not just exiled but shunned, and lives were destroyed on whims. Read almost any Hollywood memoir or history book, or any of the post-2017 coverage of the industry's abuses—doesn't that sound like how a lot of industry sets and workplaces have operated for decades?

"I find that the vast majority of people who join these groups are extremely intelligent, open-minded, kind, loving people," Jodi Wille said in a 2018 article on Mack and Nxivm. Wille directed a film about the Source Family sect, which was active in LA in the late 1960s and '70s, and observed that many striving to make their mark on Hollywood "are lost or damaged, and so if you get a predator in the mix, whether it's Harvey Weinstein or the leader of Nxivm, they're going to go for it." The fact that the industry is filled with "vulnerable, empathic artists," as reporters Rebecca Sun and Scott Johnson note, is actually helpful for abusers. After all, wherever they operate, malignant narcissists "tend to pick victims who are kind, caring, and trusting, exploiting these noble qualities to their advantage," psychology expert Kristin Neff writes. Once they've spotted these potential targets, it's time for the clever, manipulative authority figure to tear down whatever self-esteem these victims had. According to the 2018 article, "If Mack's critiques of others were scathing, her own self-esteem wasn't much better. She told her employee she would never choose to have kids of her own because she was 'so fucked up.'"

I don't always feel this way, but on dark days, I have been known to mutter, "Hollywood! Putting the 'cult' in 'culture' for a hundred years!"

When my mind runs along these tracks, I often recall an encounter I had at San Diego Comic-Con in the mid-aughts. I ended up in a conversation with actor Nicki Clyne, who played Cally on *Battlestar Galactica*. In the midst of the usual party chit-chat, she told me about a foundation or charitable group she and her friends were working with. My memories of the encounter have grown vague over time, but I can still see the idealism and passionate energy on her face. I look back now and wonder, was she trying to recruit me for Nxivm? If so, it was a soft sell.

I still speculate about whether Clyne, who became a hardcore Raniere adherent, was already in the group then. If so, what was it doing to her body and her mind, her self-conception and her will? I don't know. But I think about what she may have experienced from the industry throughout her career, and what she absorbed from a larger society that told women to be thin, quiet, attractive, obedient. What Hollywood trained her to think of herself may not have been all that different from what Nxivm sold her, and the fact that these phenomena form a continuum makes me sad.

If they are to remain in touch with the source of their storytelling power and inspiration, actors and other creative people must remain vulnerable and open to the world. On emotional and psychological levels, they can't shut down and armor up completely, even though so much of the industry seems designed to make them do so. The entertainment industry has long reinforced tremendously harmful norms, and it has told countless aspiring artists that having boundaries—not giving their *all* to the creative struggle—is bad. And then it unleashes monsters into that mix.

I no longer wonder why there are so many tales of addiction, mental health struggles, body image issues, and worse all over the industry. It's no longer strange or surprising to me that so many creative people have meltdowns, issues, breakdowns, or join creepy organizations. Not all do, of course. But avoiding the traps set by an unforgiving industry just looks unbelievably difficult to me. That so many remain so kind, inspired, and giving is nothing short of a miracle.

Individuals who ally themselves with power-mad, abusive, dangerous people, and who themselves commit damaging, terrible acts, must answer for those actions, certainly. During her time with Nxivm, Mack did things that were "incredibly intimidating, cruel and punitive," said a source in the 2018 profile. Accountability is necessary for growth and change, and if some Nxivm victims got healing from many people in the cult—including Mack—going to jail, I am not going to judge them for that.

But I look at Mack's face in *The Vow*, and I recall Clyne's eager demeanor at that party. And I think about the horror shows they and others walked into and wonder: Isn't the industry, to at least some degree, complicit in what followed? A person can only exercise their will, after all, if they consistently believe they are allowed to *have* one.

Not many people had that luxury at *Lost*.

5

Lost and the Myths of a Golden Age

I was so happy to be fired.
—*Monica Owusu-Breen*

"I got chills."

Theresa was telling me about the early days of the *Lost* writers' room, before the ABC drama premiered in September 2004. She knew in her bones it was special, long before huge ratings confirmed it. The story of a group of plane crash survivors—including Jack, a doctor transporting his late father's body home, and Locke, a flinty survivalist in a wheelchair—was going to be, she was sure, deeper and wilder and more entertaining than anyone in the audience could possibly imagine.

"Someone would say, 'Well, what if Locke walks?'" Theresa remembered. "'What if the coffin is empty?' As all that was going down, literally you got chills. We started doing the wave in the room, like, holy shit! I'd never seen anything like it in my career—that miraculous creative energy. The writers in that room were great."

"It was heaven," said Gretchen, who described an atmosphere in which ideas could come from anyone, regardless of rank. There were stresses, of course, but overall, when the core *Lost* crew was tossing around the show's foundational ideas, she said, "it was so much fun."

When it came to the highlights of that gig—the big swings, the exciting pitches, the way the show, at its best, fused sci-fi mythology and adventure elements with rich character-building—the only thing Theresa could compare it to was seeing the original production of *Dreamgirls* on Broadway. When Jennifer Holliday gave her all to her rendition of "And I Am Telling You I'm Not Going," "people were floating in their chairs," Theresa said. "When something hits a certain frequency and you know it's magic—that's what was going on in that room."

I knew that feeling. I had been writing about pop culture for years before *Lost* premiered, and when it debuted, I was a full-time TV critic. My whole life, there had been good and fun and enjoyable TV, as well as programs that were important. But something big shifted in the early aughts. In my first few years as a critic, *The Sopranos* and *Sex and the City* were going strong. The daring and politically charged *Battlestar Galactica*, which had kicked off with a 2003 miniseries, returned with guns blazing around the time *Lost* premiered. *Deadwood*, which debuted on HBO in the spring of 2004, radically redefined what a Western could be. *The Wire* and *The Shield*, midway through their influential runs, were doing the same for cop dramas.

These upstarts and many others offered provocative stories, exceptional performances, handsome locations, ambitious production values, and, frequently, characters who were not exactly role models. The vast majority of the most buzzed-about Golden Age shows featured heterosexual white dudes at the center of their sagas, which was, honestly, just a continuation of what Hollywood had been doing forever. Not until 1968, with the arrival of the half-hour show *Julia*, did a Black woman get to star in a broadcast network program that did not rely on stereotypes and racist tropes. *Get Christie Love!*, which ran for one season in 1974, represented the first time a Black woman was the star of an American hour-long show. More than three decades passed before it happened again and Kerry Washington led Shonda Rhimes's ABC drama *Scandal* to hit status.

The whiteness and maleness of the era did grate on me and other critics, especially as the decade wore on. Over time, the patterns we saw changed how a number of us approached our work. Still, even as some critics and viewers sighed at the worst excesses of the bro-tastic Big Deal shows of the time, it was impossible to deny that television was in the midst of a fertile, exciting period of growth and evolution.

For a long time, the more cautious broadcast networks struggled to keep up with this revolution, especially in the drama realm. *Lost* changed that. "It was among the most thrilling, surprising, memorable dramas in the history of American network television, and at its best it could go toe-to-toe with much of what was happening on cable during this period," Alan Sepinwall writes in *The Revolution Was Televised*, his history of the era.

Lost's pilot, which cost $13 million and was directed by cocreator J. J. Abrams, looked incredible, kept viewers on the edge of their seats, and made excellent use of its Hawaii locations. And the show was allowed to continue down that ambitious path because it was a *giant* hit. *Lost* and *Desperate Housewives*, which also premiered that fall, turned around the fortunes of an entire network: *Lost* was ABC's highest-rated debut in four years, and *Desperate Housewives* broke that record when it premiered weeks later. Despite *Desperate Housewives*'s triumph, as Joy Press observes in her 2018 book *Stealing the Show: How Women Are Revolutionizing Television*, "women remained secondary figures in [typically] male psychodramas . . . 'serious television' offered minimal scope for women either behind the camera or in front of it."

Programs that regularly won awards and landed on magazine covers and year-end Best TV lists around that time—*24, Dexter, Veronica Mars, The Sopranos, Mad Men, Breaking Bad* among them—usually had something else in common: they put people of color on-screen, but those characters were rarely the consistent focus of the story. Of course, there were exceptions—for example, *Battlestar Galactica* gave prominent roles to Edward James Olmos and Grace Park, *The Wire*'s cast reflected the demographics of the show's Baltimore setting, and Giancarlo Esposito was crucial to the success of *Breaking Bad*. But most programs of all kinds, cable or network, drama or comedy, ambitious or formulaic, had casts, writers' rooms, and director rosters that were dominated by white people, usually white men. LGBTQ+ characters and disabled characters that did not hew to stereotypes or occupy minor roles were hard to find.

Lost literally looked different: Six of its fourteen original series regulars were people of color. Four were women. Harold Perrineau was excited to get on a plane and be part of this experiment.

By the time cocreator J. J. Abrams and others on the creative team gave him the full-court press in hopes of convincing him to join the cast, Perrineau had been in two *Matrix* films and *Romeo + Juliet*. He also played a key role in TV's brave new Golden Age: he was part of the ensemble on HBO's prison saga *Oz*, another rare drama with an inclusive (though mostly male) cast. The bold, brutal, and serialized *Oz* was very much a spiritual precursor to later cable smashes like *The Sopranos* and *The Shield*. Before HBO took a chance on it in 1997, when Tom Fontana "had pitched even mild versions of *Oz* to the broadcast networks, he says he was told, 'Oh, they're all too nasty. Where are the heroes? Where are the victories?' These questions simply didn't apply at HBO," as Sepinwall puts it.

The same was true at an increasing number of ambitious networks. *Lost* was not going to be as edgy as shows like *Oz*, but securing Perrineau was, as they say in the industry, a big get. "Harold had one of the biggest careers of all of us, when *Lost* began," noted Daniel Dae Kim, another member of the cast. "He's a very talented actor. And I thought his work was some of the best on the show."

The show's marketing team was certainly willing to hype the résumés of the drama's cast. The *Matrix* sequels had just come out, and Dominic Monaghan, who played *Lost*'s Charlie, had been in *The Lord of the Rings*, and "in the very, very beginning, there were commercials and ads saying, 'From *The Matrix* and *Lord of the Rings* to *Lost*!'" Perrineau recalled with a chuckle.

Part of the reason Perrineau took a chance on the upstart ABC drama was because the creative team said they wanted to tell a story that "was really equitable," in terms of the time it would spend on its array of characters. He'd been around long enough to know, as he put it, "where the lines were, and what the ceiling was" for Black actors. But he was encouraged by what he was told and by the cast that was assembled. "We were all really hopeful about it," Perrineau remembered. "It was a bigger try than I had ever seen on broadcast TV." When he talked to the press in those early days, his enthusiasm was palpable: "I was shouting about it from the rooftops," he said. "I was such a believer."

A lot of us were. As a sci-fi nerd, I'd seen shows with genre elements get relegated to the margins, discussed condescendingly (if they were written about at all), and usually canceled too soon. So I was relieved when *Lost* was a smash: here was a character-driven genre piece willing to take risks, and it was, based on its ratings, going to stick around for a long time.

What could go wrong?

For a number of *Lost* sources I talked to, the creative highs that counterbalanced the hard parts of the job evaporated fast. A wave of dismissals (the first of many) came not long after the arrival of executive producer Carlton Cuse, an industry veteran who had worked on mainstream '90s dramas like *The Adventures of Brisco County, Jr.* and *Nash Bridges*. When *Lost* cocreator Damon Lindelof was starting out as a TV writer, one of his first jobs was on the staff of *Nash Bridges*. *Lost* was an enormous undertaking, and Lindelof was overwhelmed by his vast new responsibilities, so he asked his former boss Cuse to come and work on the ABC drama with him. It's a very common TV paradigm: a creative person who is new to a leadership role is paired up with an experienced veteran. And in this case, two showrunners were necessary, given the logistical complexity of shooting a show in one place—Hawaii—and writing, editing, and overseeing every other aspect of it in LA.

Given that *Lost* was at the forefront of pop culture for much of its run, Cuse and Lindelof were among the most well-known showrunners in American television for quite some time. (David Chase was probably more famous, but interviews with him were rare.) At convention appearances, on podcasts, and in endless media coverage, they were the avuncular, funny figureheads, fanning the flames of conjecture about certain mysteries, teasing upcoming developments, and, at times, attempting to defuse anger or confusion regarding some of the drama's twists and turns. There was drama behind the scenes too, and it was as dark and complicated as anything on-screen, if not more so.

Based on conversations with more than a dozen people who worked on *Lost* in various capacities—one source was not on the payroll but had extensive contact with the *Lost* machine—it's clear that the landmark series played right into Hollywood's most long-standing patterns, in which all-powerful auteurs wield enormous power with very little oversight. The experiences of the people I spoke to span all six seasons. They are of all races and genders, but, excluding Cuse and Lindelof, half are people of color and more than half are women. Every person I talked to is still justifiably proud of the work they did on the drama. But by all accounts, people with *Lost* on their résumés worked very hard on a job that could be quite grueling. And scarring.

"All I wanted to do was write some really cool episodes of a cool show. That was an impossibility on that staff," said Monica Owusu-Breen, who worked on *Lost*'s third season. "There was no way to navigate that situation. Part of it was, they really didn't like their characters of color. When you have to go home and cry for an hour before you can see your kids because you have to excise all the stress you've been holding in, you're not going to write anything good after that."

There are reasons these dynamics were—are—allowed to fester. And to be clear, the kind of experiences that one *Lost* source described as "shattering" did not just occur at that show, nor are they relegated to the industry's past. All over Hollywood, even now, these patterns can still play out. "You bring in a billion dollars at the box office or a series that's a winner for your platform or your network," former *Lost* writer Christopher observed, "there's lots of room for forgiveness."

On set in Hawaii, much of the cast got along really well, at least at first. "A lot of us grew very close," said Sloan, an actor on the show. "The thing that kind of created a rift in the cast was money."

Perrineau and Sloan told me that the cast had discussions about holding firm and asking for equal pay when salary renegotiations with ABC Studios began. According to both, among the cast, promises were made that centered on presenting a united front. Almost a decade earlier, the cast of *Friends* had done just that and wound up with equal pay for all six leads. But at *Lost*, the united front quickly crumbled. Ultimately, the cast of *Lost* ended up in a series of compensation tiers, and Perrineau and Sloan said the highest tier was occupied solely by white actors.

"That affected relationships," Sloan said. But the actor had no relationship with Cuse, who, Sloan believed, "didn't seem to think much of me." At least, in the midst of a work-related conversation, Cuse never berated Sloan for being "ungrateful" to the point of tears, which happened to another *Lost* actor Sloan knew.

As the twenty-five-episode first season progressed, Perrineau noticed that a few of his castmates—most of them white—got the majority of the storytelling attention: "It became pretty clear that I was the Black guy. Daniel [Dae Kim] was the Asian guy. And then you had Jack and Kate and Sawyer," all of whom got a good deal of screen time, as did Terry O'Quinn's Locke. Indeed, a writer I spoke to who worked on *Lost* during the middle of its run said that the writing staff was told repeatedly who the "hero characters" were: Locke, Jack, Kate, and Sawyer, all of whom were white. "It's not that they didn't write stories for Sayid [an Iraqi character] or Sun and Jin [Korean characters], but they were very explicit that those four characters needed to get serviced more than anybody else." This writer recalled comments like, "Nobody cares about these other characters. Just give them a few scenes on another beach," or "nobody cares about Bernard and Rose," an interracial couple who were among the show's many secondary characters.

To ensure that his colleague would understand that this observation was not just actor jealousy rearing its head, when Perrineau pointed out the story line disparities to a *Lost* producer on set, the opinions the actor offered were fairly mild. He told me he said, "I don't have to be the first, I don't have to have the most episodes—but I'd like to be in the mix. But it seems like this is now a story about Jack and Kate and Sawyer." Perrineau said he was told, "Well, this is just how audiences follow stories," and those were the characters that were "relatable."

That assertion raised the obvious follow-up question: Why were white people relatable and his Black character, Michael, was not? But Perrineau calculated that asking that question would probably unleash the same kind of frustration he felt on photo shoots, where, especially in the early seasons of the show, actors of color were often asked to stand in the back row or at the edges of the frame. (One early promotional image went through multiple layers of approval before anyone noticed that the front row consisted only of white people.) Conversations and experiences like these made the long days seem even longer. "You can feel the energy," Perrineau said. "You can feel, like, 'Oh, you're not as important as these other people.'"

When Perrineau paged through the original draft of the second episode of Season 2, "it was too much," he said. At that point in the *Lost* saga, several castaways' attempt to flee the island on a raft has gone awry, and Walt, Michael's son, has been kidnapped by a shadowy group called the Others. In this version of the script, Michael is pulled onto the remains of the raft by Sawyer (Josh Holloway), and the episode's flashbacks—a staple of every *Lost* hour—revolve around Sawyer's past. Within those pages, Michael asks about his son early on, just one time.

In that version of the script, Perrineau recalled, "Michael's asking Sawyer questions about his past, about how he feels, but he never again mentions Walt." Perrineau's reaction was, "I don't think I can do that. I can't be another person who doesn't care about missing Black boys, even in the context of fiction, right? This is just furthering the narrative that nobody cares about Black boys, even Black fathers."

He knew the risks of talking to his bosses about any of this. "That was the thing that was always tricky. Any time you mention race, everybody gets—their hair gets on fire, and they're like, 'I'm not racist!'" Perrineau said. "It's like, 'Nope. Because I say that I'm Black doesn't mean I'm calling you a racist. I am talking to you from my perspective.

I'm being really clear that I'm not trying to put my trauma on you, but I am trying to talk to you about what I feel. So can we just do that? Can we just have that conversation? Not constantly have it be like, "I'm not racist!" I'm not calling you racist, okay?'" That has been a "constant" dynamic he has faced while working in the industry, he told me.

Despite the risks, he expressed his concerns about the script to Lindelof and Cuse in a phone call. Then he brought up the on-screen equity that he had been led to expect when he accepted the job. "At the beginning, it was, 'Hey Harold, we love you. We love what you're creating in the industry. We really want you and what you do,'" Perrineau recalled.

But as a viewer, it is easy to see Perrineau's point of view: Michael does not get the depth, complexity, or carefulness of storytelling that other characters receive. In that phone conversation, he told his bosses, "'If you're going to use me, let's work. I'm here to work. I'm good at my job and I'll do anything you want. Except be "the Black guy" on your show.'"

He said he was told by Cuse and Lindelof that the episode was not about his character. "'Cool, it's not about me. I'm not making it about me,'" he remembered replying. "'I just can't have this father not care about his son. Could we put in some more lines that show he cares about his son?' They didn't. I ad-libbed some lines. I didn't give a shit at that point." Weeks later, he got a revised script—the flashbacks were now about Michael's pre-island life. Perrineau had two days to shoot those scenes, as opposed to the several days devoted to the Sawyer flashbacks. "It was fourteen-hour, eighteen-hour days. I was like, 'If you think I'm gonna fuck this up, I'm not. I'm gonna be really good.' But I felt like suddenly they were mad at me," Perrineau said.

As it turned out, soon enough, the problems Perrineau had—with that script and with the writing for his character—were no longer issues he had to contend with. A couple of weeks before shooting began on the second-season finale, Perrineau said, Cuse told him his character would not be returning. Perrineau told me he was taken aback and questioned Cuse about this, and the showrunner said he did not know if Michael would ever come back. The actor said he was then released from his contract.

"I was fucked up about it. I was like, 'Oh, I just got fired, I think,'" Perrineau recalled. "I was like, 'Wait a minute, what's happening?'"

[Cuse] said, 'Well, you know, you said to us, if we don't have anything good for you, you want to go.' I was just asking for equal depth. He's literally a one-note character—'Where's Walt? Where's my boy?'"

According to Perrineau, the response from Cuse was, "'Well, you said you don't have enough work here, so we're letting you go.'" I observed that the response seemed to indicate royal displeasure. Perrineau agreed: "It was all very much, 'How dare you?'"

During the Golden Age of the aughts, I endured my share of negative responses when I brought up biased tropes and clichés, sexism, or offensive representations of race and sexual violence. Any time a critic—especially if that person was queer, female, and/or a person of color—discussed specific examples that drove home the point that this exciting period in American television revolved around white men telling stories that were usually about other white men and that were often repetitively misogynist, racially insensitive, homophobic, or otherwise problematic, some people did not engage with the critique. Instead, as I said to Perrineau, they "just lost their shit."

"You're absolutely right," he replied. He knew the feeling.

When Perrineau's character exited the core *Lost* narrative for good, he gave an interview to a reporter whom he said quoted him fairly and accurately about various topics.

"I don't think there was anything nefarious in anything that she did," Perrineau said. "She asked me something, and I said—I don't remember exactly the quote, but I'm gonna give you a roundabout version of it. I said, 'You know, for me, as a Black person, the idea that Walt winds up living with his grandmother and not living with his father, that feels like one of those clichés—Black kids who have been raised by their grandparents, because neither of their parents are around for them. I would've liked to have seen something a little better happen, but that's not the way it went down.'"

In that 2008 interview, the reporter asked Perrineau about his disappointment in the fact that Michael and Walt didn't "reconnect before [his] character" left the show. Perrineau replied, "Listen, if I'm being really candid, there are all these questions about how they respond to Black people on the show. Sayid gets to meet Nadia again, and Desmond and Penny hook up again, but a little Black boy and his father hooking up, that wasn't interesting? Instead, Walt just winds up being another fatherless child. It plays into a really big, weird stereotype and, being a Black person myself, that wasn't so interesting." (In that piece, Cuse was quoted as responding, "We pride ourselves on having a very racially diverse cast. It's painful when any actor's storyline ends on the show. Harold is a fantastic actor whose presence added enormously to *Lost*.")

When that interview came out, it set off a furor among some *Lost* fans, but the consternation behind the scenes was worse. With those comments—which were only a portion of the interview—Perrineau said he was accused by some of playing "the race card." No one wants to be defined by one aspect of their identity, but neither do people want to feel forced to suppress who they are so that others never feel any discomfort. Perrineau was thrown because there were no good options on the table for him—again. "Time out—I get to talk about being Black, you know? 'Cause I am Black. You can ignore it. But I get to talk about it. The response from ABC was like, 'Oh, we always loved Harold, but he may be just angry that he left the show,'" he recalled. "I'm not angry that I left the show. Like, that's what I think as a *fan*."

For weeks, Perrineau went round and round with ABC, which wanted to issue a retraction of some kind. "Me mentioning the color of my skin—that just sent everybody off the rails. We came up with something, but it took weeks, because I was like, 'I didn't say anything wrong. And she didn't report anything wrong. Nobody did anything wrong.' But societally—people so loved the show. They couldn't hear one thing against it," he told me.

Perrineau had come up against one of the unspoken rules in the entertainment business: you don't question the dudes in charge—not their motivations, not their intentions, not their actions. In Gretchen's opinion, that informal but enduring industry dictum certainly operated at *Lost*, adding that in her experience, under Lindelof and Cuse, the workplace grew less flexible and more autocratic and uncomfortable over time. "Toward the end of the second season, after all the accolades came" and the showrunners' power increased, she observed, "I could see where it could be unbearable for some people to be there." Especially as an industry norm she was familiar with—that those ruling a workplace could be "vindictive" at will—was cemented into place. "An overriding thing was that they had the power to" hire and fire at will, no matter the reason, she noted, "and they used it."

But it was all okay if a show had lofty aspirations and the creative people in charge thought highly of their own goals and motivations, right? For a very long time, the creative community and many fans subscribed to the idea that good intentions—or at least not overtly bad ones—mattered more than anything else. If the "genius" or "passionate" creator had not *intended* to be racist, sexist, homophobic, or offensive in other ways, then their work could not have been any of those things (or if it was, that creator should get a pass, because creative ambition, so this way of thinking goes, forgives almost everything).

This view was not just prevalent on some message boards and comment areas back when *Lost* was on the air; you still run into it now. To an extent, I get the defensiveness when it comes to complex matters of storytelling, culture, world-building, and whose point of view matters. These things can be hard to parse intelligently in private, let alone on a public stage. And feeling embarrassed when your missteps are publicly dissected is normal. But the toxicity of the response to genuine questions about leadership, creativity, and representation can often result in high-volume screeching—yes, even now—from fans and powerful industry insiders alike. Many's the time I've been told I "just didn't understand" why a choice was made. No, I understood. I just thought it was a bad choice. And then the screeching starts again.

"For most of television, Blackness was seen through a white gaze. *Good Times* you could call authentic, but it's white-gaze authentic. Even though the idea came from a Black writer, and God bless Norman Lear, that's still a white man," creator and comic Larry Wilmore said in a 2022 interview.

Long after *Good Times* ended in 1979, "Black writers were not on white shows. The only one from those days was Saladin Patterson, who got a job on *Frasier,*" Wilmore noted. "That was huge at the time. Never happened. When I would be at those Television Critics Association things when I was doing *Bernie Mac,* people kept asking, 'Larry, how many Black writers on your show?' I said, 'Motherfucker, ask the white shows how many Black writers they have! I'm the one with Black writers. Who the fuck are you asking?'"

Six years before *Good Times* premiered, *Julia* was created by Hal Kanter, a writer and director who worked on everything from the Bing Crosby–Bob Hope movie *Road to Bali* to *All in the Family,* and who racked up industry credits well into the aughts. One of his early jobs was writing for the TV version of the popular radio show *Amos 'n' Andy*, "which was canceled in 1953 amid protests that it trafficked in minstrel-show stereotypes." For Kanter, creating *Julia*, which employed a few Black writers during its three seasons, was a form of making amends for aspects of his professional past. "I felt I was partially responsible for some of the Black image that was prevalent at the time," he said in an interview with the Television Academy Foundation. One thing *Julia* star Diahann Carroll had to make peace with—if she could—was the fact that her character's story was told through the filters of an industry that was overwhelmingly white. Those filters have haltingly begun to go by the wayside in some places, but for many Black creatives, they've been a constant.

"I always got the phone call that said: 'I have a great project for you. You're going to be with, hypothetically, Vanessa Redgrave, Julianne Moore, Annette Bening,'" Viola Davis told the *New York Times* in 2014. "Then I get the script, and I have a role that lasts for a page or two."

"I have been given a lot of roles that are downtrodden, mammy-ish," added Davis, who has been nominated for an Academy Award four times. (She won a Best Supporting Actress Oscar for her role in *Fences*.) She recalled script after script with parts for "lawyers or doctors who have names but absolutely no lives. You're going to get your three or four scenes, you're not going to be able to show what you can do. You're going to get your little bitty paycheck, and then you're going to be hungry for your next role, which is going to be absolutely the same."

Back in 2014, Davis, who studied at Juilliard, was making the press rounds to promote what may have been her most high-profile project to date: the lead role in the ABC drama *How to Get Away with Murder*. It was created by Peter Nowalk and counted the mega-successful TV magnate Shonda Rhimes among its executive producers.

A few days after that feature on Davis came out, the *New York Times* published a piece by critic Alessandra Stanley that initially incorrectly identified Rhimes, then one of the few prominent Black women in TV, as the creator of the drama. In one of her opening sentences, Stanley writes that Rhimes should title her autobiography *How to Get Away With Being an Angry Black Woman*. Davis's *HTGAWM* character, Stanley notes, is yet another "powerful, intimidating Black woman" Rhimes is showcasing in her work. Stanley also says that Davis is "less classically beautiful" than Kerry Washington or Halle Berry.

For an in-depth story I wrote not long ago, I talked to a Black writer who had been ostracized and bullied during her time working on a big-budget TV show. She was made to feel that her natural hair was unprofessional and unattractive. She was put in an office on another floor, far away from most of the staff (which, year after year, was dominated, in its upper ranks, by white men). When that showrunner's lawyer questioned my assertions on these topics, he started reeling off reasons why putting that writer on another floor was necessary—but he dropped the name of a different Black woman, not the one I'd been talking to. There was a moment of dead air on the phone as we both realized there must have been at least *two* Black women who had been physically separated from the rest of the creative team. The woman I talked to exited the industry. To her, and to so many people from historically excluded communities that I've heard from over the years, Hollywood did not feel safe, let alone reliably rewarding.

Even when white writers have questioned the treatment of race and gender, they often felt they were risking a lot.

"Some of it is subconscious, some of it's built into the system," said writer/producer Cathryn Humphris, who began working in the industry a few years before *Lost* debuted. "There were multiple shows where I would go on set and people in the crew would say, 'You're the first woman we could tolerate.' They would assume, 'If you're a woman and you're coming here, you're going to try to tell me what to do, and you shouldn't have that authority.'"

Humphris was quick to note that, during the aughts, "we were not talking about race even remotely the way we're talking about it now. The generation that was just ahead of me—that was the era of one woman, maybe, on every writing staff." But certain patterns persist: in more than two decades in the industry, she worked on one program run by a person of color but has never worked on a show created by a person of color. She cannot recall ever—including on somewhat recent jobs—being on a writing staff where there was more than one person of color at a time.

Thus it was not unusual that there were no Black people on the third-season writing staff of *Mad Men,* which Humphris joined in 2009 as a junior writer. When creator Matthew Weiner announced the show would be doing an episode in which ad man Roger Sterling would wear blackface, Humphris was assigned that episode. She panicked. "It was my second writing job ever," she recalled. "My concern was, 'How are we going to put this in an episode and not be horribly racist?'" She just didn't think she had the skills to pull it off (and she said she wasn't aware at first that Weiner extensively rewrote every script anyway). "I remember being the lone voice saying, 'Are you sure we should do this?' And there wasn't a real resolution that first day, aside from, 'Don't worry, little story editor, it's going to be fine.'"

After *Mad Men* ended in 2015, writer Kater Gordon revealed that Weiner made an inappropriate sexual comment to her while she worked on the show. Weiner has said he has no recollection of that and that he could not see "a scenario where [he] would say that." Gordon stated in 2018 that Weiner's "abuse of workplace power dynamics was rampant" and that what she said happened "should not be viewed as an isolated occurrence." Marti Noxon, known for her work on *Buffy the Vampire Slayer, Sharp Objects,* and *UnREAL,* also worked on *Mad Men.* She was among those publicly supporting Gordon and said Weiner was, as a boss, an "emotional terrorist."

Many of the industry people who've been described as toxic creatives, bad bosses, or systemic abusers came up during the '90s and the aughts, when powerful people treating those around them as expendable targets was par for the course. Almost everybody came in for a ration of abuse, no matter their cultures or identities. Writer/producer Todd A. Kessler was so damaged by working for David Chase on *The Sopranos* (where Weiner worked for years) that Kessler later cocreated a show about a manipulative, duplicitous boss called *Damages.* In his review of *Difficult Men,* Brett Martin's 2013 book about Golden Age auteurs, Phillip Maciak notes that "if it is an account of the power dynamics behind a creative revolution, those dynamics are rooted, with few exceptions, in autocracy, humiliation, and dominance."

For years, the studios—perhaps less so now—may have thought they had legal cover for these kinds of workplaces. When a *Lost* employee spoke to ABC HR about the awful, unprofessional atmosphere they'd experienced, not only did those HR people appear to have knowledge of how bad the situation was, according to my source, one of them mumbled something about writers' rooms being different, and basically ungovernable, due to "the *Friends* decision." That 2006 California Supreme Court decision had its roots in a legal action brought by

Amaani Lyle, a Black woman who had worked as a writers' assistant on the NBC sitcom.

According to a 2021 story, Lyle, who ended up leaving the entertainment industry, said she "believes she was fired for suggesting *Friends* character Joey (Matt LeBlanc) should have a Black love interest to increase diversity on the show and speaking to her superior about a racist joke made by another producer." Two decades ago, she wanted to expose "the sexual harassment and discrimination" she experienced, and in 2002, she filed a complaint with the California Department of Fair Employment and Housing. At first, she "sued for racial discrimination and wrongful termination, but after talking to her lawyer about the sexual remarks and comments in the writers' room, Lyle also sued for sexual harassment." Eventually, in that infamous 2006 decision, the court said that the writers had not violated any law by making sexual comments because they weren't directed at or said about anyone specific in the writers' room.

There are indeed nuanced conversations to be had about the kind of sensitive, sexual, or inflammatory topics that can (and sometimes should) come up in writers' rooms, but based on my conversations with dozens of industry professionals over many years, those who control various parts of the Hollywood machine grabbed onto this ruling with gleeful relief and without a shred of subtlety. BuzzFeed's reporter on the Lyle story spoke to—as I have—*many* industry employees who've experienced awful work situations, but whose complaints were shut down by studio or HR employees who cited the *Friends* ruling. In 2018, the Writers Guild of America West reported the results of a misconduct survey in an email to members, noting that the ruling "is mistakenly used to justify inappropriate behavior," despite the fact that it "acknowledges that objectionable talk may, in some circumstances, be enough to create a hostile work environment." According to folks I've talked to, so much of the industry has used the ruling as both sword and shield, including in HR sessions at various companies, that the net result was tacit or even overt green lights to "anything goes" workplaces, with predictably nightmarish results.

"They have perverted this case into something as a bullying, sort of scare tactic in a very mafioso kind of way, to mute employees and not foster an open, transparent work environment," Lyle said. As she pointed out, all over the industry, the decision was used as a "get out of jail free card" for a huge array of unacceptable behaviors, a situation that did not exactly move "the ball down the field in terms of inclusion, diversity, and eradicating misogyny, and anyone who is complicit in that is just part of the machine."

That machine was very much in place during the aughts, when speaking up to HR—or to anyone with power, really—was a dangerous (if not disastrous) gambit for most industry folks in bad situations. During the run of *Lost*, that option was simply unrealistic, many sources told me. After all, Steve McPherson, the top ABC entertainment executive during most of the drama's run, was known for his "volatile temper and expletive-laced emails," and was investigated regarding "sexual harassment": there were "alleged incidents involved several women, including some executives and on-air talent. . . . A source said [there was] an incident at a company retreat, witnessed by more than one staffer." The only consequence for McPherson was that he was allowed to voluntarily resign. And even that kind of mild outcome was incredibly rare in the pre–#MeToo era. Support staff, crews, and employees at all levels— but especially at the industry's lower rungs—even now often feel they have no recourse at all.

Like a lot of *Mad Men* writers, Cathryn Humphris only lasted one season on the show, and she told me her experience often revolved around keeping her mouth shut and trying to avoid the harsher aspects of the workplace: "The overall thing that happened in a lot of these rooms, especially if you were a woman and lower level—and I think it's worse for people of color—is that if others saw a weakness, they would find a way to twist the knife." She thought Weiner was talented but also "very egotistical and very, like, 'I make the magic, I am responsible for everything.' He had this thing where he felt he'd been wronged in every single way, and this show was his opportunity to shine."

For all those reasons, she was terrified to ask Weiner if she could swap episodes with someone else and not write the blackface episode. She told me she believed she was risking her job by asking for that. But Weiner allowed her to switch episodes with another writer, so Humphris's name is not on "My Old Kentucky Home." And of course, any creative conversation involving blackface would be radically different now, Humphris and I agreed.

But some things haven't changed. When talking to Robert, a man of color who has been in the industry about as long as Humphris, I introduced him to a term I came up with: "inclusivity cosplay," meaning the faces on the screen reflect our multicultural reality but the creative team or writing staff is almost completely—or completely—white. This still happens. "That is a Band-Aid on a bullet hole," Robert said. "I call it 'blackface writing,' to be frank with you."

Another assumption still lingers over the industry, and it involves who is presumed to have what amounts to a universal voice: "The overriding cultural view of the time was that these white men can write everything," Humphris observed. "Whereas if you're a woman or a person of color, I still feel like those writers get questioned *all the time*."

As she moved through her career, Monica Owusu-Breen heard rumblings that things were not great at *Lost*. Other writers on the show tried to warn Owusu-Breen and her then–writing partner, Alison Schapker, about the atmosphere in those offices. But having worked at the male-dominated *Alias* and at *Charmed* (where their boss was Brad Kern, whose management of a later show led to multiple CBS investigations and a post–#MeToo firing), Owusu-Breen told me she thought they could handle it.

Not only did she think she could deal with just about any work environment, Owusu-Breen loved what she had seen. She was especially excited to play in the show's "global sandbox," said Owusu-Breen, whose father is from West Africa. "I never got to write for cultures similar to those of my immigrant family. I was like, 'Oh my God, this feels so different!'"

In that third season, however, all was not well on *Lost*. Mr. Eko was among a set of characters called the Tailies, who were introduced in Season 2 and got a rocky reception. When the third season rolled around, the show contained some slow patches and time wasters such as "Stranger in a Strange Land," which is widely regarded as one of the worst episodes in the show's history. Behind the scenes, it did not take long for Owusu-Breen to realize that a lot of people at *Lost* viewed her and her writing partner as, essentially, Tailies. It became a wry running joke between them, Owusu-Breen told me: "Everyone was real nice to us for the first few days. And then they wanted us dead."

Most people I've spoken to for this book are veterans of film and television productions where off-color humor, barbed banter, and incisive, even stinging, comments are common. None have a real problem with those things, in the right settings and proportions. In fact, humor is not just itself a form of creativity, it can serve as a necessary pressure-relief valve. In any event, when you get groups of clever, creative people together and put them under a lot of pressure, razor-sharp wit, in-jokes, and the occasional harsh words are the natural human behaviors that often result. And there is a large percentage of people in the industry who, when they go too far—or are told they've gone too far—apologize and alter their future behavior.

Many people, of course, still brace themselves for punishing cultures, given how long fratty, toxic, and unprofessional cultures were accepted as the norm in so many industry workplaces. For a long time, the baseline for those workplaces wasn't great, and many could and did slide into much more scary and damaging realms. However, even for experienced professionals, what occurred at *Lost* went over or obliterated most lines. Regularly. "I went on to another show where it was not like that at all," Gretchen told me. "It was female-run and we were in at eight in the morning and out at six at night, and none of this nonsense was going on. It was amazing. So it doesn't have to be like that."

Like what? Well, what many people I interviewed endured while working there was beyond—*way* beyond—whatever skewed "norms" they were used to.

"There was this coterie of people who would find it" very amusing if a comment or joke was "offensive," one source told me. "Everything was said with a sort of sarcastic 'this whole thing is funny to me' vibe—and also a 'your discomfort is funny to me' attitude." Multiple people said that this sensibility was a cover for bullying or inappropriate remarks of all kinds, as well as comments on race and gender that crossed lines. If someone wanted to be accepted, this source said, laughing at and adding to that kind of commentary "was how you got to be part of the group. That was the terms of belonging."

Both showrunners tolerated or even encouraged the overall atmosphere, but its descent into a realm that many sources described in very negative terms appeared to arise from a couple of powerful factors: from the "sense of humor" that Lindelof appeared to enjoy, and from the showrunners' status as all-powerful entities whom no one could cross. When Cuse arrived, "that's when everything changed, in my opinion," a female source said. "It was Carlton coming in and acting like, 'I want my people and I want control of those people.'" Regarding Cuse, she said, "I don't think people really had respect for him among the writing staff," but from "Damon's or the studio's perspective, it was like, 'Oh, we have someone who's going to put everyone in line.'" Over time, this meant that the early nucleus of creatives responsible for "the ideas that everyone built on and got credit for and won Emmys for . . . a lot of those people were just tossed aside," and the culture of *Lost* "turned back to the old Hollywood way."

But an extreme version of that, certainly by the middle of the show's run, if not before. "I can only describe it as hazing. It was very much middle school and relentlessly cruel. And I've never heard that much racist commentary in one room in my career," Owusu-Breen recalled. Here is a partial roster of statements sources heard while working at *Lost* (and the first five statements were heard by another individual I spoke to):

- When someone on staff was adopting an Asian child, one person said to another writer that "no grandparent wants a slanty-eyed grandchild," Owusu-Breen said.

- When actor Adewale Akinnuoye-Agbaje's picture was on the writers' room table, someone was told to remove their nearby wallet "before he steals it," Owusu-Breen said.

- When Owusu-Breen and others were riding in a van on a trip, in answer to a question about the luggage, one writer— using a Yiddish word—said, "Let the *schvartze* take it." Owusu-Breen said she turned to that person and told them she was aware of what the N-word is in other languages.

- The only Asian American writer was called "Korean," as in, "Korean, take the board," Owusu-Breen said. (Two other sources heard this.)

- When someone pitched, "Well, maybe the Korean woman falls into the water," someone else responded, "Can Asian women swim?" During this conversation, according to Owusu-Breen (and another source), Cuse said, "'Oh wait, pearl divers exist.' And I'm like, I have no idea what land of stereotypes we're in anymore."

- When a woman entered the writers' room carrying a binder, two sources said, a male writer asked her what it was. She said it was the HR manual for the studio, and he responded, "Why don't you take off your top and tell us about it?"

- The writers kept mug shots of actors arrested for drunk driving in Hawaii on the room's walls, and at one point, *Lost* writer Javier Grillo-Marxuach, who is Puerto Rican, had to listen to a colleague "joke" that Michelle Rodriguez, who played the short-lived character Ana Lucia, "sold a white cast member to other inmates for cigarettes."

- The room's only Asian American writer was routinely referred to, "to her face, as the showrunners' 'geisha' (down to the Mickey Rooney *Breakfast at Tiffany's* accent)," Grillo-Marxuach said.

- There was apparently some discomfort around the show's cleaning staff using the bathroom in the *Lost* offices, and there were "jokes" about "putting up a WHITES ONLY sign," Owusu-Breen said.

Finally, when Perrineau's *Lost* departure came up, Lindelof said, according to multiple sources, that the actor "called me racist, so I fired his ass."

"Everyone laughed" when Lindelof said that, Owusu-Breen recalled. "There was so much shit, and so much racist shit, and then laughter. It was ugly. I was like, 'I don't know if they're perceiving this as a joke or if they mean it.' But it wasn't funny. Saying that was horrible." She began leaving the room when she couldn't take it anymore: "I'm like, once you're done talking shit about people of color, I'll come back."

But an inability to hang was regarded as a failing, Owusu-Breen noted: "My writing partner was told, 'The problem is, you don't think racism is funny.'"

Owusu-Breen and Schapker were assigned the episode in which Akinnuoye-Agbaje's character, Mr. Eko, is killed off. The actor wanted to leave the show, a situation that can be an inconvenience to producers but is a normal thing that happens on many projects. The conversation that took place when Owusu-Breen and her writing partner got feedback from Cuse on their episode was . . . not normal.

"Carlton said something to the effect of, 'I want to hang him from the highest tree. God, if we could only cut his dick off and shove it down his throat.' At which point I said, 'You may want to temper the lynching imagery, lest you offend.' And I was very clearly angry," Owusu-Breen remembered. A person who was present also recalled Cuse offering violent imagery of Eko's death in the trees in a way that immediately made this source think of lynching. This person said they definitely heard the remark about the character's genitals, but does not recall if Cuse said it or if it was said by another *Lost* writer when the episode was discussed by the staff.

It's possible, Owusu-Breen observed, that in that moment, Cuse was trying to think up a "painful death" for the character and did not intentionally bring up imagery that to her evoked lynching—but that in itself could serve as an indicator of just how damaging and routinely toxic the *Lost* culture was. Racist, sexist, and insensitive remarks were made so casually and so frequently by so many, she said, that it would not surprise her if Cuse brought that up offhandedly and then forgot he said it. "No one had the ability to call them on this stuff," she told me. "And it's terrible to this day that they get credit for any kind of racial sensitivity or inclusion. It sucks to be a person of color in rooms like that."

"I really felt sick at the thought of a Black actor who was giving a performance of real power and stature" being discussed in this way, one source said. "To toss about his death with this air of gleeful, malicious punishment" was extremely challenging on a number of fronts: It was troubling in terms of the treatment of the character and for *Lost*'s track record on representation. How Eko's death appeared on-screen was "toned down" from what was discussed, this person said, but the entire experience was deeply "uncomfortable," in part because, in this person's opinion, the showrunners "were vindictive toward their actors."

In any event, not long after that conversation, "we were put in the casting room, and then we were fired," Owusu-Breen said. She and her writing partner were told by the showrunners, "You don't fit," she told me.

Owusu-Breen has been a showrunner—of NBC's *Midnight, Texas* (among other credits, including a *Percy Jackson* TV series)—and she knows what that pressure cooker is like. "It brings out the worst in you. The person I was in my first showrunning gig is not the person I am now. I have apologized to people, because the stress is hard," she said. "But this was racism. I don't know. That doesn't feel like the kind of thing that happens just when you're stressed. There was a blood sport" aspect to how that room functioned. According to her, Lindelof "let it happen and would laugh." Owusu-Breen said her choices consisted of: "I become a dick and start making jokes at people's expense, or I'm the humorless fuck who no one could have fun around."

Four months in, when her writing partner found her in the bathroom late one Friday and said the bosses wanted to see them, she knew they were being let go. "I was so happy to be fired," she remarked.

The environment on *Lost* drove Javier Grillo-Marxuach to quit the show after its second season. He was the only person from the show's original nucleus of writers who was still in the writers' room in Season 2. Despite the show's massive success, Grillo-Marxuach had reached his limit. He told me the writers' room "was a predatory ecosystem with its own carnivorous megafauna. Those of us lucky enough to survive for any extended period of time paid for whatever scraps of the show's success we were tossed with our pride, dignity, and psychotherapy bills." Two years of what could be called the "Tallahassee Mentality" was enough for him. The term comes from characters on the show poking fun at the Florida city. One day, the *Lost* offices got a letter from the mayor of Tallahassee, who gamely invited the show's personnel to visit and enclosed brochures touting the city's attractive qualities.

"In response, Damon told the writers' room to double down on Tallahassee, and when asked why, he replied with a straight face that the only thing funnier than punching someone in the face for no reason is punching them harder when they ask why," Grillo-Marxuach said. "If you can imagine that as a management philosophy, you can understand what it was like to work on *Lost*."

"Damon once said, 'I don't trust any writer who isn't miserable, because that tells me you don't care,'" according to writer/producer Melinda Hsu Taylor. During her time at *Lost*, Hsu Taylor learned to keep eyeliner in the desk in her office. "You don't want to have to go to the bathroom to redo your eyeliner," she said. "If you cry at work, you don't want people to see that you've been crying."

By the time she arrived for the drama's last two seasons, she told me she got the impression that Lindelof had been "talked to" by someone about dialing back some of the room's worst tendencies. But she still faced a gauntlet of punishing experiences. She'd heard stories about how it wasn't unusual for high-level writers to speak "fake Korean"—gibberish that they pretended was Korean—and laugh about it. Given what I know about TV writer culture, I'd guess that sort of thing happened in other writers' rooms at the time. A different experience of Hsu Taylor's—being reprimanded by Cuse after chiming in with an affirmation of Cuse's instructions to a director during a tone meeting—was also probably sadly common. "He just totally put me in my place," she recalled. "He said, 'I don't need you to comment on anything I've said.'"

It was the kind of place where the lines of authority were clear—and in some ways, that was beneficial. Multiple people told me that Lindelof banned Cuse from rewriting him—a decision they actually agreed with, because most sources said they thought Lindelof was a talented writer and Cuse was not. "At least Damon knew what he wanted," Christopher said. "I've been in rooms where clarity from the creators is absent," which is a different kind of awful. That said, the *Lost* room was a "boys' club" atmosphere that was "cutthroat," Christopher added.

An editor once made a suggestion about a storytelling choice, and according to *Lost* employee Seamus, Lindelof made it clear to the editing team that there would be hell to pay and her job would be in danger if she ever did that again. "She wrote an almost offensively effusive mea culpa letter—'I'm so sorry,'" Seamus said. It was just one minor idea, but offering storytelling input to Lindelof, Seamus observed, was "a no-fly zone. An absolute no-fly zone."

Talent, clarity of vision, and a decisive command structure—in the right hands, these can be positive elements when deployed thoughtfully within creative environments. But it did not take long for the *Lost* workplace to drift into something else, many said—something pulverizing and often cruel. And that, sources from various seasons told me, stymied the free flow of ideas, not to mention good writing. "If you treat people well, they will kill for you, in any environment—an athletic team, a family, a job. If you foster an environment of rampant paranoia and anxiety and discomfort, that leads to bad writing," Seamus said. "And that really is the name of the game—if you are in a position of fear, you can't write well."

All these revelations about the show, dispiriting as they are, certainly explain a lot: why a show that promised an inclusive, globe-trotting adventure ended up being, in its final season, about a small group of men on interlocking epic quests. This is not in any way a critique of the show's reliably excellent actors; this is about who got the on-screen focus and why. Of course, characters of color had notable or heroic moments throughout the run of the show, but over time, they were generally shipped off the island or killed, and white male characters like Ben Linus and the Man in Black became ever more vitally important. The showrunners' "cold" treatment of Michelle Rodriguez and her character stuck with Gretchen: after the actor was arrested in that drunk-driving incident, "instead of having empathy or sympathy for her situation, they were just like, 'Well, we'll just get rid of her.'"

The show seemed unable to decide on any kind of interesting direction for Kate—who was supposedly one of the show's "hero" characters, at least for a while—whose importance and impact on the narrative was almost nil in the final season. Could one possible explanation have come from a word Gretchen used for her experience of Cuse in the show's early seasons: "misogynist"? After more than a year of reporting on all these matters, certain aspects of the show make much more sense to me. Still, though I didn't know then what I know now, by its final season, *Lost* had made me snap.

I wrote thousands of words about *Lost* back in the day, about things I did not like and things I loved (any and all Dharma Initiative mythology; Juliet + Sawyer forever). But thinking about a wretched final-season episode called "Across the Sea" still gives me a tension headache. When it aired in 2010, I was more low-key about my feminism, but that episode helped me overcome a tendency to avoid using my work to speak loudly and clearly about misogynist bullshit.

"We finally got a female character who was tied into an epic, mythologically important story line—and it's all about how her bitterness, misanthropy and evasions launched centuries of bloodshed. Fabulous," I wrote the night the episode aired. "A woman is at the heart of what first went wrong on the island. After years of putting up with lame Kate episodes, loony or smothering mothers and the killing off of great female characters like Juliet, the reward we get for our patience is . . . *this*? To say it was demoralizing is putting it mildly."

Obviously, I wasn't the only critic to point out how uneven the island saga had gotten as it entered its home stretch, and how most characters who weren't white or male didn't matter by the end. However, many critics agreed that "Ab Aeterno" was not one of the final season's weak links. It was a blast: the episode's credited writers, Hsu Taylor and script coordinator Greggory Nations, crafted a rousing adventure tale that filled in the backstory of fan favorite Richard Alpert (Néstor Carbonell). The episode was showered with praise—at least as Hsu Taylor (and I) perceived it—and that was the problem. An episode without Lindelof's and Cuse's names on it was *too* well received.

Hsu Taylor, like most *Lost* veterans I've talked to, is quick to point out that working on the show was an intensely collaborative effort. The grind of making between fourteen and twenty-five episodes of TV per season, as the ABC drama did, was so demanding that it was not uncommon for a number of writers to work together to get a script across the finish line. That's what happened with "Ab Aeterno." "We had such a talented staff," Hsu Taylor said. "I am so grateful for everything that everybody did—but my name and Gregg's name were on the script. And I did do a pass to stitch it all together and smooth things out. I wrote a bunch of the scenes too, and I was really proud of the results."

That's why she was thunderstruck when, in the anteroom to Cuse's office, she heard him on the phone with Carbonell, the actor featured in "Ab Aeterno." In Hsu Taylor's recollection, Cuse said to the actor, "Oh, yeah. I wrote that. I wrote most of that script." "I mean, it was a flat-out lie," Hsu Taylor said. "My jaw dropped. I just turned around and walked away." She was devastated.

At one point, the "Ab Aeterno" saga took a turn for the ridiculous: Cuse and Lindelof called Nations and Hsu Taylor into a room, and she recalled that they "basically [told] us how much we owed them for letting us have our names on that script. And they implied it would probably be good if we got them a little present." So Hsu Taylor went out and bought gifts for her bosses. She can't recall what she got Lindelof—probably something *Star Wars* related, given his love of that franchise. She said she bought Swarovski pencils for Cuse.

A far more serious consequence soon arrived. Some context: when a TV writer has a script taken away from them, that effectively takes tens of thousands of dollars in script fees (not to mention residuals) out of their pocket. I wish I had a dollar for every time a showrunner has taken away—or refused to assign—an episode due to some ego-driven or vindictive reason. This is an abuse of power I hear about a lot. And apparently it happened on *Lost*.

"As the episode got more and more praise, they started to get more and more tense about it," Hsu Taylor recalled. "I was up next in the rotation—I was supposed to write one of the upcoming episodes. We were in the writers' room. I remember Carlton walking around the table" while doling out script assignments. Hsu Taylor recalled feeling that he was making sure everyone was fully aware that he was skipping her. She can still remember her colleagues looking at her, their faces reflecting the embarrassment and distress they felt on her behalf. Later, when the bosses weren't around, they were even more sympathetic, she told me: "They were like, 'Yes, you're absolutely being punished for having cowritten that script.'"

As one source noted, several weeks after "Ab Aeterno" aired, "Across the Sea"—which Cuse and Lindelof wrote—was "not received as well. I think that annoyed them." But looking at the situation from a big-picture perspective, the whole brouhaha was preposterous. The two showrunners generally "got all the positive attention," this source recalled. "We were just there to kind of fill in—the jazz band in the background that nobody saw. They were the front men."

For Hsu Taylor to be singled out in that way in front of her coworkers "was humiliating," she said. "It was also the feeling of, 'All my colleagues know that this is what's happening, and we're all going to collectively not do anything about it, because this is the power structure here.' The only thing I had done was excel and get attention," she remarked. "And not in that order. They were very jealous of the attention."

To this day, Owusu-Breen is extremely cautious about what jobs she takes—she vets people she might work for and does not just talk to high-level people those potential employers have been around. She talks to assistants, support staff, anyone she can get hold of.

"I can't work for certain people and do good work. I'm a Black woman, and if you don't accept that . . . I can't change," she said. Though after she left the show, she did actually try to change *Lost*, the most "nakedly hostile" work environment she said she'd ever endured.

When Owusu-Breen and her writing partner joined the ABC drama *Brothers & Sisters*, they were required to attend a seminar on avoiding and preventing racial and sexual harassment. Afterward, they went up to the people who ran the seminar and said, "Have you done this on *Lost*? Because they actually need to be reminded of all this," Owusu-Breen recalled. "They just walked away from us, like that meme of Homer Simpson disappearing into the bush. They were walking backward, like, 'No, no, we haven't done that yet. We're going to.' You could tell everyone knew it was a toxic work environment. But it was a huge hit."

After they were fired from *Lost,* they had one other deeply surreal experience connected to the show. "We were taken out to lunch by executives and told there was no racism—it was just bullying," Owusu-Breen told me. "It was fascinating to me, because what do you think racism is?" As she sees it, "we were discriminated against on the daily. Maybe they just didn't like our writing, but it's hard to tell if you're discriminated against on the daily."

Why dredge all this up years later? Well, because working on *Lost* harmed a lot of people, and some are still dealing with the aftereffects of that personal and professional damage (including people who, after considering it, understandably declined to talk to me for the purposes of this book). "It's the sort of place where the voices still ring in your head, even now," Hsu Taylor said. "You don't know you're in an abusive relationship until you're no longer in an abusive relationship," pointed out Seamus. In a separate interview, Gretchen said almost the same thing, word for word.

Another reason to go into all this is because *Lost* is still around. Thanks to the streaming revolution, the shows of the Golden Age are available with a click or two. They're still watched, talked about, and influential. Complicating and adding necessary context to the show's legacy is important. Plus, the tendency to engage in hero worship of "geniuses" is still very much alive and well. If we don't question the more damaging aspects of our conception of "genius," we are doomed to repeat the past ad nauseam. And we'll get shittier entertainment.

"This sort of environment doesn't only poison the dynamic behind the scenes, it shows up on-screen in the attitudes of the characters, their dialogue, and the stories themselves," said Grillo-Marxuach. "It's no surprise to me that the main Latinx character in the show was frequently portrayed as feckless, ignorant, and gluttonous—and therefore the butt of countless fat jokes. It's very easy, especially twenty years after the fact, to think 'Well, it can't have been that bad or someone would have done something.' Let me say it loud and clear: it was that bad, and no one did anything because retribution was a constant and looming presence. When a showrunner makes a clear statement to his writers' room that 'I'm petty and I bear grudges,' as ours did with absolutely no irony, you know exactly what you stand to lose by rocking the boat. It is also very hard to overstate the degree to which female and POC television writers lived in a climate of uncertainty back then, with no real improvement to this day."

What remains a foundational pillar of the industry is the fact that those responsible for huge hits often get enormous passes regarding their actions, attitudes, and management styles. Very few people who are put in positions of power get the training or oversight they need to make that a positive—or at least nonmiserable—experience for everyone involved. If some powerful people want to act like despots and cruel dictators, no one will stop them, despite the fact that being decent and accountable human beings in this industry, is "not all that hard," Owusu-Breen observed.

"The notion that it could all be chalked up to inexperience alone is fucking risible," Grillo-Marxuach said. "Simple decency and managerial experience are not mutually dependent."

I've known Damon Lindelof for a long time. My career has prospered over the years for a number of reasons, but one thing that has helped is knowing that powerful people like him tend to return my call, text, or email. They want to promote their projects, and they hope for good coverage, but in many cases, there's more to it than the merely transactional. We often wonder about the same things: why some stories work and some don't; why some careers prosper and some founder. We know the same trivia, and in many cases the same people. We can lose hours gossiping about various industry trash fires. In any event, having off-the-record meals and conversations with industry people is not just useful for both parties, it's often pleasant and even illuminating.

The day in 2014 that I published a piece comparing a later Lindelof show, HBO's *The Leftovers,* to *Rectify*—saying *Rectify* was the superior drama—I got a self-deprecating email from Lindelof, who said the second season would be funnier. It was, but the HBO drama also evolved into an intense, moving saga of love, death, pain, and sacrifice that struck close to home for me. (I was going through the illnesses and deaths of my parents around then.) The drama meant so much to me that in 2017, just before it concluded, I wrote a *Leftovers* essay that is nothing like any of my previous work; it is a long, impressionistic combination of the critical and the personal that was profoundly cathartic to write and is, in my opinion, one of the best things I've ever created.

And I wouldn't have been able to conceive of that piece, let alone write it, had the show not affected me and inspired me as much as it did.

Lindelof and I were still in touch while *The Leftovers* was on the air—I wrote a lot about the brilliant second and third seasons of the show, which he cocreated with novelist Tom Perrotta. And Cuse and Lindelof were guests on a *Lost* retrospective podcast I cohosted in 2019. By that point, I had heard intimations that *Lost* was a difficult work environment. But in 2019, I did not know what I know now. What I learned in subsequent years caused me to approach Lindelof in 2021, for the purposes of this book. He spent more than an hour addressing some aspects of what went wrong.

"My level of fundamental inexperience as a manager and a boss, my role as someone who was supposed to model a climate of creative danger and risk-taking, but provide safety and comfort inside of the creative process—I failed in that endeavor," Lindelof said. In that conversation, he also addressed Hollywood tokenism that was common at the time—and is still not hard to find.

That's "what I saw in the business around me," Lindelof observed. "And so I was like, okay, as long as there are one or two [writers] who don't look and think exactly like me, then I'm okay. I came to learn that was even worse. For those specific individuals, forget about the ethics or the morality involved around that decision, but just talking about the human effect of being the only woman or the only person of color and how you are treated and othered—I was a part of that, a thousand percent."

After that first conversation, I kept talking to *Lost* veterans, and I heard awful things. It was not an easy process for any of us, in part because airing all of this out can feel, as Owusu-Breen put it, like revealing "Santa doesn't exist. People just love *Lost* so much."

They do. But the industry can't move forward unless it meaningfully changes, and that means uncovering long-festering infections in order to clean them out. To mix in another metaphor, if we don't talk about how bad it was in some cases—and why that awfulness mattered—it'd be like putting a coat of paint on a house with rotting walls. That's the analogy I used when I talked to Lindelof a second time, in 2022, when I shared the additional allegations I'd heard.

By the time I wrapped up reporting on this chapter, multiple sources—including some who heard it said in their presence—had told me they'd heard Lindelof say he fired Perrineau because he felt accused of racism by the actor. I told him the two versions of this remark that I'd heard ended with "so I fired him" or "so I fired his ass." Lindelof replied, "What can I say? Other than it breaks my heart that that was Harold's experience," adding that he did not recall "ever" saying that. "And I'll just cede that the events that you're describing happened seventeen years ago, and I don't know why anybody would make that up about me."

Lindelof said the rapid growth spurt of Malcolm David Kelley, the actor who played Michael's son Walt, factored into the showrunners' thinking about what to do with both characters. When I shared Perrineau's comments about Black families, missing Black boys, and Hollywood stereotypes, Lindelof replied that there was "a high degree of insensitivity towards all the issues that you mentioned as it relates to Harold."

Lindelof added that by the second season, "every single actor had expressed some degree of disappointment that they weren't being used enough, or their character wasn't being centered enough. That was kind of part and parcel for an ensemble show, but obviously there was a disproportionate amount of focus on Jack and Kate and Locke and Sawyer—the white characters. Harold was completely and totally right to point that out. It's one of the things that I've had deep and profound regrets about in the two decades since." All in all, Lindelof said, "I do feel that Harold was legitimately and professionally conveying concerns about his character and how significant it was that Michael and Walt—with the exception of Rose—were really the only Black characters on the show."

Lindelof told me he didn't remember any negative incident with an editor, adding that he seeks out input from collaborators and that he's "never threatened anyone's career." Lindelof also said he had no recollection of anything Hsu Taylor said about events connected to "Ab Aeterno." He said she was a "great writer who executed at a high level" and he's "stricken" that she was made to feel the way she felt at that time.

Regarding the other allegations leveled at him and the show, Lindelof said he had no memory of the incidents and comments I described. He told me he was "shocked and appalled and surprised" by the incidents I relayed to him, and said more than once that he did not think anyone was making anything up. "I just can't imagine that Carlton would've said something like that, or some of those attributions, some of those comments that you [shared]—I'm telling you, I swear, I have no recollection of those specific things. And that's not me saying that they didn't happen. I'm just saying that it's literally baffling my brain—that they did happen and that I bore witness to them or that I said them. To think that they came out of my mouth or the mouths of people that I still consider friends is just not computing."

For his part, Cuse said he was not present for nor did he hear the litany of offensive comments that I brought up, and he added, "I deeply regret that anyone at *Lost* would have to hear them. They are highly insensitive, inappropriate, and offensive." Cuse (who supplied written answers to my questions through a PR representative) also stated he had never made an actor cry and did not make the remark about pearl divers. In a letter, his attorney Bryan J. Freedman called the latter allegation offensive and false.

Cuse's comments were similar to Lindelof's on the matter of Kelley's growth spurt and how it collided with the island drama's plot. Kelley's rapid growth created continuity problems for *Lost,* hence the need—cited by both showrunners—to write him out of the narrative. And if Walt was gone, Cuse said the only thing to do with Michael was to make finding the boy his "primary mission." However, since Kelley was not coming back, that was not a story line they could "resolve for the character," Cuse added. "We did not know how to solve this problem other than to resolve Michael's story at the end of Season 2."

Cuse also stated that he never discussed matters touching on race at any time with Perrineau, and that race had "nothing to do" with the character's story line. "I do not believe he is in any way personally to blame for the way his role changed," said Cuse, who also noted that Perrineau's feedback about that Season 2 script was relayed to him by Lindelof—Cuse did not recall discussing those specific concerns with the actor—and that revisions of the script were in part intended to address Perrineau's input. "We heard his concerns and made changes to address them in the second episode of Season 2, and as we moved through Season 2 we reflected Michael's character as caring deeply about finding his missing son at every possible opportunity," Cuse wrote.

In his responses, Cuse disputed that Perrineau was fired; he said the actor was bumped down to recurring status, but that does not line up with Perrineau's recollections. The actor said after Season 2, he was released from his *Lost* contract and took other jobs. As the opening credits show, he was not part of Season 3 at all. Perrineau did appear in several episodes of the strike-shortened fourth season (for which he was under contract), and he also appeared once in the final season.

As for Cuse's remark to Owusu-Breen, this was Cuse's response to a query about it: "I never, ever made that statement above [about Mr. Eko's death], and this exchange never happened. To further add to this lie and suggest that someone was fired as a result of a statement that I never made is false," adding that the implication is "completely outrageous."

Hundreds of people were employed in various capacities by *Lost*, and not all of them have identical histories. Some had, at times, genuinely positive experiences, and that was and is a good thing. But in the engine room of the show—where decisions about theme, story, and focus were made, where characters and plots duked it out for attention—the atmosphere was often demeaning, unpleasant, confounding, and deeply damaging. At least to some. One person said of their bosses and some of their coworkers, "I think they were having a different experience of reality, which was, 'Wow, I just have a bunch of funny people I work with.' They just seemed to think they were super funny." This source felt "silenced," because it felt as though every pathway—other than accepting the cruelty, sexism, and racist commentary—was blocked. Trying to make it as a *Lost* writer was draining and "depressing," but at least this person wasn't alone in coming to that conclusion: "A lot of people had failed there. I tried to take solace in that I was in good company. Everyone who survived was almost like in a support group after that."

I kept a running list of words sources used to describe the show's work atmosphere, a word cloud I shared with Lindelof and Cuse. Among the adjectives that came up a lot: cruel, brutal, destructive, blood sport, racist, sexist, hazing, a barrage, bullying, angry, abusive, crossed lines, boys' club, hostile work environment.

"It breaks my heart to hear it. It's deeply upsetting to know that there were people who had such bad experiences," Cuse wrote. "I did not know people were feeling that way. No one ever complained to me, nor am I aware that anybody complained to ABC Studios. I wish I had known. I would have done what I could to make changes."

I also asked Cuse the following question: "It's my understanding that there were several tiers of compensation among actors on *Lost* and that, after negotiations during the show's run, white actors were in the top compensation tier. Why was that?" Cuse wrote that he and Lindelof "steadfastly believed" that the actors' "compensation should all be the same. While we did not support changes to how the actors were compensated, ultimately those decisions were made by ABC Studios."

He wrote he did not recall withholding a script from Hsu Taylor, whom he called "an invaluable asset" to *Lost,* nor did he remember claiming credit for "Ab Aeterno" or implying that she should buy presents for the showrunners. (He called the latter claim "absurd.") "Regardless of our level of rewriting on 'Ab Aeterno,' we never sought credit for our work on the episode," Cuse wrote. As for the high writer turnover—which he acknowledged especially affected early seasons—he wrote that the complexity of the show's narrative, themes, and logistics made it "very difficult for us to find writers who could accomplish all the many things we felt we needed from them. Looking back, I can understand that the high degree of writer turnover caused hurt, resentment, and frustration, and I am sorry for that. I wish we had had more time to nurture the existing writers instead of hiring many new writers, but that was not feasible due to the tremendous time pressure and demands of the show."

After I read the word cloud to Lindelof, he was silent for about a minute. He finally answered, referring to his behavior in the present: "The way that I conduct myself and the way that I treat other humans who I am responsible for and a manager of is a byproduct of all the mistakes that were made. . . . I have significantly evolved and grown, and it shouldn't have had to come at the cost and the trauma of people that I hurt on *Lost*."

Lindelof asked, "Would it shock you to learn or believe that, despite the fact that I completely and totally validate your word cloud, that I was oblivious, largely oblivious, to the adverse impacts that I was having on others in that writers' room during the entire time that the show was happening?" He also asked, "Do you feel like I knew the whole time and just kept doing it?"

I gave him a variation of an answer I have given—or wanted to give—to powerful people many times: I think he knew enough and chose not to do anything about it. But in our culture, phrases like "I didn't know," "there was so much going on," and "mistakes were made" are common ways to frame terrible patterns of behavior—many of

which are the result of terrible *decisions,* not the work of the disembodied hand of fate. Especially if the person at the center of those "mistakes"
is a high-status individual, a lot of hedges and rationales are rolled out,
and they are often couched in the passive voice. In the past decade
alone, how many times, and in how many important spheres, have we
seen wealthy or powerful people—especially white men—depicted as
stumbling bumblers who knew not what they did?

But someone who is in their early thirties—as Lindelof was when
Lost took off like a rocket—is not a child. Lindelof and Cuse were adults
when the show began, and both had been in the industry for years.
They were the two people within that workplace who had power, and
they bear the responsibility for the culture you read about here—one
that endured for six seasons. Nothing that happens consistently across
the making of more than one hundred episodes of television happens
by accident. Whether or not Lindelof and Cuse were present for every
damaging incident, the workplace environment at *Lost* was created, rewarded, and reinforced by them.

I said as much to Lindelof.

"Of course," he replied. "Yeah. Full stop. Of course, you're right."

Toward the end of that second conversation, Lindelof began specu-
lating about what would happen to his career as a result of this book.
He sounded as demoralized as I felt.

"It's not for me to say what kind of person I am," he said. "But
I will say this—I would trade every person who told you that I was
talented—I would rather they said I was untalented but decent, rather
than a talented monster."

That is a false binary: people can be talented and decent. Lindelof's
framing is one I encounter a lot, and it belies, or at least hints at, the
fundamental belief that if you're a genius, you're more or less *required*
to be a monster.

But at its heart—and at its best, it has a palpable, beating heart—
Lost tries to say that none of us have to be defined by our pasts. We're
at the beginning stages of the entertainment industry's shift to better
models, and to make the necessary changes—and to make that positive
evolution permanent—a lot of people must work hard on a number of
fronts for a long time.

What choice do we have? As the *Lost* saying goes, live together, die
alone.

6

The Myth of the Meritocracy

We are questioning the American dream.
—*Melinda Hsu Taylor*

Five people were in the room when Damon Lindelof met J. J. Abrams in 2004 to talk about joining *Lost*. As Lindelof recalled, the other people present were Jesse Alexander, Jeff Pinkner, and Bryan Burk, all of whom worked on the show in various capacities. "They were all white men roughly in the same age group, maybe a couple of years older than me—all peers," Lindelof told me. The worldviews and cultural references of everyone in that room overlapped a lot, and that helped. "I was with my people," he said.

It wasn't the first time being with "his people" gave him a leg up. Lindelof's industry breakthrough came when he was hired as a writer's assistant on the TV drama *Wasteland*. He was hired by his friend Julie Plec (who went on to run multiple shows, including *The Vampire Diaries*). "The cultural group that I ran around in advantaged me," Lindelof observed. "I could send out an email saying, 'I want to be a writer's assistant—does anybody know of any jobs out there?'" And it didn't take long for him to get one.

On his next jobs—at *Nash Bridges* and *Crossing Jordan*—Lindelof recalled that white guys were the key decision-makers each time he got hired. After *Lost*, that was the case again. "That doesn't mean that women and people of color were not part of the decision-making process," Lindelof said. "But my fundamental bosses, the people who made big bets on me—they were usually white and male."

It's worth considering Lindelof's and *Lost* writer Melinda Hsu Taylor's varying career trajectories. It took Lindelof about eight years to go from working as an assistant to becoming a showrunner. With the caveat that everyone's journey is different—for instance, Hsu Taylor was never an assistant—it took Hsu Taylor, who is Chinese American, about fourteen years to complete a similar journey.

Every creative person's path is unique, of course, but this information tracks with an array of industry data that shows that the higher one goes on a given food chain, the whiter and more male that food chain gets. Among working TV writers in the 2019–20 season, according to the WGA, 49 percent of those on the lowest level were people of color; 82 percent of showrunners were white. Seven out of ten showrunners were male. "While both women and people of color made overall gains," the WGA study notes, "these writers remain concentrated at the middle and lower levels with white men continuing to hold most of the high level positions."

The white-guy-in-charge stats were even higher a decade earlier, when Hsu Taylor was interviewing for jobs. Her journey actually paralleled Lindelof's: most of the folks with the power to hire or promote her were white, and a sizable number of them were male. A Black executive in a key position at Fox helped her get one of her early jobs, and a number of white women also gave her career major assists, she told me. But once hired, she was often the only woman or the only person of color on the staff. She was, she said, the only woman of color in the writers' room on five jobs in a row.

That kind of isolation takes a toll—a psychic cost that Hsu Taylor generally had to shove on the back burner if she wanted to get anything done. "I've sort of blocked a lot of it out," she said with wry chuckle. "You find yourself doing a lot of explaining, and you feel like you're the police and the educator. And years ago, before people got a little more sensitive and trained in the workplace, there would be comments—sexist and racist comments that I would laugh about, because otherwise you would get iced out. You would be seen as the prude or the schoolmarm. Then it would become, 'We can't be ourselves around her. Who wants to break story with her?' It was almost like a military unit—I don't want to get left alone above the trenches and not be told where the patrol was headed."

Trying to ensure her own acceptance in those spaces more often revolved around gender than race, which "didn't even enter into it because I was so busy being one of the guys," Hsu Taylor recalled. "For years, I dressed in a much more androgynous fashion, so that people wouldn't think I was too girly. I actually hid that I had kids from several jobs—certainly from the job interview process. I'd been working at *Lost* for a couple of months before anyone realized I had a baby at home." It took even longer for it to dawn on her coworkers that the baby was her second child.

Hsu Taylor has regrets about how she conducted herself at work when she was younger. "I'm not immune from the culture," she said. "There are things I regret saying early in my career, because I wanted very badly to fit in." Javier Grillo-Marxuach lives with similar guilt, especially from his time on *Lost:* "I was afraid for my career, and the stakes were enormous. I can't hold my head up high and declare that I was a 'good ally' who called out abuses wherever I saw them. I went along to get along, and I laughed and nodded when I should have balked and argued."

But at many "creative" workplaces, most folks don't have much of a choice about what to go along with. This is especially true for people from historically excluded groups; the borders they cannot stray beyond are not usually set by them, but they know where those lines are. The stereotypes Hollywood and other media industries have long reinforced about angry Black women, for example, mean that they have to navigate a minefield every time they feel rage.

"If I had a dollar for every time I've held my tongue in my career in the last thirty years, I would never have to work again," said Sarah Rodman, who has worked as a music critic, a TV critic, and an editor at publications like the *Boston Globe*, *Entertainment Weekly*, and the *Los Angeles Times*. "It is hilarious that people talk about how diplomatic I am, or how well I handle a crisis. It's simple. I have not in my entire life ever been allowed to *not* be good in these situations. I have never been allowed to be mad—ever."

Imagine the toll that takes—and then, in that scenario, add one more element to that burden: the knowledge that many of the people around you from historically favored groups think they got where they are primarily—or purely—on merit.

Franklin Leonard is a producer and the founder of the Black List, which "started as an annual survey of the industry's most-liked unproduced screenplays." Leonard said, "We built a metal detector that allowed the industry to find great scripts—to find a bunch of needles in all those endless haystacks."

The Black List exists in part because people without industry connections often asked Leonard how they could get their scripts noticed. The traditional answer—move to LA and work crappy jobs while trying to make the right connections—is not realistic for most folks. "Our goal is to reduce the cost of access, so that you don't have to pay to go to the right schools, you don't have to move to LA," Leonard said. "What should matter is that you can write a brilliant story, not who your dad went to college with."

One of Leonard's early industry jobs was at the powerful agency CAA. He could tough out a year of being paid close to nothing, but he is well aware that many can't afford to do that. "I'm an upper-middle-class kid," Leonard said. "My dad is a doctor, but I'm also a Black kid from West Central Georgia. And I'm acutely aware of the extent to which most of the opportunities in my life have come probably not because I have intrinsic merit that people have recognized, but because I fell into a social slipstream via Harvard that opened up the world to me and allowed me to show the merit that I had."

It's only in recent years that many people in the industry have come to terms with the advantages that have kept them aloft in Hollywood. What can make this discussion thorny is that, for most people in the industry, whatever their background or connections, getting something made is really, really difficult.

George R. R. Martin talked in 2022 about what an uphill battle it was to get the drama *Dark Winds* on the air that year. The program, which showcases an array of Diné (Navajo) characters and is based on Tony Hillerman's Leaphorn and Chee mystery novels, took many years of strenuous pushing from Martin and fellow executive producers Chris Eyre and Robert Redford, among others. Despite all their efforts, HBO passed on the project—even though, without Martin's Song of Ice and Fire book saga, the network's blockbuster *Game of Thrones* series (and its offshoots) wouldn't exist.

"I sat there with George and Bob [Redford] one day, and one of them said, shaking his head—I think it was George—'This is a tough industry,'" Eyre recalled. "And Bob said, 'You're damn right it is.' And I'll never forget that because it's like, even for these guys, they're saying how difficult it is to get anything made."

Still, the industry has largely danced around issues of privilege, access, and opportunity for most of its history, because delving into those

matters in a real way would be awkward and messy; it would take people who were likely already dealing with a heaping helping of stress out
of their comfort zones. So, until recently, many in the industry have nav-
igated terms such as "meritocracy" and "level playing field" with their
magical-thinking filters switched on.

"Even if you were born on third base, in order to get to home plate,
you still have to run, right? There was still an effort required to get
there," said Hannah, a writer/producer. "Once you're on home plate,
you want to believe that the run was the only part that was important,
not where you started. If you acknowledge that you and somebody else
put the same amount of effort, but you got farther than them [because
of where you started], it feels bad. It's uncomfortable to admit, and
Hollywood is an industry that avoids discomfort at all costs."

Truer words were never spoken. In July 2021, the site Discussing
Film's Twitter account noted that an upcoming short film had the following personnel in its creative ranks: Hopper Penn (Sean Penn's son),
Destry Spielberg (Steven Spielberg's daughter), and Owen King (Stephen King's son). Leonard added a few words with his retweet: "Hollywood's a meritocracy, right?"

You *might* say some discomfort bubbled up after that. "Too easy
@franklinleonard," actor and director Ben Stiller wrote in response.
"People, working, creating. Everyone has their own path. Wish them
all the best."

Stiller, the son of noted entertainers Anne Meara and Jerry Stiller,
shared a few additional thoughts: Speaking from "experience, and I
don't know any of them, I would bet they all have faced challenges.
Different than those with no access to the industry. Show biz as we all
know is pretty rough, and ultimately is a meritocracy."

(Pause for internal screaming.)

There are a lot of terms one could use to describe the industry. The
accursed word "meritocracy" is not one of them. A number of critics
and other observers made that point in their own contributions to the
social media conversation, or in think pieces and news stories written
after Leonard and Stiller's exchange.

"I was very surprised that it became a thing, and then amused, and
then a little terrified," Leonard said. But he has no regrets about what
transpired. "It became a conversation about whether Hollywood is a
meritocracy, and I think Ben handled that aspect of it really well. He ba-

sically said, 'Huh, I've never really thought about it that way. I need to do some thinking.' And we had a private conversation that continued in that vein, where he was really trying to understand where he could have missed the dynamic that I was describing and the numbers that I was presenting. What I *was* surprised by was how few industry people were willing to confirm what I was saying."

There are, of course, nuances that get lost in the whole "nepo baby" conversation (the daughter of a key grip is not in the same league as the daughter of a tremendously wealthy studio executive). Still, at the risk of overgeneralizing, I see the metaphorical blinders that many in the industry prefer to wear. In my experience, those who write about the industry or who come at it from a less insulated position are far more willing to state plainly that Hollywood is not a level playing field. Many who operate inside the industry, especially in its higher echelons, would rather dance around or avoid that reality entirely.

So that everybody hears it, maybe a white man should make the next point. According to Lindelof, whose credits—in addition to *Lost* and *The Leftovers*—include *Star Trek Into Darkness*, *Prometheus*, and *Watchmen*, "it's not remotely a level playing field. White men are systemically advantaged every step of the way, from the moment they're born to the moment they go to school, and the way that their teachers treat them. And that extends to their entry-level positions in the industry, and what's expected of them versus what's expected of those who are not white men, etc., ad infinitum."

Though people from historically excluded groups have been shouting this from the rooftops for a long time, Stiller's words are indicative of attitudes and oblivious assumptions that still exist all over the industry. When a deep-seated frustration about an unfair Hollywood power system is clearly expressed, it's not all that uncommon for a privileged person's go-to response to involve feeling personally attacked. Even mild critiques are often characterized by the powerful as someone "being unkind" or engaging in cruelty.

Some cannier folks avoid the "be kind" trap and steer clear of the dreaded M-word. Instead, they'll offer reasonable-sounding rationales about how standards should not be lowered and quality levels should not be put at risk by, you know, letting in *those people*. Of course, if you assume cracking open the gates of Hollywood's generally white, generally middle- or upper-class creative communities is sure to lower the quality of the industry's output, that's a tell. And then there is this hardy favorite that simply will not die—the one that usually contains some version of the phrase "if they just tried harder . . ."

"The view is often offered up that if someone talented wanted to succeed, they could. This, of course, ignores all the built-in advantages that the person expressing it has had," industry executive Nick told me. "The reality is that people in this industry tend to want to associate with and promote those who mirror themselves. Not *always*. But often. And to succeed in this industry takes, typically, a college education and a wealthy family that can backstop you. Succeeding without those factors is very, very difficult."

Yup. But many people—in the public and in the industry—are clearly still wedded to the idea that Hollywood is a level or at least *somewhat* level playing field, instead of a bewildering array of steep ravines, quicksand quagmires, and unscalable mountains. It's human for people to believe they got where they are through hard work and effort. And in an industry full of uncertainty and fear, it's understandable that rank-and-file workers sometimes *want* to believe that whoever is driving the car knows where they're going, so to speak. "You want to believe that everyone in these positions of power has earned their way, that they're super smart and talented and know what they're doing," said Taura, a writer/producer. "And by and large, that's just not the case."

As for those at the top, "they see the business as a right of privilege," Orlando Jones said. "They choose who is and isn't worthy. Some obviously do not see it in that particular way. But by and large, they still perpetuate the same lies. 'Oh, you're not gonna sell foreign 'cause you're Black.' You might want to tell the fans that, then. My autograph line at conventions is no shorter in France than for any of my Caucasian peers."

These mindsets, mental habits, and assumptions are very deeply embedded in the industry. One sign is that many of the usual suspects spent a lot of time in high industry perches before they even *began* confronting the following idea: hard work and talent can matter, but quite often, privilege, wealth, and connections (not to mention race, gender, class, physical ability, appearance, and education) matter more. The fact is, Hollywood tends to favor folks from certain groups—giving them a smoother ride to the top or just a glide path to the middle—while exacting enormous professional and personal costs from people who are not in the favored groups. Those individuals must cover the same terrain with fewer resources, more scrutiny, and less help.

And you don't have to take my word for it.

In 1997, Martha Lauzen, a professor of television, film, and new media at San Diego State University, began tracking statistics that documented gender bias in the film and television industries. She had become interested in the topic in the wake of assertions she'd seen in news stories about how "things were changing" for women in the industry. She assumed that assembling those numbers wasn't going to take up a huge chunk of her nascent academic career. After five or six years, Hollywood—having seen the cold, hard numbers that proved gender bias was real—would change its hiring patterns and her work would be done. Right?

Wrong.

Lauzen is still compiling those stats every year, via studies such as *Boxed In* and *The Celluloid Ceiling*. These reports track how many men and women are on-screen, what kind of roles they play, and how many men and women are senior creative forces behind the scenes. If you're a data nerd, trolling through the website that hosts decades of studies from SDSU's Center for the Study of Women in Television and Film (which Lauzen founded) is heaven. A sobering kind of heaven, in which precise numbers back up suspicions and theories that have long rolled around in my mind.

Here are some pertinent numbers from Lauzen and others who have long toiled in these data mines: White people generally still dominate most Hollywood positions of power. According to a 2020 UCLA study, 92 percent of television network chairs/CEOs were white and more than two-thirds were male; in the film world, 91 percent of studio chiefs were white and 82 percent male. The 2022 *Boxed In* study shows that women were around 30 percent of TV creators at broadcast networks and streamers—a number that is a few percentage points higher than the 2017–18 season but is, based on trends captured by the Center's studies, in no apparent danger of rising above one-third of the total. The UCLA study notes that, on cable, streaming, and broadcast, between 10.3 and 14.5 percent of shows were created by people from underrepresented racial groups, which make up around 40 percent of the American population.

One of Hollywood's largest blind spots involves depicting Latino characters and cultures, not just in nonstereotypical roles but *at all*. Latinos are "almost half the population of Los Angeles, and nearly 19 percent of the U.S. population," a news story about the 2022 UCLA *Hollywood Diversity Report* notes, "but the report found that during the 2020–21 season, they received only 4.9 percent of the top roles on scripted cable shows, and 5.3 percent of the top roles on streaming and broadcast shows." And there can be a zero-sum element to how things "change": A 2022 study found that recent seasons of TV had a significant uptick in the percentage of Black, Asian, and Pacific Islander immigrant characters—"but that coincided with a drop in Latino representation from half of all immigrant characters to just 34 percent. That underrepresents the actual proportion of U.S. immigrants who are Latino, which is 44 percent."

Things (still) tend to be worse in the film world. A 2020 USC Annenberg analysis of the top 100 films made from 2007 to 2019 notes that, while the number of lead or colead roles for nonwhite women went from 1 percent to 17 percent during that period, glaring problems remained: "The number of Black directors working in 2019 (9 movies) was not different than in 2007 (8 movies)." More than two-thirds of the top 100 movies of 2019 had no Latina women in speaking roles, and Native American, Native Hawaiian, and Pacific Islander roles were almost completely nonexistent. Some important stats have "stalled out" or gone *down*: Filmmakers from underrepresented groups directed 27 percent of the 100 top-grossing films in 2021; the next year, that number had slid down to 20.7 percent, according to a USC Annenberg study. Looking at the big picture, the same report noted that women of color directed 1.3 percent of the 1,600 films USC Annenberg has examined since 2007. That's only 21 movies.

There has been progress on some fronts: According to the Directors Guild of America, of the 2,700 episodes of television made in the 2020–21 season, 34 percent were helmed by people of color (the number was half that just a few years prior). More than a third of those episodes were directed by women, which is more than double the number of a few years ago.

But as various number crunchers keep pointing out, some data points stubbornly resist change and the top gatekeepers still look like they did decades ago. And before you get too excited about the relative improvements in some American stats, keep in mind that, just a few years ago, a UK study noted that a mere seventh of working film directors there were women. "If you look at the numbers—especially if we're looking at film—they really have not moved that much," Lauzen told me. Most of the key numbers "have never been anywhere near parity in terms of women's representation in the U.S. population, or in terms of the workforce."

If Hollywood was a meritocracy—if it even remotely resembled a system in which every kind of person had a fair shot—you would expect women to comprise half of all creators and executive producers in TV and half of all feature film directors. You would expect Black people, Indigenous people, Asian people, Latinx people, and other people of color to create a minimum of 40 percent of America's films and TV shows. That's not the case.

Hsu Taylor is now a showrunner who has worked on dramas like *Nancy Drew, Medium,* and *The Gifted.* She spent part of one of our conversations wrestling with her thoughts about a young white woman who got an entry-level job on a different show. The young woman—the daughter of two established and prosperous industry veterans—was lovely to work with and good at her job.

"But on the other hand, say that there is a kid who is really deserving out in the United States, or somewhere in some other part of the world, and maybe they're a better writer. I can think offhand of quite a few people who were hired because of their connections," said Hsu Taylor. "They happened to be white. They happened to be related to showrunners. And the people in charge would not have made that hiring decision had it not been for those connections. And there were other people of color who were more qualified who had no connections, who did not get hired, because there are only so many seats at the table."

Hsu Taylor's struggle regarding how to think about that one woman—who clearly benefited from privilege but had done nothing wrong as an individual—isn't all that surprising, given how the table has been constructed and thought about for centuries. As she observed, to interrogate the level playing field myth is to destabilize the foundational story of this nation. All these ideas about merit, worth, and who gets to sit at the table can be traced back to "the American dream—when you come to this country, if you work hard, things get better for you. If we question the meritocracy of Hollywood, we are literally questioning the American dream," she said.

HBO apparently passed on *Dark Winds* in part because the network had something similar in the works—the drama *True Detective*. It debuted in early 2014, and it caused me to snap. Again.

True Detective was atmospheric and transfixing in its debut season. It was also, like approximately nine million other shows I'd written about in the prior decade, a saga in which (white) women were not important except as dead bodies or sex partners or nags. The Black detectives in that first season were there to prod the plot along and watch Matthew McConaughey's character talk about time as a flat circle.

In a piece published by *Huffington Post* in March 2014, I wrote that the conversation around the show's issues with representation were "necessary and illuminating, but it's a conversation that has become distressingly familiar. Similar complaints have been lodged against other high-profile . . . dramas such as *Breaking Bad, Ray Donovan, Mad Men, Rescue Me, The Newsroom, Game of Thrones, The Sopranos* and on and on." I'd spent more than a decade having to talk and think and write a *lot* about the marginalization of women, people of color, and queer people, as well as the cliché-driven overuse of sexual violence (usually toward female characters). I just could *not* do the Why Is Prestige TV Like This debate anymore. So I did something else.

For weeks before that 2014 piece came out, I did the math on what HBO produced for the prior forty years. I tried to match numbers to a question that had become urgent to me. Could we pause, just for a moment, the conversation about what *individual creators* were doing and talk about what the networks and studios—what *the system*—kept doing, over and over? The two things were related, but the latter didn't get nearly enough attention.

The result of my research and calculations surprised even me: HBO's forty-year track record was exceptionally terrible. "With one exception over the course of four decades, HBO has not aired an original one-hour drama series created by a woman," I noted. "With one exception over the course of four decades, HBO has not aired an original one-hour drama or dramatic miniseries creatively led at its debut by a person of color." The stats at several other high-profile networks weren't any better. Of the ninety-seven creatives that had, over a period of many years, created dramas or limited series for all the networks I researched, twelve were women. Two were people of color.

Given the hardy endurance of some industry mindsets—time is a flat circle—I shouldn't have been surprised when, shortly after that article was published, I received an email from a high-level executive at HBO. He said that the headline on the piece—"Who Creates Drama at HBO? Very Few Women or People of Color"—was "unfair." Could I change it?

No.

It's not just that Hollywood is not a level playing field. It's that people with multiple advantages are playing a different game *with an entirely separate set of rules.*

Imagine being a woman of color who has paid your dues at a series of TV workplaces, some of them quite punishing, and hearing that your white, male boss shouted "Fuck you" at the show's female network executive—and then hung up on her. The woman who told me this story, a showrunner herself, knows that she could never do anything like that and remain employed. The male showrunner in that incident, not surprisingly, kept his job. That program was later canceled; my source suspects it was in part due to the showrunner's conduct. It's not the first (or last) time *everyone* lost their jobs partly—or largely—due to a toxic boss's terrible behavior. He's still working, by the way—he's now in charge of an important piece of IP, a TV series based on a very popular American movie.

"It boggles the mind that billion-dollar corporations are willing to hand stewardship of a globally consumed product that costs millions to people without the necessary experience to do the job professionally and humanely," Grillo-Marxuach said. "This is a major spoke in the cycle of madness, rage, and abuse I have seen repeated with depressing regularity over the span of my career."

But those jobs aren't handed to just anyone. Opportunities to paint on the big canvases—and scream at the little people—are not distributed equally. As Grillo-Marxuach noted, "if you're a white person with the slightest self-awareness, there's the inescapable truth that the casino is rigged in your favor, you didn't get here on hard work and talent alone, and that—all other things being equal—someone else could have had your seat at the table."

If we want to lift up the table, under which so many difficult truths

have been hidden, we must note that many have been broken or driven
to flee by the crushing wheel Grillo-Marxuach described. It is demoralizing to repeatedly hear about all kinds of people—especially those
from historically excluded communities—leaving the industry, but I respect and understand that decision.

As Nancy Wang Yuen notes in her 2016 book *Reel Inequality: Hollywood Actors and Racism,* white actors she interviewed were never told
to "be 'more white,'" but the artists of color she talked to were asked
"to act 'more' Black, Asian or Latin, often [in ways] based on racial stereotypes." A Black actor Yuen interviewed was asked by a director, "Can
you be more jive, you know what I mean?" For a story on *Warrior,*
showrunner Jonathan Tropper recalled Asian actor Henry Yuk thanking
him for giving him a role where he got to "use pronouns." "Because,"
Tropper told me, "he was often cast as the wise old Chinese man who
would speak in broken English."

"I think that meritocracy mostly gets invented after the fact. . . . [People]
make the false assumption that individual merit or individual talent
and effort is the main factor in production, and it isn't. . . . People make
this false assumption precisely because the inequality is already there,
and they're looking for a justification. Then, they make the further false
assumption that the variation in human merit is tremendous." Wait,
who is this sage of Hollywood?

Those observations actually don't come from an industry person at
all. They're from Matthew Stewart, author of the book *The 9.9 Percent:
The New Aristocracy That Is Entrenching Inequality and Warping Our
Culture.* In a 2021 interview, he broke down the kinds of patterns that
exist all over the place, not just in creative industries, and stated that
most of the "root source of inequality is structural, and I think much of
it goes to an economy that's no longer as competitive, where you have
oligopolies rising without significant challenge." An interesting observation, given that Hollywood is now dominated by a small number of
massive corporations.

Some of those corporations are trying—in fits and starts—to change
how their workforces look. But in Hollywood, change has been slow to
come in part because necessary conversations about who deserves what,
and who had an "easier" time in a generally brutal industry, are hard. And
race and gender are just a couple of topics in this complicated discussion.

"We're talking about religion, we're talking about age, we're talking about class, all of those things," said Robert, a man of color in a senior position in the industry. "When it comes to the system and the business as a whole, we've only really just started to scratch the surface as far as what that actually looks like and what it should look like—not just the writing staffs but the post teams, the crew."

Maybe this analogy will help: I've come to think of Hollywood as a place full of high wires. Some people go out on those high wires wearing a lot of padding, and there are so many nets beneath them that their risk of being seriously injured is incredibly low. It's still scary to step out on those wires, and to feel exposed. It's a dangerous thing to attempt.

However, we need to acknowledge that there are a lot of folks who step out on very high wires with little or no padding. They are also taking a huge chance. And all too often, they're working without a net.

All of this has gone on for a very long time. As Yuen pointed out, there were a number of structural elements that did an excellent job of ensuring white people held almost every industry position, high and low, for decades. First, "historically, Hollywood unions revolved around nepotism," Yuen said. Given that the guilds were, from the start, dominated by white people, for a long time, they stayed that way. Even now, 70 percent of key on-set roles—unit production manager, first assistant director, second assistant director, and others on the "directorial team"— are filled by white people, according to a 2022 report from the DGA. And of course, as scholar Chi-Tsung Chang writes in a 2021 thesis titled "Hollywood and the Myth of Meritocracy," "Jim Crow laws kept people of color from most but the lowest-level jobs" in the industry.

Second, by 1934, most of the industry had adopted the Hays Code, a.k.a. the Motion Picture Production Code. The code, which the industry imposed on itself after a series of controversies and scandals, limited what could be depicted on-screen: among other things, it banned interracial relationships and kept references to homosexuality oblique or nonexistent. The code was a key part of "the institutionalized culture of bias" that ruled the industry for many years, Yuen said. For instance, Anna May Wong had plenty of acting talent, but she was prevented playing the lead in MGM's 1937 adaptation of Pearl Buck's novel *The Good Earth*, "even though all the characters were Chinese," Yuen noted. The role went to a white woman, Luise Rainer.

The tenets of the Hays Code lost influence over the years, of course. It was officially on the books into the '60s, but it was quietly supplanted by a more informal code that was no less pernicious. Studios and networks would say, according to Yuen, that their advertisers wanted to appeal to "Middle America," and "the assumption was that middle Americans are white and conservative and don't want to see people of color or LGBTQ people—basically, nothing that went outside Bible Belt expectations. And this continues to this day," Yuen noted. She cited a 2022 story in which an executive with a front-row seat for the Warner Bros. Discovery merger stated that Discovery+ is a "more general audience platform that doesn't have the specificity that HBO Max was tailored to. I think Discovery [does not want to] make things that are political, topical, [and might] alienate Middle America."

When consulting in recent years, Yuen said she's been disheartened by how little she's listened to by the largely white creative teams she's working with. "I'll be in that Zoom room, laying out what I think the problems are, and I'll realize, 'Oh, they really don't care about representation,'" Yuen told me. "They just want to know if people are going to complain enough to ruin the film's launch. I was not invited back into those rooms, because I was saying things they didn't want to hear."

As I reported in a 2018 HBO follow-up piece, three-fifths of the network's directors that year were white women, women of color, and men of color. According to an in-depth 2021 report from what was then called WarnerMedia (the corporate entity behind HBO and HBO Max), the number of on-screen and behind-the-scenes creatives from historically excluded groups was, on a number of fronts, ticking upward. Other companies—including FX, Netflix, and the corporation that includes CBS, Paramount, and Viacom—have issued documentation chronicling how their hiring practices have begun to change.

Long before those companies began systematically evolving, many industry veterans from historically excluded groups were at the forefront of industry change. Larry Wilmore seeks out situations in which he can control the tone, the voice, and the lens of whatever he's working on, and he's done the same for his many protégés in the business. Grillo-Marxuach has mentored many up-and-coming creatives in various ways, including through *Children of Tendu*, a podcast he does with fellow TV writer Jose Molina. The podcast breaks down the nuts and bolts of the industry for newcomers, and a few years ago, Grillo-Marxuach published a document called "The Eleven Laws of Showrunning," which offers helpful management guidance for aspiring leaders.

When Hsu Taylor was coming up, she recalls her scripts going into a "black box" and emerging from the showrunner's grasp greatly changed—without her knowing what she'd done wrong. "I just run my show the opposite way of how those shows were run—I'm transparent with people," Hsu Taylor said. "I tell them what the batting order is and when they'll get a script. If I have a note on something, I explain it. I'll sit there with the younger writers and say, 'This is why I'm doing this. This is why I think the voice can change a little bit here. These two scenes can be combined.' Things like that."

In an ideal world, some of the people whom Hsu Taylor and many others have helped will go on to create the next wave of thought-provoking, necessary, entertaining screen stories. But we don't live in an ideal world. Not yet, anyway.

"I did not appreciate how difficult change is for the industry," said Lauzen. "It's like a big battleship turning around in the middle of the ocean—it takes a really long time. That's how I think of Hollywood. It's just taking a very, very long time to turn around." Her own work proves this: The twenty-fifth anniversary edition of the *Celluloid Ceiling* study noted that, in 1998, women were 17 percent of the directors, writers, producers, executive producers, editors, and cinematographers working on the 250 top-grossing U.S. films. In the *Celluloid Ceiling* study released in early 2023, women occupied 24 percent of those positions. (Congrats, Hollywood! Nailed it!)

Seriously, though, part of the reason it's taking so long is because a key ingredient was—or in some cases, still is—missing: "Without the will to change, well-intentioned individuals can generate a laundry list of possible solutions a mile long, and few to none of those remedies will be taken seriously or implemented," Lauzen observed. "The will to change is the key to all substantial and sustained action."

But to leave things more or less as they are, as Leonard pointed out, is to leave money on the table.

"We know how fast these companies can move when they're confronted by an intractable problem like a global pandemic," Leonard said. "What we also know is that [the consulting firm] McKinsey & Company—not exactly social justice warriors—said in a report that the industry is losing $10 billion annually because of anti-Black bias alone. Realistically, if you assume it's similar for other underrepresented communities, we're talking about $50 billion a year being left on the table. And that begs the question, why has more change not happened? More importantly, it begs the question, are the people who are currently running these companies the best equipped to run these companies profitably? If what we're talking about is merit—merit in the context of making entertainment globally—that requires a cultural flexibility, specificity, openness, inclusivity. And if you don't have those things, you're not going to be good at it. You're just not."

Perhaps the last word should be left to Leonard's father. "He had an aphorism that came out of his military background," Leonard told me. "'Don't tell me your priorities. Show me your budget.'"

7

Horror Story

Sleepy Hollow and the Myth of a
Post-racial Industry

I accepted it with enthusiasm and joy,
and I suggested I die.

−Orlando Jones

"Leftenant."

Ahhh.

Even though it's been a decade since *Sleepy Hollow* premiered, when I hear that word—"Lieutenant," said with a very proper British accent—I sigh. I feel a tiny echo of the elation many fans felt when the Fox drama was still fresh and its potential felt limitless.

But the nostalgia doesn't last. Thinking about that word, and the show, ultimately elicits a mixture of grief, bewilderment, and anger. Because what occurred at *Sleepy Hollow* is evidence of some of the worst and most demoralizing things the industry can dish out.

"There was an opportunity to elevate that show where it could have been really groundbreaking," said Robert, a man of color who worked on the show. "But that requires a desire to do that, an understanding and a skill set. But *Sleepy Hollow* was a case of, 'You do not understand the advantages and the toys and the opportunities you have.'"

Correct. Over four seasons, no matter what regimes or power structures reigned over the show, Robert's assertion was proven right time and again. And that was part of the reason he left before his contract ran out. He wasn't the only one who left early.

Nicole Beharie was, in 2013, one of the few Black women who had ever starred in an American broadcast network drama. Beharie, who played Abbie Mills on *Sleepy Hollow*, was, according to a genre expert I've talked to, quite probably the first Black woman who ever led an American horror drama. In the pilot for *Sleepy Hollow*, Ichabod Crane (played by her costar Tom Mison) theorizes he and Abbie are two Biblically crucial "witnesses brought together for a seven-year period of tribulation to defend humanity from the forces of hell." Well, the part about hell and tribulation wasn't wrong. But the time frame, at least for Beharie, was way off. Three seasons into the show's run, she was gone.

It had all started out so promisingly.

Sleepy Hollow, which ran from 2013 to 2017, depicted an upstate New York cop and—yes, this is ridiculous—a revived Ichabod Crane solving crimes. Partly because that summary sounded extra silly, before I saw *Sleepy Hollow*, my hopes for it were negligible at best. But every so often, the commercial television machine captures lightning in a bottle, and that happened with *Sleepy Hollow*.

In the pilot, Ichabod Crane—the lead character of a nineteenth-century tale by Washington Irving—was resurrected and exited his grave, much to his consternation. Crane met up with local cop Abbie Mills—the aforementioned "leftenant"—and they began unraveling a series of ancient prophecies and solving crimes in the town of Sleepy Hollow. It sounds goofy as hell, but some of the most successful properties in the history of Hollywood have preposterous premises. (Need I point out that an extremely profitable film franchise revolves around a rich guy who fights crime while dressed like a bat?)

It was easy to forget the batshit aspects of the premise, in large part because the chemistry between Mison and Beharie leaped off the screen. Shernold Edwards, who later wrote for the show, recalled being particularly impressed by one of Crane's lines to Abbie in the pilot: "You've been emancipated, I take it." To Edwards, that indicated that the show was not going to ignore the racial dynamics of the premise—maybe it was going to lean into them. She also remembered being excited by the fact that *Sleepy Hollow* devoted a great deal of screen time to two different clans: One included Abbie, her sister Jenny, and their forebears (including a resourceful free Black woman who lived during colonial times). The other revolved around the family of Abbie's boss, Frank Irving, played by Orlando Jones.

"I don't know how they slipped that through—*two* Black families—

but I saw that, and I thought, 'Oh, somebody wants to do something,'"
Edwards said. The show, especially the first half of that debut season
was, to Edwards, "magical."

"If *Sleepy Hollow* came out now, it would feel like it was right on
time," according to Tananarive Due, an expert on the horror genre. Due
has written a number of horror novels, executive produced the Shudder
documentary *Horror Noire*, and has taught university courses on Black
horror. So well regarded was her UCLA course that Jordan Peele, the
director of *Get Out*, showed up to chat with her students.

Back when *Sleepy Hollow* debuted, a wave of Black-led horror projects
like Peele's *Get Out* and *Us*, Nia DaCosta's *Candyman*, and Nikyatu Ju-
su's *Nanny* were years away from hitting the cultural mainstream. "When
Sleepy Hollow was on," Due observed, "there was no conversation about
Black horror." Another thing that set the show apart was the fact that it
was a broadcast network horror drama that was actually scary.

"*Sleepy Hollow* had some comic moments, but it definitely presented
as horror," Due said. "In fact, the finale for Season 1 was one of the
most terrifying experiences I'd ever had watching network television.
Television as a medium isn't always conducive to it—there are so many
things they won't show you on a network horror series. It's a difficult
line to walk, but they had pulled together enough frightening elements
in that finale. There was a moment where Amandla Stenberg [who
played Frank Irving's daughter] was levitating, and everything was falling apart. I felt that urge that I sometimes feel in a movie theater—that
feeling of, 'Oh my God, I don't know if I can watch this!' Which is
what I love."

That first season was, in Due's opinion, "the most direct example of
Black horror on television" that she had ever seen up to that point. The
fact that *Sleepy Hollow* seemed to "go out of its way to have an inclusive
small town," instead of the usual mostly white or all-white population,
was heartening. That's a "lazy" choice that many projects make, and to
Due, "it felt like Season 1 of *Sleepy Hollow* was going in the opposite
direction."

Viewers didn't just get to know Abbie, they learned about her sister,
her coworkers, and her ancestors. "Often on TV, you have an ensemble,
and the Black character is the person who is the least developed," Due
noted. That wasn't the case as *Sleepy Hollow* built out its world over the
course of a thirteen-episode debut season.

The drama had a wide variety of fans, and its healthy ratings reflected that (ten million people watched the show's pilot, and *Sleepy Hollow* held on to more than two-thirds of that audience during its debut season). But Black viewers were particularly vocal in their support of the show, and their advocacy helped drive *Sleepy Hollow*'s prominence on social media, which, a decade ago, was emerging as a major force in pop-culture promotion. The fandom for the show, in those early days, was full of creativity and merriment: I had a blast watching Sleepyheads create art, jokes, and memes on Tumblr and Twitter and having fun at conventions. There was a lot to enjoy, on- and off-screen, and it was particularly cool to see so many Black women talk about how they saw themselves—and their sisters and their friends—in the Mills and Irving clans.

"There was even a cultural reference to red brick dust, which is something in hoodoo to ward off evil spirits—you know, something your grandmother might talk about," Due said. "It just felt real."

"At the end of Season 1," she recalled, "I was literally dancing."

It's worth taking a step back to note that *Sleepy Hollow*'s success wasn't all *that* surprising. A number of its plot twists were certainly zany; I devised the word "bonkersawesome" to describe scenes like the ones involving a zombie George Washington. But the show was able to veer off in wacky and unexpected directions because its foundations were not just solid—they were familiar.

Shoving the fussy yet honorable Ichabod Crane—already part of American culture for two hundred years—into the mismatched-cops format was certainly not the worst idea the TV industry ever had. (Frankenstein's Monster, the Devil, and Houdini solving crimes—in separate shows? Well, one of those—*Lucifer*—was good!) In any case, you know how this format works: one person in the partnership goes by the book and follows the rules; the other is a wild card prone to getting the duo into scrapes. No matter how many times you've seen this formula, if the chemistry of the leads is right and the dialogue and storytelling are well crafted, chances are you'll sink right into the warm embrace of this Hollywood standby.

But the whole ensemble was solid. *Sleepy Hollow* "was blessed with a cast that could run with anything that was thrown at them—and then some," I wrote around the time of its first-season finale. "This world has a lot of flavors but they don't clash, they harmonize." At the center of this unexpectedly engaging creation was Beharie, who gave Abbie a quiet drive and dignity that was perfectly counterbalanced by the courtly, impassioned, sometimes troublesome curiosity of Mison's Crane. No show could possibly fail to build on foundations that were that promising, right?

Right?

The optimism that infused that first season was reflected elsewhere in the culture. Not quite a year before the show premiered, Barack Obama was reelected as president. Shonda Rhimes, who created the popular, long-running drama *Grey's Anatomy*, followed it up with (among other shows) the hit ABC drama *Scandal*, which starred Kerry Washington. That show had blossomed into a social media phenomenon and ratings hit around the time of *Sleepy Hollow*'s first season. Two years before the Fox program premiered, *The Oprah Winfrey Show* went off the air, accompanied by all manner of tributes from the biggest stars in the world. Winfrey's influence had not waned; if anything, it grew. She left her daytime show, in part, to tend to her expansive media empire, including the TV network OWN.

It was one sign among many that the TV landscape might be changing. A few months before *Sleepy Hollow* premiered, Netflix's *Orange Is the New Black* took popular culture by storm. The prison-set ensemble drama was part of a vanguard of shows—a number of them on then-new streaming services—that altered the focus and faces of television. The widely acclaimed *OITNB* was initially about an educated white lady who went to prison, but it didn't take long for the show to start telling an array of ambitious, intertwined stories about the Black, Latinx, Asian, and LGBTQ+ women locked up with her.

In the preceding decade, the rise and fall of a number of high-profile male antiheroes had preoccupied much of the scripted-TV sphere, and shows with that focus still premiered at a steady rate. But I, like many other pop-culture fiends, had longed for more variety—and between 2011 and 2015, we began to get it. Critically beloved programs like *Enlightened*, *Transparent*, *Orphan Black*, *Top of the Lake*, *Happy Valley*, *Catastrophe*, *UnREAL*, *Fresh Off the Boat*, and *Jane the Virgin* (among others) started to give some of us a little hope that the entertainment industry was beginning to embrace a wider array of protagonists, worlds, and creators. Maybe that wave of shows—some of which were buzzed-about cult hits—signaled that long overdue changes were afoot in Hollywood. Maybe those kinds of changes were taking root all over America, from the White House on down.

In that context—a context I'll dub How Naive Some of Us Were Then—it was exciting to think about the success of *Sleepy Hollow*. This wasn't a cult show, it was a high-profile drama with a big budget and a major promotional machine behind it. *Sleepy Hollow* and *Black-ish*, which was a huge smash for ABC the year after the Fox drama premiered, were as mainstream as TV shows got.

But some of the powers that be behind *Black-ish* had their doubts about the staying power of this wave. Laurence Fishburne, a star and executive producer I interviewed on the *Black-ish* set in 2016, said he thought the show was part of a trend that came around every seven years or so—and then went away again. "It's part of this new cycle where suddenly Black is the new Black," Fishburne said then. "I just finished doing a new *Roots*."

Kenya Barris, the creator of *Black-ish*, was, if anything, more doubtful. He pointed out how, back in the day, some networks had rosters of Black-led shows—which were, after a few years, replaced with so-called "'mainstream' programming," as Barris put it. "It's a fact. It's not a conspiracy. It happened with Fox. It happened with the WB. It happened with UPN."

A short history lesson: Three decades ago, the Fox broadcast network had been around for a few years but was not living up to its commercial potential. It then commissioned *In Living Color, Roc, Martin, Living Single,* and *The Sinbad Show,* which all debuted in the early '90s. The loyalty of Fox's Black viewers helped the network evolve into the broadcasting powerhouse it ultimately became—and Fox's transition into dominance was, of course, assisted by giant hits like *American Idol, The X-Files,* and *The Simpsons.*

But what's painful (if predictable) about this scenario is that Fox dumped those Black-led shows by the turn of the millennium. A few years later, UPN and the WB—which aired a string of Black-led shows in the early aughts—merged to create the CW. That upstart network featured shows that were, for many years, dominated by white people, on-screen and behind the scenes. "CW got rid of all the comedies and just became strictly a drama landscape," former UPN executive Kelly

Edwards recalled. "A lot of [comedy] people ended up having to shift into drama, or they just dropped out altogether. So we lost an entire generation of writers of color."

There was progress, and then there wasn't. It didn't stick. Black people who'd liked—or worked on—those shows were just out of luck. Given what I know now about what occurred at *Sleepy Hollow*, I understand the doubts and the wariness of Black creatives far more than I did even a few years ago.

Have you ever wondered what it would be like to make a TV show in the summer in North Carolina while wearing a wool costume topped off by a wig? "Fun" is not necessarily the word that leaps to mind.

For its first two seasons, *Sleepy Hollow* was filmed in and around Wilmington, North Carolina (for its final two seasons, it moved to Atlanta). Many of the show's characters wore elaborate period costumes made of heavy fabrics. No one in their right mind wants to wear layers of wool in the summer in the South, and certainly not for sixteen hours at a time. Most people understand that showbiz is not all glitz and glamour, but very few non-industry civilians understand what a grind it can be to work long hours on location, day in and day out—how physically uncomfortable it can be, and how long not just the days but the night shoots (a must for a scary show like *Sleepy Hollow*) can begin to feel.

The heat, the insects, the hours, all the other discomforts and logistical issues that insiders recalled—they might have seemed less daunting had the show not been beset by an enormous number of additional problems. Some of *Sleepy Hollow*'s early issues will sound familiar to anyone who has ever participated in—or written about—a TV show's inaugural season. It's rare for a program to come out of the chute fully formed, and it's even rarer for all key creatives to have the same set of priorities, working methods, and goals. First seasons are shakedown cruises, in which everybody involved finds out what works and what doesn't, what can be fixed and what can't. Some shows evolve and recover from whatever ailed them in their early days. At other shows, however, problems compound over time. *Sleepy Hollow* was in the latter category, according to multiple people who worked on the show.

In part due to turnover among the crew, the on-set hours in the first season were often "brutal," according to Frank, a man of color who worked on the show. It didn't help that there were a number of important behind-the-scenes creatives—in LA and in North Carolina—who were, in Frank's view, at odds with each other, in over their heads, or both. "It was very tense, from pretty early on," Frank noted.

There was also turmoil at the Fox network during the show's run. Less than a year after *Sleepy Hollow* debuted, Fox entertainment chairman Kevin Reilly departed, and in the summer of 2014, Dana Walden and Gary Newman, who had been running the 20th Century Fox TV studio, took over the top jobs at the network. The executive shuffle reverberated down the ranks, bringing "chaos" and "strange directives" from the network, according to Frank and Paul, another man of color who worked on *Sleepy Hollow*. There was such a level of confusion that, according to Paul, an executive once asked why Ichabod Crane was more than two hundred years old. "It was a messy time there," Paul said with a sigh.

The show's creative team had its own set of issues. Alex Kurtzman and Roberto Orci were longtime creative partners who cocreated *Fringe* with J. J. Abrams and worked on *Star Trek* films, among other credits. They, along with Len Wiseman and Phillip Iscove, were credited as cocreators of *Sleepy Hollow*. Both Kurtzman and Orci were also listed as executive producers of the drama, but their deal with 20th Century Fox TV ended in 2013, the year the show debuted. According to Paul, their departure for a new deal at CBS led to tension between them and some Fox executives. The split unfolded, in Paul's opinion, like "a bad divorce."

As if that weren't enough, Kurtzman and Orci's creative partnership fractured around that time. In the press, their creative separation was portrayed as affecting only their film work and was described as "amicable." According to industry veterans I've spoken to, the breakup of their creative partnership—which eventually included television ventures as well—was complicated and challenging.

But in the early days, four men held much of the real power: executive producer Len Wiseman, showrunner/executive producer Mark Goffman, plus Kurtzman and Orci. Paul and others speculated that the show's various issues may have caused fewer headaches had *Sleepy Hollow* had more effective leadership from Goffman.

Part of the issue was that Goffman was not, as Frank said, "a genre guy." "I got a master's in public policy from Harvard and had planned on becoming a speechwriter," Goffman noted in a 2013 interview. In the early aughts, Goffman was hired by *The West Wing,* and he went on to write for shows like *White Collar, Law & Order: Special Victims Unit,* and *Elementary.* He had bona fides in the arena of TV crime-solving, but from Frank's perspective, the showrunner's lack of familiarity and comfort with horror and supernatural storytelling contributed to the show's problems.

"I'm gonna weirdly defend Mark a little bit," said Robert. Some blame for what went wrong on the show should be laid at Goffman's feet, Robert told me, but he added that Goffman gets "probably a greater ratio of the blame than maybe is warranted." Robert continued, "I think the problem was deeper than him. There were times when serious issues were brought not just to Mark but to the powers that be, so to speak. And they either brushed them aside or they were just not handled" due to people at the top being "conflict-averse or unwilling to have tough conversations. That was not all on Mark."

All in all, though, thanks to chaos or discord on several fronts, "there was a lot of creative floundering," Paul said. Those difficulties, he added, were "exacerbated by a situation where the two leads did not want to have a whole lot to do with each other." He said the courtly bows Crane favored arose because the actors did not want to hug each other. That kind of ongoing friction between leads is not unusual in the land of make-believe; part of the magic of Hollywood is that skilled actors who do not like each other have often convinced viewers their characters care about each other immensely. But the discord between Beharie and Mison, which arose in the first season, led producers to build up story lines for ancillary characters.

Jenny Mills, Abbie's sister, arrives in the second episode of the first season, and multiple people said the importance of the character—who was mentioned in the *Sleepy Hollow* pilot—was amped up so that Jenny could serve as a possible replacement for Abbie. Lyndie Greenwood, a fine actor, made the character her own, but the initial driver of Jenny's prominence was the fear, on the part of the powers that be, that Beharie might bolt. According to several sources, Beharie seemed ambivalent about her commitment to the Fox drama—a situation many I spoke to understood and empathized with.

I understand too: when an actor is the star of a show for the first time—especially if they never expected to end up in that position—it can be overwhelming in a lot of ways. No less a titan than James Gandolfini absented himself from the set of *The Sopranos* on a number of occasions, according to *Difficult Men*. Despite being loved and admired by those who worked with him, he found the demands of the role of Tony Soprano hard to take at times, and his "sudden refusals to work had become a semi-regular occurrence." But HBO and those producing *The Sopranos* regarded those moments as "the price of doing business, the trade-off for getting" what Gandolfini brought to the table.

Beharie (who, through representatives, declined to speak with me for this book) had more reason than most to wonder what might have been if she had chosen a different path. She'd graduated from Juilliard and received acclaim for her work in the Steve McQueen film *Shame* before arriving at *Sleepy Hollow*. It would not be a surprise to hear she may have spent some of those long, hot days wondering if she'd made the right decision.

"I've seen this happen with a lot of actors, where they audition for a pilot, they get it, they do the pilot, it gets picked up, and they don't really realize what they signed onto, because of those ridiculous studio deals that sign people up for seven years," a *Sleepy Hollow* source observed. "All of a sudden, they realize they've committed the next seven years of their life to something. And that starts to get a little claustrophobic."

Even before that claustrophobia may have set in, there were problems. Two weeks into the first season, "there were serious red flags," Robert said. One of the biggest red flags involved the way that "problems were handled and the way blame was assigned—or reassigned," he noted. "There was a sense of the well being poisoned, in regard to one cast member."

"That cast member was Nicole Beharie, wasn't it?" I asked.

It was. Robert went on to lay out a dynamic that multiple *Sleepy Hollow* sources described to me. They all said that Mison (whose representatives did not reply to my queries) and Beharie both had difficulties adjusting to being the leads on a broadcast network show. And this was one where eighteen-hour days were common at first—as was conflict on a number of fronts that took a toll on a lot of people. "I probably could have been more diplomatic about things in some way," Beharie told the *Los Angeles Times* in 2020.

As noted, newly minted TV leads can have an especially rough go of it. "I've seen that with every actor that I've ever worked with, where it was their first experience doing that. It's a really tough adjustment," Robert said. But according to Robert and others, though both actors went through steep learning curves that sometimes involved friction with colleagues, Beharie's behavior was weaponized against her in a way that Mison's was not. And that process began at the start. (Two sources told me there was conflict between Beharie and Wiseman during the shooting of the *Sleepy Hollow* pilot, which Wiseman directed.)

What made Robert angry—and what helped drive his own departure from the show—was the way Beharie's behavior was depicted behind the scenes. "When a bunch of white guys say a person of color is difficult, I tend to assume that there's a lot more to that story," Robert said. "I found her to be pleasant, extremely talented, and an actor who was adjusting to being a lead. There are growing pains with that. In the time I was there, where the discrepancy came in was how their growing pains were viewed and handled." That tracks with what most other sources told me; though there were bumps along the way, many recalled Beharie as generally polite and professional, in that first season and beyond. "She didn't have to be as nice to me as she was," said a source who spent time on set in *Sleepy Hollow*'s second year. "But she was great."

However according to Robert, especially in the early days, multiple people with power at the show "claimed not to have had a good experience with Nicole. That happens." Not all coworkers click—but that wasn't the issue. What made him angry was how those negative assessments were passed on to all and sundry, including people who had not even met her. "You're basically turning the writers against one of the leads. I think it's unethical to label the person a problem before the majority of people have had a chance to have an experience with the person. And especially if that person is a woman and a woman of color—those are two groups that already have challenges to begin with," Robert told me.

"It created a very us-against-her environment from day one," Robert added. "My sense was that she felt very alone."

All in all, Beharie and Mison "were both out of their depths. No one was helping them," Orlando Jones told me. But he watched the isolation and scapegoating of Beharie that arose over time with dismay. In his view, there was a "double standard" at work when it came to the show's leads, and "she did not engineer any of that," Jones recalled.

Frank, who interacted with Beharie during that fraught first season, said he got the sense that Beharie knew she had been labeled a troublemaker. "I found her completely professional to work with," Frank recalled. "But she would say things like, 'I'm not trying to be difficult . . .' And she wasn't being difficult, at least not to me. But it was as if she was aware that was how she was already seen."

Paul agreed that Beharie "ended up getting a lot of attention for her problems," even though "Tom [Mison] was a handful too—he had his own set of issues. I've always said that on any other show, he would've been the biggest problem." But he wasn't—or, more accurately, he wasn't routinely portrayed in that light.

According to one source who spoke with *Sleepy Hollow*'s key producers in the show's very early days, they very much wanted to play up the relationship of Crane and his wife Katrina. And that struck this source as strange, because this person had instantly seen how much chemistry and potential the relationship between Crane and Abbie had. "My reaction was, 'Oh, you just don't see the Black woman on the screen,'" said this source, a person of color. The other thing this source remembered was the producers calling Mison "a star."

As Beharie noted in her 2020 *Los Angeles Times* interview, she and Mison both developed health issues during the first season. As she put it, "[We] were both sick at the same time but I don't believe that we were treated equally. He was allowed to go back to England for a month [to recover while] I was given Episode 9 to shoot on my own. So I pushed through it and then by the end of that episode I was in urgent care."

Jones observed, "What you had playing out are the politics of what it is to be a young Black actress, first time out of the gate as the star, on a television show that is struggling with all these components. First, the hair is a mess and they're having to correct it with digital effects. They did not get a proper wig with a proper hairline on her.

"From an actor's point of view, can you imagine how unstable you feel going in every day, having these people do their job and then being told that it has to be corrected, and how everybody's annoyed about that? But you have to get in two hours before [your costar] and leave two hours after—all that takes longer," he continued. "He has a driver, you drive yourself. The days are at least sixteen hours, but this girl's working twenty hours. She gets sick doing twenty-hour days while y'all painting her as a problem—while you fawn over Tom Mison and act like she's somebody's shoe droppings."

During that first season, the cast shot a baseball-themed promotional spot for the network. Afterward, Beharie and Jones went to the hair and makeup trailer (putting a baseball hat on top of the bad wig did it no favors, Jones said). A new hairstylist had recently been hired by the show, and she'd worked briefly on Jones's hair. That day, though, the hairstylist worked on Beharie's hair. Unlike Mison's, Beharie's Season 1 wig was not a custom piece, according to Jones. In his recollection, a Black hairstylist was not what Beharie necessarily wanted; she wanted a good wig that was handled efficiently, which would mean she'd have to spend less time in the hair and makeup trailer.

That day in the trailer, Jones said, he and Beharie were chatting and goofing around. They took a photo (which is still on Jones's phone) in which Beharie pretended to bite Jones. Part of their banter that day had roots—pardon the pun—in the hair situation. "You took this Black lady from the hair department, told her the Black actress was a pain in the ass, and then told her to do the Black actress's hair, as if that's going to solve the problem," Jones recalled. "That's what Nicole was laughing at—the fact that this didn't fix it. This was a 'shut this person up' move. Nicole is like, 'You can't be serious. Your solution to the fact that you don't want to spend money on a wig for me is, you send the Black lady to do some poking and prodding?' We laughed. We went on with our day."

After touch-ups, everyone—including the hair and makeup crew—walked over to the set. That night, Jones told me, a production assistant came up to him and repeated a rumor that Beharie had bitten the hairstylist. Having been around Beharie all day, Jones was incredulous; he told me that in his opinion, no physical altercation could have occurred without someone seeing or noticing.

A couple of gossip sites ran stories about this alleged incident during the show's first season, and subsequently, Jones was asked about it during an interview. He told me his reply ran along these lines: He did not know where that "stupid rumor" came from, but he did not believe it was true. He added that after the interview, a Fox PR person—I'll call her Kelly—asked him to never respond to questions about the incident again.

I asked the hairstylist for her version of events—about what allegedly occurred between her and Beharie, and about what her brief employment on *Sleepy Hollow* was like. In written responses to my emailed questions, she replied that she'd "rather not discuss in detail what happened on *Sleepy Hollow* with Nicole Beharie. I am writing about my experiences as well." Her brief answers to my questions dealt mainly with what she called "grueling" working conditions and "excessive hours." "Many accidents happened on this show, due to lack of rest. Crew was worn out," she wrote. "*Sleepy Hollow* was one of the worst projects I have worked on as a hairstylist."

I have spoken to a number of *Sleepy Hollow* veterans—and many others in the industry—who have heard some version of what is alleged to have occurred that night. I have not, to date, been able to find anyone who witnessed this alleged incident. But the gossip that sprang up that day had a lasting impact on Beharie's reputation. Some people on the *Sleepy Hollow* set—where this allegation circulated until it entered other Hollywood backchannels—believed it and some didn't, but at that stage, it kind of didn't matter, Jones told me. As matters stood, by that point in the first season, the problem was the "pre-warning that came with Nicole," which meant she never got "the benefit of the doubt. There was a witch hunt going on," Jones said.

Another thing that happened around that time: *Sleepy Hollow*—an on-screen haven for witches, zombies, and supernatural beings—was a success. Well before the drama debuted, a number of things were clearly going wrong. But the show's high profile, in some ways, fueled the problems that were present and created even more. As Paul observed, "It was a big hit for Fox and they wanted to see it keep going—they did not want to change anything" seen as crucial to its success.

Beharie and Mison's chemistry was one big element that many viewers and critics responded to, so they both needed to be on-screen. And if one of the leads left, well, that couldn't be the fault of anyone with any power. Most of whom probably, if they could have, would have voted for Obama a third time.

One name for it is the Sunken Place. When it comes to the entertainment industry, I've come to think of it as the Iceberg.

It's where real change in Hollywood founders—and has always foundered. The Iceberg sits at the center of the commercial entertainment industry. It has a different shape than it used to have. It's a little smaller. But the Iceberg is still almost exactly what it has always been: enormous, slippery, and hiding sharp things just out of view. And this is the part that may be surprising: I'm here to tell you that the Iceberg is about so much more than race. It is about that, sure, but it's also about norms and customs and culture; the operating system of how things work and have usually worked for a century. It's the thing that shaves the edges and prickles off so many stories, because many people with power tend to want what worked before.

Paul recalls an incident in which an executive wanted a couple in a story he was creating to have a big romantic smooch at a key moment. In his culture, which his characters shared, he said, that would not happen in public. If he pointed that out, he'd get the response—yet again—"'Well, that's not relatable.' What's implicit is, 'That's not relatable for a white person.'

"You realize what they really wanted was basically the same stories they've been telling all along, but instead of a white person, it's an Asian American or African American person. That is their ideal," Paul said. "Just make the lead what they consider diverse casting—but don't change the underlying story or characters."

There are more people from historically marginalized groups in more positions of influence than there used to be. But those folks did not get where they are by telling the white folks with the most power that they're wrong. Not too often, anyway.

"They're vulnerable—they have to fight multiple fights at the same time," observed Robert. "They not only have to hopefully try to bring something new to the table, but they have to survive in order to fight other battles. It kind of limits their opportunities or their ability to really shake things up."

People from historically excluded groups don't typically run things; they don't often have the kind of greenlight power that causes hefty checks to be written. The core of the Iceberg is made up of those who are either the architects of the story or *exert control over* those architects. And "the gatekeepers have not changed," said veteran writer/producer Emma. "They really haven't. If you look at who is actually greenlighting, it's mostly the same people."

But the industry changed in the wake of the 2020 protests that gripped the nation after the murder of George Floyd, right? Well, from what I've heard, Hollywood put a lot of stories about Black people into development in 2020 and 2021. By industry standards, doing that doesn't cost much. But to make an actual film, television show, documentary, animated series, whatever—that costs real money. And so, according to a number of creative folks I've talked to in the past couple years, the industry has quietly let many of those projects die.

"Black creators are not surprised by that," Robert said. "Things are said all the time, and even sometimes, yes, there's money committed to that. As a creator of color, you have to be an eternal optimist, 'cause that keeps you moving forward. But you also have to have a healthy cynicism. What the industry wants to do is revert to the mean—always. And the mean is what we've seen for the last hundred years."

That mean is what Barris and Fishburne were talking about. They'd seen this movie before.

What's it like to run into the Iceberg? Well, you saw *Titanic,* right?

A decade ago, Jones had far more on-set experience than Beharie, but the Iceberg still came for him during the run of *Sleepy Hollow.* Part of the "problem," from what he could tell, was that his character was too much of a fan favorite: "I think they were uncomfortable with what was happening between me and the fandom at that time," Jones observed. The fans, as Jones pointed out, came from all walks of life. An older Jewish lady he dubbed his "white mama" would call him and rave about the show; he got positive feedback "from all sides." He said, "It was just beautiful on every level. That's why I was such a cheerleader."

Like me, he thinks about the excellent lineup of actors on that show—"One heavy hitter after another," as he put it. John Cho, John Noble, Clancy Brown, Jill Marie Jones, Nicholas Gonzalez, Amandla Stenberg—they all appeared in the drama at various stages. Aunjanue Ellis, who garnered an Oscar nomination for her work in *King Richard,* played the Millses' mother. On top of all that, it meant a lot to Jones to guide Frank Irving's evolution from a doubter to a soldier for the Crane-Mills cause. "He became the believer who devoted himself—at a sacrifice to himself and his family. That was the soul of it." But the soul, he observed, was "ripped out by people making dumb amounts of money."

"I was excited to get on the phone to hear what my offer might be" for Season 2, Jones said, "based on the work I'd done, and not just on the acting side." Jones's companies had also worked with the show's multimedia producers and on the show's social media and promotional campaigns. And he told me that his Season 1 pay for his role on the show had been below his usual quote. He recalled his reaction when he realized the powers that be at *Sleepy Hollow* wanted to repeat that scenario in Season 2: "Your opening offer is you wish to pay me even less?" Jones recalled. "A really shitty deal was offered to me with enthusiasm and joy. So I accepted it with enthusiasm and joy, and I suggested I die."

Jones wanted Irving to die in "a blaze of glory" at the end of Season 2, and he told me key producers agreed to that, but then *Sleepy Hollow* killed off Frank Irving in the middle of the second season, only to bring him back after the fandom freaked out about the character's death. The "panicked" flip-flopping was just one more piece of evidence that "they essentially didn't value me, and I was disposable at best," he noted. Jones declined to participate in the show's third season, in part because once again, he told me, he was offered sub-par compensation. Throughout his time on the show, despite seeing how his colleague Beharie was treated, despite every obstacle, challenge, and tin-eared moment on and off set, "I never gave a note, I never changed a line. I did my job. I promoted that show like a son of a bitch in Seasons 1 and 2." He sent Fox executives a report on all he had accomplished on promotional and social media channels. And then he was gone.

All the *Sleepy Hollow* disasters we talked about for hours came down to one thing, according to Jones: "The system was set up for that outcome." When people associated with the show or the network "did press, they all told you how much they cared about the multicultural aspects of the show. But they did not. And their actions speak for themselves. The fans were right to call them out the way they did, because it's so clear that not only did they not understand it, they didn't care. And the problem with me was, I was getting too much credit for the show's success in the press."

Before *Sleepy Hollow* returned for its second season, I spent a day at its offices in LA. The more time I spent there, the more confused I became. I interviewed Goffman about what fans could expect from the second season, and there was nothing unusual about that conversation, but then I spent a while in the writers' room. Most of the people in that room were men, and almost all of the men were white. The sole woman of color in the room hardly said anything. I observed all this without much surprise because this was how the industry was. I did not know that three writers of color who had worked on *Sleepy Hollow*'s first season were gone. The show employed writers of color throughout its run, of course, but to this day I speculate about whether those three writers' world- and character-building contributions were what helped make the first season as engaging as it often was.

Anyway, during my Season 2 visit, Goffman, standing at the room's whiteboard, walked the writing staff through options for second-season plot turns, and he mentioned a proposed kiss between Abbie Mills and Nick Hawley, a new treasure-hunter character. When Goffman mentioned that, my head snapped up and my brain went into overdrive: "What the . . . *Why?! What??*" But I was self-possessed enough to stay silent. Not knowing about the discord on set, I was shocked a development like that was potentially in the mix. The core appeal of the show, after all, revolved around the relationship between Crane and Abbie.

Months later, when I watched the second season's opening episodes, I was even more confused. It felt as if one of the new goals of *Sleepy Hollow* was to make me detach from the bond between Crane and Abbie. And that could have been done, partially, delicately; I wasn't opposed to Abbie having another man in her life. Due told me she'd often hoped Abbie might get a Black love interest, "because Black love is so rare in Hollywood."

But the show didn't do much of anything on that front. Most of the choices the show made—such as getting rid of Irving and his family—were frustrating and inexplicable. And the drama assiduously avoided allowing Abbie to connect intimately with *anyone*, not just Crane. As critic and novelist Nichole Perkins wrote at one point, "How many more sacrifices does she need to make before the show allows her to give and receive affectionate love? Both Abbie and Nicole Beharie deserve better. . . . Meanwhile, we see the entire courtship of three of Ichabod Crane's relationships."

As the second season progressed, Abbie seemed to recede into the background. Characters like Hawley and Crane's wife, Katrina, got a lot of screen time, and, though it was no fault of the actors, these potential or actual love interests were not interesting. "They weren't," a *Sleepy Hollow* source agreed, and explained that their prominence was pushed by certain senior producers who wanted to foreground alternate love interests for the leads. Whatever the reasons behind the shifts, Abbie Mills became an afterthought on her own show. As the hashtag #AbbieMillsDeservesBetter began to trend regularly on social media, I wondered: What in the Four Horsemen was going on?

"All I can remember about the opening of Season 2 is that Orlando Jones's character is in prison orange, the most stereotypical image of a Black man imaginable. His family is gone. A rising star like Amandla Stenberg—whose character was, by the way, in a wheelchair, so there was disabled representation—all that's gone," Due recalled. Part of what had brought Due and other viewers joy was seeing multiple Black characters humanized and their relationships and concerns explored, at least to some extent. But she came to wonder if those aspects of the show had been unintentional. "It felt like all of that had caused some kind of weird panic attack, like, 'What have we done?!'" Due said. "The show began to focus more on Crane and his personal dramas, and it just felt like a directive from on high—'Make this less Black.'"

Among my favorite elements of the show were the bond between Crane and Abbie, the relationship between the Mills sisters, the story lines about their ancestor in colonial times, and elements of the mythology that depicted Crane and Abbie as crucial Witnesses—both vital to *Sleepy Hollow*'s prophecies and revelations. In the second season, those elements were either downplayed or gone. Those in charge didn't appear to understand what made the show special or appealing. I certainly didn't disagree with Due's reaction to the changes in *Sleepy Hollow*'s second season: "They kept wrestling to make it something it wasn't."

Why? *Why?* I asked Due the question that I have spent a decade asking former *Sleepy Hollow* fans (and employees): Why would anyone take what worked about a hit show and tear it down, brick by brick?

"Yeah, it's a good question," she replied. "And it's basically the diabolical aspect of bigotry, I guess. That's the only word I can call it. The diabolical aspect of bigotry often has people working against their best interests. During Reconstruction, when formerly enslaved people were getting elected to office for the first time and had power for the first time, there were regions where they got their first public schools. They weren't the first public schools for Black people—they were the first public schools for *everybody*. Barack Obama pushes through health care—it's not just health care for Black people, it's health care for everybody. But [through the backlashes to those developments] we can see how people work against their own interests when they're baited or scared or confused, which is what I think can happen with networks, which are very risk-averse. But—I don't know. I mean, I'm not calling any individual racist, but the process itself felt very racist."

In fact, to reduce what happened to individual bias actually might be, to borrow a word from *Atlantic* columnist Adam Serwer, "counterproductive." As Serwer said in a 2021 interview, "We've developed this consumer model of racism, where you get rid of racism by putting a black box on your Instagram, or developing yourself as a person. Racism is an institutional force. It's not necessarily about you as an individual, whether you're good or evil. That has become the preoccupation. It's a real problem, because it misleads people about how to solve the problem, and it also makes people think that this is about teams, when actually racism is a part of American society."

Those structural, foundational forces are potent. And they operate in Hollywood, where everybody is nice and nobody could *ever* possibly do or say anything that is biased. Except the Iceberg wouldn't let a character on a Quinta Brunson show ride the bus. That's not how the Emmy Award–winning creator of *Abbott Elementary* put it in an interview, but in 2022, she described just one fight that occurred when she was developing an earlier project for CBS.

"Brunson's hopes for *Quinta and Jermaine* exemplified her commitment to making television with nuanced, relatable Black characters," the piece notes. But network executives did not want a character who worked at a museum to ride the bus to work. "They thought that looked too poor to be enjoyable," Brunson explained. "Because they were like, 'Can she be in a Nissan?' It was anything they could do to not have this character on the bus. That socioeconomically represented something too unenjoyable to watch."

"I get along with these executives, but it's not about that," Brunson added. "They're still racist. It's the comfortable racism that comes from being at a company like CBS for so long that only leads to shows that are like *The Neighborhood*, that are confronting race relations more than they're about Black people."

"The needs of the white writer go to the superhuman being. At the moment, we're presenting the white Negro. And he has very little Negro-ness," Diahann Carroll told an interviewer in 1968. Back then, she was starring in the network comedy *Julia*. Carroll took a great deal of heat from all sides for the mere existence of the show. Segments of the Black community took the comedy—and its star—to task for its mild depictions of racism. Others were angry that the premise played into a stereotype by not depicting a Black father in the home. Some viewers were vocally outraged that the show existed at all.

Julia's dating life came under massive scrutiny. Whole columns were written about the fact that Julia's apartment and clothing were, in the view of some commentators, too nice. For her part, Carroll wanted to know why there were no similar criticisms of Marlo Thomas's fashionable character in *That Girl*. "She was an out of work actress!" Carroll noted. That was a minor annoyance, but many of the other criticisms were major—and they took a toll. "Very often I chose not to handle the criticism and directed the criticism to the creative powers that be," Carroll said. "I am merely an actor—I do what I can. . . . Write to Fox, NBC—the credits are there at the end of the show. Don't make me feel like I'm standing here alone. Help me." Years later, Carroll revealed that the stress she experienced at that time put her in the hospital. Twice.

"They shut down production for two weeks because I got sick," Beharie told the *New York Times* in 2020 of her *Sleepy Hollow* experience. "They sent in lots of doctors, and I had daily checkups to make sure I was actually sick because they had to get the production going. Every doctor said I wasn't doing well and that I needed to rest. That is not what they wanted to hear."

"It took five years to undo those three years," she observed.

Shernold Edwards held on tightly to the magic of *Sleepy Hollow*'s first half-dozen episodes, and she campaigned hard for a writing job on the third season of the Fox show. She knew that it was not what it had been, but she also knew the drama had a new showrunner. And she was still loyal to it—or, more accurately, to the memory of what it had been. "I think part of what saves me—and what sometimes doesn't help me in my career—is that when I think about things I like, I hold onto that," Edwards said. "And the things I don't like—or that are offensive or hurtful—I try to forget as quickly as possible."

Her reps got her a meeting with new showrunner Clifton Campbell. It was brief, but Edwards had read one of his work samples, and she'd thought it was good. She was polite and enthusiastic in the meeting. She was hired.

When she got the job, Edwards joyfully shared the news with Beharie. They had met for the first time months earlier, at the NAACP Image Awards. Edwards introduced herself and told the actor she was a *Sleepy Hollow* fan, and they took a photo together. Once she was on the staff, Edwards emailed the photo and excitement-tinged greetings to Beharie, whose reply was short but "just as enthusiastic," Edward recalled. Beharie's email mentioned some story possibilities she had discussed with Campbell, as well as emojis that signaled positive energy—"A winky face, a happy face," Edwards recalled. "We were both in a good mood at this point."

Energized by those optimistic vibes, one day in the writers' room, Edwards told Campbell that she'd been in touch with Beharie. She said she was "going to try to get together with [Beharie] and talk. I don't know if I asked him for parameters or whatever. Maybe I was just mentioning it," Edwards said. "He just went *off*. He was like, 'You can't talk to her. Nobody can talk to her. She's crazy.'"

In addition to being stunned, Edwards remembered thinking, "Well, you hired me to be her friend. How do I even do this job if you're telling me that I cannot communicate with her?"

That had indeed been a topic during her job interview—Edwards didn't recall the exact language the showrunner used, but she remembered being told that the show needed a Black woman on the staff so that Beharie would have someone to turn to. All in all, this unexpected reversal came as a major surprise to Edwards.

"I wanted this job so, so badly. I thought it would be creatively fulfilling and I thought I could contribute. I thought, 'Somehow they've lost their way, and they just need some new blood to come with new Black ideas and help them find the magic of those first successful episodes,' not understanding that they weren't interested in that at all," Edwards said. When it came to colonial history, the Millses' ancestor, and other elements of the show's lore, "I had all this cool stuff that I wanted to pitch. [The powers that be] did not care. They were not interested."

In written responses to my questions, Campbell stated that "to protect evolving conversations as the studio began to look past Season

3 and the ramifications for any subsequent seasons, I told the entire room not to share these ongoing discussions with any cast or crew. But to say that I told the writers" or any other *Sleepy Hollow* personnel not to contact or talk to Beharie is "patently false." He added that he never used the word "crazy" to describe Beharie, whom he said was "professional," "cordial and fun," and "one of the most powerful and dynamic actors I have ever worked with."

For Edwards, the statements she told me she heard were just the opening salvos of a gig that quickly turned "hellish." "I didn't vet" Campbell enough, Edwards said. "I didn't do any due diligence. I just figured he's a good writer and they hired him, and he must know what he's doing." That rosy assessment did not last.

The show continued to grapple with creative conundrums around that time. Many fans liked delving into the show's mythology, and serialization is now standard (and perhaps a little overused) in our current streaming age. More serialization would have likely helped *Sleepy Hollow* sustain storytelling energy and propel character building, but for some time, executives had wanted a procedural featuring mostly standalone episodes—something not far off from what the Fox drama *House* did, sources said. Indeed, near the end of the second season, top Fox executive Dana Walden told the press that it had become "overly serialized." In addition to that, Campbell wrote in his replies to my questions that Mison and Beharie "believed that the relationship between the characters should not evolve into a romantic relationship because they believed" that as Witnesses, the characters should have a platonic, "professional" bond.

Of course, the biggest change going into Season 3 was the new showrunner. Not unlike the first season, the second season of the Fox drama was "incredibly chaotic," and then Goffman departed. Repeating another *Sleepy Hollow* pattern, Campbell, according to an insider, had no real knowledge of or affinity for genre storytelling, nor was he ever all that interested in the mythology that had been built up over the past two seasons.

I talked to many *Sleepy Hollow* sources for hours about whether the drama's many first- and second-season problems could have been undone or majorly improved. Maybe so, maybe not. It's possible that by the time Campbell arrived, any number of issues were unfixable. But even if that wasn't the case, according to a number of sources, issues that festered in the first couple of years, including turnover in key positions, continued to be problems in the third season. It's also quite possible that Campbell, creator of the crime procedural *The Glades*, was not a great fit for *Sleepy Hollow*.

"Clifton is not a malicious guy. He's not a great manager, but he wasn't abusive. He's the standard kind of old-school TV writer who came up through the trenches of the old system," as one source put it. "Not spectacular in any way. There's a zillion people like him in television, older white guys that either continually get jobs or are brought in to manage situations."

One thing that had to be managed, or at least addressed, was that according to Campbell, Beharie said she wanted to be written off the show. But the studio resisted that, according to a *Sleepy Hollow* source. "The reason why Season 3 got so muddled creatively was because the studio would not commit to anything" regarding the character's demise, this source said. And so, a set of established *Sleepy Hollow* patterns continued: "There's a lack of coherent leadership. There's a lack of understanding about what was required in constructing narratives centered around people of color. It was a lack of empathy and foresight, including at the studio. So it ended up being this perfect storm that led to the dissolution of the show. But it'd be hard to point a finger at any specific villain. It was a series of tragic false steps."

Despite all the ongoing wrangling, Edwards looked forward to visiting the production in Atlanta. As is sometimes the custom in TV, at least until recent years, *Sleepy Hollow* writers were sent to the show's set to produce their episodes. The amount of latitude writers are given to offer input varies from show to show. The input required from Edwards was practically zero.

"I was actually disempowered from making any decisions around production, around the script, around prep, around anything," she said. When Edwards was on set the first time, she noted, Campbell "yelled at me for allowing a small dialogue change on Day 1 of shooting. The sentiment behind it was 'You don't change a line of dialogue without my okay.' So from that moment on, I didn't really participate on set or offer any opinions on any production decisions." (In response to a question about him telling a writer that she should never approve dialogue changes without Campbell's explicit permission, he replied, "I do not recall telling that to one writer at a specific time, but it was a policy that I communicated to all writers on the show.")

Edwards's sense of disempowerment extended to a Trinidadian character. The costume designer came to Edwards, who is a Canadian of Trinidadian heritage, to get her take on wardrobe choices. Edwards's picks were, she said, "insulted" by Campbell (in his responses, Campbell said he would never stand in the way of a writer's input on creative matters). Later, producers sent around emails discussing the actors who had auditioned for the role of the Trinidadian character. "It was like, 'So and so's accent is more authentic than this other person's accent.' And I was just thinking, 'Well, how would you know?'" She remained silent on the topic, believing that no one wanted her take.

"It was a miserable vibe on set," but Edwards remembered how much of "a presence" Beharie had in person. "She came in wearing her suit," Edwards recalled, "and she had this new wig on."

Black actors' complaints about the fact that many crews—which for many years were (and sometimes still are) overwhelmingly white—do not know how to light them or do their hair and makeup have bubbled up for decades. But it's taken a long time for those creatives to feel safe enough to bring up these issues more forcefully in recent years. Around eight years ago, when Edwards was working on *Sleepy Hollow*, a much more familiar scenario played out: a bunch of white people talked about what should be done with a Black woman's hair.

At one point in the writers' room, Edwards told me, Campbell and two other writer/producers—all white men—stood over her, discussing Beharie's on-screen hair situation. Edwards did not recall exactly who said what, but the discussion "was all about whether the curly hair was cute, and whether it looks good and was professional." In her recollection, those three men said things like, "'Isn't it crazy that Fox said that the straight hair is more professional? They probably shouldn't say that.'"

She was stunned—characterizing natural Black hair as unprofessional or disruptive is *not* a microaggression. "It's macro, *so* macro," Edwards said. A white male staff writer sat across the table from her that day, and she remembered the exchange they had—a wordless dialogue dominated by gestures and body language. He encouraged her to jump into the conversation. Her response involved shrugs that said, essentially, "Not worth it."

Still, Edwards wondered if the men standing over her would see her in that moment—literally *see* her. "I tugged on my hair. I rolled locs between my fingers. I was doing all kinds of things, just to see if maybe they would notice," she said. "Nothing."

Campbell wrote that the conversation was the "room reacting to the studio/network's decision" and that he was merely conveying "the studio/network's decision that she could wear her hair more naturally so long as she maintained a 'professional' look." Campbell also wrote that, for at least part of Season 3, Beharie wore "her own personal wigs, which she asked that we use" and that request was granted. One source told me there was resistance at the studio level to Beharie having natural hair on-screen, but that request was eventually granted as well. I also learned that Beharie had her own hair and makeup team starting in Season 2. Speaking more broadly about the show's leads, Campbell said that, regarding transportation and other on-set issues in the third season, there were no differences in how Beharie and Mison were treated.

For Edwards, unfortunate, insensitive, and stressful things happened at work constantly. There was another Black writer on the staff, and one day, she recalled, he stormed out when he got static for saying that two different Black men on the show should not both turn out to be evil. And then there were the times Campbell cried in her presence; once, she said, he appeared to feel accused of racial bias in the way script assignments were handled.

Here's what happened, from Edwards's point of view: For her second script, she was paired up with another writer, which is not necessarily unusual. But she told her boss that she'd been hoping to show him—via a solo script—what she had learned in her time on the show. Edwards recalled, "He teared up, his lip started trembling, and he told me that he couldn't talk about the script assignments, because he was very upset about the charges that had been leveled against him by me and the other Black writer, and that he had 'referred the matter to the studio.' And I was standing there like, 'What are you talking about? What charges? What matter? Why are you talking to the studio? What is going on?'"

She said she had not accused him of anything regarding script assignments, to the studio or anyone else. But the situation got so tense that she left the building to clear her head—all the while thinking she was about to be fired. She wasn't, but later, when a job offer came along before Season 3 ended, she leaped at it.

The other time Campbell wept, Edwards had gone into his office to ask about a line from one of her scripts that got cut. It was written for the colonial relative of the Mills sisters, and it touched on the question of whether it made more sense for Black folks of that era to fight for the British (who promised them freedom) or for the Continental Army. Even now, she's not quite sure the line captured the nuances of the situation, but she noted that she "didn't get to talk to the room about it. The whole process of writing was so isolating."

During this conversation, Edwards told me, Campbell's responses were "dismissive." "I said, 'I wish we could have talked about it, because it's important for a show like this to acknowledge things like that.' And that's when he started crying," she recalled. What she didn't know when she walked into his office was that Campbell had apparently been hearing from fans on social media about the show's handling of race.

When Campbell teared up, Edwards said, "'Do you need a hug or something?' And he said no. In that moment, instead of being my diplomatic self, I responded in real time, and I said, 'You know what, if the white assistant had asked you if you wanted a hug, I can't help but think that you would've accepted it from her.' He was like, 'Oh, Twitter's accusing me of being racist. And my parents would never let us use *that word* in the house.' He said, 'That's not how I was raised. I'm not like that.' And then he said, 'I'll take that hug now.' I had to pat him on the back and say, 'You're a good dude.'"

In his responses to me, Campbell wrote that he'd been told that "two Black writers" had said they believed his "script assignment decisions were racist. I took that as a very serious and hurtful allegation that was absolutely untrue." Due to the gravity of the accusation, he said he brought the matter to "an independent party—the Studio." (Campbell did not explain how the studio making the show would function as an independent entity in a situation like that.) In any event, Campbell, who stated that he never made any *Sleepy Hollow* decision "based on race," said that Fox HR found that there was "nothing inappropriate about the distribution of script assignments." Regarding the incidents with Edwards, Campbell said he did not cry but he did become emotional a couple of times, due to both personal and professional factors. "Anyone falsely accused of racism likely would be more emotional than average," he wrote. He also stated that the suggestion that he would accept a hug from a white assistant and not the Black writer is "false and reprehensible," and he noted that, during that interaction, they did eventually hug.

A source with knowledge of the HR investigation Campbell referred to told me that there was a system by which script revisions were handled in different ways for writers who were below the show's highest ranks. They were divided into two groups, and two Black writers were in the group in which script revisions were handled in a way that gave those writers less input as those alterations progressed. This source said that race did not enter into how that system arose—it was about getting scripts off the assembly line and fed into a "brutal" production schedule in a relatively efficient fashion. But once the discrepancy came to light, it wasn't difficult to see why it might be questioned: "If you do take a step back and look at the pattern, it looks bad. Right? It just looks bad," this source said.

When discussions arose around these topics, according to this person, the showrunner reacted in a way that, while somewhat understandable, drove the entire situation off the rails. Campbell became extremely agitated, according to this source, and said he was greatly offended by any suggestion that there were racial overtones to anything he had done. This source recalls telling him that no one was accusing him of intentional bias, but the issues that had come up regarding the script-revision process should be addressed. This person was of the opinion that the situation could have been resolved in a way that addressed the concerns of all parties in a reasonable fashion. But before that could happen, Campbell called in HR, an action that dramatically—and according to more than one source, unproductively—escalated the situation.

Campbell also took heat in the third season in the wake of interviews he'd done around the time that *Sleepy Hollow* and *Bones* had a crossover event. I've obtained an email that Campbell sent to Kelly, the Fox PR employee I mentioned earlier, dated November 3, 2015. In that note, he stated that a subset of fans—a couple hundred "strident followers"—wanted Crane and Abbie to get together romantically and that these fans had vowed to stop supporting the show if that did not happen. He was worried, he wrote, that those fans would "go negative" if that development didn't occur, and that they would declare that those making the show are "all racists who are (once again) mistreating Nicole Beharie." He went on to state that Beharie would never kiss Mison or play a romantic relationship with her costar, and in any event, that kind of plot would be "unrelated" to the goals of the program. All in all, those fans' "ire is unacceptable to me personally," he wrote.

He asked if some social media messages might help fix the situation, and then he mused that no matter what anyone might do, some fans would inevitably "lump everyone involved with the show in a category to fit their hate." He went on to state that racism remained "a horrible problem" in America and that he hoped to "deconstruct the incendiary racial element" of what was occurring around *Sleepy Hollow* in a way that was respectful. He concluded by noting, "I just hate all this hate. And would hate to see this fun, inventive show take any more bullets if we can open our arms a little."

Kelly responded to Campbell's email within thirty minutes, and noted that she would talk to others on her team and see what could be done. She replied that the "sad thing" about social media was that it let people be "trolls" and gave prominence to "the undeserving who would rather spew negativity and contempt" at a program meant to entertain than enact the change they wished to see in the world.

In replies to my questions about this, Campbell wrote he was "mainly addressing tweets from fans who were unfairly and incorrectly calling the treatment of Abbie Mills racist because they had the misperception that the producers of the show did not want a Black woman and white man to have a romantic relationship." Campbell stated that health issues for both actors created "restricted work hours," and he repeated the assertion that both actors "preferred" a nonromantic relationship for the characters. He added that he "understood why fans were angry" but that the anger was based on a "misperception" and "unfortunately translated into hateful accusations on social media." I also asked him this: When the Fox PR employee, in her reply to him, called fans "trolls" who liked to "spew negativity," did he agree with that assessment?

"I neither agreed nor disagreed," Campbell replied.

As someone who watched the show and also saw much of this play out on social media with a growing sense of alarm and sadness, it is my opinion that there is an enormous misperception on Campbell's part as well. I am aware that there are sometimes factors behind the scenes that influence whether certain fan-desired outcomes can or should occur. Sure, some folks wanted an "Ichabbie" relationship, but there was so much more to the critiques of *Sleepy Hollow*. An extensive array of reactions, opinions, and analyses bubbled up for quite some time, not just on social media but in various publications as well. Lots of folks made good points about the subpar or frustrating writing on a number of fronts. Among the elements that helped squander *Sleepy Hollow*'s potential was the apparent lack of interest in Abbie Mills. It wasn't the drama's only stumbling block, but it deserved the attention it got, because it was a complex, compounding problem that held the show back in many ways.

Sleepy Hollow did not seem to *care* about Abbie's emotional life, her interiority, her dreams, her complexities. As Nichole Perkins put it, "The audience has seen Ichabod Crane through three relationships. . . . We've even seen monsters and evil gods with romantic partners. But three seasons in, Abbie remains loveless." Speaking of *Bones*, well before those lead characters ended up together, Perkins wrote, "it didn't stop the showrunners from creating full lives for the characters, complete with sexual relationships for each."

Why was *Sleepy Hollow* so unbalanced in terms of depth and character development? If you think that has nothing to do with the fact that most of the people with power over the show—at the studio, at the network, and at the drama itself—were white, well, I just don't agree. It would be reductive to say that was the show's only foundational problem—but it would also be naive to assert that this reality didn't consistently fuel the patterns, problems, and conflicts at and around *Sleepy Hollow* for years. While I sifted through the show's troubled history, on a daily basis, versions of an idea Orlando Jones had shared kept coming to mind: Whatever the attitudes or actions of any specific individual associated with *Sleepy Hollow*, given Hollywood's hiring patterns, norms, gatekeepers, and history, it can indeed seem as though the industry was designed to produce these kinds of outcomes. And none of the reactions to this program sprang up in a vacuum. Critics and viewers—including Black audiences and genre fans—had seen these kinds of scenarios play out for years, and they were bone-tired of them.

In any event, I am unimpressed by this reductive take: that the only thing fans were after was an Ichabbie relationship. Nor is it productive to characterize the many varieties of feedback as "strident" sentiments from people who irresponsibly threw around the word "racism."

Even after I spent a decade thinking about this show and years reporting on it, there are still some things I will never know for sure,
except that some participants in this Hollywood *Rashomon* will never
agree about what did occur—or what should have occurred. I know I
won't stop thinking about it, because what played out puts the drama
at the intersection of so many problems that don't just bedevil the industry but afflict America.

I also know this: sometimes patterns of ignorance morph into systematic contempt, and while intent does matter, intent is not magic.
If you are the target of a sustained set of actions that make you (as a
viewer, an actor, or a writer) feel less-than, ignored, condescended to,
insulted, or unheard, *whether or not it was intentional* ends up being
beside the point. It still takes a toll. Another tragedy, and that word is
appropriate because I saw fans' excitement crushed in real time: many
of the people frustrated by what transpired on-screen at *Sleepy Hollow*
were Black women who had been led to believe the show might be
different. And then it very much wasn't. The thing is, thanks to social
media, their voices were louder than they would have been in the past.

But, well, where was the hug?

Abbie Mills was killed off in the *Sleepy Hollow* Season 3 finale. It was
the spring of 2016, and many critics noticed that a surprising number
of women—many of them queer or from other historically excluded
communities—had been killed off or shoved off various shows that
year. Back then, I wrote about that phenomenon, and also about how
and why things had gone south on the Fox drama. I was increasingly
irritated by these developments, and the tone of one *Variety* column
communicated that: "A lot of shows pride themselves on the idea that
'anyone can die,' but is that actually true? It doesn't feel true when . . .
Sleepy Hollow kills off its African American female lead in order to
provide motivation for the show's white, male lead—whose lifespan,
it's worth noting, now stretches more than 200 years and counting." A
few days later, I wrote that "as Nicole Beharie [has] found, [lead] status
doesn't mean you're exempt from the kind of oblivious treatment that
can stray into what can look like contempt."

I was a little surprised around that time to receive an email from
Kelly, who sent me a link to a column by another critic. The piece was
largely sympathetic to the powers that be regarding what had played

out at *Sleepy Hollow:* the vibe was that what went down was not the show's fault. Not long after, Kelly called me.

Kelly told me that Nicole Beharie was not just a disruptive presence on the set of *Sleepy Hollow*, she had bitten someone there. I was so stunned that this call had been made at all that I did not ask when this was alleged to have happened. Given the breathless way Kelly delivered the information, I assumed that *if* this incident happened, it was recent. Only during the reporting for this book have I found out this allegation first surfaced *two years earlier.* If Beharie was purportedly such a danger to others, why wait two years to write her off the show? "As someone who was there," a well-placed source told me, "I was not aware of that alleged incident" being a factor in Beharie's departure from the show.

And that alleged incident was, according to Campbell, presented to him by multiple people who worked for the show "as a fact" when he first went to work on *Sleepy Hollow.* "The first person who told me was a senior production person on the original production team," Campbell noted. In any event, during the time that he worked on *Sleepy Hollow*, Campbell wrote, "there was never any conversation about Nicole being a physical threat on set," and he was unaware of calls later being made to the press that characterized Beharie as a problem.

So why was this allegation trotted out to the media two years later? Here's my theory, which is shared by other veterans of the show: It wasn't about Beharie's behavior. It was about protecting the reputations of anyone involved in ensuring that a talented actor would end up wanting to leave the show she was the star of. As previously noted, according to Campbell, Beharie wanted off the show—but *why would she want that*? Gandolfini and men like him have been catered to in every possible way to keep them around. I understand that Beharie was not as famous or high-profile as he was. But she was the show's star, she was and is talented, and she was poised to break out. She got no such considerations, nor really much consideration at all, especially given the scorched-earth campaign that took place around the time of her departure. (I don't know for sure who made the abhorrent decision to share this allegation with the press, but I do know I was not the only media person to whom this information was given.)

In any event, the anti-Beharie campaign that Kelly participated in was effective. Around that time, another writer covering TV told me that my public complaints about the show were way off base. "Next time I see you I'll fill you in off the record on what the Nicole deal was," this person wrote in an email. "This is a case where the network, studio and particularly the producers are blameless."

Blameless. What a word.

Who is to blame, I wonder, for the fact that Beharie did not work for years after her stint on *Sleepy Hollow*? From her public comments, it sounded as though she understandably needed time for "healing." But in a much more depressing version of the themes of *Sleepy Hollow*— "Sinister forces are at work in the shadows"—it's not hard to speculate about whether those rumors set her career back a lot. Alexander, a well-known writer/producer who has worked on several acclaimed dramas, said that around the time of Beharie's exit and long afterward, the story Kelly told me was gossiped about everywhere in the industry: "It was common knowledge." He said he has come to question the narrative, but he thinks it may have prevented Beharie from working.

He brought her name up for a project he was casting, but *Sleepy Hollow* executive producers Heather Kadin and Alex Kurtzman, who were also in the meeting, spoke negatively about Beharie with a vehemence that shocked him. (Representatives for Kadin and Kurtzman denied that either made any damaging comments about Beharie at any time, to anyone.) Another source I spoke to suspects the rumors negatively affected Beharie's ability to land two post–*Sleepy Hollow* jobs.

In decades of covering the industry, I have heard about plenty of terrible behavior, far beyond the verbal, physical, and psychological warfare that was practically standard for a century. I've heard of people on sets, in production offices, at studios, and at networks punching, kicking, hitting, and assaulting other human beings, and even pulling guns on colleagues. The incidents of racism, sexism, transphobia, and homophobia, not to mention mental and physical abuse, that I've heard about could fill ten books. I know of hundreds of times that industry people put those with less power in all kinds of mental, professional, and physical danger.

But to get a call in which the lead on a project was trashed by an employee of the company responsible for that project, as part of an apparent campaign to spread damaging information about that person— very few industry developments have shocked or enraged me more. Yet it happened. And the only time I've heard of it *ever* happening, the actor in question was a Black woman. Who was, in real life, depicted by people associated with her own show as not just unprofessional but potentially dangerous.

Kelly is still in the industry. She did not return my emails asking for comment. I don't think she and others made calls like the one I got of their own accord; I think they were asked to spread that story. It was Kelly's decision to comply, and I'd like to know why she did, but I'm even more interested in the names of those who made that request.

As for Beharie, she starred in the well-regarded film *Miss Juneteenth* in 2020, was praised for her work in 2022's *Breaking*, and that year also booked a role on the high-profile Apple TV+ drama *The Morning Show*. It took years, but there is an unmistakable upward trajectory to her professional prospects. No thanks to the powers that be; having killed off her character on a show that, in the right hands, could have run for ten seasons, they almost killed off her career too. Who are "they," exactly? It's a fair question. I have theories—theories informed by extensive reporting on the topic—but I still don't know who "they" are, not for sure.

And that's the point. The insulation they have is still very much present and accounted for.

"I feel like it's taken me the last few years to really see clearly that it wasn't personal. It's about the way that these structures are set up," Beharie said in 2020. "It was very difficult to talk about at the time because I wanted to get back to work. But I was labeled as problematic and blacklisted by some people."

8

The Myth of an Egalitarian Future
The IP Strikes Back

You just can't un-see it.
—Laura Canning

The Witcher is about a gig worker trying to earn enough coin to survive in a harsh world that rejects his kind; all the while, he comes up against powerful forces that he, despite all his strength, is sometimes trounced by.

The Mandalorian is about a gig worker trying to earn enough coin to live (and find reliable childcare); all the while, he comes up against powerful forces that he, despite all his endurance and bravery, is sometimes trounced by.

Jessica Jones is about a freelancer trying to earn enough money to survive in a harsh world that inflicts great trauma on her; all the while, she comes up against powerful forces that she, despite her intelligence, grit, and strength, is sometimes trounced by.

It's just happenstance that all these shows feature people with undependable incomes facing massive challenges and taking a beating from implacable, malevolent forces with enormous reach, right? I'm sure as more and more industry workers are compelled to participate in storytelling based on giant interlocking webs of previously created content, these similarities are just one big coincidence. None of these shows could be metaphors for what it's like to work in an increasingly IP-driven Hollywood, right?

Maybe, maybe not. Obviously, the saga of a solo striver going up against a big corporate/political/intergalactic megapower is a familiar tale across many genres and storytelling venues. That kind of tale is a staple of tentpole moviemaking, which has made a beachhead in television in the past decade. Recently, that beachhead has expanded quite a bit, and has come to dominate ever-larger portions of the industry.

Big entertainment corporations that control most of the budgets in Hollywood increasingly worship at the altar of existing intellectual property, and this trend has grown so overwhelming that it is choking off the supply of original visions, premises, and stories. It's also helping to make the realms of TV and film safer and more predictable, if not a little dull and lifeless at times. (In tentpole films, to cite just one bummer, almost no one is allowed to be believably horny anymore, and that is not great.)

There are an enormous number of exceptions to these generalizations, of course. Since Hollywood began, gifted teams of creatives have forged wonderful (and weird) entertainments out of things that came before. The version of *Battlestar Galactica* that came out in the aughts was powerful, inspired, and galvanizing; that drama's creative team took a somewhat cheesy '70s TV series and spun it into a saga that was character-driven, pulse-pounding, and politically aware. It's my favorite television program of all time, and I have often longed for real-world leaders more like Edward James Olmos's William Adama and Mary McDonnell's Laura Roslin. (*So say we all.*)

One Day at a Time, in its first go-round, chronicled the life of a white single mother raising two daughters. When Gloria Calderón Kellett and Mike Royce fashioned a new version of the Norman Lear comedy, they put a Cuban American family at the heart of it. The new *ODaaT* was funny and heartwarming and, in the grand tradition of Lear's shows, it took on social and political topics with nuance, boldness, and flair. I enjoy *Peacemaker, The Witcher,* and the *Captain America* films, in part because all three use genre entertainment to challenge the underpinnings of toxic masculinity. (Eagly forever!)

But the downsides of the trend are more defined than a superhero's biceps. I have spent a lot of years talking to Hollywood writers, producers, executives, and directors, and many of them feel more and more hamstrung by the fact that it's now much harder to greenlight films and shows based on new ideas. "I do love the original movie, and I'm happy they came to me to work on this," said Molly, who, when I called her, was polishing a script for the reboot of a beloved film. "But I hate the IP trend. Everyone's so afraid of original ideas, and it's just watering down the whole industry."

"It feels [like,] more than ever, we're moving towards the middle," observed writer/producer Hannah. "When all the streamers were first on the scene, it felt like they were taking more risks, because they just needed content. That's when we had a larger swath of shows where we're like, 'Ooh, that's different. That's new.'"

TV used to do what Hannah is talking about more regularly—produce content that surprised, challenged, or shocked audiences. But eventually the quest for franchises, sequels, and blockbusters—an industry dynamic galvanized in a big way in the '70s by the massive success of *Jaws* and *Star Wars*—came for television. Streamers, like cable networks before them, took a lot of big swings when they were establishing their perch in the culture. But as they've grown up, they've become as enamored of IP as any major film studio.

One of Netflix's biggest critical successes was *BoJack Horseman,* an eccentric, emotionally acute, and wonderful animated show about a depressed horse finally facing up to the kind of accountability he owed the people (and animals) around him. It ran for six seasons and a total of seventy-seven episodes, which makes it an anomaly. In recent years, Netflix and other streaming platforms tend to greenlight shows that get short runs. ("Second and final season" is a phrase industry folk are sadly familiar with.) Those big entertainment companies are most often relying on projects with well-known antecedents or on the output of very established creators such as Shonda Rhimes or Ryan Murphy, whose content factories are themselves viewed as a form of branded IP. Lucasfilm, Warner Bros. Discovery, and Marvel going whole hog on churning out films and TV shows based on previously established characters and worlds has only accelerated the trend away from the unknown and toward the known.

When I was writing about TV before and during the aughts, it irritated me that the art form was still derided or underappreciated by the culture as a whole. But in some ways, being under the radar was one of the things that protected TV and allowed it to be challenging, form-breaking, risky, and compelling. TV is no longer under the radar. Nowadays, as Hannah observed, every big content factory is "looking for the next *Stranger Things*." And creatives have bills to pay, so they've adjusted to the new reality.

Emma was actually excited when she was hired by the company that started it all: Lucasfilm.

—

In the past, Emma had been employed by productions in which horrible behavior by toxic men was tolerated, if not encouraged. At one particularly awful workplace, she tried to report an abusive boss to those above him in the food chain, but nobody did anything. Emma left that studio and moved on to another gig, where she worked for a man who wasn't openly abusive, but the experience was still demoralizing. Once again, she was working for a boss whose mistakes, unpleasant behavior, and mediocrity were strategically ignored by the powers that be. Once again, she wondered why, despite her extensive experiences and impressive résumé, she was never put in sole charge of creative projects. Then Lucasfilm called.

Three industry trends dovetail in Emma's experience at Lucasfilm. First, she was asked to work on a project expanding a studio's existing IP, and in an increasingly precarious industry, she felt she had to take it. Second, there is, to some degree, less outright abuse and wildly obvious toxicity in a number of industry workplaces. Some of the worst behavior is being reined in (or hidden better). While she was at Lucasfilm, Emma told me, the work environment was generally professional and appropriate.

The third thing touches on a trend that has been common for some time: a highly qualified person from a historically excluded community is hired to be the "strong second-in-command" for a better-paid man who is ineffective, incompetent, and, not infrequently, less experienced. Once Emma figured out the lay of the land at Lucasfilm, she realized she had been brought in to do a lot of grunt work on behalf of Derek, a well-connected man who, in her opinion, didn't know what he was doing. He would get the glory if the project was a success, and it sure felt as though she would get the blame if it wasn't.

Executives at Lucasfilm, Emma said, treated Derek as more important than her, even though he reliably generated chaos, subpar scripts, and other problems. His management skills were questionable when they were not entirely absent. The executives supervising the project listened to Emma's complaints about these serious, ongoing issues, and more often than not, she told me, they agreed with her. But their promises about changing the situation came to nothing. "They back their creative people fully—the people they see as creative," Emma said. And Derek was the person they backed.

"It took a long time to cut through the doublespeak and figure out what was really going on," Emma told me. She had thought—and had been told—that she was going to have real creative influence over this major piece of IP. That was not the case. And Derek, thanks to his powerful connections, was essentially untouchable. Emma slowly realized that her job was to "channel" Derek's creative vision and turn it into filmable content. "I can't speak to whether it was intentional or not, but really, what they wanted me to be was a well-paid babysitter," Emma observed. "I was in this double bind where I was both accountable to them and also not creatively empowered. It just puts you in this position of feeling like the janitor."

This is a dynamic I hear about a lot, especially from folks from historically excluded communities—usually from people who have paid their dues several times over. Gillian, an experienced writer/producer in the comedy realm, is familiar with the "nervousness" of companies that want to hedge their bets by pairing creators with experienced people. But she noted, "Once I was paired with a guy who was younger than me and actually had never run a show before. I mean, what? The sexism . . . it's just systematic. And it was female executives!"

"I had an interview for a coshowrunning job," writer/producer David Slack recalled. "The interview was with an Asian woman, and I looked at her credits and her experience. And when I got on the Zoom with her, I was like, 'Hey, why am I here? It seems like you're ready for this. Do you think you need me?' She's like, 'I don't know. They think I do.' That's very, very common."

All too often, people like Gillian and Emma have to tend to the logistical tasks, management duties, and rewrites that keep a production rolling—but they don't get much, if any, of the credit for it. They frequently aren't seen as visionaries in the way the Dereks of the world are. And at Lucasfilm, in Emma's view, preference and precedence in the TV arena is given to those who have credits in the film world.

Christopher, another industry veteran who's worked in the IP realm, has seen that tendency too. "I started out as a feature writer," Christopher said. "I saw how movies got made—in the feature world, writers are like toilet paper, they've always been expendable and treated like second-class citizens. I was like, 'Get me out of here,' and went into TV, where it felt more like, 'Someone actually at least listens to me as a writer and wants to know my opinion,'" he said. But now, he observed, the IP factories—which favor short seasons and disposable if not inter-changeable writers—have put a lot of troubling changes into overdrive.

"You're not paranoid if they're really after you," Christopher said with a wry laugh. The IP pursuit "is a concerted industrywide effort that is being made to take power from writers. With the advent of stream-ing, directors and producers of these shows—they're from feature land, so they present themselves as being more familiar with big budgets and dealing with big talents—feature-level actors and directors. They're pushing out the writers from the decision-making process and saying, 'Hey, this is a *big* show, so why don't you step aside, since we've han-dled productions of this scale before and really should be in charge of how this process works.' And they're doing that because the feature model is dying and has been dying, because all they have now are tentpoles based on IP. All of these feature-level folks have migrated into streaming and television, and they miss the power they had in features. In television, traditionally, the writers have had the power, be-cause we're the ones who came up with the premise, created the char-acters, and had to generate all that story for a hundred episodes or two hundred episodes. Now, with everything IP-driven, not creator-driven, it's all changing. There is a concerted effort to strip power from writers in this business and hand it over to producers and directors who are willing to push IP over original ideas, because IP is viewed as a safer bet, and that's what sells at the corporate level."

Slack told me he didn't necessarily agree with all of Christopher's assessment; he's found feature folks arriving in TV are often "somewhat amazed by" and respectful of the power that writers frequently have there. That said, Slack thinks that not only do executives feel they're on safer ground by greenlighting projects that have already garnered success in another realm, but asking a writer to expand an existing property "helps them divorce [writers] from the moral right of authors," he noted. "If they can own the IP of some novelist or podcaster or what-ever they're developing, then the people who they hire to write it are doing it as work-for-hire. And the studio owns the sequels and series rights, as well as any consumer products, etc."

In any event, Emma wishes she'd known up front what Lucasfilm re-ally wanted. She would have said no to the job, or something like, "Call me when you're ready to fire him and give me the job. And if you're not going to do that, then great—it's all on him." She did eventually leave the gig, exhausted by the constant chaos and the fact that nobody made any meaningful moves to stop it.

Maybe the powers that be at Lucasfilm didn't feel they needed to. Before Emma took the job, a friend in Hollywood told her that Lucasfilm didn't particularly care about going over budget. Emma was gobsmacked by her friend's observation, given the penny-pinching ways of her previous employers. "But I saw it up close—that it doesn't matter how many mistakes are made or how incompetent some people are," she said. "Our budget doubled, and I'm sure it went up after I left. I've never seen anything like it."

Of course, that's just one person's observation, and others working in IP arenas have endured their share of budget crunches. But at Lucasfilm, it's not hard to figure out why the money might flow a little more freely: the company and its offshoots have had massive success in the realms of film, television, theme parks, and merchandising, among other ventures, since the first *Star Wars* film came out nearly half a century ago. And in Emma's view, the worldwide success of shows like *The Mandalorian* just reinforces the internal belief that the company can do no wrong.

Similar dynamics are in play at Marvel, according to sources I've talked to. Many TV veterans I know have taken meetings there, but a number haven't wanted to run shows for Marvel because they're not convinced they would have any real autonomy. And it's not like the company makes a secret of who is in charge. In Marvel press releases, the person who would have formerly been called a showrunner is now routinely labeled the "head writer." Marvel chief creative officer Kevin Feige and other executives who report to him are often listed as executive producers on each TV project. Those kinds of on-screen credits are not that unusual—but some aspects of the Marvel machine are.

Steve, a well-regarded TV veteran, told me executives from the mothership are often in the room while the writing team is breaking stories for Marvel shows, and he hasn't taken a job there because he'd rather not have that level of constant corporate oversight. Emma found this mindset—that the executives overseeing the IP know best—common at Lucasfilm as well: "An executive even said once, 'Well, I'm the showrunner.' That's how they see themselves."

Top executives at these big companies are, of course, entitled to run each production however they see fit. But it's worth wondering how many decisions are made to create the best story and how many are driven by other considerations, like servicing the next movie or TV series coming off the factory line.

Eliza, a Marvel insider, told me how things generally work there in the TV arena. A team of writers is assembled, with a head writer nominally "in charge"—sort of. A Marvel executive is assigned to oversee everything that the team generates, but as the company has rapidly expanded, those micromanaging the creative process are often inexperienced: "You used to be able to learn with training wheels on. Now that doesn't happen—and some of these executives should still be riding tricycles. They don't have enough experience. But there's no time for them to get that experience—there's too much going on and the machine is moving too fast," Eliza observed.

When Marvel was smaller, it was a more harmonious place to work, Eliza told me. But now, she said with a sigh, "it's not so nice. Kevin used to go around and be the problem-solver on the movies. But there's just too much going on in every area now. That's why everything is wildly uneven."

In any event, once the writers generate the required number of TV scripts, they—including the head writer—are often gone. On set, when a Marvel show is in production, it's not unusual for a different team of writers to churn out on-the-spot rewrites, Eliza said. Especially in recent years, there's frequently no writer-driven creative vision from start to finish—and that's how some IP assembly lines want it.

On one Lucasfilm show, Christopher described how "the folks who were in the trenches, the script coordinators and the writers' assistants—they never really spoke to the showrunner. When writers made revisions addressing producer and director notes, those changes would get sent to the producers and the first assistant director, bypassing the showrunner in the production process entirely." On a Marvel show some friends worked on, Christopher said, studio producers would pitch a writer an idea, give that person a few days to crank out an outline, and then the producers "would just throw it out and say, 'Go take another shot at this,' or 'Try that instead.' They'd be tasked with breaking an entirely new story without any real direction. There was no singular creative vision behind the show, no consistency. They find a writer they can prop up and they say, 'This is the head writer,'" when the time comes to promote the show. But Christopher told me that even that title can, at times, feel like a misnomer, given the transitory nature of the gig and the lack of authority it now often carries in IP-driven arenas.

"Don't get me wrong, there are some really talented writers on those shows working their asses off. And a few people, they are being given great opportunities," he observed. "But they are not running any show. They have no real power."

The IP itself is what possesses the power, after all.

To executives at these big corporations, each piece of IP is like a precious jewel. They keep a tight rein on what's being made, but if they give up even a modicum of power or autonomy to creative types, they often want those people to have established track records. They can't just hand these big properties or established titles to *anyone*.

This seems prudent on the surface, but consider this: if you want to hire directors, producers, department heads, writers, "head writers," and other important creatives with notable résumés, aren't you more likely to hire the usual suspects? Just look at who leads or controls some of the biggest IP out there—who is getting the moonshots, if you will.

J. J. Abrams has had a major hand in the *Star Trek* and *Star Wars* universes. Christopher Nolan directed a justly acclaimed series of *Batman* films, and in 2022, it was reported that another *Batman* director, Matt Reeves, was "plotting an expansion" of his universe of Gotham characters. In late 2022, James Gunn (who's led several high-profile projects for both DC and Marvel) and producer Peter Safran assumed powerful new posts as the coheads of DC Studios; they will oversee all DC film, TV, and animation projects for Warner Bros. Discovery. The four directors of the *Harry Potter* films were men (three of them white). Noah Hawley was handed creative control of a TV spin-off of *Alien*. The Amazon Prime series *The Lord of the Rings: The Rings of Power* is a billion-dollar venture. When its showrunners, J. D. Payne and Patrick McKay, were put in charge of the drama—which employs 1,300 people and had a first season that cost $700 million—they not only had never run a television show, they had no IMDb credits at all.

Apple TV+'s big sci-fi foray *Foundation* was created by David S. Goyer and Josh Friedman. The *Dune* films are overseen by director Denis Villeneuve; one of the 2021 film's cowriters, Jon Spaihts, is also a key figure in that universe (the other cowriter of that movie is Eric Roth). Villeneuve stepped away from day-to-day involvement on a TV spin-off called *Dune: The Sisterhood*, which was created by Diane Ademu-John and chronicles the female-centered Bene Gesserit sect. Before Johan Renck exited the project, he was set to direct its first episodes. Scott Gimple is the chief content officer of AMC's *Walking Dead* universe. Alex Kurtzman is head of all things *Star Trek* in the TV realm. Dave Filoni is the executive creative director of Lucasfilm, and he and Jon Favreau (who also has multiple Marvel credits) have had major behind-the-scenes roles on many Lucasfilm TV shows.

The *Doctor Who* franchise was born in 1963, and the lead creatives behind its recent TV iterations have been Steven Moffat, Chris Chibnall, and Russell T Davies. The men who led and wrote most of *Game of Thrones*, David Benioff and D. B. Weiss, were later hired to develop *Star Wars* movies. They left that gig, but now they (along with Alexander Woo) are in charge of the Netflix adaptation of Liu Cixin's sci-fi novel series The Three-Body Problem. Also at Netflix, the adaptation of *The Sandman* is led by Goyer, comic cocreator Neil Gaiman, and Allan Heinberg. The HBO series *House of the Dragon*, which is connected to the hugely influential *Game of Thrones* property, was created by George R. R. Martin and Ryan Condal.

There are some enormously talented people named in the paragraphs above, creators whose work has brought many people pleasure and catharsis. It matters that Woo is Asian American, Davies is a gay man, and Ademu-John (who in late 2022 stepped down as coshowrunner of *Dune: The Sisterhood*) is a Black woman. But otherwise, the people listed in those three paragraphs (and in the top rungs of the IP-verse as a whole) are overwhelmingly white, male, cisgender, heterosexual, and able-bodied. This all represents a terrific way to ensure that the future of on-screen genre entertainment is a lot like its exclusionary and limited past.

It's not as though zero progress has been made: Victoria Mahoney was the second-unit director on *Star Wars: The Rise of Skywalker* and is directing the second Netflix movie based on the comic *The Old Guard*. (I'm thrilled another movie is coming, because the first *Old Guard* film, which was directed by Gina Prince-Bythewood, is a personal favorite.) But generally speaking, people from historically excluded communities are just not getting the moonshots.

There's a dire history on this front. As of 2018, after more than four decades of the franchise's existence, the roster of writers and directors in the *Star Wars* live-action feature film realm was entirely white and more than 90 percent male. In 2020, Patty Jenkins was hired to direct a *Star Wars* film titled *Rogue Squadron*, but that project has been in development for a long time and, as of this writing, shows no sign of going into production. Taika Waititi is working on a *Star Wars* movie with Scottish writer Krysty Wilson-Cairns, but fans might not see it until 2025 or beyond—if it gets made, that is. As far as I can determine, as of the middle of 2022, no woman of color has written, cowritten, or directed a live-action *Star Wars* feature film.

Andor, which stars Mexican actor, producer, and director Diego Luna, was at first led by writer/producer Stephen Schiff, but Tony Gilroy took over as showrunner and executive producer. Leslye Headland was hired to creatively lead *The Acolyte,* a long-gestating show about the Jedi Order, which went into production in late 2022. Joby Harold was the creative leader of Lucasfilm's *Obi-Wan Kenobi* TV series—after screenwriter Hossein Amini left the project. Robert Rodriguez, who's made many projects on both sides of the U.S.-Mexico border, was an executive producer and director of *The Book of Boba Fett,* but all episodes of that show's debut season were written by Favreau (Filoni cowrote one installment). Deborah Chow, whose father was Chinese, is a director and executive producer of *Obi-Wan Kenobi,* but when it comes to the highest-ranking people on a creative level in IP-land, as a woman of color, she is one of very few exceptions to the rule.

In 2022, I attended a convention panel in which Harold said he was surprised by the racist backlash that *Obi-Wan* star Moses Ingram received when that show came out. Given how John Boyega and Kelly Marie Tran had been treated by a vicious subset of the *Star Wars* fandom years earlier, I wondered how anyone could be surprised by these depressingly regular developments. The *Star Wars* social accounts defended Ingram, but only after the torrent of abuse had begun. Lucasfilm, like other companies in similar positions, remained reactive and clumsy in its responses to these entirely predictable hate swarms. In any event, the ability to remain relatively—or majorly—unaware of the biases that afflict certain segments of influential fandoms constitutes a rare privilege. Thus that reaction from Harold, who appeared sincerely disturbed and upset about what Ingram endured, ended up serving as just one more indication of how cloistered and oblivious some mind-sets can be in a galaxy far, far away.

Marvel has a somewhat better track record on this front—*Agents of S.H.I.E.L.D., Luke Cage,* and *Ms. Marvel* all had men and women of color in key creative roles, and *Jessica Jones* and *WandaVision* were among a number of Marvel shows with female lead creatives. And by the way, veterans of the IP trenches do not necessarily think the men who are usually put in charge are always treated well. Emma doesn't think Derek had a smooth, untroubled ride. But having spent a long time working for Lucasfilm, she came to believe that, at that company (and elsewhere), men had more latitude and got more chances than she did. They had, as Emma put it, "an extreme degree of freedom to fail. As a woman in this business, you're held to such a high standard, and I'm sure people of color feel the same way. And yet the system is completely designed, whether consciously or not, to punish you for mistakes and to reward anyone who looks like a white guy."

It's not as though everyone is fully stuck in old-school mindsets, of course. *The Walking Dead* family of programs has become more inclusive on-screen over time, as has its roster of top creatives. In fact, author and disability activist Alice Wong, creator of the Disability Visibility Project, name-checked the zombie franchise when I asked her about some of her favorite depictions of disabled characters on the small screen. "Lauren Ridloff's character of Connie was important to me because *yes,* there are disabled and Deaf people in the zombie apocalypse!" Wong wrote in an email. "Like Daryl 'Chill' Mitchell who played Wendell in *Fear the Walking Dead,* Connie shows how Deaf people adapt and bring their talents and skills during the apocalypse, rather than the usual Darwinist tropes that only the strongest can survive." (More IP-derived characters she loves: the "scene-stealing" Maribel in *The L Word: Generation Q,* a spin-off of the popular Showtime drama, and Esperanza, a "whip-smart, witty and hilarious" character in *Raising Dion,* a Netflix show based on a comic book.)

On Lucasfilm's burgeoning TV slate is an Ahsoka Tano series, which will star Rosario Dawson, who has described herself as "multiracial," citing Puerto Rican, Afro-Cuban, Irish, and Native ancestry. Among my professional acquaintances, I can name two dozen Black, Latina, Native, and Afro-Latina women who would love to run a show like that. As of this writing, Filoni is in charge of it.

And this brings me to a tricky, sticky, complicated topic. Inclusive cast lists and director rosters are good things, and they are more likely to be found at the big IP factories these days. It's heartening that those directors and actors are getting work. But imagine if the lead creatives on each film or TV project, the "head writers" or whatever you want to call them—the people who are overseeing the *architecture of the stories and character arcs*—were a far more inclusive group. Just imagine.

Right now, at many major IP factories, that's frequently not the case. And there are numbers to back this up. According to UCLA's *Hollywood Diversity Report 2022,* leads of color made "tremendous advances" in recent years. But Ana-Christina Ramón, director of the Entertainment and Media Research Initiative at UCLA and one of the coauthors of the report, said, "When we examined the episodic budgets of all the TV series, we see a strong pattern indicating that shows created by people of color and women tended to receive smaller budgets than those created by white men, particularly" in the streaming arena, the home of many of the most high-profile and expensive IP plays.

There are other pressures that lead to the usual suspects getting the call. The powers that be want someone "established" to lead, direct, or oversee these valuable franchises. In a world where more than 90 percent of C-suite film executives and studio film directors are white, as are four out of five of TV showrunners, white people—particularly white men—are the ones who have (and keep getting) the most experience. And the harbingers are not promising on this front. As the team behind that UCLA report wrote, "Diversity initiatives traditionally are the first to be cut or sacrificed when there are economic downturns. This is already evident with the recent sale of The CW and the merger of Warner Bros. and Discovery. Many executives of color or executives who supported diverse programming were let go from their positions at these companies, and diverse shows have been either canceled, shelved, or dropped from development."

And who created the stories that are being adapted or extended, anyway? In 2020, the *New York Times* analyzed English-language fiction books published between 1950 and 2018. "Of the 7,124 books for which we identified the author's race, 95 percent were written by white people," according to the *Times*. "Non-Hispanic white people account for 60 percent of the U.S. population; in 2018, they wrote 89 percent of the books in our sample." It's not hard to find similar stats in the realms of podcasts, comic books, magazines, and so on. The things being adapted are, a lot of the time, dreamed up by white folks, by heterosexual folks, by able-bodied folks, by cisgender folks. And those realities bring with them their own set of assumptions, biases, and lenses.

It takes active effort to make sure that those conceiving, supervising, and telling these stories aren't as homogenous a group as the industry's top ranks still tend to be. We should have misgivings about whether companies devoted to harnessing IP are engaging in anything beyond surface efforts when it comes to matters of power, storytelling, and representation. That said, there are some excellent examples out there, situations in which many people at all levels (but especially in the higher tiers) worked together to make sure the worlds and stories created in sci-fi and fantasy realms reflect the complexities and realities of our present.

Syfy's *The Expanse* had *Star Trek* and *CSI* veteran Naren Shankar, who is South Asian, as its showrunner, and over six seasons, the array of people who got to be flawed, amazing, heroic, charismatic, and vicious was delightfully eclectic. The entire endeavor was a team effort that included executive producers Mark Fergus and Hawk Ostby, who wrote the show's pilot. And the goal, according to Shankar, was to faithfully transfer to the screen the vision of authors Ty Franck and Daniel Abraham (who write under the name James S. A. Corey and who were, like Shankar, executive producers). They'd imagined a future in which a range of people from a wide array of cultures settled throughout the solar system, and the drama reflected that.

"Occasionally, we would have to deal with various execs who would try to, say, convince us a six-foot tall Polynesian woman might be best played by a petite blonde, but we all always pushed back aggressively against things like that," Shankar told me. I'm glad Shankar and the producers—and the cast—put in the work: I could talk for hours about the drama's bracing takes on class, exploitation, courage, and honesty. There were many performances and story arcs to treasure, but the characters I miss the most were played by Dominique Tipper, Shohreh Aghdashloo, Frankie Adams, and Cara Gee—an array of varied but consistently brilliant actors.

But as an avid consumer of science fiction on-screen, I'm aware that show was an exception in many ways. The truth is, the tendencies of commercial Hollywood frequently lead to what professor and critic Kristen J. Warner calls "plastic representation," in which "characters on screen . . . serve as visual identifiers for specific demographics in order to flatten the expectation to desire anything more," whereas "actual progress would involve crafting a more weighted diversity, one generated by adding dimension and specificity to roles." As academic and TV critic Myles McNutt observes in a piece on *House of the Dragon,* this kind of representation is often something that skates on "the surface with no effort of exploring how race inflects identity or how it reshapes [characters'] relationships with others . . . an empty bit of inclusion that implies no deep reflection or insight into the role that identity plays" in a story.

Now, let's get weird with the Muppets.

Looking back on it now, I think what I love most about the 1976–81 run of *The Muppet Show* was how *normal* it seemed for it to exist. Ballet genius Rudolf Nureyev appeared in sketches with puppet characters and took the whole thing perfectly seriously. Peter Sellers, Harry Belafonte, Steve Martin, Elton John, Mark Hamill, various Monty Python folks—so many top talents of the era stopped by to hang out with Miss Piggy, Kermit, and Fozzie Bear. And why wouldn't they? The Muppets were the best.

I lived for "Pigs in Space" and adored the misadventures of Dr. Bunsen Honeydew and his assistant, Beaker. (I am tall, do not have much of a chin, and have red hair, thus Beaker's appearance and continual anxiety speak to me on a soul level.) If you, as a Muppets fan, didn't spend some time imitating the Swedish Chef, I urge you to make better life choices.

The Muppet-verse dreamed up by Jim Henson and his band of collaborators expanded into feature films, but it carried its core values with it. The movies were usually well made and funny but also intelligent and perceptive. The Muppets often satirized popular culture, but they tended to do it from a place of wry, bemused love, and rarely descended into bitterness or condescension. There was something humane and kind at the heart of that world, and while the classic films and shows had their issues (everything from the '70s and '80s does!), they assumed the people watching—whether children or adults—were smart. Muppets projects didn't talk down to me, and growing up, I appreciated that.

The Muppets franchise was sold to Disney in 2004, and Muppets feature films were released in 2011 and 2014; both were directed by James Bobin. Nicholas Stoller cowrote both (Jason Segel was the co-writer on the 2011 film). Dozens of Muppets characters appeared in both films; most of them were played by Steve Whitmire, Eric Jacobson, Dave Goelz, Bill Barretta, David Rudman, Matt Vogel, and Peter Linz. Louise Gold, who played Annie Sue in 2014's *Muppets Most Wanted*, was a rare female Muppets performer in that cast. Most of the key Muppets performers in the 2021 Disney+ TV special *Muppets Haunted Mansion* came from almost the same roster of men (among the exceptions were Julianne Buescher and Alice Dinnean).

ABC debuted a TV show called *The Muppets* in 2015 that had flesh-and-blood actors interacting with the Muppets. Among the thirty-one critics who reviewed it, the aggregation site Metacritic lists its overall score as 62 out of 100. I was among the critics who were dubious. In my *Huffington Post* review, I called it "puzzling." The show's attempt to adopt the mockumentary style of *Modern Family* and *The Office*, I wrote, didn't really pan out, and I *really* didn't like how Miss Piggy was portrayed. This iteration of the character was "simply mean, and not compellingly so. . . . how Miss Piggy conducts herself as a leader, an entertainer or a powerful, driven pig doesn't appear to be of much interest to *The Muppets*, which gives us the only female host in late-night but doesn't let her have good ideas or drive the stories."

According to Nell Scovell, who was a co–executive producer on *The Muppets*, it seemed that executive producer and showrunner Bob Kushell had little respect for Miss Piggy. Trying to protect the character was "a constant battle in the writers' room," Scovell told me. Kushell would dismiss Miss Piggy as "crazy," but, in Scovell's view, "Miss Piggy isn't 'crazy' at all. She's very clear about what she wants—all the oxygen in the room." She added, "I don't know how someone could not appreciate Miss Piggy's talent and achievement. I mean, Kermit the Frog loves her, so that tells you something. To dismiss her as 'crazy' is to deeply misunderstand her."

You might question why Kushell was in charge at all, given that the most high-profile job he had before *The Muppets* was as a writer/producer on *Anger Management*, a sour, misogynist, deeply unpleasant half-hour comedy that starred Charlie Sheen. When ABC announced in May 2015 that *The Muppets* would join its lineup, Kushell and Bill

Prady were announced as "co-writers and executive producers." Sources I spoke to said Prady, who has writing credits on the first few *Muppets* episodes and was cocreator of the hit CBS comedy *The Big Bang Theory*, wasn't around much, generally stopping by only once a week. Kushell was the day-to-day leader, though he left the show two-thirds of the way through its only season. Creative differences were cited in trade stories at the time. (Kushell was fired from a subsequent job at the CBS comedy *Fam* for using inappropriate language.)

While Kushell was at *The Muppets,* according to Scovell, he came into her office one afternoon and closed the door without asking permission. He then complained about how an upper-level crew member had been fired due to allegations of on-set sexual harassment. Kushell, Scovell said, "expressed sympathy for the guy, because as he explained to me, 'It wasn't like he was grabbing tits or ass.'" Kushell used gross gestures when making this statement, Scovell recalled. (I emailed Kushell about the allegations in this chapter; he did not reply.)

The showrunner continued to minimize these allegations, and in an effort to change his perspective, Scovell shared her own painful experience of having been assaulted by a TV head writer early in her career. Scovell's personal story (which she recounts in her 2018 memoir *Just the Funny Parts*) did shut down that topic of conversation, but when Kushell later stood to leave, she told me, he opened his arms and said, "Wanna fuck?" "It was obviously a joke, but we weren't in the writers' room. We were in my office with a closed door," Scovell said, adding, "There's a fine line between funny and creepy . . . and Bob's comment was nowhere near that line."

One female writer, whom I'll call Janice, told me about Kushell screaming "Fuck her in the ass!" after reading aloud creative feedback from a female executive. He also told his coworkers about his erotic dreams and made inappropriate sexual remarks, Janice said.

Comedy writers put up with a lot, and to some degree, this might all have been considered the kind of "banter" they're expected to tolerate. Kushell certainly was willing to tolerate, one source said, other writers calling a female Muppets character a "whore." But, Janice said, the banter became uncomfortable when another writer mentioned that his son had a boyfriend and Kushell responded with, "Fag!" When that writer pointed out that that word is hurtful, Kushell said he meant the word for cigarette.

Another source I talked to, Hal, cited the show's "contentious atmosphere" as one of its biggest stumbling blocks. Many different creative visions, agendas, and personalities collided at *The Muppets,* and on set, there were challenges inherent in filming actors and puppets together. This comedy was especially hard to make, even on the best of days.

In the writers' room, under Kushell's leadership, the many conflicting factions were a hindrance, Hal recalled. "There were just so much whispering of, 'I don't like this person,' or 'That person is a jerk.' It was *so* not a harmonious staff," said Hal, who told me he did not witness inappropriate conduct by the showrunner. "My take on Bob was that he was in way over his head and incredibly stressed out and just dropping the ball in general."

The comedy's creative team had to negotiate the expectations of a public that had long loved the Muppets, not to mention the dictums of studio and network executives. But other enormously powerful stakeholders—and sources of much conflict, Hal said—were people who worked at The Muppets Studio, some of whom, Hal said, played characters on the ABC comedy. In his recollection, it was not unusual for them to block, change, or object to story lines the writers wanted to put on-screen.

In 2017, Steve Whitmire, who played Kermit, complained that the staff of the ABC show didn't listen to him and his colleagues enough: "We have been doing these characters for a long, long time and we know them better than anybody. I thought I was aiding to keep it on track, and I think a big reason why the show was canceled [after one season] was because that didn't happen. I am not saying my notes would have saved it, but I think had they listened more to all of the performers, it would have made a really big difference."

Hal's not so sure about that. "You always have to deal with the studio and the network, but to have the guys who played Kermit and Miss Piggy, etc., coming into the room and giving us extensive notes all the time and telling us like what their characters wouldn't or couldn't do—it sucked. And it was extremely limiting," Hal said. "They were old-school guys. I mean, if you wanted the show to be contemporary or inclusive in some way, they were a big obstacle when it came to that stuff."

An example Hal cited: The Muppets character Uncle Deadly—like a number of Disney characters in the past half century—has long been coded as gay. On the original '70s show, he sang with Ethel Merman and talked about having been an actor. "He's a side character, but his whole schtick is that he loves theater and loves his poodle and loves scarves, things like that," Hal said. Of course, queer folks are not a monolith, and any person or character—made of felt or not, queer or not—is allowed to like poodles, scarves, and Ethel Merman. But it was important to some of the writers of *The Muppets* to take Uncle Deadly beyond what might be perceived as gay stereotypes.

This was in line with the show's mission. Whether or not you think the comedy executed well on this front, one of the goals of *The Muppets* was to make the characters a bit more real—to give their world and lives a contemporary texture. Given these marching orders, the writers came up with an Uncle Deadly story line in which him being gay was handled matter-of-factly.

"People from The Muppets Studio shot that down and came in the room and told us point blank—'He's not gay,'" Hal recalled. "We were all looking at each other like, 'He's obviously gay. What are they talking about?' They told us, in so many words, 'It's just jokes, it's just funny. It's not like he's really gay. We're not going into his personal life.' It was essentially saying, 'We want to do all the jokes but we don't actually want to experience the reality of this.'" It was a very disheartening moment, Hal told me.

Given all the clashes behind the scenes, it's not surprising that what ended up on-screen was sometimes confused and contradictory. After Kushell left, one of the tasks of new showrunner Kristin Newman was addressing "the lack of joy in the first half of the season," and by all accounts, she was enthusiastic and more open to collaboration. But *The Muppets* was canceled after sixteen episodes. Hal's feeling about any new Muppets show or film is, more or less, "good luck with that." He would never go near the property again.

"The average person doesn't understand that, whoever is writing these things or is supposedly 'in charge'—they are always going to have to deal with Bill Barretta and all those guys," Hal observed. "These guys aren't going to do anything they don't want to do. They have an immense amount of power, and any Muppets show or movie is going to pass through their lens."

Steve Whitmire is no longer part of the Muppets universe. He told the press he thought it was in part because he was a fierce defender of the Muppets ethos. But in stories about his 2017 departure, Muppets executives said Whitmire engaged in "unacceptable business conduct." Two years later, a Muppets TV project developed by Josh Gad, Adam Horowitz, and Edward Kitsis (the latter two are veterans of *Lost*) was scrapped.

In 2020, Disney+ debuted a show called *Muppets Now*, which depicted various characters as YouTubers and other modern-day influencers. The key characters were once again played by Vogel, Jacobson, Goelz, Barretta, Rudman, and Linz. Julianne Buescher, who played Beverly Plume and other characters, appears to be one of the few female Muppets performers.

"They've now had to bring in some younger guys—but by 'younger,' I mean, guys in their thirties or forties," Hal observed. "It's just more white guys. What's frustrating is—these are puppets. These are voices. Anyone can do these characters. Anyone from any background. But most of this 'newer' generation—it's just more of the same."

Muppets performer Barretta is also an executive producer of *The Muppets Mayhem*, a new show that was announced in early 2022. The creation of the TV program is credited to Barretta, Jeff Yorkes, and Adam F. Goldberg. Among the characters Barretta plays are Rowlf, the Swedish Chef, and Dr. Teeth of the rock band The Electric Mayhem. That last character will be a key figure in *The Muppets Mayhem*, which will follow The Electric Mayhem and a human music executive, Nora (Lilly Singh), as they go on "an epic musical journey to finally record [the band's] first studio album." Singh is not the only person of color mentioned in the initial press release: Ayo Davis, president of Disney Branded Television, who cited the "fun" the characters will have, is a Black woman.

The new show is under the day-to-day leadership of Adam F. Goldberg. His greatest claim to fame, prior to this gig, was creating the long-running ABC sitcom *The Goldbergs*, a show based on his own life in the '80s. In a letter sent in response to my questions, Goldberg called his new position "my dream job."

The cover letter that accompanied Goldberg's note and his answers to my questions was drawn up by the law firm of Glaser Weil. In it, Patricia Glaser stated that "the purpose of this letter is to place you on notice not only of the falsity of the claims against Mr. Goldberg but also of the potentially great harm to Mr. Goldberg and his reputation your book may inflict should you choose to publish untrue statements about him."

Well. This feels like one of the less fun Muppet capers.

The strenuous response may be related to the questions I asked, which are based on reporting I did on events at *The Goldbergs* and the professional atmosphere at the ABC comedy. Goldberg's lawyer said that he "never harassed anyone in connection with *The Goldbergs*," that he did not create "a difficult and unprofessional climate," and that he "always created a safe space for women who worked on his programs, treated them with support and respect, and never allowed lewd or inappropriate conduct to occur in the writer's room." Goldberg and his attorney shared emails from four female writers, two of whom worked on *The Goldbergs*, who spoke of positive experiences working for him.

In the course of my reporting, I spoke with more than half a dozen current and former employees of the comedy, most of whom were women, about their experiences working for Goldberg. The women said it could be a difficult environment—for some, very difficult—particularly for those who were not male or within the upper tiers of power at the show. Some people discussed positive experiences they had while working with Goldberg, but these sources generally shared the opinion that, as a boss, he allowed and enabled a culture that was frequently juvenile and challenging, and could be particularly tough on women. Multiple people told me that, especially in *The Goldbergs*'s early seasons, the attrition rate for the show's few female writers was high, and that, on the show's soundstages, writers' room, and elsewhere, unprofessional behavior by Goldberg, star Jeff Garlin, and others was not unusual.

In a 2021 interview I did with Garlin, he confirmed he'd been investigated by HR three times while working on *The Goldbergs*, and he said his verbal and physical behavior—which some sources described as harassing, disparaging, or physically problematic—was just "joking." A short time later, he exited the ABC show.

As for Goldberg, in the view of sources I spoke to, the problems at the show didn't necessarily stem from what he himself did—they often arose from what he allowed. Pranking, sexual innuendos, and jokes—normal features behind the scenes at comedy shows—regularly veered into inappropriate or uncomfortable situations that these sources told me they didn't know how to address given how much power Goldberg had. "It was a big boys' club of men who were probably always kind of the dorks in high school that got picked on, then all of a sudden, they had this power," one source told me. Another man in a senior position was one of the most vicious misogynists a female source said she'd ever come across, and she thinks Goldberg should have fired that man due to his treatment of women on the staff, but that didn't happen. (In fact, the career of the man whom this source called "a gender terrorist" continues to prosper.)

"The working environment at first—it was fun and loose and, like, dirty," but not in a way that felt truly uncomfortable, said Molly, who worked on the show. And that kind of vibe is not unusual. As Brent, a writer/producer who ran a popular broadcast-network comedy, explained, "Often the path to a broadcast-network joke is through a vulgar conversation. You laugh at something, and then somebody says, 'Is there a version of that we can say on television?'"

Taylor, a man who worked with Goldberg, said he was an encouraging boss and generous mentor. He also noted that Goldberg's comfort zone was writing and editing; he "did not go to set" a lot, where, Taylor said, the biggest problem he observed was the disrespectful and disparaging way Garlin regularly behaved toward almost everyone, including the cast and crew. If Goldberg ever did anything to address or significantly alter that situation, I did not hear about it from the *Goldbergs* employees I spoke with.

Taylor recalled Goldberg saying, during the early years of the show's run, that he thought the comedy was "toast" at the pilot stage due to Garlin's off-camera behavior. "The production side, [Goldberg] wanted nothing to do with that," Taylor said. "I think maybe he turned his head away" from that situation. Taylor was quick to add that he doesn't discount the experiences of anyone else—especially female coworkers—and indeed for some, Goldberg's behavior went beyond the "social awkwardness" Taylor mentioned.

I asked Goldberg whether he sent links to pornography to *Goldbergs* employees. "That is false and taken out of context," he wrote in response. "When the celebrity nude leaks went online, the writing staff (including the women) wanted to see photos of Jennifer Lawrence naked. I have a rule that there is no nudity or porn shown on the computers, so I sent the writers a link so they could look at it *on their own time*." The italics are in the response Goldberg sent. (Some apparently did not get the memo on that topic; sources told me of seeing images

of nude and scantily clad women on colleagues' computer screens at
The Goldbergs.)

In any case, over a year or so, I heard about a number of troubling,
unprofessional, or questionable incidents at *The Goldbergs*. As the creator and showrunner, Goldberg had a great deal of power over the
show's culture and workplace norms. I was particularly curious about
the fact that, at one point, two women on the writing staff were fired by
Goldberg. Sony—the studio behind *The Goldbergs*—later made settlements with both women, and my sources said those settlements were
related to Goldberg's conduct surrounding their terminations.

He disputed this and wrote that there was "no determination of
wrongdoing" by him. In answer to my questions about the settlements
Sony reached with those women, Goldberg told me he had fired both
of these writers at least a year before the settlements, and he defended
his reasons for firing them. Amid all that, he did confirm that Sony
"conducted an investigation into the conduct in the writer's room and
ended up settling with two women."

I asked Molly what she thought of Goldberg getting to run the new
Muppets TV program. "I don't have any reverence for the Muppets, to
be honest," she replied. "But I don't think he should be in charge of a
staff, or a show." Molly's views were at one end of the spectrum of reactions to Goldberg's actions, but I would be remiss if I did not share
another opinion: my own.

Five years after the most intense iteration of the #MeToo movement
began, I asked a high-profile writer/creator if he had shared porn with
the people who worked with him. In response, Goldberg stated that he
had indeed shared revenge porn featuring Jennifer Lawrence with employees. Lawrence has called the dissemination of those private images,
which were released without her consent, "a sex crime" and a "violation." The fact that Goldberg would offer up the fact that he sent those
photos to colleagues within what to me appeared to be a defense of his
actions—I found this jaw-droppingly tone-deaf at best.

My jaw hit the floor again while reading his responses about the two
women with whom Sony reached settlements after they worked at *The
Goldbergs*. The events he referred to did indeed happen almost a decade
ago, and I am aware that, among the numerous people with knowledge of that situation, opinions about it differ. However, his response
to me—in which he made a series of remarks intended to defend his

actions regarding the two former employees, remarks that to me read as disparaging and insulting—was written not a decade ago but *in the middle of 2022.* Whatever the differences of opinion regarding what happened among those people, I found many phrases, adjectives, and descriptions Goldberg used in his written answers not just unfortunate but deeply questionable. I personally believe those responses to be of a piece with the kind of immature and self-serving behavior that some of his employees or ex-employees described. Speaking more broadly about the culture in general, when contentious situations arise between men and women, if powerful men would not so routinely trot out responses that amount to "Don't listen to her, she's crazy," that would be nice. Or at least non-demoralizing.

In any event, we can debate for hours whether Goldberg's history makes him the right choice to take on a highly desirable creative leadership position at *The Muppets Mayhem.* This is not a hypothetical; I've actually done this. Part of the issue is that, in the comedy world, there is often so much toxicity and poor leadership—yes, still—that it can be difficult to know how to contextualize what occurred at *The Goldbergs.* The sad fact is, over the years, I've talked to many gifted creative women who told me flatly that they got out of television comedy entirely because of the horrific misogyny they encountered there.

Thus what occurred at *The Goldbergs*—at least for some—may simply be par for a toxic course. Who is responsible for that? Who is responsible for making sure biased or unprofessional workplaces don't arise now or in the future? Those are the questions that ended up serving as my North Star as I attempted to find my way out of this quagmire. This query too: If I had heard rumors about negative things going on at *The Goldbergs* for years, shouldn't executives at ABC and Disney have known—or been able to find out about—those issues?

"Look, I think he got hired because he had this huge hit, and they think he can do it again," Molly said. In her experience, if executives "can have plausible deniability" about things a high-level creative did in their past, "they don't care. If they think he can do a good job with the Muppets, that's all they care about. If the show's a success, then they won't get fired—and that's what they care about."

These *Goldbergs* and Muppets issues—and the broader questions they prompt—would have benefited greatly from some additional perspectives: those of the people who actually do the hiring. I very much wanted to hear from the executives at major media companies such as Sony and Disney, who have paid Goldberg millions of dollars over the years. What, if anything, did the people at ABC, The Muppets Studio, and Disney know about the settlements that were reached when Goldberg was leading his ABC comedy? Goldberg stated, "ABC did vet me, there were no HR claims against me from the four shows I have been the boss on." Did that vetting actually happen, and if so, did anyone at ABC, The Muppets Studio, or Disney look beyond reports from HR—which few in the industry trust—and investigate broader matters of workplace culture and conduct?

Even the most generous reading of the history of *The Goldbergs* must acknowledge that there were problems within that workplace when it came to standards, atmosphere, and leadership. How are problems on those fronts being systematically addressed, and ideally, prevented? And speaking of broader issues in the Muppets world, how many people from historically excluded communities are executives, creators, and performers in high-profile projects involving that franchise? Are there any efforts being made to create meaningful and consistent inclusion in those groups?

I emailed numerous publicists at Sony, ABC, Disney, and The Muppets Studio pages and pages of questions about all these matters. None of them emailed me back. Ever.

I'm grateful that I came of age in the '70s and '80s, when whole segments of American culture were weird.

There's still weirdness aplenty in the worlds of film and television if you know where to look. But when I was a kid, you could hardly turn on the TV or sit in a movie theater without strangeness or experimentation of some kind popping up. On *Quincy M.E.*, a show about an oddball medical examiner, there was a whole episode about how punk rock was ruining young lives. Tom Hanks made a TV movie about how Dungeons and Dragons was supposedly bad for the youth. I'm glad *Stranger Things* made Kate Bush's music popular again. My introduction to her atmospheric, impossible to duplicate vision came in 1978 via *Saturday Night Live*'s stage.

Alien came out when I was twelve. *Time Bandits* debuted when I was fifteen. The lovably loopy sitcom *Square Pegs* came and went when I was in high school. I watched (and was terrified by) the *Kolchak: The*

Night Stalker TV movies and series throughout my youth. All the old systems of media and entertainment were either rapidly changing or falling apart, and a lot of terrible tripe came out during that period of chaos, but so did quite a bit of ambitious or megaweird content. *Escape to Witch Mountain*, a major Disney release of the '70s, is "accessible," I guess, but it is also demented.

Everything felt new then; nothing was a franchise. Well, that's not completely accurate. There were a few franchise-ish entities, like *Star Trek*, which returned to TV screens (and debuted in movie theaters) in the '70s and '80s. The *M*A*S*H* TV show, which I adored, influenced me more than the excellent film of the same name.

Despite the occasional spin-off or crossover, though, things were generally singular. One-offs. I remember seeing *Star Wars* in a theater with wooden floors when I was eleven. We saw it in the second-run theater because the tickets were cheaper. I was completely enraptured; time stopped for the duration of that film, and that feeling of total immersion is what I live for. But it didn't occur to me to want, let alone *expect,* more. Properties getting extended and rebranded and rebirthed and then extended again—for a lot of my life, that was the exception, not the rule.

Am I nostalgic for an era that depended less on nostalgia? Yes, and I appreciate the irony. And obviously, no era has a monopoly on backward glances, which can leave out a lot: two of the biggest hits of my childhood—*Happy Days* and *Laverne & Shirley*—depended on rather unrealistic depictions of midcentury America. In any event, I'm not saying the '70s and '80s were *better* than now. But things were different then. Existing intellectual property, now the One Ring to rule them all, was not in charge of the culture. It was not making things less weird, more risk-averse, and more regimented.

I don't feel like I'd be carrying on the legacy of Carrie Fisher if I didn't point out that, in interviews before her untimely death, she discussed feeling pressured to lose weight before production began on *Star Wars: The Force Awakens. Absolutely not okay!* Fisher, bless her eternally, is one of the mouthy women of pop culture who gave me permission to tell the truth, push back, and have a point of view. In a way, Fisher—my indomitable on-screen mother—gave me permission to be "the asshole at the cinema."

That phrase comes from a brilliant 2012 essay by Laura Canning, and the title says it all: "Sometimes It's Hard to Be a . . . Feminist Film Critic, or; Why I Am That Asshole at the Cinema." Laura, thank you. The essay is, for me, a Rosetta stone of criticism.

The piece perfectly expresses how hard it can be to hold multiple identities in my head—feminist, woman, person, bisexual, goofball, critic, obsessive nerd, lover of silly comedy, admirer of stories that make me cry, etc. The core of the post involves Canning's reaction to the 2011 film *The Muppets*, which, as she notes, featured "Animal at an anger management clinic, [and] a barbershop quartet cover version of one of the greatest rock songs ever written." She mentions a few minor flaws but calls it a "witty and enjoyable nostalgia-fest."

But she goes on to say that there was more to her reaction, none of which she'd catalogued in the radio review she turned in after seeing the film. "Did I raise any of the points I'm about to mention now?" She did not. "Because that would have made me That Asshole at the Cinema, and sometimes I just can't take it anymore. Deep breath.

"When I see a film I have two choices. I can stop being a feminist for the duration of the film, and accept that I'm just going to enter a world in which feminism has no meaning or relevance," Canning writes. If she does this—and I have done this—then there's a prize involved: "It means I will enjoy the film as it was constructed for me, to be enjoyed, and . . . it means that nobody will call me a humourless bitch."

Or there's the other route that a critic can go—being the asshole at the cinema, which "involves me saying 'Yes BUT . . .' every ten seconds during a film, and is exhausting, thankless, occasionally interesting, but mostly alienating to others." She notes the human characters in the movie aren't more important than the Muppets—but of the three main people, Mary's arc is the least developed: "How did we get to 2012 with a public discourse about the representation of women so stunted that the one-note Mary's utter lack of selfhood . . . as a character doesn't raise an eyebrow?"

"I know, I'm taking it all too seriously," she writes. "But this is the point; either I can enjoy the film, adopting not just the 'male gaze' but 'the gaze which suggests female absence and/or character mishandling is utterly normal and acceptable' or I can be a feminist. No wonder sometimes I have to: because every film review I ever do would start with 'It's fine as long as you don't think about the female characters.' Every. One."

Now imagine if critics are from—or allies of people from—historically excluded groups. It can be exhausting to fight the tide of "You're taking XYZ too seriously." People are not taking it too seriously if their lives depend on being seen as human beings, and popular culture often determines who gets to be seen as a human being.

Thank the gods for Ellen Ripley, *Farscape*'s Aeryn Sun, and Leia—women who planted the idea in my mind that questioning authority is not just necessary but cool. I love them, and there weren't enough characters like them when I was growing up. I was in my forties when I fell hard for the cult Syfy series *Killjoys*—the first time I'd seen a woman of color as the unquestioned lead of a team of outer-space ass-kickers. If I have one core belief, it's that *everybody* should get to kick ass in outer space.

So, the Muppets: Canning *does* credit the 2011 film with allowing Miss Piggy to be vulnerable and for toning down the physical violence that was so often a hallmark of the character (which was never great). But Canning also notes that Miss Piggy has to give up her life and her career for a man. "*This is our happy ending* [italics added]. . . . It's a difficult thing sometimes, being a feminist. Once you see not just how the world works, but how all of our cultural artefacts either tacitly or explicitly reinforce the subordination of women, you just can't un-see it, though sometimes you wish you could."

Sometimes I wish I could. But I can't.

No property, big or small, can be fully separated from the context in which it was created. I can't think about Dr. Teeth and the Electric Mayhem without thinking about the hippie-dippie culture they sprang from. They represent the old, weird, gnarly Muppets; they are part of the funky shit that I grew up with in the '70s and '80s, when things were hairy, odd, and goofy, and the stakes in so many entertainment realms were lower. The fact that none of the dozens of people with corporate power over The Electric Mayhem's new show would answer my questions makes me sad.

And angry. The powers that be would rather have us all get stuck in the weeds about this or that individual and their fitness for a particular gig. What about the systemic harms, the institutional failings, the hiring of the usual suspects again and again? When they are asked about those matters, the big companies that send me dozens of press releases every week—all these corporations that say to the media and to the world, in so many words, "We Care, We Get It, Welcome to Our Ride/ Theme Park/Hotel/TV Show/App/Movie/Toy Collection, Fork Over The Cash and Have a Pleasant Day!"—yeah, all those companies tend to get *realllll* quiet.

Because I'm an asshole at the cinema, I still have a lot of awkward— and, I think, important—questions. Not just about one show or one franchise—but about the worlds and futures Hollywood is creating. From the ground up, we are all too often replicating the DNA of the past.

Of course it mattered that Kumail Nanjiani, a Pakistani American actor, writer, and producer, got to play a superhero in *Eternals*, which was directed by a woman of color. I'm not going to make the argument that the film is a classic, but I bring it up as one example of progress in the biggest cultural arenas. In a conversation Nanjiani had with Simu Liu of *Kim's Convenience* and *Shang-Chi and the Legend of the Ten Rings*, the men talked about something really important:

Nanjiani: I wanted to approach my character as an inversion of the stereotypes I saw while auditioning as an actor. We're always depicted as nerds, so I wanted [my *Eternals* character] to be cool. We're depicted as weak, so I wanted him to be seen as strong. And we're depicted as angry terrorists, so I wanted him to be full of joy. Basically, just the exact opposite of all the ways I'd seen myself represented in American popular culture.

Liu: And it's not just about the roles but their context and status within the story. How many times have I played the "Asian Guy Getting Yelled At," or "Asian Guy Getting Scared About Stuff"? I'm supposed to be playing a CIA agent, but when they cut to me, my mouth is open, I'm confused and have no idea what to do and nothing to contribute. How fucking low status is that? We have to push for higher status in our own stories.

Their context and status within the story—bingo. There it is.

People can write about whatever they want. But cultural competency matters. Context matters.

Art and storytelling expand our ability to know what others' experiences are like. I love that. A big part of the point of life is to learn and evolve. I don't know what it's like to shoot womp rats in Beggar's Canyon, but *Star Wars* made me want to do that, and also take down jackbooted thugs—and repressive empires—wherever I find them. I don't know what it's like to be a queer Cuban American woman who has a quinceañera. I *cannot* know that, because that's not my history. *One Day at a Time* helped me experience that, in part because those making it had the history and cultural competency to tell that story with wit, skill, and grace.

However, some experiences will *always be theoretical* for each of us. We all have the blind spots we have. The ability to evolve does not eliminate every single blind spot. Nor does magical thinking. All too often, Hollywood leans on plastic representation, when a better solution would be handing the creative reins to people who don't have the blind spots—the cultural or experiential gaps—that would lessen the work or suppress its potential depth, resonance, and impact.

Hollywood has been biased since its founding. At no point has a witch or a wizard magically disappeared those biases. Some visions and voices have been shut out for a long, long time, and some of the biases have simply morphed into something quieter, or gone underground. The patterns I've laid out here won't change until people actively and continually decide to change them. After all, a deeply uncomfortable fact about the commercial pursuit of IP was well stated by *The Atlantic*'s Adam Serwer in 2022, when there was yet another racist furor about Black and brown characters in fantasy sagas: "The executives in charge of these companies are typically aligned politically and economically with the American right—they simply have a commercial incentive to make things that the broadest number of people want to see. Significant right-wing cultural backlashes have succeeded in narrowing Hollywood's imagination in the past."

It certainly looks like they succeeded in *our* time, when Kelly Marie Tran and John Boyega—both exceptional actors—were both put through hell by online hate mobs when they had prominent roles in *Star Wars* films—and subsequently saw their characters sidelined in *The Rise of Skywalker,* a flaccid, frustrating film that suffers from many problems, among them their near absence. "Like, you guys knew what to do with Daisy Ridley, you knew what to do with Adam Driver," Boyega said in 2020. "You knew what to do with these other people, but when it came to Kelly Marie Tran, when it came to John Boyega, you know fuck all. So what do you want me to say? What they want you to say is, 'I enjoyed being a part of it. It was a great experience . . .' Nah, nah, nah. I'll take that deal when it's a great experience. They gave all the nuance to Adam Driver, all the nuance to Daisy Ridley. Let's be honest. Daisy knows this. Adam knows this. Everybody knows. I'm not exposing anything."

He's not. It's true. Also true: I know of so many folks who have taken refuge in romance, fantasy, and science fiction, because, at their best, these genres are a celebration of all kinds of societies, people, bodies, and ways of living and loving. When will all the folks who find comfort and catharsis in those stories routinely get chances to create— and thus mold—not just Hollywood but the future of humanity?

"Our studies including over 18,000 participants across industries consistently document that white men report lower levels of bias than every other group," the UC Hastings Center for WorkLife Law stated in 2021. The Center also noted in its findings "that white men consistently report that workplace systems are fair at higher levels than virtually every other group." This just means that within Hollywood content factories—including the IP mines—more people have to zip their lips about the questions they have, the input they have, the reactions they have to shit that is not authentic or just *not good*. The blind spots remain. The asshole at the cinema silently shakes her head.

Or not so silently. More than ever, the public has the ability to point out these gaps, omissions, patterns, and mistakes—loudly. So when these companies or their leaders' blind spots cause them to stumble, they are likely to get roasted. When Disney got ensnared in Florida's homophobic "Don't Say Gay" law in 2022, perhaps the company would not have shit the bed so comprehensively—with former CEO Bob Chapek releasing a response memo that many employees and consumers saw as tone-deaf, if not offensive—had it not been mishandling matters on this front for years.

"Chapek's 'both sides' manifesto [stated] that the biggest impact the company could have 'in creating a more inclusive world' is 'through the inspiring content we produce,'" the Daily Beast's Kevin Fallon writes. "Would that be the content that, to this day, has never featured a LGBTQ+ character in a major theatrical film role?"

In a letter to Disney management, Pixar's LGBTQ+ employees allege that the company's executives have demanded cuts from "nearly every moment of overtly gay affection . . . regardless of when there is protest from both the creative teams and executive leadership at Pixar." The letter continues, "We at Pixar have personally witnessed beautiful stories, full of diverse characters, come back from Disney corporate reviews shaved down to crumbs of what they once were. Even if creating LGBTQIA+ content was the answer to fixing the discriminatory legislation in the world, we are being barred from creating it."

There are good, smart folks working at all these IP mills. But the scramble to cash in on the past is, in many ways, antithetical to the kind of creative freedom—and rebellion—that nurtured me when I was young. The world is an unequal place. The chase for IP can reinforce that—or, just maybe, help us create a better future.

Now it's worth exploring in greater depth who is viewed as creative—and how creativity itself is regarded.

9

Launch Them into the Sun
The Toxic Myths Around Creativity

> They're just assholes.
> —Harold Perrineau

In a career that stretches back to the mid-1980s—one of his first on-screen credits was as a dancer on the TV version of *Fame*—Harold Perrineau has seen a lot. A *lot*.

"I have had some great experiences. I've met some really great people who have enhanced my life," said Perrineau, whose résumé features roles in *Oz*, *Lost*, *Romeo + Juliet,* and the *Matrix* films. Some of the people he's worked with have been gems who made the work—and the spaces they moved through—better.

Perrineau has also seen a lot of terrible behavior. He's watched actors with more power (and better compensation) show up drunk, behave abusively, use offensive language, and generally act like entitled jerks. He's also, despite his obvious skills as a performer, routinely been passed over for the kind of lead roles that his white peers frequently get, whatever their track records on other sets. For Perrineau, who plays a small-town sheriff on the Epix horror drama *From,* which premiered in 2022, things are starting to shift.

"I'm not gonna lie, I feel a little bit like the beneficiary of this racial reckoning," he said, referring to the halting attempts the industry has made in recent years to come to terms with its history of bias and exclusion. These days, producers, studios, and other key industry folks "are interested in even considering something other than a white male to play the lead in a show," Perrineau told me. "Had none of those things happened, I firmly believe that I might not be playing this character, and they would've gone to some straight white male actor.

'Cause that's the way it still goes down now, you know what I mean? Unless it's a uniquely Black story. You could try to tell the story of the *Godfather of Harlem* [an Epix drama that premiered in 2019] without Forest Whitaker, but you really can't, you know?" Perrineau said with a laugh. "Adrien Brody's not going to tell that story."

Finally, Perrineau is playing the kind of part that white actors have always been considered for—basically, just *a guy*. A lawman with a difficult past in a small town beset by frightening phenomena. It's a long-overdue starring role that amply displays Perrineau's ability to channel quiet resolve, wounded yearning, and determined resilience all at once. And it marks a notable milestone: After decades in the industry, when he walked on to the set of *From*, it was the first time Perrineau had ever been the most important actor in a production. He waited for the transformation.

"I was really excited to be Number One on the call sheet, because I was curious about whether something happens to you," he said. "What happens? What happens when you become Number One on the call sheet that turns you into an asshole?" There was that resonant laugh again.

To be clear, not every Number One in Perrineau's past was unprofessional or phenomenally irritating. But over the years, enough fellow artists with starring roles have been, to the point that Perrineau had long wondered, what button got pushed? What inevitable transformation began with that Number One status?

The suspense was killing me. "What happened?" I asked, ready for a big reveal.

"Nothing," he said, chuckling. "Nothing happened. Nothing was different. I still did the work."

The only conclusion he could come to was that the people who'd used their authority poorly had assumed that they were *really* being handed something else: the power to do whatever they wanted, no matter how counterproductive, time-consuming, money-draining, or damaging. Those people were, he said, "just assholes." That's what they were *allowed* to be, because—and I'll trot out some shopworn industry phrases here—it was "part of their process," "how they accessed their art," or "how their genius manifested," etc. Their bad behavior was considered a necessary accessory to their creativity, passion, drive, dedication, artistic boldness, and vision, *blah blah blah*. The list of excuses is endless.

The thing is, these excuses aren't rolled out for everyone—but some coast on them for decades. Bill Murray went from *Saturday Night Live* fame to huge success in the film industry despite a litany of troubling incidents that span decades. He used a massager on Geena Davis on the set of 1990's *Quick Change;* she "said no multiple times, but he wouldn't relent." As she writes in her autobiography, she still had to do media appearances with him, including an *Arsenio Hall Show* appearance where he pulled down the strap of her dress on camera.

When actor/producer Seth Green was nine, Murray, irate that Green wouldn't vacate a couch Murray wanted to occupy backstage at *SNL,* held him upside down over a trash can and dropped him in it; a "horrified" Green ran away, hid under a table in his dressing room, and cried. When filming *Charlie's Angels* in 2000, he hurled "insults" at Lucy Liu using language that was "inexcusable and unacceptable," Liu said. At *SNL* in 2016, Murray allegedly put his hands on Solange Knowles's hair after she performed the song "Don't Touch My Hair." A more recent incident shut down production on the film *Being Mortal* in 2022: Murray straddled and kissed a much younger woman who was horrified but who "couldn't move because he outweighed her," according to a news story. The woman and a colleague both filed complaints and the woman received a settlement—but she also reportedly had to sign an NDA. Murray described the incident as "a difference of opinion."

Because these kinds of litanies are not rare, I get why actor, writer, and producer Issa Rae, the woman behind *Insecure* and *Rap Sh!t,* is over it. She said in a 2022 *Elle* interview that it "feels like we're regressing, depressingly so. There are just too many enablers for there to be real change." For her, Exhibit A was Ezra Miller, the star of the Warner Bros. film *The Flash.* During the past several years, Miller has been at the center of a long litany of unfortunate or unprofessional incidents, and along the way, they had encounters with the members of the public and law enforcement that paint a picture of a person in crisis. It is possible to believe Miller is a gifted artist and to be concerned for their welfare while also recognizing that they have a history of creating troubling, unacceptable, or unsafe situations for other people. The studio behind *The Flash,* in the midst of these myriad problems and legal issues, filmed reshoots with them in 2022, and the movie was released in mid-2023. "I'm gonna be real, the stuff that's happening with Ezra Miller is, to me, a microcosm of Hollywood," Rae said. "There's this person who's a repeat offender, who's been behaving atrociously, and as opposed to shutting them down and shutting the production down, there's an effort to save the movie and them. That is a clear example of the lengths that Hollywood will go to to save itself and to protect offenders."

It doesn't have to be this way. But undoing the legacy of "creativity" will be difficult, thanks to the ideas the industry absorbed, strengthened, and promulgated for long, long time.

Nancy Wang Yuen worked as a production assistant on a film more than a decade ago, but she is still struck by a dynamic she witnessed there. The Asian American director had a white, male first assistant director who was "toxic," she recalled. "He yelled at us. He humiliated us. Everybody on set was terrified of him. We asked the director, 'Why do you have this guy around?' And he's like, 'Well, there has to be someone like him.' He believed this person had to exist on the set so he could be the nice person. The idea was that this was an important part of filmmaking. I was shocked that everyone just accepted it."

If nothing else, Hollywood needs to honestly address the fact that for people from historically excluded groups, their ability to bring their full artistic selves to a project has been hemmed in or even rejected for a very long time. For example, before Sierra Teller Ornelas took on the job of showrunner of Peacock's *Rutherford Falls*, who had offered Indigenous Canadian actor Michael Greyeyes the chance to be the cringe-inducing father of teenagers in a comedy? No one.

His character Terry Thomas is, in a way, *just a guy*—a recognizable go-getter type that has been on our screens forever. Of course, as played by Greyeyes, the ambitious Tribal casino CEO is specific, amusing, and intense. Terry not only has a plan for the future but multiple spreadsheets, timelines, and checklists, and a focused, alert energy emanates from him at all times. "He speaks almost without a filter, which is hilarious, because he's so truthful," Greyeyes told me when talking about his character, who is so tenacious and committed that he sometimes forgets not everyone is as driven as he is. Terry is also the kind of charismatic leader who does realize—at least some of the time—that some folks are a little (or a *lot*) intimidated by him.

But the nice thing about Terry is that, unlike so many Native characters in Hollywood's past, he gets to display a lot of different sides of himself, in story lines that unfold at work and in his personal life. In both seasons of the canceled-too-soon comedy, "you met people who are not scared of Terry—his own family members. His teenage daughter is not even a little bit" intimidated by her dad, who, of course, "always has dad jokes at the ready," the actor observed.

Prior to *Rutherford Falls*, which premiered in 2021, Greyeyes had built up an impressive body of work, including the acclaimed films *Blood Quantum* and *Dance Me Outside*. One of his two Independent Spirit Awards nominations in 2021 was for his work in the film *Wild Indian*. He played Sitting Bull in the 2017 Jessica Chastain film *Woman Walks Ahead*, and he had a meaty role on *Fear the Walking Dead*, among many other credits. But when he walked on the set of the Peacock comedy, he didn't have much familiarity with the rhythms of network comedies—literally. At one point, Ornelas told me, Greyeyes was asked to pick up the pace when uttering Terry's lines. "After a while, he goes, 'No one has ever told a Native actor to speak faster,'" Ornelas said.

"A lot of these Native actors have been waiting for this moment— they've just been ready," she added. When given new kinds of roles— the kinds that don't necessarily depend on somber, measured line readings—"They're so prepared, it's just like a bullet in a gun, you know?" Kimberly Guerrero, who played Terry's wife, Renee, thanked Ornelas for getting to play a character who did not die to move the plot forward. "The plight of the Native actor is that they're usually only ever offered one type of role over and over again," Ornelas said, and Guerrero had played a lot of Native women who "get killed, or they're the third-act complication that inspires the cop to figure out the case in time."

Part of the reason that Greyeyes, who is Nêhiyaw from Muskeg Lake Cree Nation, had the time and energy to figure out how to embody Terry's personality was because he didn't have another job, which many creatives from historically excluded groups are saddled with. He didn't spend any time educating his artistic collaborators on Indigenous cultures. He did not have to explain the context and constraints within which Native characters have usually operated in Hollywood. In fact, the show's writers and cast had a high old time mercilessly mocking those demeaning stereotypes in a second-season *Rutherford Falls* episode titled "Adirondack S3."

Women of color face an particularly uphill battle on the "educational" front. I've been talking to Mina, a director of Asian descent, for years. She's told me about how hard it was to book her first TV jobs, and about the many formal and informal barriers she's faced. Things are changing, she said recently—but only up to a point. "I myself have primarily been hired on projects or episodes centered on Asian characters; as more projects center characters from marginalized groups and the conscientiousness of representation behind the scenes continues to grow, the opportunities for currently marginalized directors will increase," she said. "The potential pitfalls, of course, are the ease with which marginalized directors are seen as *only* being able to tell stories about the groups they belong to. And under certain circumstances, they are expected to carry the weight of 'speaking for them' on the production side."

Ornelas is Navajo and Mexican American, and the show's writers' room across its two seasons was at least half Native, as were many of its directors. This is extremely rare; very few projects in American TV history have had Indigenous folks in a large number of key creative roles. In any event, none of the *Rutherford Falls* actors had to combat the idea that Native communities are a monolith full of people who "wear a headdress to go to the grocery store," as the showrunner put it. As was the case with Greyeyes's roles in *Blood Quantum, Dance Me Outside,* and *Wild Indian,* all of which were not just about Native characters but had Native artists in many crucial positions, he could just focus on the work in front of him and . . . be creative. "It's absolutely freeing," he told me.

Not much time passed between the moment in which he heard about the role and the day he had to turn up on the show's set, terrified and excited to take on the new challenge of being a square, driven dad with big dreams in a small-town comedy. But Jana Schmieding and Ed Helms, who also starred in the show, were generous, and Greyeyes said, "I got up to speed pretty quickly." It didn't take long, he told me, before "it was just fun."

"Fun" is not the word that leaps to mind when thinking about how many sets operated for a very long time. It's not that '60s and '70s Hollywood was bereft of enjoyment or creativity—far from it. But in reading about that era, I absorbed the idea that making movies more or less had to be a punishing endurance event. I mean, open almost any page of Peter Biskind's *Easy Riders, Raging Bulls,* and you'll find an example of awful behavior.

Actor, producer, and artist Dennis Hopper displayed some dreadful conduct on the set of *Easy Rider,* which he starred in and directed: according to cameraman Baird Bryant, Hopper "started haranguing us about how he'd heard a lot about how many creative people there were on this crew, but there is only one creative person, and that's me. The rest of you are all hired hands, slaves. He was totally out of his mind. He was just raving; probably some combination of drugs and alcohol."

It's possible that the famously wild and drug-infused set of *Easy Rider* is an extreme example, so let's check in with George Lucas on the set of *Star Wars,* which he wrote and directed near the start of his legendary career: "I realized why directors are such horrible people, because you want things to be right, and people will just not listen to you, and there is no time to be nice, to be delicate. I spent all my time yelling and screaming at people."

What happened in the early '70s, when the writer of *Taxi Driver,* Paul Schrader, was driving to a screening with Margot Kidder, then an established actor a few years from shooting to stardom in 1978's *Superman?* He begged her to kiss him, and when she wouldn't, he "slammed on the brakes and put the car in a 360 spin." Kidder noted, "He scared the wits out of me . . . I pecked him on the cheek, he pulled the car out of the spin and drove to the screening."

This behavior, friends speculated, may have had its roots in the man-crush Schrader had on filmmaker John Milius, who, in the '70s and '80s, had writing credits on everything from *Apocalypse Now* to *Conan the Barbarian* and who cowrote and directed *Red Dawn.* In Biskind's book, Gloria Katz, who cowrote *American Graffiti* and *Indiana Jones and the Temple of Doom,* called Milius an "enormous blowhard." Biskind observed that "women found him hard to take." "Unless you were going to sit there and be enthralled by him for hours and hours on end, it was incredibly boring," Katz noted.

Schrader "imitated Milius's behavior, the idea being, if you acted crazy, it scared people, and they respected you," writer/actor Kit Carson told Biskind. Throughout the book, women (and some men) sigh at a wide array of Creative Guy antics like these, many of which were fueled by insecurity and rivalry, not to mention drugs and alcohol.

Director Robert Altman "could be a miserable prick," especially when drinking; it wasn't unusual for him to make people cry. But his agent, George Litto, kept him on anyway, in part because Altman was "confrontational." To say that many (or most) people in the industry do *not* benefit—then or now—from being openly antagonistic is one of the understatements of the year. But the rules, such as they were in the '70s and beyond, were different if you were "a guy's guy," which is Biskind's description of Milius. The phrase certainly applied to many other hard-charging creative types in the book.

"We were from the same school, that Hemingway, Hammett, Chandler, hard-drinking, hard talking, take-no-shit thing," Litto told Biskind. *Easy Riders* is an impressively reported, wonderfully written book, don't get me wrong. And decades have passed since these incidents happened, and no doubt a lot of the people in its pages—if they're still alive—have changed and grown. But the attitudes and mindsets these folks venerated (or had to endure) are still around. I have talked to so many people who have encountered various flavors of miserable-prick energy throughout their industry careers, and they are, in a word, *tired*.

That said, I'd be lying if I denied that, in the past, I consumed these narratives like candy. Horrible behavior—hundreds of pages of it—in *Live from New York,* the oral history of *Saturday Night Live*? Of course I devoured the whole thing. When I was coming up, not only as a consumer of popular culture but as someone who wrote about the industry, these narratives—dishy stories of industry people behaving badly—were, in and of themselves, a popular subgenre of entertainment.

Premiere magazine ran its share of puff pieces in its '90s heyday, but it also published serious stories, like a 1998 exposé on the abusive, harassing culture at New Line Cinema. Journalists Kim Masters and Nancy Griffin wrote the smart and engaging 1996 book *Hit and Run: How Jon Peters and Peter Guber Took Sony for a Ride in Hollywood,* and Julie Salamon's 1991 book *The Devil's Candy,* a clear-eyed assessment of the making of *The Bonfire of the Vanities,* is rigorous, well-crafted, and deeply reported. Scouring every issue of *Entertainment Weekly,* which came along in 1990 and was the go-to source for movie and TV obsessives for a long time, wasn't just enjoyable, it sent the message that you knew the score. When you read books and publications like these—and there were so many good ones—it showed you weren't naive. You knew how the sausage got made.

Some of that sausage-making—it was really bad. All right . . . a *lot* of it was bad. In writing this book, it did not take me long to stumble over a problem that industry reporters before me have tripped over many times: everyone in Hollywood has dozens of stories about awful things they've experienced, witnessed, and heard about. Or hundreds of stories. Rachel Abramowitz's 2000 book, *Is That a Gun in Your Pocket? Women's Experience of Power in Hollywood,* is packed with this kind of testimony: "Almost every [woman] had a story to tell . . . of job interviews that began, 'Take off your clothes' and of bosses who started each morning with a call announcing 'I'm holding my big, veiny dick in my hand.'"

It does stray into the laughable—a parade of men who, in the pages of so many of these books and magazines, bought in to the big-swinging-dick myth of Creative Guy behavior. But it was still jaw-dropping to read in Abramowitz's book how the rare successful women in the industry were treated when they displayed competence on the job. Jodie Foster, who brought in *Little Man Tate* a million dollars under budget, was still screamed at by producer Scott Rudin, and she had to throw him off the set. (Rudin, naturally, disputed that account.) Callie Khouri told Abramowitz she was "treated like a nonbeing" and was only reluctantly allowed on the set of *Thelma & Louise*—which she wrote—an experience she recalled as enraging and "humiliating."

Studio head Sherry Lansing had to proceed with "her own ambition . . . carefully veiled," lest she threaten the men around her. At one point, Lansing's creative hopes rested on the 1995 film *Jade*, which was directed by her husband, William Friedkin: "Reams of explicit sexual footage were shot but never made it into the U.S. version of this psychosexual, violent phantasmagoria by Joe Eszterhas about a married psychiatrist who doubles as a high-class call girl," Abramowitz writes. This, too, was part of a pattern: in a speech she gave in 1990, Meryl Streep lamented that women were paid less than men, that they had fewer options for roles, and that her own creativity was limited by being repeatedly asked to play sex workers.

The few women who got past the gates often decided that if you couldn't beat them, you *had* to join them. High-level executive Dawn Steel, Abramowitz observes, "aped the testosterone-fueled antics of the town's men—yelling, screaming, controlling, demanding fealty and obeisance from all who came into her purview."

For years, these kinds of histories and backstage chronicles—this saturation coverage of assholery—led me to a set of assumptions about creativity that were faulty, at best.

I do think suffering certainly can be and often is part of the creative process. The immensely destructive thing Hollywood has done for a century is normalize *externalizing* that suffering and those difficulties *on the wrong targets at the wrong times.*

Doubt, neurosis, panic, nervousness, worry, fear—these are all feelings that people are likely to experience when taking on a new role, designing a costume, trying to land a director of photography job, writing a script—whatever the creative activity might be. Those reactions and emotions are normal, as are anger and frustration when things go south. As is talking about them with friends, professionals, and possibly even collaborators, within the appropriate settings and situations. Maybe there's venting in the group chat, or maybe whoever is feeling the jitters or frustration needs a night on the town. Or maybe, as happened on the set of Beyoncé's *Homecoming,* people need to be told—in a professional, direct way—that some of them are not hitting the correct targets.

Humans need to process and deal with the hard parts of being inside a creative endeavor. But physically taking out one's frustrations on others, verbally harassing or abusing them, using one's status or power to make everyone in the vicinity suffer, again and again, manipulating people and abusing them—that's not creativity. Nope, nope, and *nope.* Also not creativity: *any* of this Jared Leto nonsense.

"Jared Leto was so committed to playing Michael Morbius [in the 2022 film *Morbius*] that even when he had to go to the bathroom, he would use his crutches and slowly limp to get to the bathroom. But it was taking so long between for pee breaks, that a deal was made with him to get him a wheelchair so someone could wheel him there quicker and he agreed to that," director Daniel Espinosa said about the actor's activities on set when asked by entertainment reporter Mike Ryan (no relation).

"I think that what Jared thinks, what Jared believes, is that somehow the pain of those movements, even when he was playing normal Michael Morbius, he needed, because he's been having this pain his whole life," Espinosa responded. "Hey, man, it's people's processes."

Rather than rolling my eyes to the point that they pop out of my head and fall on the ground, I'm going to let *Uproxx* editor at large Brian Grubb take this one:

There's a lot to unpack here, some of which we can knock out via bullet point, so let's start there:

- This is deeply funny
- Imagine how much all the other people on set hated this
- Actors seem like very exhausting people, generally

There's also the other thing, which I point out because I have a for-real disability and use a wheelchair because I have to: Please knock this off. Please. Just act. I understand you want to get into the character's mind so you can comprehend their situation, but also, no. Get up. Jared. Listen to me. Do not do this.

Also, somewhat related, but still: Please consider casting actual people with disabilities in roles where a character is disabled. . . . let's go back to the bullet points again here:

- It's not like disabled actors can super-easily play non-disabled characters, so there's already a limited pool they're working with
- Some people defended Leto by pointing out that Daniel Day-Lewis did similar stuff on the set of *My Left Foot,* but I'll just go ahead and say it: that doesn't make either any better
- Let me play Batman

If you think the point of this book is to advocate for a pop-culture columnist from Pennsylvania to take on the role of Batman, you are not wrong. In all seriousness though, we can't look past the fact that Leto's unfortunate behavior was considered acceptable by his own director. This kind of knee-jerk enabling happens a lot.

One result of these tiresome mentalities is something that has come up in conversations with many creative people over the years: being well-adjusted, kind, unproblematic, and efficient often does not help them get ahead. Hollywood, they suspect, *wants* the jerks.

As one experienced writer/producer told me, "being an enfant terrible is still rewarded. There are far more brilliant people who are nice, but the industry is still not incentivized toward positive behavior." Hannah, the former assistant turned writer/producer, mentioned the career trajectory of a man she knows and respects. He's done okay, she said, and she certainly doesn't endorse him or anyone else acting like a monster. But in her view, he's not wrong to suspect that being a good egg has not been great for his career. "He doesn't have any of the markers of what Hollywood considers 'genius,'" Hannah observed. "His approach to work was to show up on time, to try to be under budget and then everybody goes home. He's not 'difficult.'"

Maybe he's too nice to be truly creative? I honestly think that is the mindset of any number of Hollywood gatekeepers. The truth is, the industry has barely begun to dismantle this noxious belief. Many, many people want to believe that the suffering they went through—or witnessed others go through or dish out—was worth it, because of "art" or whatever.

"I guess they have to excuse these things, somehow," Hannah observed. "Because when you have a bad experience, you have to consistently tell yourself, 'This is worth it because of some X factor. This is worth it because this person is a genius.'"

Is Jeff Garlin such a genius?

In the fall of 2021, I had what I thought was a simple question: Was Garlin still employed by *The Goldbergs*, a long-running ABC sitcom? I naively thought that there were only two possible answers to that question: yes or no. I had not allowed for a third potential answer: clusterfuck.

As I noted in chapter 8, I'd heard for years about a difficult environment at *The Goldbergs*. When word bubbled up again about Garlin and *The Goldbergs* in 2021, I looked into whether he'd left or been fired. For weeks, I could not get a definitive answer from anyone, including Sony, the studio that makes the show. Then Garlin emailed me.

Eventually, we ended up talking on the phone for nearly two hours. I asked Garlin, at length, about a confrontation with a stand-in, his habit of engaging in physical behaviors that made people uncomfortable, and his pattern of saying offensive, unprofessional things in the workplace. In the resulting piece, I cited sources who said that *The Goldbergs* could indeed be a punishing environment, especially for women. Garlin told me he was "a hugger" and he'd stop doing that. But he said the rest of his behavior is intrinsic to his creativity.

"We have a difference of opinion, Sony and myself. Okay. My opinion is, I have my process about how I'm funny, in terms of the scene and what I have to do. They feel that it makes for a quote 'unsafe' workspace. Now, mind you, my silliness making an unsafe workspace—I don't understand how that is," Garlin told me. When I said I'd heard that he'd been investigated by Sony HR, he stated that he had been—three times. The complaints HR brought to Garlin were, he said, "basically a lot of things that I disagree with—that are silly."

Again and again, Garlin told me, his behavior on set was both harmless and necessary. He also quite vehemently insisted that anyone who ever reported his behavior on any set should do so using their name. My explanations of why people probably did not want to use their names—as a well-known and well-connected industry figure, Garlin had far more power and influence than almost anyone who might want to report him—just did not land. In any event, within a few weeks, Garlin had exited the sitcom for good.

After that interview was published, my inbox filled up—again. Sources at *The Goldbergs* were not happy that Garlin had downplayed the stand-in confrontation, which they said was anything but light or funny. (Garlin was "angry and intense," in the words of a source who added that there were numerous witnesses to what occurred, one of whom called HR.) Before and after the piece came out, people who observed Garlin's behavior told me that they regularly found him to be a disruptive, disrespectful, or rude presence whose "process" often involved using unprofessional, vicious, or offensive language. The day after an HR session that was called because of a complaint about Garlin's behavior, one source said, the actor made sexualized comments to a female employee at *The Goldbergs*. As for Garlin's claims of respecting women, "in general, he is a nightmare for most female directors," this source told me.

In the 2021 interview, one of Garlin's defenses was that he was well-liked and behaved appropriately on the set of the movie he directed, *Handsome*. However, one person who contacted me said that was definitely not her experience and that the actor was unprofessional to her and other women on that set.

I spoke with more than a dozen sources during my reporting on Garlin and the vast majority shared the same view of his toxic workplace behavior. A few people I talked to during months of reporting had no issues with Garlin's behavior (but all understood that others did and respected those people's accounts). During the phone call with Garlin, I myself was all over the map. It was intensely frustrating when he did not—or would not—recognize how his behavior affected others and how protected he was by his status. At times he appeared to be genuinely trying to understand where he'd gone wrong, and if nothing else, he was at least willing to answer my questions, which is more than I can say of many other people with questionable industry histories.

I ended that call with mixed feelings that were tipped into a more negative region by the reports that reached me after the interview was published; they lined up with the earlier stories I'd heard about frustration with his conduct. And Garlin's claim that the *Goldbergs* crew universally loved him was not correct. A source who reached out after Garlin talked to me said he "uses his power and status to intimidate and demean everyone on this crew." Many sources praised *Goldbergs* star Wendi McLendon-Covey who, on social media, described Garlin as "someone who doesn't want to be there and wants to leave mid-scene." As for his work at *Curb Your Enthusiasm*, Garlin had a "very vindictive energy" there, a source told me. HBO HR had investigated complaints about Garlin's behavior multiple times, sources said. I heard from more than one person that there was at least one legal settlement with a former *Curb* employee regarding Garlin's conduct.

In the fall of 2022, Garlin stated on his social media that he lives with bipolar disorder. It is always my hope that anyone with a mental illness diagnosis gets the help that they need. Every person working for every entity in Hollywood deserves to have their boundaries and their mental and physical health respected. This philosophy also applies to all of Garlin's coworkers, past, present, and future. If anyone engages in patterns of behavior that are disrespectful, harmful, or unprofessional, employers need to step in and take meaningful actions to preserve and enforce a safe and acceptable work environment for all.

I reached out to Sony about the additional allegations here; they never replied.

What follows are allegations that three sources with knowledge of events at *Curb Your Enthusiasm* made to me in 2021 and 2022: that Garlin used demeaning, graphic, sexual language in the workplace; that his behavior was investigated by HBO; and that those investigations touched on the harassment or mistreatment of people connected to the show. I also heard that Garlin (an actor and executive producer on *Curb*) requested the names of people who had complained about him, and that it was not unusual for him to behave in an inappropriate, unprofessional, or vindictive fashion. I asked HBO about all these matters.

This was HBO's entire response: "Any reports of inappropriate conduct on our productions are investigated fully and addressed. Jeff Garlin remains a cast member and executive producer on *Curb Your Enthusiasm* and will return for any subsequent season."

I asked Garlin's PR representatives about these allegations as well. They did not reply.

New Line Cinema was the HBO of the '90s: brash, cool, and on a creative roll. It churned out popular hits like *Blade, Austin Powers, The Mask, Dumb and Dumber,* and *House Party;* in the early aughts, it won the box office and lots of Oscars for Peter Jackson's *Lord of the Rings* film trilogy. New Line was also, per the 1998 *Premiere* article mentioned earlier, a disastrous place to work if you were a woman.

I reread that piece in 2019, when Glenn Kenny, a critic and a former senior editor at *Premiere*, wrote about it for the *Columbia Journalism Review:* "A story about sexual harassment, assault, and a skewed power hierarchy, it had a good deal in common with the journalism that inspired #MeToo. But it didn't have the impact we had hoped it would at the time." That makes me sad, but it's not surprising. The world was a different place in 1998. As Salon editor in chief Erin Keane put it in her pop-culture saturated memoir, *Runaway,* Hollywood's reflexive romanticization of transgressive behavior by powerful men was one reason "why the arts and entertainment press, myself included, had refused for so long to understand that they were also working a crime beat."

By the time the HBO oral history *Tinderbox* came out in 2021, from one of the authors of *Live from New York,* I had been working that crime beat for a long time. All the industry anecdotes I had eaten like candy in the past—this time they tasted of ashes.

One phrase deployed a lot in stories and profiles during the television Golden Age that lasted from the late '90s until around 2012, was "making decisions from a place of fear." Top creatives and executives, you see, didn't do that. They were strong men who made strong, bold art. They were not cowed by normal-person emotions like fear. Manly Creative Guys ate fear for breakfast!

The industry has only recently—and haltingly—begun to contend with the knowledge that many people in the industry have been forced to make any number of decisions *based on fear*, because they'd been mistreated in the past and expected more of the same. Because they were the only person of color or disabled person or queer person in a space. Because biased encounters, abuse, and even violence, psychological and physical, were always possibilities. Because they were afraid of men like Harvey Weinstein, Bill Cosby, or Les Moonves.

Or Chris Albrecht, who physically assaulted women on two different occasions. The first incident—which took place within the offices of HBO itself—resulted in a settlement that the company hushed up. According to *Tinderbox*, Sasha Emerson, the HBO employee whom Albrecht assaulted in Los Angeles in 1991, later regretted not going to the police.

The second violent encounter occurred on a 2007 trip to an HBO boxing match in Las Vegas. Albrecht was arrested near a valet stand; the police report describes a "white male grabbing a white female by the throat with both hands." The attack occurred because "she 'pissed me off,' Albrecht told the police."

When news of both these situations hit the press, it created a firestorm in the media, and eventually Albrecht was out as head of HBO. Three years after departing, he consumed alcohol in front of a reporter and told her that the cover story put forward in 2007—when he'd talked about seeking help from Alcoholics Anonymous as he left HBO—was a useful fiction. He had no issues with alcohol, he revealed to the reporter. It had all been spin.

At least that 2010 *GQ* profile—in which Albrecht claimed "no one got hurt" in a physical assault that included a "loud thump" heard outside Emerson's office—gave space to a voice that had not been heard from, that of Emerson. "Chris Albrecht's lies about me and those events have endured for twenty years," Emerson said. "For him to comment on whether or how I was hurt is colossal hubris. I'd expect nothing less from someone as delusional as he is. He needs to believe his own narrative."

Albrecht wasn't alone. Powerful segments of the industry clung fiercely to that narrative for a very long time. After his stint at HBO, Albrecht made a great deal of money running the pay-cable company Starz and, beginning in 2019, had a series of powerful executive roles at Legendary Television. All this occurred despite the fact that, in that 2010 profile, he was described by "numerous sources" as a man whose interactions with women "could also be belittling—even destructive."

HBO undoubtedly has employed many very smart people and made a great deal of outstanding television. Throughout my career, I've dealt with a number of people from HBO whom I think are perceptive, thoughtful, and extremely capable. It has not been fun in the last few years to watch particularly ferocious waves of industry turmoil destroy or thoughtlessly disassemble much of what set HBO apart for so long.

All that said, HBO is also a network that very frequently has depicted women as naked sex objects, and not just in marquee shows like *Entourage* and *Game of Thrones*. A baseline misogyny was in its DNA from the start. In the '80s program *1st & Ten* (which had O. J. Simpson in the cast), producer Gary H. Miller said, "We had nudity throughout the show and I tried to work against it. They'd say, 'Let's have a party scene so the waitresses can walk around naked. . . . This is what people want to see.'" The creative team for the early HBO show *Dream On* was regularly told that some episodes didn't have "that cable edge," which executive producer Kevin Bright realized meant "it didn't have any nudity in the script." When the show was on the air, *Dream On* producer John Landis told the media that "we have breasts in the script just for the sake of seeing breasts. Excuse me, but what's so bad about that?"

Overall, there was a "frat house" feeling at HBO, where a boss summoned a secretary by saying, "Get your tits and ass in here," HR executive Shelley Fischel recalled. Both *Tinderbox* and 2022's *It's Not TV: The Spectacular Rise, Revolution and Future of HBO* go into how many affairs and relationships (and divorces) occurred thanks to HBO. "I was never involved with Michael [Fuchs, early CEO of HBO], but there were a lot of women who were," former HBO executive Ilene Kahn Power said. The implications of a culture like that—where bosses regularly slept with underlings whose careers they controlled—are sobering, especially when you consider the usual power disparities in industry workplaces. Especially when Fuchs's attitude, in his own words, was "there was one fucking shooting star at that company, me."

There were many tough, tenacious women at HBO; *Tinderbox* and the far superior *It's Not TV* make that clear. But it's hard not to speculate about the psychological and professional cost of that "toughness"—and about the fact that, no matter what era we're talking about and no matter how much they tried to fit in, women were far less protected than those inside various bro cliques. "For women, Michael was not easy to work for. I can still get enraged when I think of the awful jokes we women had to listen to at staff meetings," Fischel said.

Right from the start, all of this contributed to the programming decisions that were made. Fuchs thought broadcast networks catered to female viewers to an "absurd" degree, and the whole point of HBO was to be the "anti-broadcast network." Executive Susie Fitzgerald lobbied for shows about female protagonists, but she said "we would go to research meetings, and they were like, 'The man controls the remote control, and the woman will watch what they watch.'" As HBO's lineup of stand-up comedians began to include women, she asked why one couldn't lead her own show. "But they're not going to take their tops off," Albrecht told Fitzgerald.

Well beyond the '90s, HBO was a punishing environment for anyone who was not part of the chest-thumping boys' club. Carolyn Strauss, a top executive during the network's most celebrated era, could be enigmatic, which is far from a crime, but she was summarily fired for reasons that still don't make a lot of sense. "If Carolyn was a man, she would have never been let go," Sue Naegle said. Keep in mind that if it weren't for Strauss, Naegle, and Gina Balian—all of whom advocated for the show and its creative team at key moments—there's a good chance HBO's *Game of Thrones*, one of the biggest hits in the history of television, would not have survived its long, challenging development process.

But Naegle herself had a short tenure at HBO. She said, "I was never able to get a show on the air written by a woman or run by a woman except for *Girls* the entire time I was there." She attempted to land the drama *The Affair*, but that did not go well. In a meeting, the show's cocreator, Sarah Treem, talked about how the drama would explore infidelity from various perspectives, including that of a married woman. HBO executive Mike Lombardo "was just like, 'That's immoral. . . . That's disgusting,'" Naegle recalled. Agent Rick Rosen "just stops and says, 'Mike, the most successful show in the history of the network is about a gangster adulterer, murderer, mafia boss.'" Tony Soprano behaving badly, that's creativity. A woman using her sexuality on her own terms? Disgusting.

Sheila Nevins accomplished a lot as the longtime head of HBO's documentary division. And that is why it was particularly jaw-dropping and disappointing to read many of her comments in *Tinderbox*. She said that sleeping with a man in order to get an early industry job "didn't ruin my life," and she dismissed Albrecht's actions because "he wasn't Trump." "Even if it was true that he fucked everybody in sight, so what?" Nevins asked. "He left me alone." This defense of an often-appalling workplace culture was especially hard to take given that, within the pages of *Tinderbox*, Nevins's own brutal ousting was recounted. The culture that she explained away, if not defended—it sure didn't defend her.

Then again, *Tinderbox* wasn't a book in which the most tiresome iterations of chest-thumping "creativity" were questioned in any meaningful way. The tone of credulity and wide-eyed appreciation ended up making it come off as yet another endorsement of how things operated at HBO. The vibe of the book was, "But it all worked out, because look how much good work came out of that place."

Some questions that big chunks of the media have been bad at asking: What good or great work *didn't* we get from HBO and other high-end culture purveyors due to how those workplaces operated and who they rewarded? What shows did Sasha Emerson dream about making? And what kind of mark would she have made on the industry, given a real shot at the top? What programs and films and documentaries would we have gotten from those who were driven out or *never hired* by these kinds of macho, vindictive workplaces? The overlong *Tinderbox* is dominated by many who quietly—or loudly—endorse the big-swinging-dick school of Hollywood creativity; it often reads like a bunch of men crowing about how they made systems of exclusion, domination, and brutality work for them. As a story supposedly about creative ferment, it ultimately began to feel not just demoralizing but deadeningly predictable.

The lack of pushback—or just a minimal amount of skepticism—especially informs the section on Albrecht's ouster. I have no doubt some HBO colleagues felt complicated emotions, including grief, at his departure. But that section reads as so sympathetic to him that you'd be hard-pressed to keep one fact at the forefront of your mind: *Albrecht inflicted physical violence on two different women in work-related situations.* Lots of people knew about one or both of those incidents, and seemed to be just fine with all of it. The book treats his ouster as though it's a tragedy—for Albrecht.

Who, at HBO, was forced to *operate from a place of fear*—could it have been junior employees? Women? Anyone who wasn't white? Anyone who wasn't one of the big-swinging-dick guys? What was it *really* like for the majority of people who worked there—or were driven out or excluded by these kinds of mindsets? And how much did this predictable, exhausting, reflexive veneration of brutality seep into the work?

The authors of *It's Not TV*, thankfully, ask many of these questions, and, through their rigorous reporting, made me abjectly furious when I learned more about who Emerson was and what she was put through. She grew up going to all kinds of theater productions and ended up at the Yale School of Drama; when she moved to LA, she got to know an even bigger group of creative people through her work as a CBS TV movie executive. When Emerson took a job at HBO, she drew on her wide circle of collaborators to work on anthology series such as *Tales from the Crypt* and *Vietnam War Story*. Later, in her role as creative leader of HBO Independent Productions, a studio designed to make shows for other networks, she instigated the creation of the TV show *Roc*, starring her Yale Drama friend Charles Dutton. The Emersons of *Roc* were "one of the few stable Black families on American prime-time TV," *It's Not TV*'s authors note. And the clan was named after the executive who helped them get on the air.

Clearly, Emerson was on a trajectory that could have taken her to the heights of the industry. But that didn't happen. She and Albrecht had an affair; after it ended, "in an apparent fit of jealous rage, Albrecht attacked Emerson, charging at her from across the room, grabbing her by the neck, knocking over her executive chair, and strangling her down to the floor," according to *It's Not TV*. "Before she could lose consciousness, he let her go."

Emerson took a settlement and left, but HBO and Albrecht were not done. Later that year, a trade story floated the fiction that she left HBO because she and management had "differences of opinion." There's that phrase again, the one Murray and Garlin and so many others have trotted out over the years.

Emerson understandably viewed that shiv in the back, delivered via a trade paper, as "a violation." Her attempts to rebuild her career were challenged by the "whisper campaign" that Albrecht led against her, according to *It's Not TV:* "It's almost as if the stigma of being battered at the HBO offices had attached to Emerson rather than to her attacker." One HBO employee witnessed "firsthand as Albrecht made up all sorts of false things about Emerson, saying she was unhinged, unprofessional and worse." A TV writer told the authors that "there was a real campaign to blacken her" reputation and make her seem like a "chaotic, problematic person." She took another job—at New Line, of all places—but later left Hollywood to pursue a career in interior design. I understand that decision. But I wonder about—and feel grief to have missed out on—the stories she might have brought into the world in the last couple of decades.

As for Albrecht, in 2011, at age fifty-nine, he married a twenty-five-year-old woman who'd been a competitive equestrian alongside one of his daughters. Jeffrey Bewkes, an HBO veteran who was then Time Warner CEO—and who described the network as a "boys' club"—stood up in Albrecht's wedding. Also in attendance: Leslie Moonves, Brett Ratner, and Harvey Weinstein. Around that time, Albrecht's efforts to buy Playboy Enterprises ran aground, but his support among a large array of the industry's power players was unwavering. The men who determined the content of an enormous amount of television and film, those with not just the power to greenlight but who had great power over how women "were depicted on screen," offered "a showy phalanx of support for . . . Albrecht, the celebrated TV executive and admitted batterer."

In October 2022, around the time that *The Hollywood Reporter* revealed some of the contents of *It's Not TV* pertaining to Emerson and Albrecht, Legendary Television placed Albrecht "on leave"; two months later, he departed the company. The fact that it has taken decades for his well-documented brand of "creativity" to face any meaningful consequences—and the fact that "consequences" for men like him are often temporary at best—is ample evidence of how much has *not* changed.

It's yet another demonstration of who gets to have a vision, protection, power, and a massive paycheck—and who gets to be afraid.

If we don't challenge the idea that creativity is often, in Hollywood, linked to a whole range of awful behaviors and attitudes, we end up with tinpot dictators no one has even heard of. The passes that men like Bill Murray and Chris Albrecht got for decades eventually trickled down to garden-variety assholes who were—are—convinced their patterns of shitty behavior have something to do with creativity, passion, vision, *blah blah blah*. The irony that causes me to cry-scream frequently is that the output of these people is typically intensely mediocre and derivative. Let's hear it for Art!

In any event, I have a few ideas about why the conflation of art with abuse lingers, especially in the realm of commercial Hollywood. We have to remember one big truth about the entertainment industry—not just as it is presently constructed but as it has always been constructed. Those who run it care about power and money. Profits that used to be measured in millions now are measured in billions. Every penny has to be squeezed from every possible corner of the industry. People don't talk about that in their acceptance speeches when they win awards, but that's the foundational concept from which everything else flows. Those at the top want to acquire, retain, and grow their power, and they will go to almost any length to protect that—and their fortunes.

"HBO had already helped to bury the story of Albrecht strangling one woman," the authors of *It's Not TV* observe of Jeffrey Bewkes's attempts to salvage Albrecht's 2007 Vegas debacle. "Perhaps the company could be convinced to look past another." Not recent enough for you? In 2017 and 2018, "CBS and its senior leadership knew about multiple allegations of sexual assault made against Mr. [Leslie] Moonves and intentionally concealed those allegations from regulators, shareholders, and the public for months," New York Attorney General Letitia James's office stated in November 2022. By the way, CBS approved senior PR person Gil Schwartz selling a block of stock in June 2018, and James "said the action constituted insider trading because Mr. Schwartz had known about the accusations against Mr. Moonves, which could potentially sink the company's stock price."

These attitudes and actions, these kinds of cover-ups—they are par for the course, or long have been. If those with power think it saves money to ignore monstrous behavior—if it saves money to not care about who gets damaged, broken, or otherwise abused during the creative process—well, that's what happens. With almost six hundred scripted shows on the air in 2022 alone, and dozens of films and shows getting greenlit every day, the motivation to enable bad behavior—and call it by a more respectable name—remains strong. How does the belligerent boys' club mentality trickle down to the rank and file? Well, in 2018, I reported that CBS showrunner Brad Kern talked about wanting to hire a specific actor because Moonves wanted "to fuck" her.

Having observed the industry for a long time, I have seen that a lot of what I'm describing here is about preserving careers, not saving money. After all, according to *It's Not TV*, what Bewkes was worried about in 2007 was the effect of Albrecht's violence on Bewkes's professional ascent. Speaking of budgets, perhaps this is the right moment to mention that, not long before Albrecht choked a woman in public on a work trip, a high-end sex worker claimed that Time Warner's chief financial officer at the time was not only a frequent customer but used his corporate "salary to shower her with luxury gifts." There are waves of cost-cutting in the industry at times—one is gaining steam as I write this—but in my experience, they tend to gravely affect assistants and other working stiffs, not guys like that.

In any event, I don't think harboring abusers *does* save money in the long run. High turnover, missed deadlines, people afraid to do their best work for fear of being bullied or abused, people avoiding a company or a set due to miserable working conditions—these are just a few of the reasons putting up with toxic, abusive people is not just a terrible idea but often an expensive proposition. Sometimes that price is viewed as worth it: The abusive showrunner who drove away many colleagues who had pay-or-play contracts—that guy was costly as hell on many fronts, not least because those coworkers had to be paid even when he told them to stop coming to work. But that particular asshole was connected to a much more powerful mogul the studio wanted to keep in the fold, so those checks were written. The abusive jerk I'm thinking of was a mediocrity who enjoyed misusing his status, and his awful, sexist, racist behavior was not just tolerated, it was *rewarded*, with more shows, more power. With every credit added to his résumé, he got worse. I wish I could say he's the only one who fits that profile.

That jerk is out of the industry for now but I periodically hear about his attempts to return—which might work someday. After all, the myths around creativity may have endured a few punches in the past few years, but they live on, in part because they are useful. They allow people to scurry away from the moral consequences of what they've enabled or ignored. Many's the time I've heard about what some Hollywood "creative" is doing with their power, and thought, "Why don't they just retire? Go play golf? They've got to be richer than rich." And then I remember that some people are in the industry because it supplies them with not just power but *an array of largely powerless targets*. And by calling the worst things they do part of their creative "process," they're able to get away with a lot of what they do, for a long time.

Nope. Plays, movies, and TV shows were still made after Scott Rudin "took a step back" from the industry. People still got to star in awards-bait films after Harvey Weinstein went to jail. People at CBS still churned out procedurals after men such as Les Moonves, Brad Kern, and Peter Lenkov were bounced from that company. Chris Albrecht departing his Legendary job won't kill television.

Maybe it'll help Hollywood. Or at least make it a little safer for a few more people.

Evan Rachel Wood told me that every day she worked on the set of HBO's *Westworld*, she felt respected. She also found a safe haven among her collaborators on the HBO limited series *Mildred Pierce*, which she worked on during a very dark time in her life.

In 2018, Wood began talking publicly about the assaults and domestic violence she had experienced in an intimate relationship that had ended by that time. Afraid for her career and for her safety, for years, she avoided naming Brian Warner, a.k.a. Marilyn Manson, as her abuser. But people knew they had been together, on and off, for some time. "I would believe every single thing she has said about Marilyn Manson, because we were there," *Mildred Pierce* producer Ilene Landress said.

All in all, it was not difficult to connect the dots about who Wood was likely talking about when she testified before legislative bodies in Washington, DC, and in California, in 2018 and 2019, respectively. In her testimony, she described being beaten, raped, and abused by that intimate partner.

People at her talent agency and at HBO had known she had been with Manson. Thus she was shocked when the aging rocker—whose work in TV picked up as his music career waned—was cast in HBO's *The New Pope* in 2019. For some time, Wood told me, she avoided going to HBO parties because she was afraid of running into Manson. One of the stars of an HBO show was, through no fault of her own, operating from a place of fear.

"It threw me for a loop," Wood said of *The New Pope* casting. "It made me feel really unsafe."

Despite that fear, and despite the messages she'd absorbed from the industry about not making waves, Wood decided to do something genuinely brave. On February 1, 2021, she joined several other women who, via social media, named Manson as the man who'd hurt them. There were many motivations behind that act, but a primary driver was something that happened after she gave her public testimony on domestic violence: she found out that there were other women whose experiences with Manson echoed Wood's own. She learned they were trying to make what they'd endured public but weren't getting much traction with the press.

"Once I realized that a number of other people had experienced what I had experienced, it was an earth-shattering moment," Wood told me. "I thought that I was the only one that this had happened to. And that idea was reinforced by the media who—while I was being abused—was calling me crazy, was calling me a whore, was saying 'What's wrong with her?'"

In 2021, Wood and the other women received support from segments of the public and some in the industry, but anyone who followed the story on social media also saw reactions like these: "They had it coming," "They're lying," and "He's a rock star—what did they expect?"

This was a Creative Guy—why was anyone surprised?

I should not have been shocked by how vile so many of the reactions were, but that subset of comments threw me. Not least because I've been in bands, I've written scripts, I've spent decades around musicians, filmmakers, designers, artists, creators, and writers. The best ones are human, flawed, messy, all of the things; but in my experience, they are often wonderful people. Or at least they manage to hit the baseline known as "not consistently damaging to be around." But so many powerful people in the industry, for so long, through their own behavior and through that of the people they enabled, have propagated a message that has sunk into every corner of our culture: creativity usually comes packaged with a side of abuse.

Few people in the industry know more creative people than Wood, who is active as a producer, musician, and actor. She's gone on tour and she's met lots of famous rock stars. "Some of them are really sweet. They have families. They go home, they watch *Family Guy,* and eat grilled cheese. And they leave it on the stage," she said.

Creativity and empathy, kindness and goodness can be found—and she's found those things with many of her HBO colleagues. But within the industry as a whole, having a creative spark and being able to express it without trepidation—working from a place of security and not *fear*—that's not guaranteed.

"That's just always been the war—between the creatives and the money people and who has the power, and how far can you get ahead without playing the game in some way, or how far can you get ahead with integrity," Wood said. "I still believe that integrity has currency and a lot of people think that it doesn't, and that you're only going to get ahead by playing the game and by compromising who you are. But I beg to differ. I think it's just a slower burn, and there are good people that gravitate towards that. But it's hard. You're going to have to sit a lot of rounds out because you're not going to play the game. You just have to be okay with watching from the sidelines sometimes."

Harold Perrineau is a wonderful actor, and *From* is good TV program, and nobody had to be abused for that to be the case. That said, Perrineau and Daniel Dae Kim told me they were dismayed by something they have both witnessed. As people from historically excluded communities have risen in the industry, they sometimes adopt the behavior of the kinds of toxic people who, for decades, didn't just set the tone but enforced a set of awful norms.

It's as if those people have absorbed the worst messages about "how successful Number Ones act. It's really unfortunate. Especially if you come from one of these historically excluded groups, because right now people will be on your side. They're looking for you to succeed," Perrineau told me. "But the message some people got is, 'I have to act this way, and then I'm really successful.' It's usually abusive. And it causes toxicity where there might not necessarily be any."

"There are many different ways people can wield power inappropriately," Kim said. "It's not limited to men or white men. There have also been women that I've worked with, including on *Lost*, whose behavior might today be considered toxic. Bullies can come in all races and genders."

They certainly can. But speaking of power and the ways it can be wielded poorly by a member of the industry's most elite and established tier, it's time to talk about *Saturday Night Live*.

10

Live from New York

The Persistent Myth of Comedic Liberation

I would want something to be done,
and I don't think that that happened.

—Jane Doe

She wanted to work in comedy. The mordant wit she displayed throughout our three-hour conversation, which sometimes went to dark places, showed she may have made it in that world. When she called the defendants in the civil suit she'd filed "jabronis," it was unexpected—and funny.

Here she was, taking on a gigantic media company—NBCUniversal—and one of the most powerful and legendary men in the American entertainment industry, Lorne Michaels (among others). But Jane Doe, like so many survivors I've talked to, was anything but humorless.

She recalled, two decades ago, going to an official *Saturday Night Live* afterparty, where she chatted with Michaels about the Jimmy Fallon fan site she ran. After another such gathering, she and Horatio Sanz headed to an after-after party. She consumed alcohol at both parties, and she alleged that at the latter, cast member Sanz put his hands on her breasts and genitals, in full view of several *SNL* cast members.

"My control top pantyhose did more to keep me safe than any of those people that I idolized," she said.

Later that night, she passed out in a taxi on the way to Penn Station. She told me she woke up to Sanz's vigorous efforts to remove her pants. (I contacted Sanz's attorney, Andrew Brettler, with questions about the allegations in this chapter; he did not reply. In other news stories, through Brettler, Sanz has denied all misconduct, and the attorney has said Doe's allegations are "categorically false.")

Jane Doe was seventeen. She'd been in the orbit of Sanz and *SNL* for more than two years.

Studio 8H was smaller than I thought it would be. That was not necessarily surprising; in three decades of covering the entertainment industry, I can only think of a few instances in which sets were larger—or people were taller—than I expected them to be.

I visited in 2008, but *SNL* still goes out live from the same space, which is, in my somewhat timeworn recollection, around the same size as a suburban Costco.

Like Costco, *SNL* deals in bulk quantities. Come 2025, the show will be fifty years old, a milestone reached by few other pop-culture commodities. *Doctor Who* has been around since 1963 in various forms, but the sci-fi institution has taken breaks over the years. The James Bond franchise puts out 007 films regularly, but they're not a weekly part of our lives. The *Star Wars* franchise—born shortly after *SNL*—has only recently begun to release live-action projects more frequently.

SNL, on the other hand, is close to racking up one thousand total episodes. Hundreds of people have taken its stages during that time. And like *Doctor Who*, *SNL*—a flagship property for NBC and its parent company, Comcast—has turned the cast regeneration process into a subject of fervent speculation. The interest is there because its stages and the ranks of its writers have, for decades, launched an enormous array of creators, directors, producers, and performers into the upper tiers of various comedy and entertainment industry ecosystems.

All these factors make it difficult to write about *SNL* as an institution. During its lifetime, it has showcased a staggering variety of performers, ideas, and comic tones. Recently, a lot of what *SNL* has churned out has felt more than a little tired and predictable. But a critic offering that assessment is itself predictable. "A Prosperous *Saturday Night* Grows Tame" is a headline from 1993.

As a comedy nerd and an observer of the industry, Grant, who wrote for the show, kept circling the idea that it was nearly impossible—no, *definitely* impossible—to write about *SNL* as an institution. As a cultural force and as a place of employment, there was simply too much to examine, synthesize, and distill. Anyone attempting to write about the show would have to find a way to slice off a smaller segment and focus on that.

I'll attempt to do that by focusing on one person, and, to some degree, another mistake I made. For decades, I too easily accepted certain narratives surrounding *SNL* and its key executive producer, Lorne Michaels. I will only indict myself, but I don't think I'm alone in having gone down a mistaken path; I believe I have a lot of company on that road. That's how good Michaels has been at playing the game for half a century.

Michaels is one of the rare people in the entertainment industry who is far more powerful than his public image would indicate. "Executive producer" is hardly a title that does his many roles justice; it'd be like designating the late Queen Elizabeth II a "notable Briton." For almost fifty years, Michaels has decided who got hired at *SNL*. Staffers advise him on who the hosts and musical guests should be, but he makes all the big calls. Generations of comedy performers have spent thousands of hours sweating where Michaels will place their sketches in the show's lineup.

But that's just the start of Michaels's role as a kingmaker. He and very frequently his company, Broadway Video, have credits on *The Tonight Show Starring Jimmy Fallon, Late Night with Seth Meyers, Wayne's World, Mean Girls, 30 Rock, Los Espookys, Portlandia,* and *Saturday Night Live* itself. And that roster is just a tiny slice of industry projects Michaels has had a hand in the past half century.

For all these reasons, during many different NBC regimes, his power has been near-absolute. Or, depending on whom you talk to, absolute. When Grant joined the show in the '90s, he observed that "the lighting designer was an eighty-something World War II veteran who worked there until I think he was in his nineties, and whose vision was failing. And he was the lighting designer of the show!" During Grant's time at *SNL,* the rules, such as they were, were "insane." People smoked in their offices in the early aughts, Grant said, despite the existence of a Manhattan indoor smoking ban.

This was all part of Grant's argument that "it's a little bit reductive" to examine the program as if it's any other show; it's a "weird Hollywood outcropping" that somehow lasted for a long, long time. "You can't just say, let's look at *SNL,* because *SNL* is fourteen different shows spread out over fifty years." I do understand that take; it makes sense.

Yet the unifying force behind almost every iteration is Michaels. That lighting designer and others had such long tenures at *SNL,* which is located in Manhattan's 30 Rockefeller Center, in large part because Michaels is, as Grant put it, "the prime minister of his own nation. He has his own laws and his own rules." Grant and I disagreed at times, but we were in harmony on one point: the idea of Comcast or NBCUniversal executives having meaningful power over Michaels seems naive at best.

"All of the current Comcast executives, when they talk about him, it's like he's, I don't know, Mandela or something—you know, this *figure*, who looms largely over show business and entertainment and NBC," Grant said. "He's the last real direct connection between what we have now and what we had then, this magical, mysterious, nostalgic time—the halcyon days of television."

All the more reason to examine the image and legacy of Michaels, who has spent many years exerting massive power within the center of the entertainment industry and who resides at the epicenter of the New York media scene. The image he has constructed, in my opinion, is the product of conscious effort and strategy. Grant did not agree.

"He likes the living in New York part of the job, and the working in 30 Rock part, and the connection to old Hollywood and old show business," Grant said. "He has a reverence for the history and he likes the stars, and he likes being in a place that culturally matters." But, in Grant's view, outside of the moves Michaels makes to protect his late-night fiefdom (which, as noted, includes Fallon and Meyers's programs), "I don't think he sits there and says, 'Here's how I'll maneuver.' He's not a maneuverer. He's a guy who likes wearing black Prada suits and getting recognized and eating at fancy restaurants and being a part of a cultural institution."

Regardless of what Grant or I think, the pose struck by Michaels in the many books and articles in which he is quoted is impressively consistent: the cast are the stars, he is merely the majordomo, trying to help them make the magic happen. "It's very hard, and you don't really know what you're doing 'til the day of [the broadcast]. But we have a really talented group of people and the cast has been amazing and the writing staff has come through. So I think everybody cares about it. There's a certain pride in doing it." That's a quote he gave me in 2008, and it's very typical of this subgenre of journalism.

In part because Michaels has so often been so quick to share credit, it is easy to infer that he runs a shop that reflects the public image he has built: low-key, modest, cerebral, hardworking. For nearly fifty years, Michaels has offered the US media a mild-mannered, soft-spoken, extremely Canadian image—he's positioned himself as the anti–Scott Rudin, if you will. "Toronto in the 1950's was a very safe and ordered place, so the chief thing to be overcome in my childhood was boredom," Michaels told the *New York Times* in 1993. "Defying authority in a small way is a big Canadian thing."

There is merit in humility, whether it's real or a pose. If nothing else, not hogging the credit that belongs to those who write the jokes and perform the sketches is laudable. And *SNL*'s legacy is certainly studded with joy and wild, smart, goofy humor. "It's a one-week performance camp where everybody's operating from a sense of just incredible amounts of glee and manic energy as well as vast amounts of fear and flop sweat. That's *Saturday Night Live* and there is absolutely nothing like it," Tom Hanks said.

Michaels, as the ringmaster of that circus, has been a lot of things to a lot of people over the years. *Live from New York* is full of another ritual of *SNL* coverage: people trying, in dozens of ways, to describe Michaels's influence, personality, and management style. Was he caring, pompous, helpful, supportive, a good listener, aloof, a remote father figure, arrogant, a hard worker, a distant egoist, or a cruel tyrant? Yes. All those things have been true to someone, or to multiple people, at one time or another.

I do understand that when you attempt to say a definitive thing about a film, a show, or a creative person, you risk flattening that entity. But after nearly five decades, isn't *SNL*—which Michaels has run for most of its long life—ripe for an examination that bypasses the romance of its history and engages in at least a little rigor?

"Of course, yes. Any institution that's been around as long as it has and has the power that it has—and has had intermittently, but somewhat consistently—for fifty years deserves scrutiny," Grant replied. "There's no question."

SNL does receive some forms of scrutiny, but with a few exceptions, there's not much variety or depth to it. People in the press—an overworked group at the best of times—have usually grown up with *SNL* and are likely to have affection for it. These days, there isn't a ton of serious coverage of *SNL;* it's sort of like a slightly tedious aged uncle you treat politely due to his sheer longevity. The coverage, what there is of it, is typically about ascendant cast members, or consists of posts aggregating *SNL* clips and so on.

Various books have exhaustively chronicled the making of the show, and especially the infighting and inspirations (and illegal substances) that fueled *SNL*'s early days. But even the *yikes* stuff that has come out in books, magazines, profiles, interviews, and other coverage—those revelations don't stick to Michaels, or even the show, really. If anything, they burnish *SNL*'s cool-kids aura and Michaels's legend as the gray eminence of North American comedy. By not taking credit for the show's output, he's cleverly divorced himself from any of the consequences for its missteps. It's a neat trick that not many other industry kingpins have successfully managed, certainly not for this long.

Nobody wants to be the killjoy that pokes holes in the joke-makers' stories of themselves. But I will be that killjoy, one who'll point out that Michaels's long tenure as a power player and *SNL*'s enduring importance are intertwined with a culture of impunity within the world of comedy, in which abuse and toxicity are not just permitted but often celebrated.

These days, millionaires holding forth in podcasts and on sold-out comedy tours regularly talk about how they are persecuted and silenced while holding microphones in their hands. This idea that comedians are truth-tellers who should have special status has roots in the comedy of the '60s, '70s, and '80s, when certain stand-ups—and *SNL*'s Not Ready for Primetime Players—made their marks as shit-stirrers. In 2020, Michaels was asked about the fact that younger people are now, as they did in the '60s and '70s, "seriously questioning institutions," and about the fact that *SNL* is itself an institution. How does he reconcile those things?

"I think in exactly the same way," Michaels answered. "We came on in '75, and the last helicopter of Saigon was '75. And there was Watergate, of course. When I got here, the city felt abandoned and broke. But it was also a really exciting time to be in New York, and we were part of the rebirth."

That's the myth of *SNL*, which is intertwined with the cultural mythology of Lenny Bruce and George Carlin and Eddie Murphy, who were among the people who did, in their heydays, test the limits of what was acceptable in the public discourse. At *SNL*, some sketches over the years have contained memorable political fury and bite. But the idea that a comedian, an improv performer, or a sketch writer is *inherently* a rebel in pursuit of noble, truth-telling goals—that is an assumption that Michaels is still putting forward, long past the point when a lot of other folks have begun to question whether it's true.

Still, as it amplified and rode that simplistic message—that it was the admirable (and acceptable) face of rebellion—*SNL* produced a huge number of stars. And in both fan and media realms, "a lot of people have this mindset of, 'Well, it has put all these great comedians into the world, which makes up for its flaws,'" said Seth Simons, who has done in-depth reporting on the comedy world. On top of that, "many people have this mindset of watching comedy as sports—you watch to see whether the sketches are funny or how the host does or what characters they do. There's no culture of critical thinking or consumption around comedy, the way there is slightly more of that around television or film or theater."

There are occasionally pieces that take on comedy and those who make it with searching intelligence, but Simons is largely right. And that's troubling, given the comedy world's reputation for inflating its importance as a force for good and downplaying its long-standing status as a haven for bigoted or abusive people. There have been some important examinations of how biased and sexist many comedy institutions have been—including the Chicago improv mainstay The Second City, which has begun reckoning with alumni who have called it to account for a legacy of entrenched racism—and many stories about assault, toxicity, and harassment in comedy circles have been published in recent years. Just one example: Gilbert Rozon, head of Toronto's Just for Laughs festival, has faced numerous allegations of harassment and sexual assault. In 2020, he was acquitted of criminal charges in one case, but there are still several civil suits regarding women's allegations of assault, including one woman's allegation of being "brutally raped" by him.

Despite the many scandals and exposés of systematic misbehavior, bias, assault, and toxicity, the myth of comedy as a meritocracy full of brave, admirable rebels fighting for justice and freedom simply refuses to die. In fact, it's not uncommon for those who've succeeded in comedy to describe it as an important set of harbingers, a weather forecast system that tells us what we're going to experience next. As Jon Stewart put it when he accepted the Mark Twain Prize for American Humor in 2022, comedy is "a bellwether. We're the banana peel in the coal mine"; in that speech, he also warned of the dangers of authoritarianism.

These kinds of "bellwether" ideas are typically voiced in comments meant to laud the bravery of a joke, a comedian, a sketch, or the comedy profession as a whole. And we can all point to jokes, shows, and bits that have not just been funny but paradigm-shifting. But it's not all noble; far too many comedy scenes, clubs, and mindsets are, at their roots, far from purely admirable. If we're going to talk about the canaries sent into coal mines to see if the air was safe, we need to acknowledge that *sometimes they died.*

A lot of the "revolution" in comedy, especially in the past decade, has sought to cement the status and unassailability of certain comedy performers and creators—most of them heterosexual men—who want to speak, act, and conduct themselves with total impunity, no matter how harmful, actively damaging, and noxious their actions or views.

"To the extent that comedy has been the canary in the coal mine, it has been telling us exactly how bad things are going to get," Simons told me. For pointing out that, as he put it in a 2021 essay, "comedy is a safe space for abuse"—one in which sexual assault is common, in which racism is common, in which transphobia is common, in which a number of bookers, podcasters, and club gatekeepers have strong links to inflammatory right-wing figures—Simons has been consistently harassed on social media and doxed in real life. As have members of his family. I have also been harassed when I've shared his work, much of which thoughtfully and deeply examines the questionable values, assumptions, and power disparities within a number of commercial comedy worlds.

"Ten years ago, the great intellectual discourse in comedy [was] about whether it was okay to make fun of Muslims and tell horrible rape jokes," Simons told me. "Now, the last few years, the grand intellectual discourse has been about whether it is okay to say trans people are bad and not real. And we're just going headlong into that awful direction. As a society, I think comedy *has* been predicting things for us—not really predicting, but it's a preview. It's the space where it has been okay to be a horrible person."

What any number of comedy figures, in quite a few different realms, have consistently rebelled against in recent years is the idea that other people matter; that those other people are human beings worthy of consideration; and that those other people get to *have a reaction* to the harmful, shitty, and dangerous things that stand-ups and comedy performers say about them.

Of course, those doing comedy are free to say what they like. But people get to respond to those statements. And these days, if people don't like what they hear, they're able to communicate, on any number of platforms, that what a comedian said was dumb, poorly formulated, tired, racist, biased, sexist, or whatever. An enormous percentage of these comedy "rebels" can't handle that. They regard communication with their audience as a one-way street. The audience is, of course, allowed to laugh and clap—but that's it.

Some comedy elites—and those who aspire to the perches they occupy—have very much decided on a policy of "free speech for me and not for thee." The result of all these trends in comedy cultures is a form of "liberation" that revolves around the enabling and cheering on of just about anything certain performers do—on- and off-stage. No matter how damaging, no matter how dangerous to other people's safety.

Who exactly gets to enjoy that freedom? Well, when it was pointed out by many (including members of the cast) that *SNL* has very rarely hired Black women—an issue that finally made the headlines a decade ago—*SNL* put text on the screen saying this was "not an ideal situation and [producers] look forward to rectifying it in the near future." This was *almost forty years after the show premiered.* As I've said elsewhere, that situation was not inevitable, nor was it the work of the disembodied hand of fate. This was the result of a series of choices, decisions, and preferences, all of which were made plain over a long period of time.

The awful but logical outcome of many of these comedy-world dynamics—and the voices they elevate—is that when Louis C.K. came back to the comedy scene, a group of comedians at a club chanted, as the sole female comic on the bill listened, "Fuck the #MeToo movement!" "I left to cry and quickly wash my face before performing," Sara Wren wrote.

The result is many observers feeling, as comedian and survivor Julia Wolov put it, "There has been zero change in the way comedy is run. . . . Nobody cares." It's hard to refute that assertion. Somewhere along the way, the idea that those who work in comedy should be able to push boundaries and explore difficult topics morphed into something wretched: the myth became a weapon. It was transformed, over time, into the idea that those with power or status in comedy should be able to do whatever they want to anyone else they encounter, and face no consequences for their actions or words.

SNL is not solely, or even mainly, responsible for these toxic mind-sets and dynamics. But within the halls of 30 Rock, I personally believe Michaels has done his share to enable them. And fuel them.

Whether or not creating an awful work environment was Michaels's goal is irrelevant. For decades, *SNL* has been a frequently terrible, punishing experience for a lot of people who worked there or ended up in the show's orbit. This fact is in full view, in any number of books, interviews, and other coverage of the show. What is wrong is systemically and institutionally wrong, and Michaels runs that institution. He has had the power to change the *SNL* culture for the better on a number of fronts, but the hours, the pressure, the lack of inclusion, the punishing, manipulative atmosphere—not enough changes have been made to prevent the worst excesses of all that from negatively affecting many people, for many years.

I'd challenge anyone to come up with a truthful history of the show that does not include stories of gross misconduct, racism, sexism, abusive dynamics, various forms of assault, substance abuse, and mental health struggles exacerbated by punishing working conditions. Nobody has cared much about the people affected by these things, not in general. At least that's how it looked to me, when I spent months talking to people who have worked there and reading what many of them have said, often on the record.

A 1995 *New York* magazine piece on *SNL* quoted cast member Ellen Cleghorne as saying, "There's no black writers on the show—this is 1995, and I feel like I'm in a really bad sci-fi movie where all the black people already got killed, and I'm next." Colin Jost and Ellen Cleghorne don't seem to have a lot in common, but even Jost wrote about finding the environment frightening. He felt anxiety when he talked up sketches that he liked, but that Michaels might not like; he worried about what might happen to the writers of those sketches, a fact that indicates that he couldn't necessarily protect those people's jobs, despite the fact that Jost was one of the show's head writers for years. This resulted in the kind of panicked response that required medical help: "My heart was racing and skipping beats and I didn't know what to do," he writes in his memoir, *A Very Punchable Face*. "I lay down on the couch outside Lorne's office and his assistant brought me water and called for a doctor. I remember thinking, *If I die, will they mention me in the show on Saturday?*"

Janeane Garofalo described waiting in Michaels's office for hours, which prompted an epiphany: "You've shown him your weakness. You've shown him that you will wait four or five hours and that you'll take it. There's your first mistake," the one that will ensure that "he can't respect you."

Setting up a meeting and talking to Michaels "like an adult" did not produce results, cast member Harry Shearer noted—a better strategy was to "act out." "I believe, and I think the evidence pretty much shows, that Lorne's approach to the cast was to try to infantilize them," Shearer said. "I was a mess my first three years. . . . There was no escape, so I was like crying all the time," Cheri Oteri observed. "I had no idea that people could be so tired and miserable—because of so much pressure—and still be good and still be funny," Darrell Hammond said.

Grant said that working at *SNL* "sent me to therapy. My life was so weird and my anxiety levels were so high that I had to start going to therapy for the first time, in order to make sense of why it was that I felt sad. I was working at *Saturday Night Live* and making a good living—and I was miserable."

In a world where there's just so much media of almost every kind, curation systems matter more than ever. Getting hired by *SNL* as a writer or a performer is a message to not just the public but the industry: this person has the potential to write a good TV comedy, star in a funny movie, win Emmys and Peabodys and Oscars.

SNL jobs are not just gateways to paid work as a comedy performer, something that has always been in short supply. Once you've been picked by Lorne Michaels—the most important gatekeeper of commercial comedy in North America and one of the most powerful people in the industry at large—you have access to an array of possibilities and opportunities that would be much harder to find via any other route. "Instantly people respect you in a way that should maybe take you much longer," cast member Aidy Bryant said.

She's not wrong. People get meetings that would have been nearly impossible to get before *SNL* was on their résumés. Agents, managers, lawyers, creative people, and industry executives—they're all much more likely to take a chance on and write checks to people who have been through the *SNL* system first. That system is not an easy one to endure.

"Everyone's anxieties about the show and problems with the show are exactly the same, which is weirdly reassuring," said Grant of talking to *SNL* vets from different eras. "You can talk to someone who worked there in 1978, and you can have the same exact conversation with a person who's in the cast now. Which is how you know that it's not personal."

What is "it"? Well, this: "It's completely and utterly Darwinian. It has no institutional interest in helping the people who work there be better at the job. You just get thrown into this pit and you kind of have to fight your way out," Grant told me. "I was living in a sort of *Mad Max: Fury Road*–style sink-or-swim environment that was utterly unconcerned with my well-being and my happiness and my sense of safety and just general holistic health."

When Grant arrived at 30 Rock, no one told him where the bathrooms were. "Nobody told you how to do the job. You either figured out how to do the job, or you washed out," Grant said. "And because of that, the environment could be incredibly unwelcoming, even for a straight white dude. Even for me, it was an incredibly unwelcoming and unkind place to work." He's thought a lot about what it must have been like for the few people from historically excluded groups who made it on to *SNL*'s writing, performing, and producing rosters. It probably involved the fear and stress that everybody felt—but, Grant said, "times ten."

By the time Grant arrived, Tina Fey's *SNL* career was ascendant. Even though men outnumbered women in the writers' room (and that's consistently been the case), he recalled Fey, Ana Gasteyer, and Molly Shannon dominating the first half hour of the show, when the most high-profile sketches typically appear.

"At that time, just the fact that the show skewed female at all felt very cool," Grant observed. "Of course, now, if you look back on it, you would think, 'Well, every single one of those ladies is white.' I don't think there were maybe any people of color on the writing staff at all, or certainly no women of color."

Things were pretty awful on multiple fronts in the '80s, '90s, and beyond. Terry Sweeney, the show's first out gay cast member, lasted one season, during which Chevy Chase, a former cast member who had returned to host, "insulted everybody" and behaved like a "monster" (nothing unusual there). At one point, Chase suggested Sweeney star in a sketch where he was weighed to see if he had AIDS. Chase was "really furious" that he had to apologize to him, Sweeney said. When Chase hosted some time after that, after being introduced to a female writer, "he made some reference like, 'Maybe you can give me a handjob later,'" Will Ferrell said.

"There's no word for when you castrate a female," *SNL* writer Rosie Shuster said of how Garofalo was treated when she was with the show for a brief time in the '90s. "But that's the feeling I get watching what's happening to Janeane." Her first few years were "fabulous" and then "my last year [at *SNL*] was one of the worst years of my life," Julia Sweeney said. "I found being a writer on *Saturday Night Live* more nerve-wracking than being the host of *Late Night* and replacing Letterman," Conan O'Brien observed.

There's going to be pressure in any high-profile gig. But surely the show could have had a healthier culture and still been funny. The fact that the environment often is, for so many, unpleasant or even terrible seems not just unnecessary but, as Bob Odenkirk said, weird.

"I mean, the whole thing was weird to me," former *SNL* writer Odenkirk said in *Live from New York*. "To me, what was fun about comedy and should have been exciting about *Saturday Night Live* was the whole generational thing, you know, a crazy bunch of people sittin' around making each other laugh with casual chaos and a kind of democracy of chaos. And to go into a place where this one distant and cold guy is in charge and trying to run it the way he ran it decades ago is just weird to me." That tracks with something that former employee Ben mentioned—that the *SNL* work processes were usually "extremely regimented." That may have been partly necessary to keep the trains running on time, but Ben also described an overall culture where stepping out of line in any meaningful way was frowned upon.

The conversation around the show blew up in a big way in 2013, when Kenan Thompson said he no longer wanted to play Black women on *SNL,* and he and fellow cast member Jay Pharoah expressed "displeasure at the absence of black women in the show's cast." Black performers have been, for the most part, few and far between: in the '90s, "I got hired because *In Living Color* was on," Chris Rock said.

"I don't think it's meant to be easy. I also think that being in a forty-year-old institution that is predominantly white, as a woman of color, it's a different journey," Natasha Rothwell said in a 2018 interview that touched on her one-season stint on *SNL*'s writing staff. "I was, like, working alongside amazing, smart, funny people in an environment that wasn't for me. Like, some people thrive there. You know, so it's like no shade, but it just wasn't for me."

Just five years before Rothwell gave that interview, only one of the show's twenty-three writers was Black. According to a 2013 *New York Times* piece, *SNL* had hired only three Black women "for its main cast . . . in four decades."

And as comedian Kerry Coddett pointed out, not only did the show go for long stretches without Black women in the cast, it often handed them roles that traded on demeaning stereotypes. Yvonne Hudson, who worked at *SNL* in the 1980–81 season, played "a maid, a nurse, a slave," writes Coddett. Danitra Vance, "a classically trained Shakespearean actor who also performed at the famed Second City Theater," had two recurring roles. One was Cabrini Green Jackson, "a 17-year-old welfare mother who gave advice about pregnancy. . . . In another sketch, 'That Black Girl,' Vance plays LaToya Marie, a black actress who will do anything to get famous." Vance only lasted one season in part "because she resented routinely being cast as a maid or a prostitute," according to a story written at the time of her 1994 death.

In 2018, Awkwafina became the first female Asian American *SNL* host in eighteen years. Two years earlier, stats compiled by *IndieWire* revealed that between 1975 and 2016, more than 90 percent of hosts were white. Less than 7 percent were Black and 1.2 percent were Hispanic. The most recent all-white hosting season ended in 2011. "Because it lacked Asian cast members, the show has for many years had to call on a longtime production designer, Akira Yoshimura, to play the part of Sulu in *Star Trek* sketches, and in one instance, he played Connie Chung," the *New York Times* reported in 2019.

"*SNL* doesn't have a strong record of reaching out to diverse voices, either in hosting choices or in casting its ensemble," Mark Lieberman notes in *IndieWire*. His piece also points out that Sasheer Zamata, who was on the show from 2014–2017, and Leslie Jones, who broke out in a big way in her 2014–19 stint, were hired around the time of the scramble to add Black women. Both are now gone from *SNL*.

Kate McKinnon and Bowen Yang, two out cast members, are among the most acclaimed performers in recent *SNL* history, but the show's overall track record on the LGBTQ+ front is, in a word, dreadful. Vance was not out while she was on the show, which is understandable, given the environment she was in, and how homophobic the industry (and the world) could be. As Denny Dillon, a gay woman who was in the cast for a short time in the early '80s, observed, "It wasn't safe to be out in Hollywood for a long time."

"We were on the show when Reagan shut off any research for AIDS or HIV. It was a real homophobic era, that time. We didn't have any gay writers. We didn't have any gay cast members," late '80s cast member Nora Dunn said in a 2015 Salon interview. As far as I can tell (NBC declined to answer my questions on this and other matters), between the departure of Terry Sweeney and the arrivals of Kate McKinnon and John Milhiser in 2012 and 2013, respectively, for around a quarter of a century there were no out LGBTQ+ people in the performer rosters of *SNL*.

Dunn left the show in 1990, and in her 2015 interview, she discussed what led to her exit. Working at *SNL* is "a traumatic experience," Dunn said, "kind of something you have to survive." "Women are hard to write for, that was the anthem I heard for five years," Dunn said in 1992—many years after, the piece notes, founding cast member John Belushi was heard to yell "women aren't funny" in the halls of *SNL*.

Dunn boycotted the episode Andrew Dice Clay hosted, and her analysis of that situation, which contributed to her departure, is worth quoting at length, given that it addresses how power operates at *SNL*. Almost any topic can be the subject of comedy, Dunn noted: even challenging "subject matters can be handled because satire is ridicule, and satire is smart. And if you're really performing satire, you have to be intelligent. It's how you do it. Look at *All in the Family*—they handled that material brilliantly. They handled racism, all of that stuff, and it was very smartly written. . . . Andrew Dice Clay, the character, who was an abuser of women and he was a homophobe. And his material was terrible. He just wasn't smart enough to handle that material. And our writing staff was not the writing staff to handle that material either [when he hosted the show in 1990].

"Lorne said, 'Andrew Dice Clay was a phenomenon worth examining.' And yeah, he was a phenomenon, but if you're going to examine him, he shouldn't be the host, you should write an article," she added. "We didn't examine the hosts of *SNL*. We supported them, we wrote for them, and we made them look good. Otherwise you'd never get a host. You're there to make them look good."

She didn't care that Clay was foulmouthed, she added: "My objection to Andrew Dice Clay was that his character was only about one thing: abusing women and laughing about abusing women. There was nothing else behind it. There was nothing else about it except to make him look harmless." At the time of the Clay controversy, Michaels called the protests regarding the comic's humor "sadly humorless."

More than two decades later, *SNL* did its level best to make another aggressively biased bully seem harmless.

Donald Trump, whose reputation was in eclipse just after the turn of the millennium, had his career revived in 2004 by the NBC reality show *The Apprentice*. The program earned millions for Trump—not just in money but in free publicity—and though the original show ran out of steam after several years, a Trump edition of *Celebrity Apprentice* aired on NBC as late as 2015. On June 16 of that year, Trump declared his candidacy for the presidency, and in his remarks, said that Mexico was sending criminals and "rapists" to the United States.

Days later, NBC said it was cutting ties with Trump and would no longer carry the Trump-produced Miss USA and Miss Universe pageants. "Due to the recent derogatory statements by Donald Trump regarding immigrants, NBCUniversal is ending its business relationship with Mr. Trump," the network's statement said. "At NBC, respect and dignity for all people are cornerstones of our values."

About five months after making those offensive comments, Trump hosted *SNL*. I was working as the chief television critic for *Variety* at the time, and I could not quite believe that NBC had broken its promise so quickly. Nor could I believe what I saw, which was not just uninspired but leadenly unfunny: the sketches were particularly "weak, timid or predictable," I wrote then. It still stuns me that after supposedly "breaking with" Trump, the network used one of its most high-profile platforms to position candidate Trump as an eccentric buffoon, not as the dangerous racist demagogue he was (and is).

Morale in the week leading up to the Trump show was awful, according to Ben, who worked at *SNL* in a low-level job. "The cast was upset," Ben recalled. "It is truly the lowest moment of my career and probably will be for the rest of my life. And it was not a choice to be there. I was not allowed to be like, 'I don't want to work this week.'" Not coming into work, Ben said, would have put him in danger of being let go.

Grant, who was no longer with the show by then, theorized about why Michaels wanted Trump to host that fall. "When I was there, I saw him, over and over again, say, 'This is the thing the country is talking about. This is the thing we need to have a take on,'" Grant recalled. "You take the person the country is talking about and you put them on live TV. If you put the DNA of the show in a centrifuge and boiled it down to its essence, that's it."

The Trump appearance "was an absolute blunder of the highest order," Grant told me. "Everyone I talked to had the same thought, which is, this is a calamitous error in judgment." Grant speculated that Michaels's thought process may have gone something like this: "'I've known Donald Trump for thirty years. He's a funny, harmless idiot. He's a New York real estate shyster. We all know these guys. We're going bring him on because that's what this show does.' And he absolutely should not have."

In his memoir, Jost guesses "Lorne would not have asked Trump to host if he had known how insane and divisive Trump would later get," in a passage that has a light, dismissive "whoopsie!" tone. "But Lorne is also very contrarian, so maybe he would have!" In that section, Jost observes that by "the end of the week, I think most people at our show thought, *Huh. This guy isn't a monster after all*"—an assessment that doesn't track with what Ben told me of a very demoralized cast and staff (and some in the latter group fielded verbal abuse and threats, he said, via scary phone calls to *SNL*'s offices). Jost spends no time considering Trump's racist rhetoric, which was very established by that point, or NBC's decision to "cut ties" with him months earlier. No matter; for Jost, Trump was "incredibly charming and fun to talk to."

Not only did Michaels or the show face no real consequences, Michaels's authority only continued to grow over time. In 2015, NBC aired a special devoted to *SNL*'s fortieth anniversary, and to one former cast member, it reaffirmed just how powerful Michaels had become.

"When Seth Meyers left the show [in 2014], the dynamic changed quite a bit," former cast member Taran Killam said in 2018, two years after he departed *SNL*. "He was the last person there who I witnessed really collaborate with Lorne, as opposed to just kind of do what Lorne says. . . . And I also think the 40th really sort of affected Lorne in that I think it was exciting and I think it was flattering and I think he was really able to sort of relish in this incredible institution that he's responsible for and all these amazing iconic careers and all of his famous friends, and it had to have been the most potent overwhelming boost of a 'this is your life' experience ever. And then it all went away, and then it was back to this cast who's all 40 years younger than you and aren't as famous as Tina Fey or whatever, and my experience was he became very impatient."

A few years later, the theory that Michaels runs his own country— one without meaningful oversight or guardrails—got another workout, through *SNL*'s response to the COVID-19 pandemic.

Like most of the industry, *SNL* shut down for months during early phases of the pandemic, but it opened back up in the fall of 2020, long before vaccines were available. And it had an audience.

"What makes *SNL* so important that it was permitted to continue hosting live audiences even as the state shut down indoor dining earlier this winter?" asks Simons in an early 2021 piece. "If audiences are required to wear masks, why not the performers sharing a room with them for over an hour? What are audience members supposed to be, anyway, cast or employees?" Simons tried to find answers to these questions, from NBC and from New York City authorities, but they were muddled or hard to come by, and in any event, "the unmistakable appearance [is] that *SNL* is getting special treatment."

Simons points out in an October 2020 story that the tests administered to audience members were not fully reliable and that those audience members were not, per mandated guidelines, sitting six feet apart in all directions. *SNL* maintained that it had, throughout the pandemic, "observed all safety protocols throughout their return to the studio."

But as public health expert Lisa M. Lee told Simons, "We do not yet have an effective vaccine or treatment, so gatherings that are nonessential will continue to put people at risk for COVID-19 and death. There are things we can do to make essential gatherings as safe as possible, but we should carefully consider any non-essential gathering."

Why in the world was having a live audience essential? "Laughs are the clear indicator" that a joke writer or performer got it "right," Michaels said in the fall of 2020. Is that worth running the risk of getting—or exposing employees to—a potentially deadly disease? I wouldn't have thought so, but clearly I'm a harpy who hates laughter.

Late in 2021, when the Omicron variant of COVID was surging in many cities, including New York, Ben kept hearing from friends at *SNL* that people were "dropping like flies" but that the show "was refusing to stop." On December 11, 2021, Billie Eilish hosted and was the musical guest. Days later, she appeared on Howard Stern's show and said that, while she was there, "Lorne was sick, coughing everywhere. Mr. Lorne was coughing and coughing and coughing."

On December 18, 2021, the day of the last *SNL* taping of the year, the *New York Post* reported that four performers "tested positive for coronavirus—and 'three others' have called out because they are now 'fearful' about coming to NBC Studios at 30 Rockefeller Center." Though some sources told the *Post* that Michaels had gotten COVID-19, others said that was not the case. Regardless, multiple members of the cast were not part of the episode that eventually aired. "Everyone is fearful here," one person told the *Post*.

According to Ben, who was in touch with friends at the show at that time, "it took people literally storming off the set for Lorne to be like, 'Fine, we will show some of these pre-tapes'"—versions of sketches that had been filmed earlier in the week.

If that is not a clear demonstration of values—i.e., the *only* thing of value is the comedy show that is transmitted to the public on Saturday night—I don't know what is.

As I noted in earlier chapters, difficult, if not toxic, industry environments often thrive when many people in a workplace are young, powerless, or inexperienced—or all three. For people from historically excluded groups, the bias and gaslighting they come across can be even more isolating.

Patterns of mistreatment, bias in hiring, cast members and writers abusing and harassing young female employees within a "treacherous" culture, per a 2022 *Business Insider* article about *SNL*—none of it ever gets laid at the feet of Michaels. I still can't quite figure out why. Maybe he's just been, for decades, *that* skilled at portraying his long-running character—Humble Canadian Guy in New York.

"For someone so concerned with nurturing his power, Michaels casts himself as amazingly passive," according to the 1995 *New York* magazine feature on *SNL*. There's little difference in a 2021 *Washington Post* piece that came out when Michaels was feted by the Kennedy Center Honors. When asked about the show's power, Michaels replied, "We're a comedy show. We can influence, but we don't determine."

Asked three times about "the power you've created for yourself" to "start and stop careers," Michaels "resists the question" and "sidesteps again. He prefers not to talk about his own power; he'll focus on the power of the voices he chooses to elevate. He prizes truth-tellers, he says, especially in moments of national unease or confusion . . ."

Oh, *please*, that "truth-tellers" thing again. Give me a break. Either comedy is so crucial that it must be protected at all costs, or it's a wispy nonentity, so unimportant that no part of it needs to be held to account in any way. Just once I'd love for one of comedy's toxic yet powerful gatekeepers to tell us which of these rationales they'd like to permanently hide behind.

In any event, you'd never know that three months before that *Post* profile came out, Jane Doe filed her civil lawsuit against Michaels, Sanz, and NBCUniversal. "Horatio certainly is the main character here, but he didn't abuse me in a vacuum; he abused me all over *Saturday Night Live*," Doe told Laura Bradley of the Daily Beast, who wrote one of the few major pieces on her case.

Doe's story did not get blanket coverage, but it got enough. It would certainly have come up in a Google search that you'd hope a reporter would do before talking to an important subject. But if Michaels was asked about this lawsuit—which was filed just a few months earlier—there's no evidence of that in the *Washington Post* piece.

Jane Doe met Jimmy Fallon at an event for a book he wrote. Her mom drove her to the New York bookstore from their Pennsylvania home; Doe was fourteen. "It was me and some adults and some people who lived in New York and his family members," Doe said. "I stood out—I was the only kid at that thing, and I had that energy of, like, a Beatles fan."

That superfan energy had previously led her to create a website for *SNL* cast member Fallon, one that posted scoops about who upcoming hosts and musical guests would be. (She told me she got that information from Sanz.) Not long after she turned fifteen, Fallon and Sanz, using an NBC employee's email account, got in touch with her to praise her for her efforts to promote Fallon and *SNL*. She told me that, over the next few years, she got swept up into the show's world, attending parties and getting to know fellow fans and people who worked at *SNL*.

On occasion, she would roam the halls typically occupied by writers and performers, and it was not unusual for her to attend the official after-party that follows every episode of the show. (She was not the only one to do so while underage; Ben said he did so once as well.) At one *SNL* event, Jane Doe recalled, "Jimmy Fallon introduced me to Lorne after we had consumed alcohol together." Earlier that night, Doe said, she told Fallon and his agent what Sanz already knew—that she was a high school student. Another "perk" of knowing the cast was being invited to after-after parties like the ones that were, around that time, occasionally hosted by Tracy Morgan.

The attention from cast members, other *SNL* people, fans, and members of the public who visited her site—it all made Doe feel special, for a time. But those years also created enormous damage that she is still trying to process.

Doe said that there was an NBC page who had been "aggressive" all season about "trying to sleep with me." One night in the *SNL* offices, after she'd consumed alcohol, he got her to go into a stairwell with him. "He wanted to hook up with me, and I wasn't sure. And then he said dismissively that he wasn't going to rape me, so I went into the stairwell with him." Like so many teenage girls before her, she was afraid of being disliked or being labeled a prude. The page, who was around twenty-two, she said, stuck his tongue down her throat and pushed her against a wall. Doe said that those actions and others felt like "much more than I wanted," but her understanding of consent, like that of many teens (then or now), was very different from what it evolved into later: "Like, you just had to agree to hook up with someone and hope they weren't going to do anything violating, you know?"

In her lawsuit, Doe states that Sanz put her "on his guest list for *SNL* after parties where she continued to be served alcohol and engaged in drug use," and describes being assaulted by Sanz at one after-after party in full view of a number of *SNL* employees and cast members. (Two witnesses said, per the suit, "Are you f***ing serious?"). Doe told me that in a taxi on the way to the train station, she awoke to the assault that involved the attempt to remove her pantyhose.

"I just know that as an adult now in her thirties, if I saw a colleague fingering or getting a minor drunk, getting a fan drunk, and I saw that clearly unbalanced power dynamic. . . . Sanz was clearly pursuing me, physically pursuing me across years of these parties," Doe told me. "If I saw my colleague doing that with a teenage fan, I would absolutely intervene or I would go up the chain of command and I would want something to be done. I would want it to be handled. And I don't think that that happened. And I don't know if that was because no one said anything at all. And I don't know if that's because, maybe, *Saturday Night Live* selects employees who happen to be funny and also happen to be the type of people that aren't going to say anything when bad things happen to people—they're just going to keep their mouth closed. I don't know if Lorne just has such a stronghold on everyone."

In the middle of 2022, around the time Doe added documents to her suit claiming that Tina Fey, Maya Rudolph, Rachel Dratch, Ana Gasteyer, and Seth Meyers saw Sanz assaulting her at that after-after party, representatives for all five *SNL* alums "did not respond" to requests for comment from the Daily Beast.

Other survivors of industry wrongdoing have received statements of solidarity, but when she and I spoke in early 2022, Doe told me she had not felt supported at all. She cited the way that the cast of *Sex and the City* spoke out when assault allegations against costar Chris Noth came out. (He has denied the allegations but lost his job on the CBS drama *The Equalizer*.) In that case, Sarah Jessica Parker, Cynthia Nixon, and Kristin Davis put out a statement that acknowledged "that it's hard for the survivor to come forward and we support the survivor," Doe recalled. "None of the people who were at *SNL* at the time have had one word to say, not one person has said, 'Oh, I remember that—that was wrong.'"

She shut down the site she'd made for Fallon after Sanz assaulted her, but she told me that she was occasionally in touch with Sanz for a very long time afterward. In recent years, however, she has come to see his behavior not as friendship—which is how she viewed their relationship when she was in her twenties—but as another form of manipulation and even attempted damage control. In her view, Sanz wanted to shape how she saw both him and their relationship, and she said she came to see their later contact as an "emotionally abusive" relationship.

"He steered me into thinking that everything that happened—when he tried to rape me in the cab after that party—was my fault," she said.

In the end, Doe remarked, "I forgot about that fifteen-year-old girl that used to have confidence."

NBC responded to her suit by telling the press her allegations were "meritless," and asked for the case to be dismissed. (The network, Comcast, Michaels, and NBCUniversal declined to answer my questions about these matters.) In late 2022, the legal action came to a close and in news coverage of this development, Doe's attorney stated that the "parties have resolved their dispute and have moved on."

When Doe and I spoke almost a year earlier, the concept of "moving on" sounded like a complicated, ongoing challenge for her—something I understood, given all that she'd experienced. She told me she wasn't overly interested in money, and I learned that, regarding the legal case, she did not sign an NDA. The resolution of the legal situation does not mean that what she experienced no longer affects her life, of course, and I continue to feel compassion for her for many reasons. At least in part because I understood a topic we discussed at length: what she wanted was for people to explain themselves—to be accountable.

"When people are like, 'Don't you just want all this to go away?' I'm like, 'This has been my life,'" Doe said. "I would rather be involved in this lawsuit than let them go on being these mega-successful people who are not held accountable to anyone at all."

In thinking about the Jane Doe situation, I have reflected on what Dr. Richard "Bo" Travis told me when I interviewed him about abusive personality types and how they operate. He delved into the topic of cognitive dissonance—the idea that human beings don't like to dwell on pieces of themselves that they can't easily integrate into their preferred self-portrait. And that when we encounter facts or assertions that fly in the face of the identities we've crafted for ourselves, we often minimize or disregard the things that don't fit.

With the exception of a flurry of pieces about the legal filing in 2021, stories from Simons, and in-depth Daily Beast coverage, Jane Doe's story has been frequently ignored by the media. Five years after #MeToo, there was *a lot* of silence around her lawsuit. And taking a wider view, there are the occasional aggregated posts but vanishingly few in-depth dives into *SNL* as a workplace. Because cognitive dissonance can affect entire cultures.

And also because, in my experience and Simons's experience, people who *don't even work there anymore,* let alone people who work at *SNL* now, are afraid to speak out. I don't think a culture of fear and silence is a net good for the industry. It is not my job to judge each individual who felt they could not cross Michaels over the Jane Doe situation or anything else. It *is* my job to say that it's unbelievably tragic and depressing that some of the most famous people in the American entertainment industry felt they could not say a single word about any of her allegations or the gross, demeaning culture described in that *Business Insider* article. Where's all that bold freedom of speech now?

No, I'm not a fan of the ongoing replication of Hollywood's worst and most damaging patterns of silence and submission—however uncomfortable—to patterns of exploitation, deeply unprofessional conduct, or abuse. Just as the toxicity of Scott Rudin's operation affected whole generations of Hollywood strivers, what was accepted (or venerated) at *SNL* wasn't contained to its offices or Studio 8H; the culture and norms that were born there radiated outward. An experienced New York writer/producer who has not worked for Michaels told me he still feels familiar with the mindset and culture of *SNL,* because "to the extent that *SNL* is a training ground, that means that its culture has been replicated all over the place, in lots of other shows' offices."

As I said a while back, we're not even at the end of Act 1 of this story. In recent years, Horatio Sanz booked roles on the Disney+ drama *The Mandalorian,* the children's film *Clifford the Big Red Dog,* Showtime's *Black Monday,* and the HBO series *Curb Your Enthusiasm.* His career appears to have hit a drought once the lawsuit went public, but who thinks that drought will last forever? And even if it does, the culture of silence—the one that enveloped the industry after those Rudin stories came out, the one that enveloped almost the entire system of popular culture and commentary when it came to allegations of deep toxicity and assault within the world of SNL—*that* persists.

Doe's story shows what can happen when a culture of impunity festers and we don't want to look at the results. They are, I admit, hard to look at. I'm embarrassed that I didn't look at *SNL* more closely for this long. I'd bought into the show's reputation as a more or less acceptable haven for hard-partying rebels, and I was wrong to do that.

I wish more people were willing to use their high perches to support meaningful change, and to question the culture that Michaels helped create and presided over for so long. But once again, a vast silence speaks volumes. On and on a broken system goes.

What would be truly rebellious, at this point, would be to question all these histories, all these norms, all these cultures, which are just one culture. It would be revolutionary to burn down the toxic machinery, and put something better in its place.

PART
TWO

There was nothing less for Lady Russell to do,
than to admit that she had been pretty completely wrong,
and to take up a new set of opinions and of hopes.

—*Jane Austen,* Persuasion

11

The Path Forward

What Does Centering Survivors, Cleaning Up the Industry, and "Doing the Work" Actually Look Like?

There is a bar to clear, and the bar is really high.

—Rabbi Danya Ruttenberg

It sounds like the setup to a joke—a shrink, a screenwriter, and a rabbi walk into a bar. Richard "Bo" Travis (the shrink), Kyra Jones (the screenwriter), and Danya Ruttenberg (the rabbi) are three experts I greatly enjoyed talking to. Travis is a licensed clinical psychologist who has spent years evaluating and treating sex offenders; Jones is a performer and writer who has been through a restorative justice process; and Ruttenberg has literally written the book on the processes of repentance, forgiveness, and making amends. What I hoped to gain from them were insights and possible answers to the thicket of questions that have lingered in the wake of Hollywood's various reckonings, some of which have barely stumbled out of the starting gate.

How should those who have been harmed within the industry be treated? What should be done about patterns of transgression, bias, and damage, and who bears responsibility for eliminating them? What values, philosophies, and practices should the entertainment companies and communities adopt as guides in these situations?

Addressing the needs of survivors of harm should have priority, obviously. But so many of us have been trained to consider instead what powerful perpetrators need—and how to protect ourselves from their wrath when they are called out. To move forward, survivors must come first. But how does that actually work? How can we make that routine?

Eventually we are going to have to ask this question too: What is the path back (if any) for harm-doers? Many of us in and around the industry have been deeply frustrated by that question for some time now. When that is the first—and often the only—question that gets asked after damage has been done, it's both unfortunate and illuminating. It usually reveals that the person asking the question has fallen into the trap of putting the perpetrator first and sees the survivors of misconduct and abuse as afterthoughts (if they are seen at all).

That's part of the point, actually—no matter our status, education level, belief system, or capacity for forgiveness, a lot of us have been thinking about a lot of these things in ways that aren't productive or helpful. Many people, including me, need to uproot or change the assumptions, instinctual responses, and dynamics that have led to iffy or just plain bad outcomes over and over again. That said, if you think this chapter will supply a hard and fast set of rules and guidelines that are applicable and effective in every situation, think again.

It will contain as much helpful, concrete advice as I can cram into it, of course. But the point of writing this book is to delve into situations that are complex and that sometimes resist one-size-fits-all answers. The people I talked to for this chapter have smart things to say about how to conceptualize and reframe the assumptions many of us have made about what constitutes justice, consequences, and change. They've been thinking deeply on these matters for a long time, as have I.

Among the people who raised me were the Springfield Dominican nuns who ran the high school I attended outside Chicago. This wasn't one of those schools where one or two nuns were on the staff; the majority of the people who taught me about writing, poetry, biology, chemistry, and the novel were habit-wearing, educated, articulate, and witty women who lived in a building attached to the school. They did not meaningfully answer to any men, as far as I could tell.

I'm a Buddhist now, in part because I retain a strong interest in the workings of morality, grace, and karma, a semi-obsession that my Catholic education initially fed. As an Irish American woman who was born on the South Side of Chicago, I'm also culturally and possibly genetically drawn to the topics of punishment, injustice, and undying vengeance. As the daughter of a cop, it eventually dawned on me that I had, without fully realizing it, appointed myself a Hollywood cop. In the past several years, I've also turned into some combination of therapist, trauma worker, lawyer, HR official, and private investigator, and I cannot overemphasize how few qualifications I have for—and how much profound trepidation I have about—most of these roles. I had excellent instructors in journalism school, but nothing in my training prepared me for *this*. And by "this," well, I will never be able to sum up what the last several years have been like, but I sort of mean "the psychological equivalent of holding unexploded (or exploded) bombs in my hands while people talk about shocking, awful, or excruciating things that have happened to them."

I've learned a lot about how to interact with survivors and how to navigate the swirling rapids of the reporting process in these difficult realms, but there's still so much I don't know. So I wanted to ask people who know what they're talking about: Now what? Given my penchant for truth-telling women of God, let's start with the rabbi who flipped me the bird.

I first became aware of Rabbi Danya Ruttenberg not long after Hollywood was engulfed in the #MeToo movement (a term that was originated by activist and survivor Tarana Burke). In 2017 and beyond, as I read and reported stories that centered on pain, abuse, and misconduct in Hollywood, I kept seeing Ruttenberg's Twitter threads on what meaningful apologies should look like. She also frequently addressed the topic of making amends, and wrote on social media and elsewhere about how we might create different kinds of communities—fairer ones, ones that don't systematically dish out sympathy to perpetrators and cold comfort to survivors.

As her social media following expanded and her inbox and DMs flooded, Ruttenberg realized "people were looking for a language they didn't have. People were looking for a set of tools, and my traditions seemed to have something useful to offer the conversation." So Ruttenberg wrote a graceful, practical, and necessary book, *On Repentance and Repair: Making Amends in an Unapologetic World*, which came out in 2022. In it, she describes hearing innumerable stories "from people who have been hurt and were told by their teacher, parent, pastor, or partner that they should just forgive, that reconciliation is important, or even that they should return to an abusive situation with an open heart. These emotional letters drove home to me the extent to which American culture emphasizes letting go of grudges and redemption narratives instead of obligations of a perpetrator of harm and the recompense that is due to one who has been harmed or even traumatized."

People, Ruttenberg explained, were looking for "a different model."

That different model does not include letting terrible deeds slide. "No, you don't have to forgive your abuser, especially if they haven't repented," the Chicago-based Ruttenberg told me. Kyra Jones, who learned a great deal about restorative justice through a process that included her rapist, a man named Malcolm, offered a similar take: "So many people talk to me about restorative justice and they're like, 'I could never forgive the person who assaulted me, the person who harassed me.' I never forgave Malcolm." Jones has written extensively on her assault and the process that followed, and "in all the statements," she noted, "I wrote that I do not forgive him. And the community does not have to forgive this person."

But many kinds of outcomes are possible, because there are as many offenses, contexts, and circumstances as there are human beings on earth. Even so, some principles and framing devices—many long studied within various Jewish traditions—can help us navigate these complexities. Of course, to put the game plan Ruttenberg describes in her book into action, a person does not have to be Jewish. They just have to be willing to supply, as Ruttenberg said, "crisp" and specific descriptions of what needs to happen after harm has been done. No "loosey-goosey ideas about what 'doing the work' really is." As she puts it in her book, "we must not be too generous with participation trophies or cookies for people doing the bare minimum." Patience is a must as well.

"It's going to be messy. It's going to be uncomfortable. You're going to make mistakes," Ruttenberg told me. And "the person who caused the harm isn't the one who gets to decide" when the work has been done. Does the person who was harmed "feel like they got their needs met? Do they feel better?" Those are key questions.

"There is a bar to clear, and the bar is really high. There has to be rigorous accountability. When we center those who have been harmed, then we know what to look for," she said. "Feeling 'sorry,' skulking around for a bit, having your publicist write an apology for you, having a time-out of some kind"—nope, nope, and *nope*. An apology—written by a PR team or not—is not even the first thing that should happen. It's the *fourth* step in the five-step process the rabbi outlined.

Ruttenberg based the five-stage process described in her book on the work of Maimonides, a medieval philosopher who "took a lot of ancient Jewish thinking from the Torah and from other sources and organized it in a particular way to set up what he called the laws of repentance," she said. And the first step is for transgressors to fully and completely own what they did.

"My fans are so disappointed in me," "This has been really hard on my family," and "I'm sorry you took offense at this reasonable thing I did"—I tried to restrain my pained laughter as she offered these familiar bits of Hollywood-speak (which can, of course, be found in other arenas in which high-powered people offer self-absorbed non-apologies). None of these unfortunate statements qualify as true accountings of harm. When in "taking ownership" mode, there should be "no narcissism, no denial, no hedging your bets, no trying to make yourself look better," Ruttenberg noted. "Name it. Own it. Say it."

To the extent that a harm was public or semipublic, taking ownership of the act should be public to the same degree. "If, in your marriage, you are having an issue, you don't have to put that on Facebook," Ruttenberg said. "But if you said something racist in a staff meeting, then your confession has to be heard by everybody who heard that. Put it on the company Slack, acknowledge what you did at the next staff meeting—whatever is appropriate to the venue in which the harm was done." If it's possible, it may actually be better if the confession is somewhat more public than the harm that was done, because then the person who did the damage "is telling people that they need to be accountable."

The second step may sound easy, but it's the hardest one, and it can take the most time, if it's performed in a meaningful way: the perpetrator must actually change.

A person must do whatever needs to be done "so that they cannot be that person [who caused harm] anymore," Ruttenberg said. "How long this process takes depends on what the harm is. Someone who committed rape is going to have a different process than someone who told a not-funny joke and who needs to get the memo on that." (Travis will address a lot of these topics in a bit. But for now, let's move on to the third part of Ruttenberg's process.)

Step three features many potential pitfalls: the person who did the damage should ask those whom they harmed what they need—and if the survivor(s) are responsive to a dialogue on the topic, the harm-doer should then make every effort to supply those things. Even if the person or people harmed aren't open to that conversation, valuable work can still be done.

"If you did a cultural harm, you can do a cultural good," Ruttenberg said. "You caused a rip in the cosmos—how can you do some healing of the cosmos?" She knows an Orthodox rabbi who was part of a rabbinical court "that let an abuser go back and work with teens, with young adults. The guy was eventually arrested. When that rabbi finally got the memo about what he had done, he has spent the rest of his life advocating for victims. He can never undo what he did, but it's not even about him going to each individual victim. It's about dedicating his life to making the world better in targeted ways related to his mistake."

That's why, "if you stepped on somebody's toe, you'd better pay their medical bill," Ruttenberg said. "If you masturbated in front of somebody and as a consequence, their careers have since gone sideways, because they're now publicly known as the survivors of that, what might be welcome amends could be money. It could be connecting them with your producer or a big streamer or studio, in order to get them a special, to get them those meetings. Maybe they never want to hear from you again, but you're donating $2 million toward helping out women in comedy or to prevent sexual violence."

As you may have guessed, that last set of examples wasn't chosen at random. In 2018, what had been long rumored and hinted at in smaller publications was made plain in the *New York Times:* comedian, TV creator, and filmmaker Louis C.K. engaged in harassing and intimidating behavior by masturbating in front of multiple women. The survivors said that for years, they were silent because they were afraid of C.K.'s power in the entertainment world, as well as that of his extremely influential manager, Dave Becky of 3 Arts Entertainment. Two survivors spoke of the "backlash" they faced in the industry, and "said they understood from their managers that Mr. Becky, Louis C.K.'s manager, wanted them to stop telling people about their encounter with" him. Becky told the *Times,* "I never threatened anyone." C.K.'s acts were violations and he did not have consent, and none of that is up for debate, despite what a large subset of comedy-world edgelords appear to think.

When the *Times* piece came out, C.K. issued a non-apology about how he was going to go away and think about what he'd done. Then, having had a time-out that lasted about a year, he returned to performing comedy at clubs. At first, venues allowed him to take the stage without giving patrons advance notice, which means that the assault and harassment survivors in the crowd had the presence of an admitted serial assaulter sprung on them with no warning. It was not just an echo of what C.K. had done, it was a profoundly thoughtless and harmful choice on the part of those who ran those clubs.

But thoughtlessness was the order of the day. C.K. had an enormous mailing list; he had a site he used to drop specials and TV shows; he had influence, reach, and a huge megaphone—and he could have used all those things to make meaningful amends. He could have used his joke-writing and storytelling skills to be ruthlessly honest about what he'd done, and maybe he could have prompted some men in comedy spaces—and in the world—who idolized him to understand why all the things he'd done were terrible and not to be emulated.

He did none of that. In 2020, he released the comedy special *Sincerely, Louis C.K.*, in which, according to *Variety*'s Elizabeth Wagmeister, "he poked fun and downplayed his own sexual misconduct," and the following year, he went on a comedy tour that was sold out in two dozen cities. In 2022, he won a Grammy for *Sincerely, Louis C.K.* On our Zoom call—which took place before that Grammy win—Ruttenberg's profound disappointment with C.K. was palpable.

"The feminist pretender thing really just kills me," Ruttenberg said. "He could have just handed that mailing list over to women comics for a few years, right? He could have decided that he was going dedicate the rest of his career to dismantling rape culture. He had this whole list of possible choices he could have made that he did not make. The true test of whether somebody has done the work of repentance is if they cause the harm again. He went back to the ego-stroking limelight. He could not resist the opportunity to go back to the place that made it so easy for him to do the harm."

The path C.K. and his enablers took—one that compounded existing harm and created new damage—is common in Hollywood, especially if the transgressors are rich and propped up by prominent companies and influential power players. All of these people and entities operate the way they do because they do not generally subscribe to the notion that they should atone, make amends, and prevent further damage.

Time-outs are usually all that most transgressors get; a rich person

going on what looks like a vacation appears to be a sufficient consequence to many with power. A magic amount of days or months are
spent out of the spotlight—a time frame determined by some toxic
wizard I've yet to locate—and then, presto! The harm-doer and their
support systems can get back to the work of acquiring more money,
more opportunities, more glory, more chances to pretend nothing ever
happened. And was it really that bad? (That's a real question an agent
asked about a man I reported on, less than a year after that man was
fired for gross misconduct.)

"What is maybe uniquely toxic about Hollywood and industries like
it—it's the whole system. The number of people who make money off
of a single human being is huge," Ruttenberg said. "The enablers are
there. The number of people who are willing to tell you that you're doing okay, the number of people who are willing to tell you that you're
doing *great*, rather than holding you accountable—it's profound. All
those people who know perfectly well what's going on and are not saying anything—they have their own repentance work to do."

Absolutely correct on all counts. Those who hurt others are a problem, obviously. But in entertainment circles, the people with at least
some power—if not a great deal of power—who silently endorse the
existence or return of abusers are just as big a disaster. Some enablers
who don't even make any money off harm-doers and abusive people
are still very clearly invested in terrible status quos because they don't
want to face up to the deep rot in the systems, cultures, and institutions
they're part of.

These are the people who often go to the individual experiencing a
pattern of harm, bias, or damage, and say things like, "Well, that's just
the way it is." "You know how it is." One of my favorites: "We talked to
him."

Oh, word? *Fantastic.* Seriously, not tremendously helpful, as these
things go.

There's something particularly dispiriting when enabling mindsets
are couched in the language of comfort, sympathy, and support. There
are just so many ways that people around an abuser—or who know
about an abuser's tendencies—can make certain painful dynamics even
worse.

"I've seen this up close," Ruttenberg said with a sigh. In the world
of big-money donors to Jewish causes, "it's sending the development

person in to the donor that everybody knows is a sexual harasser without giving her a heads-up. And then when she comes out, everybody shrugs. And then when she says, 'Please don't invite him to the gala—that would be traumatic,' he's [still] invited to the gala. And her chair is moved to the very back of the room, away from the people she needs to be talking to" for her work.

Ultimately, "we privilege bringing the perpetrator back into the ecosystem because he's either got money or talent that we perceive to be more valuable than whatever the victim has going on," Ruttenberg said. And that's not just wrong—it's ridiculous, given how competitive commercial creative industries are. There are so many qualified people who could do most jobs, hundreds of qualified candidates for just about every gig. Why not pick the ones who don't have a track record of harming others?

"They're like, 'Well, that person made us money,'" said Jones. "But it's like, the industry is constantly turning out new stars. Why are you so attached to these problematic ones, when you can have a new one in five seconds? I don't get it." Nor do I. But let's return to Ruttenberg's plan.

Next, we arrive at step four: the apology. That garbled set of words that a celebrity taps out on the Notes app, or has their team write for them, before gearing up for an awards campaign or a red carpet, or heading out on a comeback tour. All exhausted joking aside, when someone messes up, there is a big difference between saying some version of "I don't want to feel bad about this anymore," and sincerely understanding the damage done and stating "I'm profoundly sorry I harmed you." As I said to Ruttenberg, those are very different statements.

"Exactly," Ruttenberg answered.

One of the great things about the rabbi's plan is that it is full of concepts a child could understand. She said, "I've trained my kids—when they screw up, which is daily—that the first words out of their mouth should not be, 'I'm sorry,' but rather, 'Are you okay? What do you need?' It's 'What do you want?' And *then* it's 'I'm sorry.'"

The fifth step is also not especially difficult to understand: "Drumroll, please," Ruttenberg said. "Not doing the thing again."

That's not easy when we're talking about Hollywood, where, as I said, "the identification of a problem is often mistaken for the solution to the problem."

Ruttenberg sighed in agreement on the Zoom screen. I then grumbled about those articles you see about disgraced industry figures who have caused massive harm. Inevitably, one of the rich friends of the rich transgressor (who hasn't, as far as anyone is aware, meaningfully made amends or apologized to *anyone*) wonders aloud about where society's compassion and mercy have gone, *yada yada*. Justice, mercy, and compassion are valuable concepts, of course; I would not have talked to the people in this chapter if I didn't believe that. But in that moment, my frustration with people, especially connected industry people with *all kinds of resources*, who are not willing to do this kind of genuinely valuable work, individually or as a community . . . *grrrr*. As my rant petered out, the rabbi responded with sage wisdom, and at the end of her response, the Chicago jumped out.

"As a rabbi, I will say, firmly: Nobody is ever beyond redemption or repair. Rabbinic lore teaches that the heavenly gates of repentance are always open, and I sincerely hope they choose to walk through them someday and attend to the needs of their victims—and their own need to face what they have done, and to change and transform into better people. And I sincerely hope their own communities will hold them accountable until they do. But hey, we all contain multitudes, and speaking as a feminist, if these people don't do anything meaningful, well . . ."

Ruttenberg held up her middle finger with one hand. "Here is my mercy," she said. And then did the same with the other hand. "And here is my compassion."

Bo Travis, the psychologist, lives in Florida but travels to Chicago a lot. Much of his work involves the correctional system in Illinois and, for a while, that of North Dakota. He evaluates people convicted of sexual crimes who have served their sentences and makes recommendations on what should happen next.

"Even though they've finished their sentence, the state is afraid to let them go because they think they might offend again," Travis said. He evaluates them in order to help the state decide what to do next. Among the options: the person is released with some restrictions and monitoring; they are released with serious monitoring and oversight (including a GPS tracker); or they undergo a civil commitment, which means the state keeps them locked up even though they've served their time.

To do a proper evaluation, Travis told me he reexamines the nature of the person's crimes. He looks at other, nonsexual violent behavior they've ever exhibited. He does research to determine if that person has engaged in patterns of antisocial behavior. If he was ever out on parole, how did he do with supervision? "Is he just not a rule follower?" Travis asks. Did he respond to the kind of intensive treatment that can, in some cases, cause clinical narcissists, sociopaths, and other harm-doers to change their behaviors? Or does the convicted individual continue to be "a person who's going to take what he wants from people without regard to anybody?"

Even when men—and Travis deals mostly with men—undergo a civil commitment, "this isn't to warehouse them," he said. "This is to treat them and prepare them for release back into the community." Maybe. He told me that Illinois has around six hundred people who are either awaiting civil commitment trials or civilly committed—some for more than twenty years. Certain individuals just do not get with the program, and must be, in the opinion of professionals like Travis and the state, kept away from the rest of society.

Those who are released with strict supervision are reevaluated regularly, and even those who graduate to less intense oversight will remain on the sex offender registry forever. The morning of the day Travis and I talked, he'd met with a man who'd been out for about a year. "The state knows where he is every second of the day," Travis told me. "The state is paying for his housing while he is getting a job, so he can support himself." I asked what the guy's mindset was.

"He's humble," Travis said. "He said, 'I'm trying to see my community management team as allies. I go to them for everything, every problematic thought I have. I seek their assistance.'"

The man might be lying. He might reoffend. But there are a set of employees, programs, and oversight mechanisms to keep him on the straight and narrow—and if that fails, there are all sorts of systems that will kick into gear. But the simple fact of having been to jail could well have changed the equation for him.

Travis told me that, according to the research literature on this topic, a sizable number of those who are convicted of sexual crimes—or even just arrested—do not reencounter the criminal justice system. There are many caveats attached to this information, of course, all of which Travis readily conceded. Many crimes, especially sexual ones, are profoundly underreported in the first place. Some offenders and reoffenders just don't get caught. But Travis was very clear on one point, which he said his professional experience reflected: peer-reviewed studies support the idea that a notable percentage of men "who experience legal consequences for their sexual offending are not detected committing another sexual offense."

And change is possible for some of those men, Travis told me—but *only if they encounter those meaningful consequences.*

"If there are no real consequences for anything they've done, then they aren't going to be fed up. That's why you need consequences. That's the way to get people to the point where" they are ready to commit to significant change, Travis said. Both those elements—consequences and a sustained desire to change—may, with arduous effort, keep them on a path that leads to a substantial evolution.

So . . . if people are rewarded for their toxic, abusive, harmful, and narcissistic behaviors with lucrative contracts, fame, awards, and luxury gifting suites, uh, what then?

Travis laughed. And I laughed. But we both understood that the way Hollywood often rewards and even encourages harmful behaviors is not funny.

We then talked about the things that are often, in entertainment industry spheres, viewed as "doing the work"—getting a life coach, going to a spa or a high-end retreat, reading a self-help book or two. He shook his head when discussing these things. And he was emphatic on one point: no HR department (in Hollywood or elsewhere) has the experience, resources, or training necessary to identify and profoundly alter clinical narcissists or abusive personalities.

"This is not easy work. It's not 'hang out with a life coach or a guru.' It's not going to be done with affirmations or a cleanse," Travis remarked. "It's a difficult process, and it takes time."

The first step is learning about their cognitive distortions—"human thinking errors," Travis said, that most of us make at one time or another, but in abusive narcissists, have morphed into rigid and deepseated thought patterns around "power and control" that lead them to excuse the awful things they do. In many cases, these folks' outlooks and personalities revolve around, as Travis explained, "a victim stance. That's what leads to the entitlement—'I was hurt, therefore "fill in the blank." I can do whatever I want.'"

"The narcissist's need and demand for respect is constant. Because narcissists are always trying to hang on to that elusive feeling of high self-esteem, the wrath that descends when their precious ego is jeopardized can be truly something to behold," according to Kristin Neff, PhD. "When narcissists receive put-downs from others, their retaliations can be fast and furious, even violent." Joseph Burgo, PhD, the author of *The Narcissist You Know*, concurred: "All [extreme] narcissists care about is proving they are superior to you—a winner to your loser."

If they do change—a situation experts say is rare—it's the result of a hard slog. It can take a very long time before people Travis works with even *recognize* the cognitive distortions that they must then learn to manage. One reason Travis advocates for group therapy is because people can often identify unhealthy thought patterns in others before they recognize them in themselves. "They can't see it at first. Their ego-protective mechanisms keep them from seeing it," he observed. And "narcissistic injury"—which can occur when an abuser is confronted about their behavior—can create moments of aggressive and abusive behavior. (After the publication of some stories, through various channels, I've been made aware of the reactions of people at the center of those pieces; often a major theme of those reactions is narcissistic injury. I don't reply. Burgo's advice is to "not play" their game.)

Elements of these people's behavior is recognizable, however. Every human being, even a well-adjusted one, at times "finds all kinds of ways to avoid seeing true things," Travis told me. With narcissistic and abusive personality types, the shielding can become "impenetrable. Those defenses can be pierced, but they are so strong," even when the person is engaging in behaviors that others find "extremely objectionable."

If these people are fed up enough to really change, they need to understand the path will be a long and difficult one—one that may result in more sanctions if they reject the truth about their behavior. And they won't necessarily gain back the reputation, money, access, and opportunities they had in the past. "Psychopaths and narcissistic personalities are very resistant," he told me. "You can accept that troubled souls are sometimes very creative, but you can still place limits on their behavior. They should not necessarily have power over others." And that's if they come back at all.

We also talked about the culture of enabling that I still encounter—the mindset that people should endure abusive, exploitative, and damaging behaviors because it will "give them a thick skin." Many in creative industries continue to assume that if an action is not physical, it's probably not over the line. I described the behavior of one man I reported on—some of his verbal manipulations and lies—and Travis instantly described it as "sadistic."

"Psychological harm can, in some cases, be worse than physical harm. It often lasts longer," he said. I also described some horrific things that powerful industry people have said to their employees. "That's psychological abuse," Travis responded. "Abuse has to be identified and labeled as such, and it has to be met with consequences." If those things don't happen, then any attempts to alter the larger culture are likely to come to naught.

New ideas about culpability, abuse, and responsibility are trickling through the industry, but, in some cases, toxic people have adopted those terms and concepts to their own ends.

"I can tell you firsthand, the bullies have gotten smarter," said writer/ producer Christopher. "The second you try to stand up to a bully, now you can get painted as being the problem. The pendulum has swung in a direction where automatically, the first person who says 'I'm offended' is the person who gets the platform. I've seen a situation where a person who has a lot of power passive-aggressively bullies a production to get what they want—playing people against each other in these power-hungry games, saying one thing to one person, and something else to another. And when you try to call them on it, they go running up the chain, saying, 'This person's being negative.' In a way, I'm like, 'Whoa, that's clever—getting out in front of it.' There are all kinds of crafty, cunning people out there."

This move does not surprise experts like Travis. "People like that think they can manipulate your mind. And here's why—because they've manipulated a lot of minds before," he noted. And when feeling persecuted and misunderstood is core to an abuser's identity, it's quite easy for them to adopt the language of victimhood. "The bullies have always had victim language," Travis observed. "That's how they got to be bullies."

And part of the reason perpetrators resist meaningful change is because it represents an existential threat. "People don't know who they're going to be when they change. It's like the self they know dies, and what replaces that self—not knowing that is scary," Travis said. "This is all very much amplified with the narcissist, because they don't know who they are in the first place," so the idea of radical alteration leads to terror and resistance. In those who are actually willing to do the real, deep, "painful" work, "there's a way they can identify these thought patterns when they rear their head," and they can make better choices, Travis said. Those with destructive tendencies must manage them, and "people who can't or won't learn to do that—they shouldn't have a place in the industry, because they are going to hurt everyone around them. Continually." And while they are undergoing treatment regarding their damaging patterns, they should not have power, Travis added.

Unfortunately, there are people in this world—some remain in Illinois jails, some are industry millionaires with shelves full of awards—who do not resist but venerate and *nurture* the cognitive distortions that result in many forms of pain and damage for others. Those individuals stay locked into the belief that "other people are not people with hopes and dreams and wishes," Travis said. "They are not real people who can be hurt." The mindset remains "I'm the only one who matters."

Kyra Jones is, among other things, a prison abolitionist. Jones, a filmmaker who has acted on *The Chi* and has written for shows like *Queens* and *Woke*, told me she does not believe calling the police and putting people in prison meaningfully alters communities experiencing harm and violence for the better. For that reason, after she was raped, she agreed to go through a process called restorative justice (or transformative justice); it was led by author and activist Mariame Kaba, the author of *We Do This 'Til We Free Us: Abolitionist Organizing and Transforming Justice*.

Whatever you think of prison abolition, Kaba's work and writings on this and related topics are thought-provoking. She and other activists have explored ways to rethink and rebuild systems of justice, violence prevention, and community care, all areas of American life that are certainly in need of enlightened change. And her work is relevant because Hollywood, like many communities in the United States, would often rather focus on the "one bad apple" theory of wrongdoing instead of getting to the bottom of the whole troubling barrel.

In a 2021 interview, when discussing the trial of Derek Chauvin, who murdered George Floyd in Minneapolis in 2020, Kaba said, "We devolve to the individual so often because the structural and systemic feels so daunting, and how are we going to actually shift and change that? Also, because it feels so good to enact vengeance on people who've harmed us. Part of the conversation we don't have is just how much liminal pleasure people get out of vengeance, which is a big part of why it's so hard to uproot that feeling and that desire within us as human beings."

During my years of hearing about the actions of people in the entertainment industry who have harmed others—and I know of far more instances of abuse, damage, and violence than I've been able to publicly write about—I've felt those emotions. I have fantasized about going John Wick on a few individuals. I never would do that, of course (damn you, Buddhist nonviolence). But I've felt rage when I hear about what survivors have endured at the hands of nightmare people whose reigns of terror were barely a secret. On top of all that, Hollywood itself has trained many of us to think we're entitled to vengeance, under the right circumstances. Or under almost any circumstances, really. The final act of every superhero or action film is, after all, usually just a whole bunch of punching, shooting, and killing.

But there is a difference between vengeance and justice, and there's a big difference between exposing the abuse of one person and changing an entire social, cultural, and corporate apparatus for the better. I care about both, but I'm writing this book because I (and others) desperately long for the latter.

That said, it's hard to remove one person from a system in which they are creating harm with impunity, and harder still to change an entire system that has tolerated (or rewarded) that person for the way they act. It just feels impossible at times. But Kaba is also right about this: "There are many consequences that can be offered that aren't the criminal punishment lane." And Jones got to experience what one of those other lanes was like.

Another reason her experience is exceptionally relevant is because very few entertainment industry transgressors have gone or are likely to go to jail—or even be charged with a crime. Harvey Weinstein is in jail, and Bill Cosby also served time but was released on a technicality in 2021. They are exceptions to the usual entertainment-industry rule.

For decades, Hollywood employed fixers to make sure their stars weren't charged with crimes, or if they were, many mechanisms were in place to ensure that power players generally avoided major legal and criminal consequences for what they did. After a rash of scandals in 1920s Hollywood, famous people "did not suddenly become less prone to scandalous behavior; the cover-up and management strategies simply got better," Anne Helen Petersen writes in *Scandals of Classic Hollywood*, adding that over the years, "the methods of containment may change, but the pattern endures." She's right about the lack of change. Allegations against Cosby were reported on by various media outlets—including *Philadelphia* and *People* magazines—starting in 2005, but he got a new TV deal at NBC in 2014.

And then there's the toll that going through the criminal justice system can take on survivors. "How many decades did it take before the police got involved" in the Cosby and Weinstein situations, Jones asked. "How many survivors coming forward, dozens and dozens and dozens—and how much public pressure was there before the police and the courts got involved? And even if you were one of the few people who does end up with the person who harmed you going to prison, they're gonna get out." Within the restorative justice process Jones went through, the idea was that three entities would end up significantly altered: Jones, Malcolm, and the communities they were part of. On many fronts, she told me, the process—which was fascinatingly chronicled by key participants at transformharm.tumblr.com—was a success. But it also had its challenges.

"It's hard. It's difficult," said Jones. "It's not really about, 'How do we redeem the person who caused harm in the eyes of the community?' That doesn't matter. And it's not focused on punishment, because punishment . . . that's just the simplest term. Like, 'You did a bad thing to someone, so a bad thing also has to happen to you.' That doesn't actually help anybody. But there are consequences" related to the harm done—a concept very similar to what Ruttenberg laid out.

"For example, 'This person caused harm to a child and they are a teacher. This person should not be a teacher anymore,'" Jones said. "Even if they finish the restorative justice process, they should not be put in the environment where they get access to the type of people that they harm. So when people in the industry are like, 'Why does this person have to lose their deal? Why are they losing their TV show?' Because they caused harm to the people on the TV show. So they don't get a TV show anymore. It's not a punishment—it's a safety measure."

Major parts of the process she went through, Jones explained, involved having the communities that she and Malcolm were part of help determine what amends to her would look like. There were also efforts to educate Malcolm on what he did wrong and how he could change, with an emphasis on the fact that the process of changing his behavior would require major commitments of time, energy, and attention. And there were efforts to ensure that the circles they moved in did not offer Malcolm more opportunities to prey on young women. That part of things hit some snags, Jones told me.

Even before the formal procedure had ended, Malcolm was being invited to gatherings in the kinds of "spaces that allowed him to be around the kind of women he targets. He was specifically targeting Black women who are in the organizing community and the arts community. He weaponizes the language of the movement and mental health and feminism to make women feel safe, so that he can assault you," Jones said. "I made that very clear in my letter [to these communities]. And people were like, 'Let's have him come and do these poetry readings.'" The organizations, she said, "put him on a pedestal" for admitting to the harm he'd caused. "And then we found out he was still raping people."

I hadn't been expecting that. My first response was to wonder— incorrectly and insensitively—if the process hadn't worked. I apologized to Jones for some inept word choices, and then she patiently explained that she still believes in the process, in large part because it centered on what *she* needed. "I mostly engaged in it for me," she said. "I don't care about him. If I got my pick of what happened to him, I'd push him in a volcano." It caused Jones to pay attention to "all of the ways that I had not been prioritizing my own care and healing, and I was thinking about what would restore the harm that was caused to me."

If she'd gone to the police, "chances are, nothing would happen." The stats on that front support that assumption. According to RAINN, "out of every 1,000 sexual assaults, 975 perpetrators will walk free." And the truth is, all kinds of processes of addressing harm can and do fail sometimes. There are, after all, those who commit crimes, go to jail, and then commit crimes again. What happened was "not the fault of the process, it was *his* fault." Jones added that she's aware of many other restorative justice processes that resulted in "the person not continuing the harm."

"When I talk to people who are considering transformative justice processes, I do say, 'You have no control over the result, over whether that person continues the behavior or not.'" Jones also worked as a sexual assault survivor advocate at Northwestern University, and she recalled that "so many times, survivors say, 'I just want to make sure this person never does it again.' And I'm like, 'That is out of your control. You can only control what you are doing.'"

"I tried," she said. "At the end of the day, I attempted—or the community attempted—to prevent this harm from happening again. Mariame [Kaba] says all the time, restorative justice is not going to work on everyone. It's not going to be the right solution for everyone. But we need more options. We need to explore more ways of addressing harm."

In any case, our conversation landed in a similar place to my conversations with Ruttenberg and Travis. People committing harm, abuse, and violence need to face consequences. Whatever process they go through, even if they're addressing what they've done, it "doesn't mean they get to have the same cushy life they had before," Jones said, "and have all the types of power and access they had."

Every so often, a phrase or sentence lodges itself in my memory bank permanently. During one reckoning about harm done in a community of film people a few years ago, a woman with the Twitter handle Spacecrone came up with this indelible formulation: "compassion without boundaries and accountability is a form of enabling." Ten words containing *so much truth*. Another brief but memorable phrase: "Vengeance is a lazy form of grief." That's from the movie *The Interpreter*, and though it works, the following sentence works just as well, in my experience: "Vengeance is an *understandable* form of grief."

Compassion, boundaries, violence, grief, vengeance: all these things are messy and complicated, as are many cases of misconduct and patterns of abuse, whether those situations are adjudicated in or out of the public eye. All these matters reside in or near our deepest, primal, and most intimate selves. But the kind of guardrails and guidelines laid out here may help serve as lights that lead survivors and their allies out of the darkness.

The good news is that the thinking and suggestions and ideas these experts offered are proof that the industry does not have to resort to binary solutions—the only two options are not "permanently disgraced" or "protected forever." There are situations with shades of gray in them, in which people need to learn and grow, and once they've completed those evolutions, many will need help—and also require serious, consistent monitoring—to stay on the right path.

But even as I acknowledge the gray areas and the varied range of solutions that can be brought to bear, I need to underline a big, uncomfortable truth. For a hundred years, the entertainment industry has not had a reliable way for people who have experienced harm to report that harm, formally or informally, and get any kind of real relief, let alone amends. Very powerful executives admitted to me that the systems they had in place until very recently—the methods employees were supposed to use to report abuse, misconduct, violence, and all the rest—were bullshit. They didn't use those words, but that's really what they were saying. Those "systems" were shams. They were part of the problem. And in some cases, they still are.

Many people have lost money, time, and careers, and have gone through hell, all to make things on flickering screens. It never had to be that way; all that harm was not inevitable. It was not the unavoidable byproduct of harnessing creative energy. So, *so* much of the damage that was done happened as the result of specific, active choices that people and companies with power made over a very long period of time. Those people and companies need to reckon with—and atone for—the vast damage done. Not that all of them will.

Even so, the industry's patterns of moral evasion don't need to serve as the roadmap for where we go from here. The changing and fixing that still needs to occur can happen on many fronts—individuals can change, communities and social groups can change, ideas about leadership and creativity certainly need to change a lot. Decision-makers in the industry have much to do before integrity, safety, respect, and amends for harm done even approach being the norm for the people who work for them.

But our ideas about kindness and tolerance need to change too. Those qualities shouldn't be eliminated, of course. But we all need to be aware of how easily they can be manipulated. What I know after talking to hundreds of people who've come across industry narcissists, abusers, and bullies is that *these people weaponize the niceness of good people every chance they get*. The industry attracts a lot of good-hearted, empathic people. And those qualities are turned against them by industry abusers all the damn time. The matters I've explored in this chapter (and this book) can be complex, but simplicity can be found in this territory as well: Some people hurt, abuse, manipulate, and damage other people because they want to. And because they can. And in some cases—too many cases—they won't stop on their own.

It's going to take a lot of work to make sure the industry has the guardrails it needs in the future. Those with real power need to own that, and fix what's broken. If you're in the process of *truly* fixing these systems, keep fucking going.

12

A New Day for the Death Star

What Industry Companies Must Do to Foster Real Change

I really think something has shifted seismically.
—*Lesli Linka Glatter*

The actor was harassing people on set. Tale as old as time, right? Well, the ending of this story may not be the one you expect.

Complaints about this actor's pattern of harassing women rose through the ranks, and the people at the top of this project's food chain became involved. They recognized his behavior as unacceptable. Relatively quickly, as these things go, the actor was confronted about his behavior. He was not only told it was a problem, he was offered guidelines and support, on the assumption that he might need those things to change his unprofessional conduct.

He was not interested in changing. He minimized his harassing actions, portraying them as normal, if not expected. He dismissed the complaints out of hand. "Therefore, we had no faith that it would stop," said Patrick, the high-level industry executive in charge of the company behind this production.

Those in charge—a group that included the project's creative leads but was ultimately headed by Patrick—briefly discussed giving the actor an on-set minder, to make sure he didn't behave unprofessionally. This likely would have been an expensive solution, and it was ultimately deemed an impractical one as well: "You can't devise a perfect system of monitoring" one person's behavior with every single person on set, Patrick noted.

As ludicrous as that "solution" may sound, I'm aware that other

Hollywood workplaces have indeed assigned "don't mistreat colleagues" minders to people. You might think it would be more efficient to either *not hire* or eject harassers who make it clear they are not going to follow the rules of commonsense decency. Many other industries get by without relying on toxicity nannies for adults. But . . . well, this is Hollywood. When "names" are involved—not even A-list names—it's an understatement to say that common sense does not routinely prevail.

And that is one reason the story of this actor—the harasshole in question—remains an object of fascination for me. Some industry executives (yes, still) expend a lot of time and energy to keep around problematic people who have expended little or no effort on meaningful change. Thus it's not hard to imagine the actor in this scenario expecting an ancient Hollywood tradition to play out: people bring a concern about his conduct to him, he tells them to get lost, the end. Roll credits.

Except . . . he was fired.

"We said, 'Even though it's going to cost us a lot of money to reshoot the part and recast it, we're going to do it,'" Patrick told me. And that's what they did. (This incident is not about Frank Langella's 2022 firing for alleged harassment on the set of a Netflix program. The situation I'm describing happened a few years prior to that.)

What melted my brain about this situation is that executives didn't wait for the actor to harass more people or wreak vengeance on those who reported him. The people with power just bounced him. A high six-figure sum was spent reshooting his scenes with a new actor (who, speaking as a critic, was excellent in the role).

These actions, more than any press release or corporate manual, told workers that they were seen and heard, that they had value and worth. The company not only said it believed they deserved a respectful workplace, *it acted on that belief*. I still don't think that that's the message industry workers typically get. Need proof? Five years after #MeToo broke open in Hollywood, 70 percent of respondents to a Women in Film survey said the industry's culture of abuse and misconduct had "improved somewhat"—but 69 percent said they had experienced abuse or misconduct within that time frame.

Patrick is understandably worried about legal exposure should the actor's name come out in connection with this book. Even without that identifying information, this story is worth telling. But I have more complicated feelings about the incident than I did when Patrick first told me about it in 2018.

Back then, we were a year into the turbulent changes wrought by the #MeToo movement. I'd been reading what felt like an endless series of stories about industry abuse and the widespread enabling of toxicity, assault, and gross misconduct. I had done major reporting in these realms as well. During that shell-shocked time—when a lot of us who'd covered the industry had our assumptions about it rocked to the core and then rocked some more—I latched on to the story Patrick told me as a possible beacon of hope. I wasn't naive, of course. When I first heard the story, I knew that a damaging situation resolving in that way was the exception, not the rule.

But could this story point the way toward a better future? At a painful time, I wanted that to be true. After months of wading hip-deep in swill, I was tremendously wary of having hope, but I also desperately wanted at least a few data points that allowed me to think even a glimmer of guarded optimism was possible. I also knew that for a hundred years, Hollywood had resisted meaningful reforms of all kinds while distracting everybody with shiny, pretty things. Had I been distracted by a shiny story and taken my eye off the ball?

Four years later, I was still thinking about the story Patrick had told me, because my continued reporting on the industry had forced me to look at every seam and stitch on that ball. Over excellent salmon, I pressed Patrick for more details. I was very hung up on one part of the narrative: He and the rest of the people overseeing that project didn't wait to fire the guy? Really?

"No, of course not," he replied.

I was silent for a few moments after he said that. Part of what stopped me cold was that Patrick did not think he'd done anything unusual. He and his team didn't wait for more people to be demeaned or damaged while they dithered. In my experience, dithering is far more common than decisive action. But in that 2018 case, more people did not have to sacrifice more time, energy, and thought to this problem, or risk their mental, physical, and financial health because nobody with real power wanted to make a decision. It was just . . . *over*.

Patrick was surprised that I was surprised it went down that way. But there were a number of points at which the entire situation could have gone (and often does go) wrong, and I broke all that down for him, piece by piece:

- The people on that set recognized unprofessional behavior for what it was. This is changing, but in many industry workplaces I've covered, people have been trained (and gaslit) into not identifying what they were forced to endure as the harassment or misconduct that it definitely was.

- The coworkers felt empowered to talk to one another about the unprofessional behavior they were experiencing. It's not all that rare for industry folks (especially crews and lower-level workers) to recognize behavior from others as problematic or wrong but feel unable to bring it up to colleagues, let alone to anyone with real power. It is a hallmark of many abusers, after all, to keep people isolated in separate silos of pain.

- Those with power and status listened when concerns were raised. They not only heard people out, those with power at no point enacted revenge, overtly or covertly, on the people who spoke up.

- As this information rose up the food chain, those with power and influence accepted that the behavior was unprofessional and unacceptable; as happens too often in other cases, they didn't try to convince those enduring the behavior that they were imagining or overstating things. There was no minimizing, shaming, or victim-blaming.

- Those in authority got all the information they needed to make a decision, and they made it. The situation did not fester.

I do realize, of course, that the actor could have just said, "Oh no! I had no idea my behavior was wrong—I'll stop," and then not stopped. That happens with depressing regularity. But, if nothing else, a number of industry companies now know they are sitting on potential time bombs if they don't take these situations seriously. Industry workers can and will use every means at their disposal, including social media, to call out transgressors, as happened with various online allegations of misconduct against director Cary Fukunaga, which were later chronicled more fully in a 2022 *Rolling Stone* article. (When asked about allegations of using and "abusing" his power to pursue and harass young, powerless women on set and off, Fukunaga's attorney told the publication that Fukunaga has "'not acted in any manner that would or should generate' an article focusing on claims of misconduct made against him.")

Some companies, sometimes, are monitoring certain workplaces more closely, to determine whether people who've caused serious problems—and who weren't let go—actually did stop doing unacceptable things. Do those companies still fuck up? Yes. Are things changing? Yes, but from an incredibly toxic set of norms.

That said, workers have a much better sense now that there can be strength in numbers, and many are less willing to put up with the kinds of mistreatment that have been routine for a long time. I was feeling low one day, wondering aloud whether the work that reporters were doing was having any effect on the industry at all, when a Hollywood activist said this: "You're helping change the expectations of the people who are coming up."

I do think those expectations have evolved. And when it comes to those who run big corporations, at least some of their calculations have changed as well.

For one thing, executives I spoke to now readily admit that it's not easy to get employees to believe that using the reporting channels at their companies—formal and informal—can be trusted not to backfire on them. That's because using those channels *has* backfired on workers, *a lot,* for years. An industry veteran named Ron told me about a friend whose agent said not to list any of the numerous problems with his boss in his exit interview. "If you are the person coming forward, and they have invested millions in him as their showrunner, you coming forward alone probably won't accomplish anything. And this is something they are not going to want to hear," Ron said his friend was told. As Ron put it, "You can have all the reporting mechanisms in the world, but where is the incentive on our end?"

It's a good question, one I don't have a definitive answer to, except to say that it's going to be a long, slow, difficult process to get industry workers to regularly trust the mechanisms that are being put in place in some (certainly not all) workplaces. If I could boil down my advice to those in power, it would be this: all entities that have power over industry workplaces need to show *meaningful accountability over time*. Making people feel safe at work will not be a speedy, easy process—many still understandably think they are risking a lot if they attempt to register complaints about all manner of unprofessional behavior, from the less serious to the very serious.

So the work is not done yet (and it's barely begun in some places). But one thing that's heartening is hearing some top executives say that getting the rank and file to trust reporting pathways will take time. "It has been a very complicated process," Paramount's David Nevins told me. "You've got to create countervailing forces. One is a clear laying-out of expectations—what is expected, what is acceptable behavior."

And that change is beginning to happen, according to writer and creator Mike Royce. "There's more education about what the standards should be," said Royce, executive producer of *One Day at a Time* and *Men of a Certain Age*. "There's greater awareness about the fact that we're in a workplace, meaning certain behavior is unacceptable and can't just be written off as 'part of the creative process' or some previously accepted excuse."

Still, things can and do go wrong. And not every workplace allegation is the same. Someone who made one inappropriate comment should not receive the same consequence as a person who regularly makes people feel unsafe. Not every corrective action will be the subject of a press release or an internal memo, nor should every person accused of misconduct be fired. But when weighing the tensions inherent in these complex situations, Nevins told me, "A big thought in my head is always, How is this going to play to that cadre of people who experienced it or who know about it, or who heard about an investigation?"

Protecting those folks from retaliation—from anyone at all, and certainly from the person they reported—is now recognized by some as a critical goal. It's "the bare minimum," Nevins told me. And then executives have to decide what to do: "The right thing might be corrective action. The right thing might be a change—maybe it's 'remove this person.'" But in each situation, he said, "I want to maintain trust. I don't want lower-level employees saying, 'This got swept under the carpet.'"

"What's difficult about this is you have to ask yourself, 'What is an unforgivable offense versus a forgivable one, and what is a teachable problem versus an unteachable problem?'" FX's John Landgraf observed. "It turns you into a cop and you don't want to be a cop. Fundamentally, you don't go into this industry because you want to be a policeman. But you have to come to the reluctant acceptance that every system needs an internal affairs department, and that basically policing is a part of leadership. I don't think it's a standard that's always met everywhere at all times, but you have an obligation to provide a safe working environment. You just do."

Over the years, a lot of people have confided in me about compromises and decisions that left bitter or guilty tastes in their mouths. Witnessing misconduct, abuse, and acts of cruelty takes its own toll, and many of those folks wrestle with agonizing questions about what they could have done differently. They often tell me about trying to change bad situations, but in many cases, they had to leave the relevant workplace as an act of self-preservation. Christopher told me he was "haunted" by one work experience that he exited (despite being offered an extremely large raise to stay). The erratic and chaotic man he worked for showed no signs of dialing down his (well-known) abusiveness, and Christopher knew the colleagues he left behind were in for a rough ride.

I asked him, "Were you the person or the entity in that situation with the most power?" He responded, "No." And I said, "Then responsibility for changing that situation was not on you."

I know the workplace Christopher left very well, and I also know that powerful people connected to that production knew how awful that boss was—and they left him in place for a decade. The odds of Christopher alone being able to change that ranged from slim to none.

If feeling guilty or even partly complicit in the existence of wretched workplaces means many industry people, as they rise, work hard not to be like the worst colleagues they've known—and many are indeed trying to be the change they want to see in Hollywood—that's not a bad thing. But my most stringent assessments regarding patterns of industry misconduct are reserved for the people and the companies that, in a given situation, could have done the most to fix a bad situation—and that would have been the most protected from any potential blowback. My most savage industry burn does not, perhaps surprisingly, contain any swears: "You could have done more, and it would have cost you nothing."

A variation: "You could have done more, and it would have gained you a lot." Any number of abusers have cost industry companies and productions a great deal, either in hush money or in lost time, high turnover, and productivity derailed by some blend of inefficiency, cruelty, and stupidity. It's possible that encouraging survivors of mistreatment, violence, and abuse to come forward—if that's the right decision for them, of course—might well save money. Evan Rachel Wood is deeply sympathetic to the fact that some people might not ever be able to talk about their negative experiences publicly or even in some private contexts, due to fears about their safety or their careers. But if the industry encourages an atmosphere of accountability and respect, it's likely to lead to more positive outcomes and, ideally, fewer awful ones. "We can tell great stories and be efficient and save money without abusing people," Wood said. "That's the thing—you'll save more money because there won't be damage control."

There are other reasons to weed out people who consistently engage in heinous, unprofessional, or abusive behaviors—aside from it being the right thing to do. Those individuals might also be doing other bad stuff. I first learned about the Al Capone Theory of Sexual Harassment in a 2017 piece from tech-industry veterans Leigh Honeywell and Valerie Aurora. They note that, despite his many other criminal activities, the government only succeeded in convicting Capone of financial improprieties. The authors made the connection to a string of men in the tech industries who not only acted inappropriately to colleagues but were found to have flouted a series of other policies and rules.

"Initially, the connection eluded us: why would the same person who made unwanted sexual advances also fake expense reports, plagiarize, or take credit for other people's work?" they write. "Then we realized what the connection was: all of these behaviors are the actions of someone who feels entitled to other people's property—regardless of whether it's someone else's ideas, work, money, or body. Another common factor was the desire to dominate and control other people." Well, this certainly sounds familiar.

Honeywell and Aurora go on to note that "organizations that understand the Al Capone theory of sexual harassment have an advantage: they know that reports or rumors of sexual misconduct are a sign they need to investigate for other incidents of misconduct, sexual or otherwise. Sometimes sexual misconduct is hard to verify because a careful perpetrator will make sure there aren't any additional witnesses or records beyond the target and the target's memory. . . . But one of the implications of the Al Capone theory is that even if an organization can't prove allegations of sexual misconduct, the allegations themselves are sign to also urgently investigate a wide range of aspects of an employee's conduct."

Does every allegation need to result in this kind of wide-ranging inquiry? No. But some do. Here's one way for executives to reframe most employee complaints, whatever channel they arrive through: *these people are trying to help you avoid being nuked from orbit.* If companies have early warning systems and don't use them wisely—if they use them instead to stifle employees and drive them away—then these firms are likely to end up inside a big, stinking scandal that looks worse with every new story that comes out.

One thing that might help speed up the process of reform is something like Callisto, a reporting system that is available to students on dozens of college campuses. The service—offered by a nonprofit that is independent of those colleges—allows people to file encrypted reports and supplies survivors with information and resources on a number of fronts.

"Any serial perpetrator can be detected, regardless of their university affiliation," Callisto's site says of its Vault Matching System. "Over 90 percent of sexual assaults on college campuses are committed by repeat perpetrators, who offend an average 6 times before they graduate; yet less than 10 percent of student survivors report their assault."

Callisto isn't fully anonymous—it requires people to submit an email address and other contact information—but the service does not share information with a survivor's college (and those using Callisto can delete their reports at any time). Users can be paired with Legal Options Counselors, "third-party attorneys who advise survivors of repeat perpetrators on their range of options to seek justice. . . . This could include reporting to their school, obtaining a restraining order, contacting the police, confronting the perpetrator, engaging in restorative justice, etc."

A profoundly frustrating industry dynamic is watching people with bad track records on any number of fronts get ejected by one employer only to be hired by others, if not *lots* of others. The idea that Hollywood couldn't afford to implement something like Callisto is nonsensical. The biggest companies in the industry are doing fine. And companies like GoPro and Zillow have made the reporting tool AllVoices available to their workers, and they still manage to be successful businesses. Speaking of success, as Jason Kilar said in 2022, just before exiting a top job at what became Warner Bros. Discovery, that corporate team had just brought in "the highest revenues in the 99-year history of the company last year in the face of a pandemic, in the face of theatrical closures, in the face of cord-cutting of five to seven percent a year." That firm is now servicing a lot of debt, true, but for the biggest entities in the industry, the cost of implementing an effective reporting tool would barely be a rounding error in the corporate budget.

Attempts to offer a service like Callisto have been made—and a big attempt is supposed to follow a smaller one that launched a few years ago.

Actor and producer Jessica Barth was one of the driving forces behind Voices in Action, a survivor-led organization and reporting service created in 2018. VIA "has helped hundreds of people privately and safely document incidents of sexual abuse and misconduct" and was "directly involved in bringing dozens of perpetrators into the spotlight and removed from their positions of power," according to the group's site. VIA, which relies in part on donations and a GoFundMe, in a 2022 blog post encouraged attendance at two high-profile Los Angeles trials "to support the women assaulted and lives altered by Harvey Weinstein and Danny Masterson."

Of course, VIA was just one of many reform efforts that sprang up in the wake of the #MeToo movement. Many people are aware that Time's Up, the high-profile advocacy group founded in 2018, messily imploded in 2021; the majority of its leadership resigned and most staffers were laid off. Various issues came to light when it was discovered that some senior figures at Time's Up had consulted with advisors to Andrew Cuomo, the governor of New York at that time, who was accused of harassment and a string of other serious transgressions. The problems at Time's Up went deep, as a report written by an independent consultant found.

"The organization was riven by disputes, sometimes between different groups of staff, over what the organization should be, with one participant saying in a listening session for the report, 'I don't know what we do, and I really should,'" notes a 2021 story in the *Washington Post*. "Some of Time's Up's employees and many of its stakeholders viewed the organization as 'distracted or unfocused,' the report found." It's not that the organization didn't notch some wins—and its separate Legal Defense Fund appears to have assisted survivors of abuse in many industries—but the group's original wave of energy is spent. Time's Up formally ceased operations in early 2023.

If an organization more effective than Time's Up arises as a force for positive change in the industry, no one will be happier about it than me. But we'll have to see. What's never been in doubt is the sturdiness of this cycle of events: the industry says it wants to reform, and then things just quietly go back to more or less how they were.

Whether that's going to happen this time remains an open question. As director Lesli Linka Glatter said to me, "There were times in the past I felt that reform slid back, but I really think something has shifted seismically in our culture."

Part of that shift may have been driven by the rise of formal and informal reporting and industry hotlines. The advocacy group Women in Film offers workers in TV and movies a hotline that supplies "resources and support, including referral to pro bono legal services, low-fee therapy, and free support groups," among other types of assistance. The Screen Actors Guild–American Federation of Television and Radio Artists (SAG-AFTRA) has an online reporting portal for members of that union, and Glatter said that more time, staff hours, and resources have been assigned to the Directors Guild of America's reporting hotline. In some cases, representatives for the DGA told me, instances of misconduct that came through the guild's hotline resulted in people being fired.

"I think it depends what it is," said Glatter, the president of the DGA. "Every situation has to be properly investigated. But sometimes, yeah, the action has to be extreme."

Many observers I talked to are hoping for a seismic and ideally permanent shift courtesy of an organization called the Hollywood Commission, which is working on an industrywide reporting tool that could finally start tracking not just abuse and misconduct but the industry's repeat offenders.

The Hollywood Commission was founded in 2017, and it's a less high-profile but very well-connected endeavor that came out of the movement to reform the industry. On its board are Lucasfilm president Kathleen Kennedy and well-connected industry attorney Nina Shaw; its chair is author, professor, and activist Anita Hill. The Commission's values, as stated on its site, are laudable: "We believe in the value of diverse, inclusive and equitable workplaces. . . . We believe that creating a climate of accountability for abuse and bias . . . begins with leadership." The Commission put out a series of reports in 2020 and

2021, and on its site offers guidelines and recommendations regarding how workplaces should operate. In a statement to me, the Commission noted that it had developed trainings and held panels, workshops, and roundtables to help educate industry workers about safety, inclusion, and anti-harassment strategies.

I am grateful that, in its reports, the Commission put some statistical heft behind things we know—that industry workers face racism, sexism, homophobia, mistreatment, and various kinds of unprofessional conduct on the regular. I've often found that in tough situations, numbers can help. They can make unfortunate truths about hiring, promotion, and culture undeniable; where arguments and persuasion fail, math occasionally triumphs.

But one of the most surprising things about covering the entertainment industry is that it is positively *awash* in numbers that tell us how bad things are (or, occasionally, how some situations are improving). USC, UCLA, Pay Up Hollywood, the WGA, the DGA, GLAAD, SDSU's Center for the Study of Women in TV and Film—these are just some of the organizations that regularly put out statistics and reports on various aspects of the industry. For a long time, industry reporters have been swimming in data—and I'm not saying we should turn off the data pipes. They provide key tools for those trying to make the industry even marginally responsive and accountable.

But at this point, what would help, even more than another study or set of numbers, is a tool that undeniably *works*. I have long believed that a well-funded, well-publicized, functional, and effective industry-wide reporting portal could be revolutionary. In 2020, the Commission said it was going to unveil its reporting portal the following year.

"People feel there is a lack of accountability for misbehavior," Hill told *The Hollywood Reporter* in 2020. "As many as 64 percent of our sample said they thought people in power or authority would not be held accountable for harassment that was found to exist." The story notes that "ninety-one percent of respondents to [a Hollywood Commission] survey expressed a need for such a reporting platform."

"Both victims and bystanders indicated to us at the rate of 70 percent or so that they believe reporting is too risky," Hill said. "They fear retaliation. . . . This is an important start in instilling some confidence and trust in the system. It's not the end of what we will be doing, but it is a start."

That start has taken time to arrive. In a mid-2022 statement, the

Commission told me it is "prioritizing getting it right, including a trauma-informed approach. The user interface, IT infrastructure and technical aspects of the platform are nearing completion, as are legal and regulatory reviews." Initial user testing was scheduled to begin in the third quarter of 2022, and feedback "from user testing will be incorporated during our phased launch." The statement added, "The goal is to launch in beta later [in 2022] with evaluation mechanisms in place to ensure the efficacy of the platform."

The Resource and Reporting Hub will reportedly have many similarities to Callisto and services like it: it is supposed to feature an anonymous chat function offering advice and resources; secure and confidential communication; and once matches are made among people reporting the same person, "users are notified . . . and provided an opportunity to participate in the investigation," according to the statement the Commission sent me.

An independent, reliable, and robust tool like this, properly implemented, publicized, and consistently supported, could be a game-changer. But we'll have to see. I understand how a desire to get the platform right, not to mention the pandemic, may have led to some delays, but the length of time it's taken to get this tool to the workers who need it has made me wonder, again, if the most powerful people, entities, and companies in the industry genuinely desire the real, lasting change that Hollywood unquestionably needs. I hope they do. But if this long-awaited reporting system ends up being one more broken promise to entertainment industry employees, at least we will know where to lay the responsibility—at the highest echelons of Hollywood.

Of course, no one tool, rule, or change will fix the entire industry, so here is a grab bag of other suggestions. This is not an exhaustive list of what can or should be done to reform Hollywood. But it's a start.

Meaningfully vet the people you hire for positions of authority.

It is immensely frustrating when people whose terrible, bullying, biased, wildly incompetent, or harassing track records are hired again and again, long after their reputations were common knowledge. Many's the time I've muttered, "How is it that *I* know this person is a nightmare, and these industry executives don't?" Sometimes they know but pretend they don't. Sometimes they don't ask.

If you're hiring someone in any position of power or authority, call around to multiple people who worked for this person in various capacities. Don't just hire based on someone's IMDb profile: A lot of toxic, abusive, or ferociously incompetent people have, for one reason or another, well-regarded entries on their résumés. Their résumé alone is not a reason to hire them. Find out about their behavior from those who know what it was like to work with those individuals. And if you don't talk to at least a few people from historically excluded groups as part of the process, that's a problem. If you can't find that many—or any—instances of a person working with people from those communities, well, that is another problem.

These red flags—they are out there, sometimes a whole sea of them. Please put reporters who write about industry abuse out of work by paying attention to the seas of flapping red pennants. If you're not going to do that, please, just stop issuing press releases or giving speeches that state that you value your employees.

Train and supervise the people you put in positions of authority.

"It's hard to think of many industries where somebody goes from sitting in a room in front of a word processor, writing alone, to sitting in a room with eight other writers, to running the multimillion-dollar company" that is a film or television production, John Landgraf said.

"It's not like it's rocket science, but it's a lot to learn and consume," writer/producer Meredith Stiehm said of being a showrunner. "The volume of the job takes some getting used to. And the network model that I spent years in was very much like, 'Here are eight people watching me every day, learning from me, I hope I'm setting a good example so now they can go do this.' And that is not happening for many people these days, and that's a real void."

It is. And when people are put in all kinds of high-stress jobs—not just showrunner—with no training, well . . . imagine that in half of the cars the automotive industry manufactured, the brakes didn't work. What could possibly go wrong?

"We promote people into management and we just hope that they figure it out. And then we stand, mouth agape, when things go sideways. And this isn't just a problem for our new managers. We are 40 years into this strategy and now the overwhelming majority of the workforce came up through this same form of occupational hazing," said Melissa Nightingale, in an interview in Anne Helen Petersen's newsletter *Culture Study*. Nightingale and her husband, Johnathan, worked at Mozilla and are now management consultants who've written a book, *Unmanageable: Leadership Lessons from an Impossible Year*. Almost everything they said in that interview had a great deal of relevance regarding how Hollywood has typically functioned (or, more accurately, not functioned).

"There's a very sad stat that most leaders, not just [in] tech but across all knowledge industries, go about 12 years in the role before they get any management training," Melissa said. "You didn't have to look too hard to see that the ramifications weren't slightly less productive orgs. The impact was unchecked harassment, workplace trauma, and a massive flight of marginalized groups from the sector." Add to that Hollywood's general attitude toward its workforce—it's disposable—and you have a recipe for the kinds of constant yet avoidable abuses we've been reading about for years.

By the way, that's not just me saying the industry views its workers as disposable. Glatter agreed with that assessment. Patrick observed that, for a long time, in various ways, the industry ensured that "you ended up with a very small number of people who were fundamentally" seen as necessary to the production, "and a very large group of people who were seen as replaceable."

Writer/producer Terrence noted, "The studios treat each production like a cocktail party instead of a place of business. There are very few rules—and what rules exist are seldom enforced, especially for the most powerful people on set. It's within their power to make every workplace and set and writers' room safe and healthy and, you know, an ordinary workplace. And they don't do it because I think they think it will cost them a little extra money."

At the moment, the WGA is one of the only entities that regularly provides formal training for aspiring showrunners. (Sony Pictures Television began its own training program in 2021 with nineteen participants.) Anecdotally speaking, there are always more people who want to take the WGA course than can be accommodated (and that program has some requirements that candidates must meet before they're accepted). As noted, the typical apprenticeship path for TV showrunners—gaining experience in various skills as they ascend the ladder—has largely gone away, due to shorter seasons and short overall runs. The Nightingales offer a training program—which is "five or six" weeks long. "That's honestly as fast as we can go to give people the room to do work that will actually last," Johnathan Nightingale said. (The sad fact is, their training course lasts as long as some writers' rooms do these days.)

Hollywood's longtime approach to apprenticeship—watch someone do the job long enough to learn how to do the job—is simply not what it once was, certainly in the TV realm. As for the industry's other method of helping new showrunners and directors—pairing them with a more experienced veteran—that can go well. Or it can go very poorly.

Joe, a high-level executive, told me about various instances of pairing up new showrunners (most from historically excluded communities) with more experienced hands. In one situation, the veteran and the younger creators of a show worked well together, and that alliance helped in the propagation of a much buzzed-about hit. In a second, a new creator was paired with two different people, and didn't click with either. Eventually a third was tried, and it worked, but there was a lot of wrangling and difficulty before then.

In a third situation, a new creator was left largely to flail alone and problems developed. In stories that later came out in the press, Joe felt some of the issues at the program were skewed or overblown, but he also blamed himself for not assisting the young creator more. Eventually, he canceled the program because "the popular attitude towards the show had gotten so poisoned among the audience that we needed to for that show to succeed," he said.

Too often, still, things spin out. And I ask this question, not as a condemnation or from a place of bitterness, but with sincere curiosity: Would that show be on its fifth season if that creator had participated in an effective six-week management course?

**If you want to change the makeup of your employee
rosters, change the gatekeepers, and if your organization
is snowcapped, address that.**

When people of color are hired in key roles, they hire more people
of color in all kinds of industry jobs; the same is true of white women.
In television, Martha Lauzen said the numbers she tracks move when
directors and executive producers come from these groups; in film, the
gatekeepers who usually matter most are producers and directors. "The
findings have shown that it makes a big difference," Lauzen said. "There
are nontrivial differences in the numbers."

But when organizations have not cultivated the kind of meaningful
change that leads to true inclusion, they often find themselves, as consultant Mistinguette Smith says in a 2019 article, with "snowcapped"
structures: "places where staff of color carry the focus on equity and
justice in frontline, mission-related work, while being clustered at the
bottom of the institutional hierarchy. They have little voice, inconsistent
influence, and lack the power to change the rules about how the organization works. The decision-makers on strategy and resource allocation
sit at the top of the organizational hierarchy like the snowcap on a
mountain, mostly white and white-haired people over 50."

Smith was writing about the nonprofit world, but her words are just
as applicable in Hollywood. If your company finds itself unable to retain qualified workers from historically excluded communities, it might
be because snowcapped organizations can be, to supply the obvious
analogies, frozen in place, not to mention cold and unwelcoming.

**If various kinds of exploitation are a cornerstone of
your business, not only is that bad, people are going to
notice and quite possibly make noise about it.**

"In mid-century America, corporations struck a much more equitable balance between profitability, executive compensation, and worker
pay," *Popular Information* reported in 2022. "In 1965, for example,

American CEOs made 15 times more than the average worker. Today, the CEO-to-worker pay gap at America's largest low-wage employers like Starbucks is closer to 670 to 1, according to a report published this month by the Institute for Policy Studies. The pay ratio at Starbucks is even more extreme. Starbucks' former CEO, Kevin Johnson, raked in $20.4 million in 2021—1,579 times more than what the typical Starbucks worker took home."

It's like they're not even trying. As previously noted, Warner Bros. Discovery CEO David Zaslav's compensation package was almost $247 million in 2021, or around $675,000 *a day*. Support staff at Warner Bros., according to Pay Up Hollywood's 2021 survey of entry-level workers, made about $185 per day. The CEO making 3,600 times more than the lowest-paid worker—seems fine, right? Nothing to see here, move on.

In 2022, at Netflix, chairman and co-CEO Reed Hastings made $34 million and co-CEO and chief content officer Ted Sarandos made $40 million. Netflix has also tried to combine four entry-level jobs into one extremely grinding job. "A lot of showrunners have tried to say: We need one person per one position," a Netflix insider told *Vanity Fair*. "But Netflix has been insisting on these god-awful combinations that are basically burning through assistants and treating them as though they are a renewable resource: When one burns out, you just replace them with the next one." Netflix, not surprisingly, had no comment for that piece.

Pay Up Hollywood—like many other industry movements—arose on social media. It began as a hashtag, but now it is an organization that puts out yearly reports on what support staffers are paid and how they're treated. "We took this idea that as assistants and support staff, you should be grateful for every crumb that you get, and we made it okay to call out the abuses in the jobs," said Liz Hsiao Lan Alper, one of its founders. "One of the things about social media that has been great is that if you are alone in something, you know, for better or for worse, you can find other people who feel the same way you do very quickly."

As Patrick said, holding up his phone at lunch, "These devices and social media have made the world more transparent." He's right. Social media has any number of ills, but it has also allowed industry folks to connect with one another and with reporters. And that is not going to change. "We've so often been divided and cornered and isolated, so that we think that what we're going through is normal and okay," Alper said. But now folks are "getting a chance to connect with one another in a much more meaningful way. That allows us to recognize that the issues we are facing are not individual—they're systemic."

They are. Industry companies and their boards remain quite free to prop up systems in which the rich continue to get a whole lot richer, those on the lower tiers need to have trust funds to survive, and the industry's middle class fades away. They can subject people to serious physical and psychological harm. But the more megaphones that allow people to make situations like these widely known, the more companies will get dinged for not practicing what they preach in press releases. Companies who say they value their employees are going to actually have to start doing it, or the discrepancies between words and actions are likely to be pointed out more and more forcefully.

Pay Up Hollywood has certainly notched some wins, in terms of getting assistants and support staff higher pay at a number of workplaces. By using social media, IATSE made not just the industry but non-Hollywood civilians aware of how bad things can be for crews. None of these trends are going away, so if companies are not going to eliminate and prevent exploitation and abuses, if nothing else, they should expect to take their lumps in the public square.

Don't deploy solutions at the wrong time.

As noted, not every offense in Hollywood is worthy of being fired, and some effective actions are taken out of the public eye. Having said that, when I hear the words "we talked to him" or "HR talked to her," steam comes out of my ears. A lot of the time, this approach simply empowers people with patterns of bad actions to keep doing what they've been doing, and because they realize nothing meaningful will be done about their behavior, it's not rare for them to double down. In any case, all too often, "we talked to him" or "we got her coaching" is what happens when companies want to appear as though they did something effective about a problem, when, realistically, they didn't.

"We talked to him" can take many forms, of course. "Leadership coaching" is what *Bull* star Michael Weatherly and executive producer Glenn Gordon Caron received after the "relentless sexual harassment" of actor/producer Eliza Dushku by Weatherly. Dushku eventually settled with CBS for $9.5 million after her experiences on that show. In a press session months after the Dushku matter came to light in 2018, Kelly Kahl, then the president of CBS Entertainment, noted that the "leadership coaching" those men got was not even compulsory.

In 2021, when I was in the midst of reporting that, after an investigation, Caron had been let go by the network and his overall deal had been canceled, I asked CBS what they had done to repair and change the work culture at *Bull* in the past few years. CBS declined to answer several of my questions. In that story—in which I noted not just Caron's departure but the exit of *Bull* actor Freddy Rodriguez after an investigation—multiple employees described a workplace that was extremely disrespectful on a number of fronts. I wonder if the company can get a refund for that leadership coaching?

Also not apparently effective: the coaching executive producer and coshowrunner Greg Spottiswood received courtesy of Warner Bros. after a series of complaints at the show *All Rise*. A year after the *New York Times* reported on turmoil at *All Rise*—and the coaching and training that followed—I learned that he had made a deeply inappropriate comment on Zoom, among many other troubling incidents and mismanagement that multiple sources described in a story I wrote in 2021. What happened for months after that Zoom comment, which was made *after* all the extensive coaching? Nothing much, because the sources I spoke to said that by that point, they were too intimidated to bring up anything to HR.

Coaching, management training, apprenticeships of all kinds, and leadership courses have their uses. But for those coming into positions of responsibility in Hollywood, training of any kind is usually absent at the outset—and then comes into play *far* too late. Chats from the boss or from HR may be helpful to right things in a workplace that has not yet tipped over into abuse, terror, or toxicity. However, there are very serious limits to what those things can accomplish, and there must be teeth behind these early-stage strategies. Abusive, inappropriate, or potentially dangerous people must know that hot air is not the only blowback they'll face.

Listen to your employees when things are going wrong—but not only then.

One thing bosses can do for free is, well, care.

Landgraf is of the opinion that there is a finite number of world-class storytellers and "there's no substitute in the industry for finding those people and elevating them into positions of power. But when you do that, you have to have a mechanism that monitors the job they are doing as bosses, not just through the prism of the output," he said. What should be assessed is not just the creative product, its financial cost, and its efficiency (or lack thereof), it's also "how productive and nurturing an environment it is." And without systems for surfacing problems within a work environment, it's easy for things to go awry.

Many industries employ 360-degree reviews that allow all kinds of employees to (safely) give feedback on those they've worked with. Hollywood should use them more, especially for high-level positions, but it doesn't use them much, if at all. "In over thirty years working in TV and movies, I've never had an exit interview or contributed to a 360 assessment," writer, director, and creator Nell Scovell wrote in 2017.

As for exit interviews, they should be standard for all industry jobs. Not everyone will tell the truth, but enough people might, and that could make a real difference at some workplaces. Also, rather than just allowing the powerful to fire anyone they want at will—long a perk of most industry power positions—every single boss should be made to explain why they're firing someone, in writing, every single time, and the employee should have a chance to respond.

Make amends to survivors of industry abuse, harassment, and misconduct.

One way to make amends to survivors: hire them. "If you're going to hide behind 'We can't drop him if no formal charges were filed,' it's like, you don't formally drop survivors, but you certainly don't give them as much work," Evan Rachel Wood said. "It says so much about the systems that are in place when I as a survivor feel like I'm hyper-aware of that [status], and I don't feel like the abusive people are treated the same way. The industry is more scared to hire survivors than we are abusers."

Eve, a survivor who has worked with a string of toxic, harassing men, is even more blunt: "Speaking publicly about a powerful man's abuses of power completely derailed my career progress. No one in the industry has reached out to reduce the harm they or their colleagues have caused me or to try to remedy the blacklisting I've experienced by offering me opportunities to audition or work. Not that I am at all looking for handouts, but doors have been shut and continue to be shut because people don't want to be associated with survivors who speak out unless they were already famous and bankable."

In an interview with *Variety*'s Elizabeth Wagmeister in 2021, Sarah Ann Masse said she has been "largely frozen out of the more main-stream parts of our industry" since going public with misconduct allegations against Weinstein. "In the three-and-a-half years since she came forward . . . she's had roughly a half dozen auditions. Prior to speaking up in 2017, she says she was auditioning at least four times a month," Wagmeister notes. Masse created an organization called Hire Survivors Hollywood, which attempts to right this wrong, but as she said, "retaliation and blacklisting are alive and well."

It took two decades for Mira Sorvino's career to even partially recover after she was sexually harassed by Harvey Weinstein in ways that left her "afraid and intimidated," and then told someone at Miramax about what had occurred. "Obviously, I knew that Harvey was angry with me," Sorvino told *Vanity Fair* in 2021. "But I did not know he had the reach that he had—that he could chill my entire career so that I could not work in studio films anymore. That threw me into a tailspin. . . . To find out [in 2017] that it wasn't random; it wasn't fate. It was a malevolent hand that altered the trajectory of my life and my career." Sorvino added, "This is the problem with sexual harassment: It is not an annoyance or a nuisance or something that women have to fend off. It shapes their entire lives and their potential. A man being able to stunt your career, to get you fired or not hired for refusing to comply with sexual demands, sexual predations—it's the destruction of so many women and men. And I'm just one of millions of people that this occurred to."

—

Here's a grab bag of ideas to create safer workplaces, some from industry contacts and some from a roster of suggestions writer/producer Marti Noxon and writer and activist Kater Gordon published in 2020 (Noxon and Gordon, by the way, published that piece in part because FX had begun development on a new project with Matthew Weiner; the project was later dropped):

- Ban alcohol and drugs from the workplace, because, as Gordon and Noxon point out, they increase "incidents of harassment, aggression, and disrespectful behavior."

- Have a succession plan prepared for a change of leadership. Often companies are not prepared to protect their projects— and the jobs of their employees—in the case of reported and confirmed abuse.

- Bench a leader while a neutral party (along the lines of a substitute teacher) comes in and runs things. In TV, this could involve a showrunner going to "behavior rehab," as Melinda Hsu Taylor put it.

- Anyone who has been benched "comes back on probation. If it happens again, they get fired and their name is taken off" the project—an action that could affect episode credits, royalties, and/or "quotes for your next contract negotiation," Hsu Taylor said.

- Have agencies donate the commissions from abusive or toxic clients to organizations that provide training and jobs for people from historically excluded groups. This action would give "the agents skin in the game" rather than having them participate in the process of "moving abusive priests to different parishes," Hsu Taylor said.

- Require in-person, or live, bystander intervention training that addresses sexual harassment, discrimination, bullying, and racism for all employees.

**Understand that changing industry cultures will take
time, and if you don't commit to the long haul, it'll fail.**

The only time I have ever seen Evan Rachel Wood flummoxed is when I asked if she had ever been on a set that was not majority male. Startled, she repeated this sentence twice: "All sets are majority male."

She did note that HBO's *Mildred Pierce* had a lot of women in prominent positions. But otherwise, she recalled being on sets where women advocated for themselves—and they were *not* engaging in the kind of destructive "creativity" that from men often gets a pass—and the reaction from crews was, all too often, chilly at best. "I just see their skin crawl, and the cringe—it's like they're being scolded by their mom," Wood said. "It's so deeply rooted in sexism, and a lot of it is unconscious."

Conscious or unconscious, the result of intent or inattention, there is still a lot going wrong in the industry. In some places, that is haltingly changing, but turning that battleship around is an enormously difficult process. Hollywood's focus, to put it mildly, has never really been the conditions employees work under.

Until recently, the industry had not looked at anything aside from the results it was after. In other words, if the film is in the can, if the TV show came in more or less on time and on budget, that's all anyone really cared about. "If you have a chemical plant and you don't look at the pollution it emits and the cost of that to the surrounding communities, then you're not actually measuring the true cost of it," Landgraf said. "We as an industry, I don't think, have looked at all the externalities," i.e., the damage created by allowing abusive people—and systems—to run amok.

He added that he sees around him "genuine and meaningful attempts at reform" and people trying to create "a better set of guardrails," and all that has brought about what he believes is a meaningful evolution. "There are unique talents—there are certain writers, directors, actors, and others who have those unique talents—and you have to create systems and environments where they are both supported and accountable," Landgraf said. "In the time I've been in this job, the length of time somebody could get away with bad behavior—and what they could get away with—has changed, because the monitoring system for being aware of and investigating that behavior has become much more acutely tuned."

I was encouraged by how many times Paramount's Nevins used the words "institutional" and "systemic" in our conversation. He talked about all the ways in which his company reinforced to recalcitrant or reluctant people that things were not going back to the way they used to be. "You do have the white guy over forty-five saying, 'What's the deal? This used to be okay.' Or, 'I'm not one of the bad ones,'" Nevins said. "If you assume not everything is the result of bad intent, just modes of behavior that need to change, it can come down to articulating, again and again, 'We're not doing that anymore.' It's about changing the expectations in this new world, and following through." And putting people who may not have gotten as many chances as those dudes "in a position to succeed."

These were not the kinds of conversations I was having with reactive, rattled PR people and executives in 2017 and 2018. I'm glad about that. But I need to offer up one more observation about the industry: "less bad" does not equal "good." There's still work to be done before things are routinely and reliably respectful, healthy, equitable, nonexploitative, and safe. We are definitely not there yet. I mean, look at where the industry started from.

"When I was starting out, I worked on a major studio production where at least 250k was hidden in the budget to pay off women who might 'claim' sexual harassment against the director," writer/director Lulu Wang tweeted in 2021. "I was an assistant and I knew. Everyone knew. Because the director constantly bragged about how he got the money built into his deal. Going rate was about 20k per woman who complained. I know this because that's what I was told I'd get offered if I wanted to make a report. But then I'd be blacklisted, I was told. Choose wisely: 20k or your career."

And then there's this, from Juliette Lewis, who shared these thoughts during the lead-up to the IATSE strike vote: "I personally was conditioned in TV/film business since a teenager to never take a sick day off, or it would cost tens of thousands of dollars. And you'd be labeled 'problematic' . . . so I've worked through a flu, I've worked through migraines, I've worked through walking pneumonia on *Natural Born Killers* for two weeks where I thought I might die . . ."

And speaking of recent developments, Terrence told me that in 2022, he heard of a studio that proposed a "pencils down" writers' room—where no one would write anything down, so nobody would have to be paid guild minimums. "I wish I could say I'm surprised," he said. "They just constantly make up stuff like this and it's always up to us to stop them." The reason Terrence thinks that no well-funded, industrywide reporting tool had been launched as of mid-2022 is because "I don't think they want a record of how poorly they run their businesses. Things are broken, and some people want them to stay broken."

In the final analysis, what Hollywood employers—from the largest to the smallest—need to do isn't all that difficult to describe. It can be summed up by Ed Zitron, who writes a newsletter about work, management, and employee satisfaction (or lack thereof): "If you want loyal workers, you pay and treat them well while also making their job as easy to perform as possible. This involves (but is not limited to) making sure that their tasks are clearly set, that they are managed by people that know how to manage, and that any difficulties they face are met with an attempt at reconciliation rather than immediate damnation.

"When someone is loyal, it's because they feel like the company gives a shit about them and that they're getting a fair deal in working for them (as this is a transaction of labor for money)," continues Zitron. "Elder generations have lionized suffering as a necessary part of labor—a belief that very rarely survives the simple test of asking 'How exactly did that help you?'"

13

The Sun King Is Dead
A New Model of Creative Leadership

It's not going to be the same as it was.
—*Kyra Jones*

Everybody has bad days. But some bosses and workplaces are genuinely good. A sizable number of industry leaders—rising or established—not only lobby for higher pay for support staff and others, they supplement their assistants' salaries out of their own pockets and help them revise their work samples and make useful industry contacts. Good bosses, mentors, and leaders do exist in the industry, and they always have.

Then there are . . . the other bosses. This is not comprehensive, but here is a partial list of things that people working in the entertainment industry *do not want to do*:

- Have sex with their boss

- Constantly fluff their boss's ego

- Obtain drugs for their superiors

- Be the frequent object for whatever anger, frustration, or angst their superiors feel

- Massage any body part of anyone they work for

- Be hit or otherwise physically injured or menaced by their superiors or managers

- Be assaulted by bosses

- Be coerced into watching porn with supervisors

- Provide unpaid caregiving services for a supervisor's family and friends

- Dress "sexy" because someone they work for urged them (or told them) to do so

- Be shown dick pics (just . . . *no*)

- Provide constant praise and positive commentary about their boss's work, leadership, or physical presentation

- Purchase the services of sex workers for people they work for

- Be a supervisor's audience as that person processes thoughts, emotions, and ideas, for hours and hours on end

- Repeatedly hear their boss's opinions about their own physical appearance

- Be harassed, demeaned, bullied, humiliated, or othered by those they work for

And finally, they do not want to be forced to be the friend of someone they work for. People often *end up* friends with people they work with. This is potentially a good or great thing. We've all met friends through work. *However.* Being forced to be a powerful person or supervisor's "friend"—having one's time, mental energy, and companionship be constantly demanded, if not extorted—that happens in the industry way too much. That's not friendship.

In any case, this list is a mere sampling of the things people have told me that they were expected to do in the course of their industry jobs. The lower folks were on an industry ladder, the less they were paid to do or endure these kinds of things. Doing the kinds of tasks listed above is not as unusual as it should be, and that's bad.

The goal here is not that everybody should do their jobs with grim efficiency and have no fun at all. What would be the point of that? Enjoyable and fruitful collaborations can be the best part of being in this industry. The point is, *bosses, supervisors, and others with power should not ask workers for things that are not theirs to request.* Hollywood employees have no desire to be the forced friends, unwilling therapists, rage targets, or unpaid bartenders of people with power over them. Workers at all levels do not exist as objects to be manipulated, controlled, or dominated; their abject fealty is not indication of an individual's value, desirability, or worth. They are *employees*. They don't owe anyone adoration, fear, worship, every waking hour of their lives, or anything else. They owe their employers their work, completed in a timely, professional, and appropriate fashion. Nothing else.

Those with power in an industry workplace "have a responsibility of creating safety. That's what all artists deserve," said actor Claudia Black, who has appeared in programs like *Farscape* and *The Originals*. "It's like women birthing, we want to have that proverbial cave that we're birthing in where someone is standing like a sentinel at the mouth of the cave, keeping watch to make sure we can get quiet and feel safe to go into this very sort of primal process. And that's what creating is like too. If we're going to hand over our greatest vulnerability to people, that has to be treated with reverence and safety. And we have to be in a container that creates that and affords that, and makes that possible."

Well said.

I know from my own life that when it comes to damage, trauma, and other personal and mental health issues, the only way out is through. "Through" does not mean "through damaging or destroying other people and their mental and physical health." It does not mean "through terrorizing a workplace or its employees." It means "through the appropriate channels, at the appropriate times, with the appropriate people or professionals."

On the other side of "through" you are likely to find—and generate—better workplaces, better relationships, and better *art*. I am sure Melinda Hsu Taylor would agree.

Noga Landau has been around Hollywood long enough to know that "this industry can turn anyone to the dark side." She has resisted that, as have her most trusted collaborators.

After writing features and working on shows like *The Magicians*, Landau cocreated a *Nancy Drew* series with industry veterans Josh Schwartz and Stephanie Savage. Once it was picked up to series, Landau knew she'd need help to run the CW drama.

When Landau and I talked in 2021, she described the early days of 2019, when she was in a new-mom haze and taking a series of virtual meetings with potential coshowrunners before production began on

Nancy Drew. "I was in a fog," Landau recalled. But hearing Hsu Taylor talk about her management style cut through that fog.

"She told me about her approach to leadership, and I was, like, slurring, 'She's the one!'" The duo survived making the pilot—when they met up in Vancouver, Landau had a baby strapped to her chest and Hsu Taylor had presents for Landau. The partnership worked out so well that they extended it when the CW picked up a *Nancy Drew* spin-off, *Tom Swift.* That show premiered in May 2022 and was canceled just a month later. (Suffice to say that the CW, like many other industry entities, went through a lot of turmoil in the wake of the lengthy Warner Bros. Discovery merger.)

That was all in the future when I sat in on some of the early meetings of the *Tom Swift* staff in the fall of 2021. On a Zoom call, Landau and I talked just before the start of a mindfulness and meditation session that had been lined up for the first week of the writers' room. Not long after that get-together, the writers and support staff had a long, in-person session with Birgit Zacher Hanson, an executive coach. These and other efforts were part of Landau and Hsu Taylor's attempts to, as Landau put it, "create a Hollywood writers' room that is not a pressure cooker. It's about trying to have a sense of community, even through COVID."

In both sessions, there appeared to be some getting-to-know-you jitters, the normal kind that occur in any professional group coming together for the first time. How to navigate a new workplace can be tricky under any conditions, but the pandemic made those kinds of situations even more challenging. Yet it was clear that both sessions allowed people to break the ice with their coworkers in ways that didn't feel too awkward or invasive.

I was particularly fascinated by the session with Hanson, who, on her site, states that her "aim is to assist leaders in creating a promise-based culture in which people value diversity, collaborate and hold themselves and others accountable for results." In Hsu Taylor's home that October, Hanson asked the assembled group of more than a dozen people to play a series of games and answer questions that shed light on their workplace styles. Some people offered answers and ideas quickly, and it took others longer to offer up feedback and input. There was quite the gamut of personalities, thought processes, and interpersonal styles.

And that was the point. By the time the session was done, everyone in the room had a better idea of who their coworkers were and *how they operated best* within a creative setting. Not only did Hanson's encouraging words urge everyone to honor their colleagues' differing modes of engagement, they gave everyone data points that were likely to make the workplace more efficient, collegial, and productive.

Having come up in a system in which Hsu Taylor was often the only woman or person of color on a staff, she and Landau had assembled a team that was majority people of color. A number of people at these meetings mentioned being LGBTQ+, which made sense for a show about a queer Black entrepreneur. It's a shame the drama got canceled so quickly, but it's encouraging to know that, for one season of television at least, these folks got to witness modes of leadership that were, if nothing else, wildly different from the ones other reporters and I hear about all too often.

Lost was not the only challenging work environment Hsu Taylor endured: Another one was the 2005–11 drama *Medium,* where she worked for Glenn Gordon Caron. Hsu Taylor told me she learned valuable writing skills from Caron, but within a workplace culture that often left her self-esteem and peace of mind in tatters.

For much of the industry's history, this has been how it worked: There was little or no formal training, and not many limits on how powerful people behaved as they set an example for the next generation of creatives. If they behaved badly, there were generally no consequences, especially if they were well-connected. If any creative growth or learning occurred on the job, it often came in combination with major stress, panic, and trauma. When I talk to industry leaders, they regularly start sentences with this formulation: "I learned how *not* to be a boss from . . ."

But the industry's attitude was—and still is, in some places—if learning one's craft comes with an enormous cost to many people's psyches, careers, and physical health, so be it. Hsu Taylor could have done what so many have done in the face of this kind of belief system: adopted it as her leadership style. It's worth recollecting how young Samuel Laskey was when he went to work for Scott Rudin: eighteen years old. "At thirty-one, I absolutely wouldn't put up with it," Laskey observed. "At eighteen, I treated it as, 'I guess that's how it's supposed to be.' I grew up on a farm. I didn't know Hollywood. I didn't know what the rules were."

The rules were nonexistent, for a long time. Hsu Taylor said she did encounter a lot of good, encouraging, and kind producers, writers, and executives along the way. But her choice to be a good boss was absolutely that: a choice. In my travels through the industry, I've learned that being a good boss in Hollywood is kind of like being an avid composter or a knitter. It's nice if you want to do it—it's cool if that's your fun little hobby—but no one's going to *make* you do it. Not until somewhat recently, at some places (definitely not everywhere), and the enforcement of the "rules"—which are still plenty hazy—is inconsistent at best.

But one reason I have hope is that a lot of people who could have hidden behind the excuse "but this was done to *me*" or "the job is just too hard" have decided to not replicate the past. Those who at least try to break the industry's most pernicious patterns have learned the first lesson of being a good industry boss, which is . . .

Whether or not you think you are a mentor and a role model—guess what? You're a mentor and a role model.

If you're in a position of power and/or people's boss, "your job is to lead and teach" and your role is to give "your employees an environment in which is it safe to try, and both succeed and fail." Even if you never particularly wanted to be a mentor, leader, or tutor, "this is the duty that fate has thrust upon you." Those words come from "The Eleven Laws of Showrunning," which Javier Grillo-Marxuach published online in 2016. In this essay, he helps demystify how a good boss should act—and why that can be difficult in an extremely non-nurturing industry.

"Leadership is not an easy thing," Patrick said. "When you have a really demanding work product and schedule, and you're making something that costs a lot of money and there's a lot of pressure on performance, for somebody to locate the right amount of accountability, kindness, supportiveness, discipline, forgiveness, and encouragement—it's very challenging." Yep. And if a leader screws up, it is not necessarily from any kind of evil intent.

"A big takeaway for me of studying dysfunctional leaders and leaders who fail: Human beings, we all have a dark side and have behaviors that could probably derail us, and which are problematic for those around us," organizational psychologist Mary-Clare Race said. Race analyzes the corporate world, but her findings have a good deal of relevance to Hollywood. She has found that toxic leaders are often promoted not despite their problematic behavior but *because* of it. Employees who take big risks and who have "stellar personal performance tend to be promoted quickly into positions where they manage other people, since management is still the most accepted way to attain higher status and get paid more. But management may not suit their skills . . . [and] we do so little for leaders to help them manage" the problems that they have.

The fact is, however you rise (or don't rise) to the challenges of your job—those around you will not only notice, they may ape how you behave, as some of Rudin's former employees did. Screaming and verbal abuse still occur in the industry, but these are not, you will be shocked to learn, helpful communications strategies. Which leads to the next point . . .

You're in a creative job to communicate something to the world, so you need to know how to communicate effectively.

Grillo-Marxuach, like Hsu Taylor, also worked at *Medium* and *Lost;* during his three decades in the entertainment industry trenches, he has been a showrunner, an executive, a comic book creator, and more. He knows creatives have baggage. And he knows that when they are calling the shots, as much as humanly possible, they need to leave that baggage at the door in order to run safe, efficient, humane, and professional workplaces. Showrunners in particular, as Grillo-Marxuach explains in "The Eleven Laws," must make decisions in a timely fashion, competently promulgate those decisions, and give those around them the time, resources, and information they need to do their jobs effectively. They must, again and again, lay out what their vision is and stand behind their choices, while considering and, at times, incorporating the input of those around them in a respectful and encouraging fashion.

"This is a difficult task that requires intellectual and creative rigor . . . and that you make a discipline out of talking to other people and being on message at all times. As a showrunner, you must communicate your vision so that everyone understands it, and then preach it, day in and out, to the point of exhaustion until everyone feels it in their soul like a gospel," writes Grillo-Marxuach. "And here's the great part of successfully communicating a shared vision: your employees will love you for it." This behavior may go against the grain for some in the industry, but if you want to employ other people or manage workplaces, you have to learn how to do these things.

We wouldn't have TV shows, plays, films, poems, books, paintings, and all the rest if human beings weren't trying to tell one another something important or valuable about the human condition. The ironic thing is that artists are not always the best communicators. But this makes a certain kind of sense: if you want to make good art, tell a good story, or do anything creative at a high level, you have to spend a lot of time inside your own head, figuring out how best to create that vision or story.

One of the problems with the industry is that it takes people who are not necessarily great communicators, managers, or leaders, and puts them in charge of dozens, if not hundreds, of other people. And the industry's preparation for doing that job consists of saying "good luck" as a newly minted leader is flung out of a plane, grasping a parachute they have never seen before.

I don't have the full answer for how to fix that—as noted, the companies that make the commercial storytelling we consume don't usually set aside the time and money for the effective training, support, and resources leaders need. But you can read "The Eleven Laws." If you're in a position of responsibility, ask friends and colleagues for help. Ask the company that employs you for help. You're going to need it.

And when you ask for help, you're actually modeling something good, believe it or not, because . . .

Humility can be a core element of effective leadership.

In an industry in which leadership has long been linked to toxicity, bullying, domination displays, and all manner of bad behavior, in which winning at all costs has been the default mode that most were taught to worship, talking about humility might sound weird, naive, or stupid. But humility is not weakness. It is, deployed correctly, one of the most useful tools in a leader's toolbox. From what I have seen up close, a sizable percentage of people who've succeeded in the industry have displayed this kind of leadership, in some cases for decades. But it doesn't make headlines, so we don't hear about it as much as we should.

Humility is being able to take feedback and respond in a productive and professional fashion. You can have a vision and a strategy and still listen, and it's certainly possible to be both decisive and humble. You can even politely reject input that doesn't fit your vision in a way that does not destroy someone's confidence or willingness to contribute. These modes involve making alterations as necessary, based on input from others and changing circumstances, all the while not taking revenge on employees (or fans) who make a point you hadn't thought of or offer information you don't like.

"This grief people feel when marginalized people bring up concerns where it feels like such a personal attack, where it feels like 'hate'—I think, honestly, just take a deep breath, put on your big-girl panties and listen," Tananarive Due said. "Because however painful it is for you to hear that someone thinks you've made a mistake, imagine how painful it is for people who have to live this. It's not about you. It's about growth."

When I spoke to Judy Reyes on a panel at the ATX TV Festival in 2022, she talked about working for Bill Lawrence, who was her boss on *Scrubs* and who went on to be an executive producer of *Ted Lasso*. I asked her to weigh in on the complicated question of when someone else's creative process becomes an impediment to others. She responded, "That's the showrunner's job . . . to accommodate and balance [varied approaches], and it takes somebody really skilled to do that." Lawrence "is not only able to balance it but make fun of everybody's process while respecting it at the same time."

But she would still get nervous when asking questions, she said. In the first season of *Scrubs,* she had a question about her character, Carla: "Is she Mexican? 'Cause I'm Dominican. If she's Mexican, I gotta know . . . so I can do the proper accent. One of the things that drives me crazy is . . . you know, Latinos are a culture, not a race, it's not a monolith, and not everybody's from Mexico or Puerto Rico or Cuba." In Reyes's account, Lawrence said Carla could be Dominican—a fact that writers forgot in later seasons, when scripts would make references to Carla's Mexican family. The writers would always make the changes, but she said it could be nerve-wracking to ask about that topic and others. (She definitely had issues with a script in which her character was supposed to put her mother in a nursing home.)

"I'd prepare a speech . . . I was like, 'Oh God, he's going to have to change a script.' I have to ask for this. Is it okay? I didn't realize what a safe environment that was," Reyes said. Being a person of color makes these requests even more daunting, but Lawrence "always responded." And being heard allowed her to do a better job in the role she'd been hired to play. At work, she said, "You don't feel like you're part of it until, you know, you continue to be" able to give feedback.

Joe Henderson, who, with Ildy Modrovich, ran the long-running drama *Lucifer,* approaches his job in a way that flips the usual industry script on its head: "My philosophy as a showrunner is, the room doesn't work for you. You work for the room." Henderson said, "Once I cemented that as the core idea I was working with, it changed everything."

Henderson, like many other established writers, producers, and directors I've talked to, considers mentoring the next generation of creative people part of his job. To that end, he regularly checks in with everyone on the staff, so that writers being summoned to speak with him is not a rare, terrifying event. "Every writer should get honest, useful feedback given in a nice, professional way. In my experience, they want that! They want to get better," Henderson said. In those meetings, "we'll talk about how I can be a better boss or what they might need from me."

The need for humility can and should extend to the people who are learning the ropes, Daniel Dae Kim noted. "Sometimes I think we're in danger of an overcompensation—where any critique of someone's work is regarded as 'toxic.' An example of that kind of thing is when you have someone with no experience who feels entitled to promotions and praise that have not been properly earned."

In the main, however, Kim—who is an actor, a director, and an executive producer of *The Good Doctor,* among other projects—said most people he's encountered are responsive to feedback delivered in a helpful, professional fashion. And building good workplace cultures from the ground up can be done—as long as everyone in power is on the same page.

"As you progress in your career and you have been the victim of hazing or mistreatment, you have to turn around and say, 'That's not how the business should be run,'" he said. "Changing the paradigm requires finding people who believe—from the beginning—in a friendly, respect-based workplace." And that is likely to lead to better outcomes on a number of fronts.

> **A healthy, well-led workplace is likely to be more efficient, more productive, and more cost-effective. More creative too.**

Not long after we first "met" via email, Hsu Taylor forwarded me a note she sent to a potential new hire for the writing staff of *Nancy Drew*.

Hsu Taylor's note contained her "personal touchstones" about "how to foster a writer- and family-friendly environment that also results in better work and a more fulfilling daily existence." She mentioned that the team would be working with Hanson, the workplace coach, "to discuss how we'll . . . establish norms and protocols for creative interactions and decisions." There would be a volunteer session with kids at the local elementary school, helping them tap into their storytelling powers.

She brought up a metaphor that would help explain how the *Nancy Drew* workplace would operate: She described a petting zoo where the children were excited and wired, but the goats they were petting were very chill. The goats were mellow, Hsu Taylor wrote, because there was an adjacent paddock that the goats could retire to when they needed to relax and not be around rambunctious little ones. "Every goat here in the petting zoo *wants* to be here, *and knows it can leave anytime*"— that's what the zookeeper told Hsu Taylor.

"Same principle applies to writers' rooms," she said in her email. The leadership team would always "let people know they can leave the room for school events and doctors' appointments and development" meetings. The room would start on time, end on time, and there would be transparency about due dates and other work matters. The idea, the email said, was to "remove unnecessary stress and uncertainty, and be extremely respectful of people's time and personal lives, which results in better morale and better work."

The goal was, she wrote, "an atmosphere of possibility." She concluded the note with a quote from Antoine de Saint-Exupéry: "If you want to teach someone to become a great shipbuilder, don't teach them how to hammer a nail. Teach them to love the sea." To the writer thinking of joining the show's staff, she then said, "I sincerely hope that you will give us the chance to increase your love of the sea. I believe that having you on our team will only increase our love of the sea as well."

The point of this email is not that it made me a little weepy (I was working on a very hard story at the time). The point is that *Nancy Drew* could not offer this person the amount of money that other shows could. The recipient of the letter joined the *Nancy Drew* team, not surprisingly.

Treating people well: It's not just the right thing to do. In the long run, it saves time and money. Speaking of time . . .

Putting unreasonable demands on people at work, and not allowing them time to tend to their lives, is bad for creativity and bad for humans.

According to many sources I talked to, Bathroom Guy, the showrunner of a long-running broadcast-network procedural, got angry when people left the writers' room to relieve themselves. "He would say, 'If you really cared about the show, you'd get a catheter,'" an ex-employee told me. "Or he would say, 'We need to put a diaper on her.'" These remarks were supposedly jokes, but everyone in the room understood that he wasn't kidding. "It was ridiculous," a different former employee told me. "You had a bunch of adults who were afraid to use the bathroom. We were not children ditching class. This is a bodily function. It felt punitive."

I wish that this guy was the only person who thought this was reasonable behavior, but employees of talent agencies and on-set crews have also talked about feeling coerced into not leaving their posts to relieve themselves. If there's one thing a sizable chunk of Hollywood is good at, it's making workers believe it's okay to consistently downplay or ignore their physical and mental needs.

Everyone knows Hollywood HR departments are usually nobody's friend, but even so, you might wonder why these people didn't report Bathroom Guy's conduct to HR. They did. Studio HR, you will be shocked to hear, was unable to conclude that this individual engaged in discrimination or harassment. But not to worry: HR said in documents shared with employees that it took appropriate action. Nothing changed, of course. Bathroom Guy continued to hire and fire people at will, often for reasons that had nothing to do with their job performance. Bathroom Guy was eventually fired, but it took *years* of people going through hell to bring that about.

Bathroom Guy is out of the industry, but there are so many petty dictators like him still around. Still, some of the most experienced and successful people I've talked to are fully aware that working on TV shows and movies does not need to be a miserable endurance test.

There are people that think that good work can only be "born out of pain. That to be an artist, you have to suffer. I think that's a load of shit," Lesli Linka Glatter said. "As a director, I want to create a very positive working environment. No one is disposable and you treat everyone with respect. I feel the best work comes out of that. Also, I want to live in that world, and work in that world."

Glatter has a favorite kind of workday: ten hours, with one break, and then everyone is done. Director Paul Feig is also a fan of so-called French hours: "We do it on most of my projects. Ten-hour days with no lunch break but food constantly circulating on set. People drive home awake and see their families." What a concept! (That said, I have talked about French hours to a number of industry professionals, many of whom have complex or wary feelings about them; some crew members have concerns about the version of the practice that does not include the important hour-long break, and some have expressed concerns about how that kind of workday can affect their compensation.)

In any case, Glatter told me that those kinds of workdays tend to be more common in European productions. But in general, Glatter, a director on *Homeland* (among many other credits), said long hours are disastrous on a lot of fronts, a point on which many sources concurred.

"On the last project I did, we did a ten-hour workday and one hour for lunch. We never went over that. That is somewhat sane," Glatter said. "Now that's still a lot of hours, but when I was coming up, a twelve-hour workday plus one [hour] for lunch—that's a thirteen-hour day, you know? And then if you go over, which happened, you're working fourteen, fifteen hours. That that is not good for humans. It's a safety issue."

Accidents are more probable when people are tired; during the lead-up to the IATSE strike authorization, social media was full of stories of crew members nodding off on the way home or being injured due to exhaustion. And by the way, after sixteen hours on set or in the office, how fresh will anyone be after only a few hours to recharge? In my thirty years of covering the film and television industries, no one has ever made the case that people's best ideas arrive after 10 p.m., let alone after 2 a.m. Quite the reverse. And some are trying to lead the industry in a better direction on the work-life balance front.

When I visited the headquarters of the CW musical comedy-drama *Crazy Ex-Girlfriend* in 2018, I saw something heartening: an on-site space for employees' children. It was a bright, cozy room where kids could hang out with their parent or childcare provider. I'd heard tell of these kinds of spaces but, despite having covered the industry for a long time, I had never seen one in the wild, so to speak. Back then, I talked about the reasons behind the room a bit with the show's creators, Aline Brosh McKenna and Rachel Bloom, and in 2022, I revisited the topic with McKenna. The room was established, she told me, partly because there were so many employees with young children as well as parents who needed a place to nurse or pump. She added that it felt "paltry compared to what we should be doing" for parents, and she said she wishes there were far more robust systems of support in the industry for parents and other kinds of caregivers. But she and Bloom did their level best to create a workplace that was fun and that made people "excited to go to work," she said.

"The number one thing we did for parents was, we had regular hours," said McKenna, who is also a director and who wrote the screenplay for *The Devil Wears Prada*, among other credits. "Parents want to know when they're getting to work and when they're leaving, and they want to know they can leave on time for the dance recital. In general, people want to know what they're doing and when it'll end, and not feel like they're in a psychological experiment, you know?" In any event, I wish I'd come across more concrete examples that employers understand that people have responsibilities outside the workplace that don't magically vanish when they turn up in production offices, in writers' rooms, or on set.

I do think that's changing, to a degree. When Jac Schaeffer was appointed showrunner of Marvel's *WandaVision,* she had never run a show before. But in a way, she writes in a 2021 piece, that freed her to do things differently. "Visions of a utopian working environment filled my head: a culture of respect and inclusion, big ideas and even bigger feelings, clarity of purpose, lots of laughing, and . . . a 10 a.m. to 4 p.m. workday."

A lot about the job scared Schaeffer, who cowrote the film *Black Widow.* "My kids were ages 2 and 4 at the time I was hired," she writes. "I had no idea how I was going to do this job. But there was no way I was turning it down." She not only didn't turn it down, she made reasonable workdays a reality. "It still makes me sweaty to see those hours in black and white," given that Schaeffer had been trained "to demonstrate my commitment to work by pretending I had no commitments at home."

There were a few "planned" all-nighters, she noted; not every workday ended at 4 p.m. But she observes, "The room was healthy and the work was good. It's possible to have both." The sane approach to workdays certainly didn't affect *WandaVision*'s creative output negatively; it remains one of Marvel's best-reviewed shows.

On the *Screaming into the Hollywood Abyss* podcast, writer/producer Joe Henderson talked about how there is actually no requirement for the gig of showrunner to be "all-consuming." He said, "You can work normal hours, you can live a normal life. The key is delegation—the key is trust." It can be scary to delegate, he noted, but doing so means that people in high-powered jobs can actually have lives. Showrunners in particular should "make ourselves necessary via our writing, our craft, our leadership, our ability to get the best out of people. As opposed to the bottleneck that everything must go through," Henderson said.

Managed right, this leads to not just better quality of life but even more creative satisfaction: "There have been so many people who have written [the character] Lucifer in ways I would not have written him. And then a season later, I am writing him that way. Because they have taught me a side of him that I would never have found otherwise."

In a later conversation, Henderson told me with a laugh that mentoring and delegating are actually "selfish": "Not only are people learning how to become a showrunner themselves eventually, it's less work for me if other people know a lot and grow their skills. The work gets better, the work experience gets better."

When something goes wrong and someone speaks up, don't make it about you: Fix the problem. If you fix it while demonstrating accountability, integrity, and respect, people will walk through fire for you.

"Well, this is embarrassing."

That was Melinda Hsu Taylor's response when a Black person in the cast for one of her shows said, as Hsu Taylor recalls it, "Nobody knows how to do my hair." This occurred relatively recently, and after pausing to feel terrible, Hsu Taylor and the other producers—assisted by executives at CBS, the studio that makes the show—addressed the situation. "We had to look for a person who knew how to do Black hair in Vancouver. There's a narrow pool of skilled candidates, but [executives] were really supportive and talked to the actors who were being affected by the lack of expertise in that department. They talked to the hair department, and they were great. Everybody was rowing in the same direction, and we got it done," Hsu Taylor said. She added that it shouldn't have happened in the first place—she regrets that the actor was placed in the uncomfortable position of having to speak up—but the situation was dealt with forthrightly.

One of Shernold Edwards's most rewarding work experiences involved being heard on several fronts by a boss—even when things got awkward. "It was the most creatively fulfilling job, because the showrunner was interested in telling the story I was interested in telling," Edwards said. She was intrigued by the ways race played into certain aspects of the show, but she told the showrunner in her job interview, "I can write for everybody. Please don't hire me to be your single Black writer. I don't want to do that anymore."

Her wishes were respected, but there were other bumps: she did not understand why the showrunner was pushing everyone so hard to get their scripts done early. It took a while before her boss confessed that she'd had to essentially write the previous season of the show by herself, a punishing experience that left her physically ill. Edwards said she wished she'd been told that earlier, because she and the rest of the staff really wanted to help their boss.

She and the showrunner also differed on how frequently Edwards should have brought up a complaint about a story element that touched on race and that Edwards found offensive. Edwards brought up her objections two or three times, and then the showrunner decided to keep the version of the scene that had already been crafted. When that episode was in production, another producer saw an upset Edwards leaving the set and asked her what was wrong. Conversations ensued about this aspect of the episode, and eventually, the production went back and—despite the fact that it cost a tidy sum—reshot that sequence.

According to Edwards, the showrunner asked her why she hadn't brought up her objections more forcefully. But as Edwards remarked, her experience at *Sleepy Hollow* had left her "smarting" about how industry workplaces often silence the voices of those without power, especially if they are from historically excluded groups. "It's very risky," she said.

"'I wish you had pushed harder,'" Edwards recalled this former boss saying. "And I said, 'I was never going to do that. This is your show. And you had made up your mind.' And then there was a lot of silence." And yet, all in all, she considers that job a fruitful, creative experience. She has complex feelings about that former boss but called her a "brilliant" writer and "terrific" showrunner.

Part of being a good leader, after all, is hanging in there and listening, even when things get awkward and difficult. But . . . this is the way.

> **Rejecting the old, toxic models and bolstering better ways of working might be scary, unknown territory— but that path could be the key to not just job satisfaction but lasting success.**

One of the challenges of Lesli Linka Glatter's early directing career was that she was not, and could not force herself to be, a dominating, larger-than-life Creative Guy. Not only was she not a man, she did not want to be the kind of blowhard, abusive personality or "miserable prick" the industry has long venerated—or, at the very least, has treated as a necessity. And when she moved on from her first career choice—dance—to directing, she realized that the popular stereotype of the cruel, overbearing director didn't necessarily have a basis in fact. At least not on some sets. She shadowed Steven Spielberg and Clint Eastwood while they were filming *Amazing Stories*, and she told me she didn't see them act in that imperious manner. But their working methods were also unique to them and their sets.

"What became clear to me is that these two guys are really brilliant directors and they have completely different styles of working," Glatter said. She had grown up with "the image of the director who was the strong man who controlled everything and knew everything and behaved a certain way." She couldn't be Spielberg or Eastwood or the All-Knowing Director or a miserably mean Creative Guy. Who would—who *could*—she be, creatively speaking?

She had to be herself, ultimately. There was not really anyone to model herself on, because she had so few female peers. "I can't tell you how many times I've heard, 'We hired a woman once and it just didn't work out'—there was no embarrassment or irony about saying that," Glatter recalled with a laugh.

For her, being a creative leader means coming to work very, very prepared while also remaining open to ideas that bubble up on set. Moreover, she knows that she's setting an example for everyone else: she will not do so publicly, but if anyone in the crew is inappropriate or cruel, she takes them aside and tells them that her sets don't operate that way. Aside from that, a lot of her process is about listening.

"I don't need to be the smartest person in the room, but I want to be in the room with the smartest people," said Glatter, who has directed *Twin Peaks*, *The West Wing*, *ER*, *Mad Men*, and the film *Now and Then*. "If I get a good idea from the key grip or the craft-service person or whoever, if it's going to make the story better," Glatter will consider it. "And then, even if you don't use it, but you thank that person for throwing it out there, they'll feel like they were seen and heard, and they're going to do their job well. They'll feel like they're part of it.

"I prepare like crazy so I can be open to the life that is happening on set," she added. "Having humility is a huge part of that. You've got to do your homework, but if you leave yourself open, things will come to you."

Leaving herself open was not always an option, however. "We have a horrible past history in the film business," said Glatter. The industry is getting better, she noted, but she also told me there were times she did not always feel comfortable at work. And pre-#MeToo, she said, "I wouldn't have reported something." If she had, she feared she'd never work again. Even being pregnant was something she felt she had to hide.

And time and again, she said, she has encountered what I call the *Highlander* mentality—the idea that, as in the genre classic about a singular avenging hero, "there can only be one." This mentality still exists on many fronts—if, for example, a studio has a modern-day rom-com featuring South Asian characters in development, it will turn down a period piece with South Asian characters, even if it's very different in tone and content. The *Highlander* mentality, which creatives of color deal with a lot, dictates that a company only needs one project at a time set within a specific historically excluded community. The *Highlander* mentality also, for decades, extended to hiring decisions. One woman or one person of color in a writers' room or on a directing roster was seen as sufficient.

"I never bought into that, because I came from dance, and dance is primarily female," Glatter said. "I never saw other women as the competition. I know that is not how it is with younger women. They help each other out."

> **Positive change can be hard to implement, and it can be easy to use your position to hold it back. But industrywide change is possible if enough leaders make up their minds to consistently support it.**

Cordelia was shooting the breeze, as one does with colleagues. This was not all that long ago. The showrunners were a white man and a white woman, but the colleagues she spent the most time with were male. "I was super open with them and talked a lot about how sick I was of the status quo and only watching/telling stories through a male lens," she recalled. "One day the female showrunner pulled me out and said she was worried the men in the room felt discriminated against because of my comments. She told me it wasn't appropriate for me to say things that belittled them. I explained we were having general conversations about the state of the business, and I was never targeting my comments toward anyone specifically. She asked me to stop saying those types of things."

Cordelia suspects the coworker who reported her "belittling" comments was a male colleague who occasionally fell asleep during the workday. "I'm guessing he felt I was the kind of woman who was cockblocking him from the rich career he deserved," she said. "I think that experience shook me as much as any harassment ever. [The showrunner's] instinct ran so deep to protect the men around her, and keep me under control. When I tried to explain that I couldn't believe she'd put me in an environment where I was the only woman and then accused me of sexism, she got really upset."

Cordelia said she felt that "I am still not safe to be myself, be honest, and move past all the gender discrimination and harassment. We're an industry that now pretends to get it and be inclusive . . . but to succeed, you have to play along as much as you ever did, with maybe the added caveat of pretending all the problems are solved."

There are many different ways Cordelia's boss could have handled that situation, and she chose the one that made Cordelia feel not just singled out in a harsh and unfair way but also gave her grave doubts about her willingness to continue in the industry. There are a lot of bosses like that out there, and not being honest about that would be a disservice to the realities of the state of change in the industry. It's tentative, and sometimes the change is only skin-deep.

But I'm not without hope, in part thanks to people like actor and writer Kyra Jones. "I have learned even in the short amount of time I've been a professional screenwriter, don't meet your heroes"—that maxim is true at least some of the time, Jones said with a laugh. "But I want to say, I've been so fortunate that the vast majority of people that I have met so far in the industry have been genuine and wonderful and really do want to change Hollywood for the better, in terms of the stories they're telling and also how they're treating people."

She's had all kinds of mentorship opportunities—"Wait, what's up with you, straight white man going to bat for me?" she said, laughing again. In a more serious moment, she talked about what the industry hasn't made her do: hide or fundamentally alter who she is.

"Part of the invisible harm in the entertainment industry is, like, you cannot be vocal," she observed. "They tell you, you cannot and should not be vocal about the things you care about. Just be a blank slate, be whatever is popular. And you have to shrink your identities and what you care about to fit into Hollywood. And I think that is not true. I am unapologetic about my Blackness and my queerness and that I hold people accountable." And ultimately, being clear about who she is and what she believes and "being able to be that voice in a powerful and funny and nuanced way" is what gets her work.

Not that everyone appreciates what she brings to the table. "I've just had my first experience with the shit in the industry," she noted. She was in consideration for the writers' room for a comedy, but the white woman showrunner didn't hire her because she apparently thought she wouldn't be able to say anything that sprang to mind with Jones in the room. "She wanted to be able to say whatever racist, sexist, transphobic jokes she wanted to make in the room, I guess," Jones said. She isn't sorry the job didn't work out; there are some people "I definitely don't want to be working with," she noted. But being exactly who she is has also been "attracting folks who are interested in having my voice in the room and having my voice in a script."

One thing's for sure: she and her friends do not want to re-create the worst of what they've found or propagate the mindset that "everyone must suffer because I did." Creative people coming up, at least from what she's seen and heard from her peers, are creating better work environments and more readily admit when they make mistakes.

"I was just talking about this with some other Black writers who just wrote on their first or second show," Jones said. "We found each other. And we were like, 'Let us promise to each other that we are never going to be like that.' Once we are there, it's not going to be the same as it was."

And that's crucial. Find your people.

14

Mad as Hell and Not Going to Take It Anymore

What Industry Workers Need to Survive—and Thrive

I thought it was a mistake.
—Lucy Luna

In 2021, Lucy Luna was fried.

"I really needed a break, because I was experiencing burnout," said Luna, a television and film writer who was born in Mexico but who now lives and works in Los Angeles. During the time she set aside for recovery and healing, she worked on a movie script but she also took care of herself. Simple pleasures like cooking and going to the gym were big priorities. It was a relief, she said, to no longer have to navigate the kind of chaos she has experienced at some workplaces in the industry.

The time off transformed Luna, but one experience made her realize just how far she had yet to go, at least when it came to her expectations around the entertainment industry. That year, Luna's representatives received a "great offer," without her reps having to claw and scratch for the right promotion and proper recompense. Luna told me that this felt very strange at first. "I thought it was a mistake," Luna said. Part of what was odd, she told me, was that she "felt very valued."

How do we get to the point where workers are routinely valued—financially and in every other important way? How do we get that to happen without a whole lot of people having to first endure chaos, bias, or other negative things—possibly for years?

I have some thoughts on that. But first, a warning.

—

I want those who aspire to work in the entertainment industry to shoot their shot.

But people entering that arena should know that they are likely to deploy as much creativity and energy to ensuring their own survival as they do to their work. All these truths apply to a lot of folks in a lot of places, but especially in creative industries where serious gatekeeping, massive inequities, and brutal forms of "paying your dues" are common. But there are lots of harsh elements and rejection baked into film and television in particular. It's a hard, hard industry to break into—and almost harder to stay in these days. If people don't take care of themselves, and seriously prioritize what they need to get by, things can go south fast. I truly hope those going to Hollywood have (or create) all kinds of support systems. They'll need them.

The thing is, there are folks in and out of the industry who think its problems are pretty much solved (or were overblown by the media). But the structural, institutional, and cultural problems all over the entertainment industry are deep-seated and still quite real, as are the backlashes to even moderate progress on some fronts. I'm not saying people should cover themselves in the armor of cynicism or despair. But they should prepare for a way of life that can be quite demanding and draining, if not demoralizing, on a regular basis. If Disney was willing to subject Scarlett Johansson to a "misogynistic attack" in 2021, when she asserted she was undercompensated for *Black Widow,* what is it willing to do to others? *Anything at all.* And that can take a toll.

Seamus recalled going on job interviews after his bruising run at the hit drama where he worked. "I'm going, 'I'm the king of this room. I'm nailing this meeting.' Meanwhile, I'm exuding this energy of pain and frustration that is so palpable," he recalled. "No wonder no one would hire me."

He worked through all that baggage, but it took time, effort, and energy. And his story is not unusual. Folks I know in the industry have good and great times; that's what keeps many of them in it. But many aspects of Hollywood can also be daunting, if not overwhelming, on a regular basis, so having mentors, allies, friends, and resources is important.

Here are some ideas on how to find your people.

Find your people: The guilds

"The hope for a more equitable, democratic, and prosperous society lies not with enlightened corporations, but with organized workers." That is not a quote from union organizer Mother Jones circa 1912. It's from Adam Serwer, a writer for *The Atlantic,* in 2022.

As Serwer points out, when a company is "notoriously exploitative" and routinely offers "low pay; long shifts; few breaks, even to go to the bathroom; and a high injury rate," unionization efforts are not just predictable but necessary. "Such conditions reflect the corporation's leverage over its own workforce—without the protections of a union, it is difficult for employees to secure better working conditions."

If you think the comparison between a warehouse worker and a Hollywood assistant, grip, or writer are unfounded, you're mistaken. I'll remind you again that, at a number of entertainment companies, overages that exceeded the designated food budget were taken out of the assistants' pay. Many of these folks were, at the time, making just about minimum wage in Los Angeles, a city in which living costs have gone up tremendously during the years I've covered Hollywood.

"Unpredictable hours are bad for marriages, bad for long-term partnerships, for being present in your child's life. There are health ramifications associated with sleep deprivation," according to Kate Fortmueller, a professor at University of Georgia. She was not discussing gig workers at an Amazon warehouse or people hustling rideshare jobs on the side; she was interviewed for a 2021 article about the working conditions of many Hollywood employees.

She observed that, many years ago, Hollywood strikes usually centered on day-to-day working conditions, but from around the '60s onward, unions were chiefly pushing for larger residuals. "It's interesting, in 2021, we are returning to those same conversations" about hours, meal breaks, and punitive workdays that pushed Hollywood guild members to march on picket lines a century ago. The last major crew strike was in 1945, Fortmueller noted, but she thinks that more might be coming down the road. Some of her former students are in the industry and told her they have foot issues from standing on sets all day. For these young people (and others), she said, "it's really a question of, is it worth it?"

All these things, of course, are part of much bigger trends in society. As labor reporter Kim Kelly pointed out, as the waves of the COVID-19 pandemic rippled through the world in 2020 and 2021, they "pushed the economy—and the social fabric of the United States—to a breaking point, [and] sick-outs, public calls for support, wildcat strikes, and militant action dominated the labor landscape. Millions were left jobless or thrust into contact with a deadly disease without adequate protection," a set of conditions that certainly describes some folks' experiences in Hollywood, where, despite precautions that were supposedly taken, COVID broke out in a large array of workplaces.

Hollywood took center stage in this larger wave of labor unrest when, after overwhelming "yes" votes on strike authorizations, the WGA and SAG-AFTRA went on strike in mid-2023. Notable solidarity within and among Hollywood guilds resulted in meaningful gains on a number of fronts when the strikes finally ended that fall. But the curtain hasn't fallen on this saga yet. Having spoken to a lot of union members on and off picket lines during the long, punishing strikes, I'm aware many industry folks remain deeply concerned about their futures.

The pain of the last few years—which includes lower income and difficulty finding steady employment—lingers. That said, many workers spent time on picket lines comparing notes and realizing they were not alone in their struggles. A lot of big employers ended 2023 in retrenchment mode, but guild militancy is not waning. One harbinger: the WGA was, in 2020, willing to take on a complex action that many thought would not work (spoiler alert, it worked). Another sign: IATSE members (who, along with Teamsters, showed crucial solidarity to picketers in 2023) voted to authorize a strike in 2021. It didn't happen, but I wouldn't rule out guild walkouts in future. All in all, we're in a new Hollywood labor era, one that has deep conflict baked into it.

In the past decade or two, I have watched the Writers Guild of America go through a transformation. Today, it is far more cohesive and focused on the needs of the average guild member than the WGA that existed when I first began writing about the industry decades ago. The WGA has long been regarded as a more hard-line union, as Hollywood guilds go, but in the past, it has sometimes appeared to prioritize the concerns and agendas of its highest-paid writer-producers. That's no longer the case. Many have watched streamers with big pockets dismantle the systems of apprenticeship, residuals, and compensation that gave some in the industry at least some job security. And now many of those platforms are not only in cost-cutting mode, they are adding commercials to some of their service tiers (among the big players that have or are exploring putting ads in some plans are Peacock, Netflix, Disney+, HBO Max, and Paramount+). Of course, TV had advertising for decades—back when many more creative people had a better chance of sharing in the revenue that their work generated. As writer/producer Lila Byock put it on Twitter, "The streamers keep trying to reinstate the linear TV model without reinstating the compensation that linear TV creators used to earn."

As for the Directors Guild of America, as labor expert Robert W. Hurd wrote a decade ago, "union critics of the DGA deride them as a willing management ally," an image that wasn't altered by the quick deal the guild made with studios in 2023. Still, many Hollywood workers (including some in the DGA) are wary about where the industry is headed, and I think a number of leaders in various unions are more aware of how the rank and file view the major changes and consolidations that have roiled TV and film in the past decade.

The DGA, the WGA West branch, and SAG-AFTRA were all, as of mid-2022, headed by women. And of course, having a woman in charge does not necessarily ensure that workers will be protected. But this trio of women have all publicly stated that they don't want to propagate the bad ways of the Before Times. Fran Drescher, who won a bruising battle with actor Matthew Modine and now leads SAG, is not just an actor and a producer but also a survivor of assault. SAG, which has 160,000 members, not only offers its members a portal for reporting abuses, it has also issued guidelines aimed at the training and activities of intimacy coordinators on sets. Consequences for perpetrators of harm do not faze Drescher, who said in 2022, "Nobody, as we see now, is that important. Kings fall."

Glatter's father was an organizer with the International Ladies Garment Union, and when she and I talked, she expressed the same fear that I often have: that progress in the industry, especially on conduct and inclusion fronts, could "slide backwards." "We meet with every studio and network and talk about hiring and inclusion statistics," she said. "There are still areas that need a huge amount of work, like Latino hiring, Asian American hiring. Things are better overall, but is our work done? No."

She told me she hopes an industry coalition can be convened to issue guidelines that cover a range of subjects on all areas of safety, including (but not limited to) the treatment of animals, car chases, stunts, gun safety, misconduct, and other matters. Right now, she pointed out, there is no uniform standard for how safe, professional sets should operate. "We're in the traveling circus, you know—I'm an itinerant worker, going from set to set and studio to studio," Glatter said. "And right now, someone can go to one set where things are horrifying and dangerous and unsafe, and another where everything is well done." If all the guilds and employers come together, through the Hollywood Commission or some other body, to create a unified set of standards "with some teeth in it, then everyone has skin in the game," and an entire production or studio can be held responsible when the rules aren't followed, Glatter said.

Though the DGA has its own reporting hotline, Glatter said she supports an industrywide reporting tool, "so there's some common database and if some individual has been reported over and over again," there will be consequences. Directors themselves, of course, usually have a good deal of power on sets, which is why she has stood behind the guild's efforts to educate its membership on matters of conduct, bias, safety, and inclusion. Ultimately, "all our employers have an obligation to keep people safe," Glatter said. "And we have to be able to hold them accountable for that."

The WGA isn't as big as the DGA, which has around 19,000 members; all told, in the WGA East and the WGA West, there are about 13,000 people covered by the guild's Minimum Basic Agreement with the studios. Still, despite its smaller size, the Writers Guild has often been in the vanguard of the labor movement in Hollywood. I covered the industry's one-hundred-day strike in 2007, which came three years after David Young joined the WGA West as its organizing director (he is now its executive director).

There's no doubt that the 2004 arrival of Young, a former garment-worker organizer, galvanized the WGA in many ways. As one guild insider told me, at a prior job, "the Mob burned his house down. He's deeply and profoundly unimpressed with Hollywood. And it drives them crazy." "Young was widely credited for running a well-organized strike [in 2007–'08] featuring extensive picketing and rallies that benefited from strong support by the Screen Actors Guild and the Teamsters," *Variety* wrote in 2018. "The work stoppage forced a halt to most TV series in the middle of a season," and in the end, the guild ended up with some notable gains, particularly around the internet and then-nascent streaming.

There were also some advances made when the guild nearly struck in 2017. (There was a round of WGA negotiations in 2020—the union secured paid, portable parental leave for its members—but a number of major issues were kicked down the road, given that COVID was raging at the time.) What did happen in 2019 was the start of the WGA's packaging fight, which was conducted by the guild with a great deal of discipline. It's not worth going into all the details of the packaging wrangle—suffice to say, the talent agencies, years ago, thought up a way to stick their hands in creators' pockets, to the detriment of those creators. An executive at one of the major entertainment companies—for once not the bad guys in a Hollywood guild battle—called packaging "fucking evil."

As part of the packaging battle, WGA writers all fired their agents (a big deal, given how hard most creatives work to get representation in the first place), and during the campaign, which lasted a year and a half, some writer-on-writer spats broke out here and there. But in the main, the union hung tough. And won. The WGA ended up securing a new set of agreements with the agencies that eliminated packaging going forward, which went into effect midway through 2022.

The big kickoff to the packaging fight was the guild filing a lawsuit against a talent agency consortium, and one of the key names on that lawsuit was that of *Cold Case* creator and *Homeland* writer/producer Meredith Stiehm. She is now the president of the WGA, and she told me she'd like to see the guild's rank and file get a bigger slice of the billions that the big industry conglomerates are making. As she said in her candidate statement, "The downward pressure on income that we are all feeling is not a byproduct of the model—it is the goal."

"We're kind of working under an old model. The streaming model is new, and we have to kind of wrangle it and understand it, and figure out how to have a different kind of contract around that," Stiehm told me. And though she agreed that there have been positive changes in the industry in the past couple of decades, she's wary of believing that employers have fully understood how tired rank-and-file workers are of mistreatment.

"If you're on a toxic set, they don't care about that, because they're not there," Stiehm said. "It doesn't affect the product. If it doesn't affect their product or their profit, they can kind of pay lip service" to the idea of worker safety and dignity. "I don't think they're very motivated to change things if they're still getting what they want at the end."

The industry people I tend to talk to at length—admittedly a self-selecting group, given my track record as a reporter—care a great deal about creating healthy and productive workplaces and modes of leadership. More than fifty well-known creators and showrunners have signed the WGA West's Safe and Inclusive Workplace Pledge, which involves, among other things, promising to take training courses and endorsing the WGAW's Community Standards. Those commonsense standards include some things that should not have to be said, but, well, they actually do have to be said: "No porn at work. No sex toys at work. No miming sex at work. No running jokes about having sex with someone at work. No nudity at work. Descriptions of sex should only take place if they are pertinent to the story."

The pledge and the guild's educational efforts are admirable, but the entire industry needs more robust countermeasures, given a century of routine misconduct that was hidden when it wasn't glorified. Though I'd heard rumors over the years that the WGA was exploring the creation of its own online reporting portal, Stiehm only mentioned the guild's hotline during our conversation. She said that the guild can advise and provide support if people call that number, but in the end, "the employers are the enforcers. If there's sexual harassment going on at a studio, it's their job to fix that. We can't do that work for them."

I noted that the WGA had taken on packaging and won, so I wondered out loud: Couldn't it do more when it comes to those engaging in flagrant and unrepentant workplace misconduct? Over the years, I have floated the idea—including in a 2018 column—that repeat offenders should have their union cards pulled, temporarily or permanently. I haven't abandoned that position, but I realize that those kinds of moves are extremely tricky for guilds. For a few reasons, it's unlikely to happen.

As several union insiders explained to me, preventing a fellow guild member from working—for any reason—can put a union in hot water; the legalities are too complex to go into here, but they pose significant concerns about this kind of action. Another issue is that investigating or ejecting fellow guild members could damage the united front unions need to successfully address the many pressing issues they face. "Our collective bargaining power comes entirely from our ability to build solidarity among our members," Terrence observed.

When I mentioned these matters to Stiehm, she pointed out that "the huge difference in the agency campaign was, that was about a contract we had influence and authority over. It was within the sphere of what we do as a union." She added, "I mean, we do care a lot about workplace culture and toxicity. We talk about it at every board meeting. But it's not really our sphere of influence. We can say, 'We support the principles of equity, anti-harassment, anti-discrimination—and you can't be a bully.' We cannot regulate workplaces." The MBA—minimum basic agreement, which creates floors for various kinds of writer compensation—"That's our lane. That's where we can make change every three years," Stiehm said.

And indeed, for some folks I talked to, falling compensation and the inadequacy of certain guild protections in the current era are even more urgent issues. "The guild only exists to determine minimums, and I mean the bare minimum," said Kali, a WGA member. "The networks and streamers don't have to act in good faith. They don't have to play fair ball. They have all of the leverage. The guild has to adapt" and fight hard for members in the brave new world workers are in.

Kali supported the packaging action, but at this point, she regards it as "an old fight"—not a battle that really addressed the many ways in which creatives have been profoundly and painfully squeezed in recent years. Not only have the old training pathways fallen away, paychecks and residuals are often smaller than they used to be. The shred of hope that many used to nurture—that a job on a twenty-two-episode show might provide a measure of job security—is, for many, pretty much gone. The solidarity and gains achieved by the 2023 strikes were impressive, but the need for all guilds to adapt to the profound structural changes affecting the industry is not going away any time soon.

And while it might be very hard to change all kinds of long-standing norms, addressing these issues could radically shift the industry's quest for inclusion.

"Costume and makeup aside, many of the unions . . . are commonly white-male-dominated industries. Who is excluded from doing 18-hour days? I think for all these issues people care about—accessibility in Hollywood and diversity in storytelling—you need a production culture than can support a wider array of people participating in that work," Fortmueller said.

Another thorny issue unlikely to be resolved soon: the issue of free work. What has "long been an issue for screenwriters" is now a huge problem for TV writers, especially in the streaming realm, according to writer/producer Robert Hewitt Wolfe. He, like many writers I know, has major issues with the "protracted auditions during which dozens of writers are asked to pitch their takes on IP they do not control, often over the course of multiple meetings for months on end. . . . Even for the winner of a pitch sweepstakes, actual payment can be months or even years away, contingent on a network sale or securing financing and distribution. Closing these deals requires more pitching and more unpaid work."

It'll certainly be interesting to see how—or whether—the guilds continue to rise to these interlocking, complicated challenges. Fortmueller, who is a historian of Hollywood labor practices, pointed out that the streamers largely driving the industry now have roots in the tech industry, which is "known for its horrible working conditions. . . . If you watch television, if you watch films, you should think about who is making them and under what conditions. If you care about how your iPhones are made, and I think a lot of people do, you shouldn't see this any differently."

Given the headwinds they still face, my sense is that many industry workers have come to view strikes or other kinds of job actions as potentially necessary, if not nearly inevitable. "One of the big myths is that the losses incurred by a strike can never be made up, no matter what," writer/producer David Slack said. "And that's just patently false."

Find your people: Grassroots alliances

"I knew I had a decision to make," Liz Hsiao Lan Alper said.
In 2019, a hashtag—#PayUpHollywood—took on a life of its own.

That year, John August and Craig Mazin, writer/producers who cohost the industry podcast *Scriptnotes*, got an email from a listener asking them to focus on the plight of assistants. August then reached out to an industry group that Alper was part of, asking if people had relevant stories. "I was immediately like, 'Oh boy, do I!'" Alper recalled. This was not long after she had been elected to the WGA West board; she said, "I had a platform for kind of the first time in my life." She went on Twitter and "ranted" about her own harsh assistant experiences, and asked others for theirs. A large part of what she wanted to do was "clarify why most employers, showrunners, and supervisors didn't understand the situation that assistants are in, because it was so ingrained in everyone that these gigs are meant to prove people's worth through suffering—whatever creative torture people can think up."

Alper's online recollections launched a "massive wave" of stories and testimony, and "when it exploded, I started fielding a lot of interviews, and people kept saying, 'What comes next? What comes next?'" she said. "I realized, at this moment, we either figure out how to keep working on this, or we let the momentum die and nothing changes."

Did she consider the latter option? "Many, many times!" she answered with a laugh. At the time, she was unemployed and had just amicably split with her writing partner. "I was sitting there going, 'I'm broke, I don't have a job, and this is something that could prevent me from getting work in the future.'" But she kept the momentum going, cofounding Pay Up Hollywood with Deirdre Mangan and Jamarah Hayner. Why? "This sounds so gross and idealistic, but I was just like, 'This is the right thing to do.'"

The activism of Pay Up Hollywood has changed the equation for a lot of entry-level workers; many are now paid more than they were, though getting even remotely fair wages for all of them is an ongoing battle. To some degree, what Pay Up Hollywood has done is old-fashioned organizing and education. "There are times when people simply do not know how bad things are," Alper noted. "People were hearing what assistants were making and going, 'That's what I made fifteen years ago, when rent in Los Angeles was a third of what it is now.' People just didn't know, in some cases." Those efforts to educate employers—and workers—have led to a reconsideration of not just how those jobs operate but who gets them. As Alper and others have pointed out, if entry-level jobs favor the wealthy, then the industry's main intake pathways will be packed with educated people, most of them white, whose relatives may or may not be studio executives or tentpole-movie directors.

"If nothing else, the mindset of 'blame the assistants for not wanting work hard enough' is waning," Alper said. "It's much more about, 'Why don't we look at the employers who may be putting them through hell and are paying them nothing?'"

Pay Up Hollywood's annual reports make for fascinating reading—some support staffers recount how their jobs have changed for the better, others list the objects that have been thrown at them. And there are other grassroots efforts that have changed the industry in small and large ways.

Activist April Reign kicked off an enormous change when on January 15, 2015, she tweeted about the Academy of Motion Picture Arts and Sciences's list of Oscar nominees: "#OscarsSoWhite they asked to touch my hair." The hashtag was relevant again the next year, when the acting nominees were once again all white, and in 2020 too, when Cynthia Erivo was the only person of color nominated for a major acting award.

The Academy responded to various waves of criticisms with the announcement that "a wider breadth of actors and filmmakers [would] join their ranks by 2020, which would ultimately make the Academy Awards voting body more diverse in gender, race, and ethnicity," Imaan Yousuf wrote in an #OscarsSoWhite explainer. As of June 2020, the Academy board announced that it had actually surpassed its goals of inclusion, and the new 2020 member class was "45 percent women, 36 percent underrepresented ethnic/racial communities, and 49 percent international from 68 countries."

#DisneyMustPay is another campaign that has scored some successes; it advocates for writers who have been, according to the group, systematically shortchanged by the corporate behemoth. The product of an alliance among a number of author-focused trade organizations, the group's site, WritersMustBePaid.org, noted in 2021 that Disney "still refuse[s] to recognize [its] obligations to lesser-known authors who wrote media tie-in works for Marvel, for *Star Wars*, for *Aliens*, for *Predator* . . . [It's] failed to pay these writers royalties they're legally owed and have not given them the courtesy of royalty statements and reprint notices."

The group also pointed out that the pandemic was "hard on creators. Surveys by the Authors Guild and the Society of Authors have shown 71.4 percent of writers' incomes in the USA and 57 percent in the UK have declined since it began. Inflation is growing, bills still need to be paid. Honor the contracts." That effort is still a work in progress, but I have seen it gain traction on social media time and again—and it's been covered by industry trades and other publications.

Some online efforts have also altered the conversation around representation: #StarringJohnCho, which was created by writer William Yu, was an ingenious way to get folks to notice that the actor has a big range and should not be limited in the kinds of roles that he is usually offered. As someone who knows a lot of reporters and media types, I can say that this creative campaign didn't just stop many of us in our tracks, it got a lot of folks to think about how we write about—and how the industry treats—actors of color.

Find your people: The media

The media can certainly act as one of the entities holding the industry accountable. That will always be the case. But going to a reporter is not a feasible solution for everyone who needs help, for a lot of reasons.

I try not to talk too much—publicly, anyway—about the difficulties inherent in researching, reporting, and writing major pieces about systemic industry issues or abusive people in Hollywood. Like most people who do this work, I want the focus to be on the survivors of the abuse and the changes that are necessary to prevent more damage. But here's a behind the scenes truth: these pieces are profoundly hard to do—and in many ways, that's for good reason. Sometimes we are taking people's careers in our hands, so reporters are as diligent, meticulous, and comprehensive as we can possibly be. That means doing dozens of interviews, getting responses from studios and powerful individuals, and melding the information we've gathered into a judicious, readable, fact-checked narrative.

It sounds straightforward; it is not. It's not uncommon for powerful companies and people—or their lawyers, PR teams, and representatives—to drag their feet when it comes to responding to repeated queries, to not respond at all, or to bombard me, the legal teams I work with, and my editors with calls, emails, spin, threats, and other responses that are more designed to throw reporters off their game (or get a story killed) than get a piece over the finish line. I've come to know all too well the highly compensated cadre of industry and industry-adjacent professionals whose core job appears to be frightening people into giving up on that whole "speak truth to power" thing. Witnessing the courage of stalwart sources is a genuine reward, one I'm eternally grateful for, but much of the rest of the process is stressful, time-consuming, and scary. Each time I have done a big, wrenching story, I have vowed to never do it again.

And we shouldn't have to do it, because the industry could and should put abuse reporters out of business. As editor, writer, and former reporter Sarah Rodman asked, "These are large corporations employing these people. Why do we need to be your janitor, taking out your trash?" It's a question I've often asked myself. Especially when I've suspected that big companies were waiting for the press to ask about someone so that they could be spared the blame for *finally* taking decisive action regarding those folks' reigns of terror.

But not many people know reporters, or know which reporters they can trust; in addition, the media industry is itself more unstable and prone to layoffs than ever. "Economically, newsrooms have been hemorrhaging jobs over the last decade," Ronan Farrow said on an HBO panel I moderated in 2022. "The old kind of advertising-driven revenue models are not working across a lot of journalism in a lot of different formats. There's really promising experimentation happening with subscription-based models and other, newer ideas. And thankfully, some of those are causing good journalism to flourish. I think it's really important for all of us, as a country, as a culture, to back journalism that we believe in and pay for those subscriptions." But he added that, no matter what, "there's always been the struggle to resource the work of journalists who do that kind of reporting."

That's absolutely true. I've been lucky enough to work for supportive publications that assisted me greatly in bringing rigorously edited and fact-checked stories to the public. I'm grateful for everything that credible news organizations and book publishers have done to support excellent, necessary reporting on Hollywood. That said, the kind of work I and other reporters do in these challenging arenas takes time, and the media as a whole is not incentivized in that direction. For many publications, the goal is to churn out a lot of pieces that get a lot of traffic. Spending many months on one story—a thing I've routinely done—is just not a realistic thing that most freelancers (or even staffers) can do. If I was not married to someone with a stable job far away from any media-related industry, a lot of the work I've done in the past few years probably wouldn't have happened.

And though I'm immensely proud of all that dogged reporters and their sources have accomplished in the past several years (and before), good journalism alone will not fix the industry from the ground up. It can create change—of that there can be no doubt. But there are limits to the kinds of changes it can bring about.

As writer/producer Ron said, many truly incorrigible industry people don't see themselves in the stories of systemic abuse and mistreatment that do come out. "I don't think anyone who was running a [Peter] Lenkov-like room who read your story on him was like, 'They're coming for me next,'" Ron said. "They read that and thought, 'Another innocent man railroaded.' They're not terrified of going down for things they did that were wrong—because they don't think they did anything wrong."

To combat this kind of myopia, it's good to have peers who have your back.

Find your people: Peers, mentors, and allies

Now for something fun: I regularly hear about industry people having a good time while creating together and having one another's backs. The popular image of Hollywood might lead you to think it's a dog-eat-dog world, but that's not what I've found. Yes, there are assholes and jerkbags who do bad stuff (hence this book), but a lot of people in the industry routinely offer others their services as sounding boards, teachers, activists, and allies. If those senior to you offer—in a non-creepy way—to help you gain the skills you need, take them up on it. Because those opportunities are not necessarily easy to find.

Peers and leaders can also prevent people with shitty track records and no apparent inclination to change from ascending the ladder. "I'm always brutally honest" when asked for a recommendation, writer/producer Christopher said. "I don't sugarcoat. I never recommend anyone who I don't think is, first and foremost, a terrific person."

"I'm the ultimate pragmatist and I have always begged my agents, just be honest with me," Monica Owusu-Breen said. "Do they like Black people? Do they like women? I don't want to play a game. I just want to know. But the information is so hard to come by."

That might be changing, out of the public eye, at least some of the time. "People might not be tweeting about it, but the culture of silence" around destructive people in the industry is not nearly what it used to be, Terrence told me. "Instead of telling maybe one trusted friend about someone like that, they're probably going to tell a lot of people." More of the time, when someone's name is raised for a job and there are serious concerns or allegations about them within the creative community, "you'll probably hear about it."

Find your people: Those who can create from all kinds of lived experience; those who know some worlds, contexts, and cultures more intimately than you

Harold Perrineau's role in *From* wasn't constrained by stereotypes about Black men, nor did the character's journey revolve around historical traumas inflicted on Black Americans. Telling the latter kind of stories is important, of course. But no community wants their experience perpetually flattened to the worst atrocities perpetrated against it. Hollywood is in a transitional state on this issue. We are seeing more nuanced depictions of not just marginalized groups but individuals from within those communities. But it is still all too easy for storytellers to fall into the traps of blandified story lines and inauthentic characters.

Here's one example: Andy Weir, whose book, *The Martian*, was turned into a hit film starring Matt Damon, wrote a subsequent book called *Artemis*. In *Artemis*, his protagonist, Jazz, is a woman of color; she is of Saudi Arabian descent. That's an inherently political act in the world we live in, given the West's history of exclusion and inequity. But Weir insists his geeky, science-soaked books are apolitical. Thus a Saudi

Arabian woman is important, but we, as readers, are supposed to think her culture, context, and history are not.

Hollywood does this a lot right now: it wants credit for its inclusive casts but doesn't do much with the implications of those characters' identities and cultures—and then it bristles at the criticism it receives for falling short. The fact is, Hollywood still does not routinely infuse characters from historically excluded groups with the nuance, background, connective tissue and layers they deserve.

"There's a word for this lack of discussion: *erasure*," *Wired* writer Justice Namaste says of *Artemis*, in a thanks-but-not-quite-there critique. "[Weir] does create a society in which people are of different races, which is a step in the right direction. And people from a variety of ethnic groups have power, and interact. But the book glosses over those interactions, and how race might inform them, and inform people's identities, in a way it doesn't gloss over, say, the physics of explosions."

I bring this up not to ding Weir for having a woman of color protagonist. It was good of Weir, whose work I enjoy, to make that effort. But we have to talk about the entertainment realm's good intentions versus its execution. Good intentions aren't enough. When people are writing or creating outside their lived experience, extra care must be taken to bring granular, thoughtful authenticity to the process of building backstories, worlds, and characters. Artists and creators from historically excluded groups can do this if you give them the space, time, and resources to do it. The key is treating their contributions as intrinsic and critical to the creation of the work from the start, not as an ancillary or a "would be nice to have" extra. If nothing else, think about this: storytelling and drama thrive on conflict, so why not use the fuel provided by differing cultures, priorities, and historical contexts in intelligent and thoughtful ways?

We're finally past the point when there was one person of color in most casts and that character got the smallest amount of screen time (though this still happens, of course). Even so, I cannot count the number of times I have seen a Black person in a film or TV show who, for example, does not appear to know any other Black people. Latinx characters still are often maids, gangbangers, or service workers of some kind. A lot of projects pat themselves on the back for having queer representation that flits by quickly, or that involves a character that does not appear to have a place within a larger LGBTQ+ community. This is weird! Most queer folks know a lot of other queer folks.

An Asian character, if one exists in the story at all, should be more than a silent assassin, a tech geek who provides the exposition the heroes need, or the third-most important detective whose culture matters once a season (if that). "There might be a special episode where they go to Chinatown or Koreatown, and that's it," said Jeff Yang, who cohosts the podcast *They Call Us Bruce* and cowrote *Rise: A Pop History of Asian Americans from the Nineties to Now.*

A pet peeve for Orlando Jones is casting notices that erase the specificity that might help an actor build a role. "Why would you send out a casting saying 'All ethnicities welcome'?" Jones asked. "When Neil Simon sat down to write a play, he had a very specific idea who these characters were and how they talked and moved and fit into the world. And that's part of what makes him so wonderful as a writer. So you're telling me you're gonna take all that away, and all these characters are just racially ambiguous, and in no way connect to a culture, to a specific language? What are you talking about? 'It could be any race.' Wait—so there's no one in the room who understands that the way I have to approach this role as a Black man is likely going to be different than the way that a woman or trans person would approach this, right? It's our individual uniqueness that makes us artists! Get out of my face with your generic gibberish!"

These are all the awkward, complicated, and potentially contradictory things we'll have to delve into in any discussion of creativity and how it is defined and displayed. There is a history behind what a Black American man or a queer woman or a disabled person brings to a role, and what it means when someone from one of those communities directs or writes that role, given that they were long prevented from doing so.

Whoever they are and wherever they're from, good characters are not bland props or empty vessels; they're not narrowly defined, predictable, or one-dimensional archetypes. The same goes for characters from historically excluded or marginalized groups, and to be clear, in a number of recent Hollywood projects, these matters are being taken more seriously. It's about time. The fact is, we live in a world in which some fans erupt in a racist frenzy (that they deny is racist) when a Black woman plays a singing mermaid, as Halle Bailey does in the live-action

Little Mermaid. As we move forward, we ignore the intertwined histories of Hollywood and America at our peril. As sociology professor and *New York Times* columnist Tressie McMillan Cottom puts it, "There is no hierarchy of oppression. But there is a context for all speech."

And there is a context for all creation, characterization, and casting too. Genuinely inclusive casting is a good thing, of course; everyone should get a fair shot at the meatiest and most rewarding roles. It was astonishing, and a little heartbreaking, to learn that when Sandra Oh got the pilot script for the drama *Killing Eve,* she assumed she was being asked to play a supporting character of some kind—despite her successful career on *Grey's Anatomy* and elsewhere, it took her a minute to realize she was wanted for the title role. "After being told to see things a certain way for decades, you realize, 'Oh my god! They brainwashed me!' I was brainwashed! So that was a revelation to me," Oh said in 2018.

Adjoa Andoh plays the imperious Lady Danbury in *Bridgerton,* a huge Netflix hit from the Shonda Rhimes empire. Before Andoh was cast, she had understandably absorbed the "rule" that period dramas were a no-go area for UK actors of color. (I watch everything with corsets, and this was so true for *so long.*) "And so typically, actors of color think, 'Oh, another job I won't get,'" Andoh said. "I needed to know that this was an opportunity to be in it—and also, that I was expected to be myself, a Black woman, not a Black woman pretending to be white."

There's no rule that says a project absolutely *must* delve into the histories, cultures, and identities of each character and community; everything depends on the needs of the story being told. But I cannot think of many projects that balance all these considerations more spectacularly than the Oklahoma-set *Reservation Dogs,* which follows the lives of four memorable and extremely varied young people who are messing up, processing grief, finding their places in the world, and, in the course of doing all that, sometimes just being goofballs. In the show, which is run by cocreator Sterlin Harjo, there isn't a "very special episode" about being Native, just as, on Lisa McGee's *Derry Girls,* growing up during Northern Ireland's Troubles is simply the backdrop of the characters' lives.

These shows are wildly different in tone, but both are created by people who grew up in those places, and specific cultures, histories, and traditions are organically part of moments big and small. Within the worlds of both *Derry Girls* and *Reservation Dogs*, sometimes the most challenging aspects of the young people's lives don't come up, and they're simply talking about the movie *Lost Boys* or trying to get to a concert by a favorite pop artist. Other times, the shows draw on the spirituality, humor, deep wells of pain, and cultural touchstones characters are very familiar with. And those moments often resonate profoundly, because they clearly come from complicated and empathic lived experience. Through specificity, both programs get at emotions everyone knows: loss, grief, hope, frustration, and humor as a pressure-relief valve.

A 2022 episode of *Star Trek: Strange New Worlds,* on the other hand, was an utter delight for a different set of reasons. There was nothing about anybody's real history on-screen: "The Elysian Kingdom" used one of those classic *Trek* premises—everyone was put into a fantasy scenario because a space entity felt like doing that, basically—and the cast clearly had a blast playing queens, kings, knaves, wizards, and warriors. It was a heartwarming, light adventure that turned emotional and moving at its conclusion, and it was cool—and yes, still somewhat unusual—to see Black, disabled, and Asian actors get most of the big moments in the episode. In that installment, I especially loved the co-medic stylings of Bruce Horak as Hemmer, the ship's sarcastic, brilliant Starfleet engineer. Hemmer is blind, as is the actor who plays him, but the character is never defined by that fact. He is hilarious, cranky, and wise—and specific.

Perhaps that's the upshot here: specificity and authenticity matter. I first connected with Alice Wong, editor of *Disability Visibility* and author of the memoir *Year of the Tiger: An Activist's Life,* because we are both TV fanatics. (Social media has many ills but reading thoughts from—and meeting—Wong on Twitter remains a high point.) I had to ask her what her pet peeves are when it comes to characters with disabilities. "The first is the pervasive practice of casting non-disabled people as disabled characters," she replied in an email. "Second, characters [who] are sidekicks or tokens with little effort to give any depth or meaning to the character's motivations. Third, inspirational stories about disability that are clearly used as a device to teach or valorize the non-disabled main character. Fourth, narratives that living with a disability is a fate worse than death or an anomaly that must be fixed or eliminated."

A mainstream show she thinks has done a great job with its depictions of disability is *Call the Midwife*, a popular UK drama (it's currently available in the United States on Netflix). During its long run, it has depicted the various challenges disabled people face, including "stigma, discrimination and inaccessibility," Wong noted. But that's not all it's done. "More importantly, there are multiple storylines, disabled characters, and themes that are organically integrated throughout the show's 11 seasons. The show doesn't dwell on the tragedy or difficulties disabled people face—there is joy, love, and care," she observed. Reggie, a favorite character played by Daniel Laurie, "exercises his self-determination and asserts his autonomy with his parents. He's also a loving son and member of the community who has dreams and desires like everyone else."

Find your people: The public

I don't know that I would have found the courage to come out as bisexual a few years ago, had I not witnessed the bravery of many LGBTQ+ fans who have campaigned to make the industry better. In the spring of 2016, Lexa, a fan favorite character on the CW drama *The 100*, and the show's lead, Clarke, acted on their attraction and slept together. Moments after that long-awaited consummation, Lexa, a powerful warrior queen, was killed by one of her retainers.

Queer women and their allies unleashed a wave of protest, the likes of which I have rarely seen—and that anger was justified. Lexa's death played into just about every Bury Your Gays trope in Hollywood history. The alarming frequency with which queer female and femme characters have been brutalized or killed off has taken an incredible toll on LGBTQ+ audiences for decades, and the poorly handled killing of Lexa caused that dam to burst. Understandably.

It's very easy to dump on the excesses of online controversies. (I'm a woman on the internet, no need to explain how bad it can get.) Yet I was at the core of this situation, and the overwhelming majority of fans were eloquent, heartfelt, and yes, angry—but also focused on changing the narrative about queer women in entertainment. They churned out essays, studies, statistics, and personal stories, and they were all powerful.

During that difficult time, I learned—and a lot of other people learned—from folks who, despite their pain, did an enormous amount of work to educate all of us about these damaging tropes and how persistent they have been. It worked: there is no doubt in my mind that those who set out to educate the media and creatives about these clichés succeeded in raising awareness about how pernicious and awful they are. So before I get to the next thing I want to say, I need to reaffirm: I think fans of popular culture are entitled to their responses to what the industry releases. I want there to be less toxicity online, of course, but people, especially those from historically excluded groups, should be able to speak their truths.

All I want to do now is perhaps inject a note of caution about where those responses are directed. When it comes to feedback or input you have for some product of the entertainment industry, it might be worth asking yourself this question before offering that feedback: Am I directing this at the appropriate entity—or at the *available target*?

During the protests surrounding that episode of *The 100*, I tried to get folks to understand that Hollywood workplaces are not democracies. There are exceptions to this rule, but executives and showrunners generally control the stories their programs tell. Only a few people control what's in a studio movie. *Almost nobody else who works on any Hollywood production has real, meaningful, ongoing decision-making power.* Most, if not all, people below the rank of showrunner, director, high-level producer, or important executive have no sway at all.

The bigger and more important the industry property, company, or franchise, the less likely you are to find that the real decision-makers are active online. If they're high enough on any industry food chain, they're likely having their online accounts managed by someone else. They are often protected in ways that rank-and-file workers are not, online and in real life.

What follows is a huge generalization, but the truth is: the industry folks most active online—the ones likely to read your messages and possibly even reply—are usually not the ones with meaningful power. That creative decision you hated in that movie or that TV show? The person you're messaging or tagging *may well have argued your exact point* to the powers that be and lost. But they can't say that. They can't say, "Many people internally also hated the thing you're mad about." If they do, they might not ever get hired again.

Look, I get it: it's hard to see harmful patterns enacted by the industry. But where the response is directed matters. It may be pointless to say this several decades into the monetization of online harassment, but I am tired of seeing creative people driven offline by responses to situations, decisions, or storytelling they don't control. It's especially dispiriting when those folks are already dealing with all kinds of hurdles, personally and professionally. After enduring a wave of harassment for saying she liked the movie *Dune,* author Fonda Lee notes, "I imagine it's satisfying for some of those who feel voiceless or overlooked to lash out in ways that falsely feel productive simply because the punishment actually lands. BIPOC and other marginalized creators who disappoint you are not going to fight back. They have no weapons. I'm not going to doxx you, hit back with racial slurs, or set my legions of asshole friends with Pepe the frog avatars on you. All I can do is take it. BIPOC creators are just trying to keep our heads up."

As noted previously, some innovative and savvy fan campaigns and some online (and offline) advocacy do real good. If you want to produce that substantial, positive change—if that is your goal—throwing abusive, cruel, or toxic comments and vitriol at the people *who did not make the decisions you don't like* won't change anything. As Lee writes, "nothing about the underlying structures of power or representation are actually changed and the only real result is exhausted creators withdrawing."

> Look, I know that hope is hard. But at the same time,
> it's kind of the best.
>
> —*Michelle Lovretta (writer)*, *"Last Dance,"* Killjoys

During the pandemic, I watched the scrappy sci-fi show *Killjoys* more than once. Don't judge me; it's a show about space bounty hunters having a great time while kicking oppressive forces in the nuts. Metaphorically and sometimes literally. If you found a better thing to do during those hard years than watch a show that featured not only space bounty hunters but *gay space pirates*, I congratulate you. In any event, before I end this book, I want to speak this truth: not enough shows have gay space pirates.

To return to my main point, one reason I love sci-fi storytelling in all forms is because it allows us to think about all kinds of futures. To see other paths and possibilities. And that brings me to one vision of how the entertainment industry could operate going forward. What if, for all industry workers, things worked like this?

You are an employee or contractor working for a company, organization, or production in the entertainment industry. You've typically had bosses and colleagues who were professional, kind, thoughtful, and super-creative. For a long time, you were living the dream. *Yay!*

But you experience a pattern of bad behavior from someone with more power than you. That pattern of behavior has a negative effect on you, and it does not go away. The fact that this is happening at all surprises you, because you're aware that those with power in your industry are required to go through extensive training in order to be put in positions of responsibility. This is also mystifying in part because there are a number of complementary systems in place to protect people in the industry. They have worked effectively for a while, everyone knows about them, and they've had a deterrent effect on those who attempt to engage in patterns of bias, toxicity, abuse, assault, and mismanagement. Everyone knows that if you repeatedly make people feel harassed or unsafe, and if you don't change those ways, the consequences are serious and potentially career-ending.

But the problem keeps happening. So you go to the union, trade guild, or professional organization that you're part of, and make use of the robust systems of advice and resources that it offers. You consult with trained professionals as many times as you need to, as you think through your options. Since the problems show no sign of ending, you decide to report the person in question through the well-publicized, third-party reporting system designed for all industry workers. It is not controlled or administered in any way by the company you or the problematic person work for.

In this reporting process, you have some control over what you want done. You can alert the person's employer without the person knowing it. You can request an investigation, or you can request an investigation after a certain number of other individuals report the same individual. This is all explained to you in a clear, cogent fashion, and you are given the choice to remain anonymous. Even if you want to be anonymous, there's a way for investigators to contact you if they need to hear from you. If there are a lot of complaints about this person—in the present or future—you will be told. If at some point you want to delete your report, you can.

If there is an investigation, it is handled by a discreet, experienced, and helpful third-party company skilled in these matters. No company or executive the problem person works for has any control over events that transpire in that investigation. While this is ongoing, you are offered meaningful mental health support and other kinds of help.

The good news: The negative pattern of behavior ends. The person has been made aware of that pattern and has been told they are no longer allowed to engage in those behaviors, and they stop. Or the person, despite being offered resources, support, and education, does not change the behaviors. They are removed from that job, temporarily (in order to receive more education and training), or permanently (either because they consistently reject education and training, or independent auditors find that the training and/or consequences didn't work).

At no point were you ever made to feel unsafe because you reported this person. Though it was unfortunate that you experienced the damaging behavior, you don't fear that you're likely to encounter it at many future workplaces. What you went through was rare. And handled. (And if a lot of what I've outlined had turned out to be untrue, you could have gone to the press, where thoughtful, considerate, experienced reporters would have taken on your story.)

Anyway, you had this experience, and then you went on with your career. You were compensated fairly and well for the hard work that you did. You worked with people who behaved kindly and professionally—and so, so creatively—while you brought to life the stories and images and ideas you burned to share with the world.

And I thank you.

15

To Be Continued

A Season Finale, Not a Series Finale

It's like in the great stories, Mr. Frodo, the ones that really
mattered. Full of darkness and danger they were, and
sometimes you didn't want to know the end, because how could
the end be happy? How could the world go back to the way it
was when so much bad had happened?

But in the end, it's only a passing thing, this shadow. Even
darkness must pass. . . . Those were the stories that stayed
with you, that meant something, even if you were too small to
understand why.

But I think, Mr. Frodo, I do understand, I know now.

Folk in those stories had lots of chances of turning back,
only they didn't. They kept going, because they were holding
on to something . . . That there's some good in this world, Mr.
Frodo, and it's worth fighting for.

—The Lord of the Rings: The Two Towers

I cry every time I watch that scene. I get a little misty when I just read
those words. Even when they're on a sheet of paper cranked out by my
home printer. When I read that speech by Sam Gamgee, something in
my soul shifts.

Every. Time.

Why does it move me? I could list the reasons, but they wouldn't
fully explain it. It's not just the words, it's the performances, the framing of the shot, the light, where that moment comes within the story.
But also, here's a confession: I don't know.

I've been writing about things on screens for decades, and the truth is, I still don't know how they do the magic trick. I've learned a lot, but I'll never fully know, because that is the nature of magic.

That's really the thrill of the job of a critic—we spend all this time constructing word palaces, playing around with similes and metaphors, and trying to make the reader understand—*feel*—what we feel. Because somebody else felt something and they just had to put that story, those emotions, into the world.

That creator wanted us—a bunch of strangers—to experience something. Critics try to make those connections, to bridge the gaps between artists and artisans and audiences. If film and TV storytellers build fantasy castles in the sky, we are the housing inspectors who come along to make sure the foundations are up to code and the roof doesn't leak. What an absolutely ridiculous, presumptuous job. It's preposterous that grown adults do this.

I love it. I have no regrets. Because I get to cry at work. Sometimes for good reasons.

Yet I am sorry—no, enraged; no, exhausted—when I think about all the things I know now. What I know, years later, about how many of the things I liked and loved were made. I'm gobsmacked that so many people often created good work under terrible working conditions. I'm sorrier than I can say that an industry many people believe is glamorous routinely and even casually treated so many so unfairly, so unjustly, so *wrongly*.

My parents sent me to Catholic school, and I cannot unlearn the habit of thinking about sin. It was wrong—it was a sin and it *is* a sin when human beings and their inherent dignity are simply . . . disregarded.

The process of change in Hollywood—it's nowhere near done. And if you're expecting me to have a pithy, neat wrap-up in these closing pages, this finale will leave you hanging.

Two events demonstrated why that is the case. After I wrapped up my interview with Lesli Linka Glatter in the middle of 2022, a DGA spokesperson sent me numbers clarifying something we'd talked about. In the TV season that ended in 2013, 28 percent of TV episodes were directed by women of color, men of color, and white women. In the season that ended in 2021, that number was 60 percent. Progress.

Less than twenty-four hours later, I saw the first news reports about Eric Weinberg, who'd been a writer/producer on *Californication* and

Anger Management. During his lengthy career, "he displayed egregiously misogynistic and inappropriate behavior in writers rooms and on sets," according to an in-depth story on him. "Weinberg, who on October 25 pled not guilty to 18 counts of sexual assault including rape, was able to use his credentials as writer and producer on such sitcoms as *Veronica's Closet* and *Scrubs* over the course of years to entice women to photoshoots where they allegedly were violated," Kim Masters and Samuel Braslow wrote in their November 2022 article. Since news reports about him had surfaced months earlier, "dozens of possible victims have contacted law enforcement."

"It's all wrong." Sam Gamgee again. "By rights, we shouldn't even be here. But we are."

But we are.

Months after I was assaulted by a television executive, there was no answer, there was no solution, but in a diner near the Los Angeles airport, two friends held my hands. I held onto them, and to what we told each other. And to what one friend said: "Put it in the work."

I kept going, because I was holding on to something.

I have put it in the work. The rage, the pain, the confusion, the desire to help someone, somewhere. The need to make it better for someone else, maybe lots of someones. The desire to mirror the love, support, and recognition I got—from people and from stories—at my lowest moments. So many times, I reread words written by Tressie McMillan Cottom in 2019 about how she approaches certain kinds of storytelling: "I will never feel comfortable trading on the story of my loss purely for personal gain. That is why I decenter the trauma to focus on the culture that produced it. . . . If your hell was only ever about you then it was a hell of your own making. I want to be better than that."

I want to be better than that. And . . . I tried.

We talked for three hours. That afternoon in 2022 in Evan Rachel Wood's backyard, despite the hard stuff we talked about, it was an exhilarating day. We both knew what it was like to interrogate the powerful industry institutions enabling the worst shit, to poke into very dark corners and hear the growls of the biggest monsters. And yet . . . we were still here.

The golden quality of those hours in her yard—not unlike the sunlight on the *Friday Night Lights* set—made them feel like . . . an arrival.

Was this the catharsis I'd been waiting for? Maybe everything so many people had been through, all the pain that had been channeled into stories and posts and testimony and truthful, painful reckonings of all kinds . . . maybe it had all been worth it. I wish that pain had never happened. If I were a god, the spinner of myths and the holder of lightning bolts, I'd banish all of it. And then I'd bring back every good person driven out of this industry by evil shit.

But maybe, just maybe, something new was taking shape.

The moment that got me—I didn't ugly cry, but I welled up—was when Wood talked about how different she felt on February 2, 2021, the day after she and other survivors named their abuser.

"My child, the very next day, looked at me and said, 'Why are you acting so weird?'" Wood recalled. "And I said, 'I'm not. I'm just free.' He had never seen me without that hanging over me. He could see it in my entire being, the very next day. If I never worked another day in my life, it would still be worth it, because it was the greatest gift I ever gave to myself."

Not everyone in the industry has Wood's privilege and perch, a fact she is well aware of. What she and others did was still scary, and there were hard consequences. But she told me she has no regrets. Like a lot of other industry folks I know, in high and low and middle places, she has taken risks in an effort to enact systematic change. Real change, for *everyone*.

It has been my privilege to talk to a lot of people who have done the same thing. The script coordinators, the assistants, the managers, the executives, the crew members, the actors, the writers, and the survivors who are, together, attempting to burn down the old temple. It's a long, unglamorous slog, but there are many incredible people forging these better—these *necessary*—paths.

In late 2022, Stacey Pinkerton sent me links to accounts of ongoing legislative efforts by the Consent Awareness Network to define consent into law; one press release from CAN, on the battle to alter military law, contained statements of support from Pinkerton and from Andrea Constand, who was among the first to bring Bill Cosby's history of sexual assault to light. Pinkerton's work with CAN—"we are working on each state," she told me—is part of the educational and activist work she has done for years. Our first conversation took place not long after we both appeared on a Zoom panel for *We Need to Talk About Cosby*, the Showtime documentary in which the stories of Constand, Pinkerton, and many others were told.

"If the Cosby survivors had not spoken out when they did in 2014 and even before then, we most likely would not have seen Weinstein convicted, and a lot of other cases afterward," Pinkerton told me. "Our voices helped open those doors and helped supply that courage, and then everything else had a domino effect. The more we speak up, set boundaries, recognize predatory behavior as abuse of power, demand appropriate education, and most importantly, change the laws against these predators, the less likely we will have such institutional abuse. And the more we keep doing these kinds of things, the more the world will know we're not going away."

Something I don't have the words for: the courage of those who look the toxic gods in the eye and throw the thunderbolts right back at them.

Here's the magic solution to fixing all the terrible stuff: there isn't one.

There's no button to push, no One Big Thing that needs to be done. Some big things do need to be pushed much more diligently and much further. But a lot of the changes that matter most—they happen in the small moments. Many are not that small, not really.

In the past few decades, especially in the past six years, I have had the honor of getting to know hundreds of industry sources. The connections and conversations I've enjoyed—they've been among the most meaningful and consequential of my life. So many people have put themselves on the line for a goal that is much bigger than they are. I keep a list of sources, and I look at it sometimes, and I send my gratitude into the universe. Because they changed something. Not just me. The *world*.

I want to burn Hollywood down some days. I really do. And then I fall in love with a TV show or a movie and I want to know everything about it.

And then I remember I *don't* want to know everything about it, because what if my heart gets broken again? I do not want to keep finding out that bad things happened on productions where the final product meant a lot to me. Seamus and I talked several times, and he never told me the name of the huge star who he knows is a huge asshole. I never asked. We both have mental lists of Bad Names that are long enough.

So what do we do now? We burn it all down.

I'm well aware of how terrifying fire can be. I was once woken up on a wintry night by what I thought were post–New Year's fireworks. I looked out the window and our garage was on fire. It was really scary. About a decade later, my son came into my home office and asked if I was burning a candle. I was not, but I had noticed a smoky smell. I pulled aside the curtain and saw that our next-door neighbor's house was on fire.

The fire was more than a dozen feet away, but it felt much closer; I could feel the heat from where I stood. It was terrifying. The flames seemed *alive*. My reptile brain was sure they were clawing at me. We ran.

We watched the progression of the flames for hours, from across the street. The fire was sneaky. It crept up inside the house and hid in the eaves; the firefighters fought the blaze all day. Our neighbors ran out of the house without shoes on. They were all okay, but they lost everything. So yeah, that kind of fire—not good.

But not all fires are the same. If I ever abandon this line of work, I'd love to be a landscape designer or full-time gardener. I said before that Buddhism is my faith, but my true religion is composting.

As many cultures have known for thousands of years, fire's good for the soil. Even now, you can find folks doing controlled burns as part of a program of thoughtful stewardship of the land. An educational sign in a forest preserve near my house describes the various workers that are involved in its controlled fires ("burn boss," "torch operator"), and notes that the blazes create "large open areas of black soil and ash that absorb more heat from the sun, speeding up the growth of native plants."

"By ridding a forest of dead leaves, tree limbs, and other debris, a prescribed burn can help prevent a destructive wildfire," *National Geographic* tells us. "Controlled burns can also reduce insect populations and destroy invasive plants. In addition, fire can be rejuvenating. It returns nutrients to the soil . . . and can help young trees and other plants start to grow." Some tree seeds, it turns out, need fire to kickstart their growth.

When I gave this book its title, it came from two places: These were words I frequently (and furiously) texted to friends during the past several years. I also know that fire can renew. It can be a source of warmth, beauty, and comfort. You have to have a plan, and you have to use it the right way.

We can do it the right way. And we must.

When people say, about some kind of industry bullshit, inequity, or misconduct, "that's just how it is," nah. *We make things how they are.* We make choices, big and small, that determine how the world works going forward. People I respect in the industry are doing things to try to make it better. I know that process can be messy and hard, and I fear, every day, that it's not enough.

It might not be. I can't know. I can't be everywhere and talk to everyone (though some days, it feels like I have). One thing I do know: I don't have it in me to write a lot more about industry misconduct and abuse. The job title "burn boss" sounds cool; experiencing the paralyzing fear and dread that often accompanies this kind of reporting—not cool. At all.

When a survivor recently told me she wanted accountability, I understood. But I also offered this advice, unprompted but gained through brutal experience: If you destroy yourself in an effort to get accountability, what did you really get? If you do that, they win.

The best news I can offer her—and you—is that we are not alone in this fight.

The world, more than ever, is a scary place, but I'm going to trust that all of us together, if we keep pushing, can sustain and nurture real change. Our fire will feed what we want to thrive. The seeds will burst and bring forth healthy new growth.

And then, we will have not just the good stories and delightful diversions and moving sagas we all need but a better world.

Our stories tell us who we are. And we deserve the best.

Acknowledgments

In 2019, Sara Baker Netzley and Cory Barker asked me to give the Robison Endowed Lecture at Bradley University. It was an offer I was happy to accept, and I had a great time. The title of my speech was "The Myths of Hollywood," and it ended up contributing a fair bit to the structural foundations of this book.

My book agent, Sonali Chanchani, approached me in the spring of 2021, and since that time has been one of the most supportive, effective, and dependably kind people I know. Thanks for everything, Sonali.

Rakia Clark not only took a chance on this book, she made it decidedly better, and I'm deeply indebted to her for that and for her support, wisdom, and advocacy. Thank you, Rakia. Sincere gratitude to Dale Brauner, Sarah D. Bunting, Trina Hunn, Rachael DeShano, Ivy Givens, and Pilot Viruet for helping in so many ways to improve this book.

For many years, I have belonged to an awesome book club and I have long aspired to write something worthy of the time of these wonderful, supportive, perceptive friends. Thanks (and happy reading) to Marcie, Ann, Curt, Peggy, Renee, Ellen, Susan, and Carolyn.

After many adventures and misadventures in the media trenches, I'm glad to have landed in a welcoming place. Cheers to the whole *Vanity Fair* crew, especially Radhika Jones, Mike Hogan, Jeff Giles, Katey Rich, Hillary Busis, Kase Wickman, Julie Miller, and Joy Press.

A disclaimer: Being mentioned in this section does not necessarily mean any of these people helped me with prior stories or with the reporting for this book. It just means they have superpowers.

I am extremely grateful for the kindness, friendship, and support of Melanie McFarland, Lana Kim, Jenny McGeary, Tom Pazen, Tara Bennett, Paul Terry, Mere Smith, Alan Sepinwall, Linda Holmes, Tara Ariano, Dave Cole, Sarah Rodman, David N. Patton IV, Erin Keane, Jo Duren-Sampson, Melissa Urbanski, Andrew Halaby, Sarah Gura, Betsy Edgerton, and Robert K. Elder. I am beyond fortunate to know, as mentors and friends, Kim Masters, Jim DeRogatis, and Greg Kot; their encouragement and the tenacious, compassionate examples they set are priceless. Extra super special thanks to J.

People in various media, legal, education, and entertainment trenches have freely and kindly shared their wisdom, experience, insight, and expertise with me for many years, and a lot of folks have also, through their work, encouraged, enlightened, or inspired me. I can't list all the people I'm grateful to here—there are *so* many—but here's a shoutout to some of the folks who made the journey better: Joe Adalian, Sam Adams, Emily Andras, Kate Aurthur, Angelica Jade Bastién, W. Kamau Bell, Marc Bernardin, Elizabeth Bridges, Taffy Brodesser-Akner, Monica Byrne, James Callis, Laura Canning, Tim Carvell, Jen Chaney, Justin Chang, Tressie McMillan Cottom, Joe Darrow, Felicia Day, Eric Deggans, Andy Dehnart, Kayleigh Donaldson, Kether Donohue, Tananarive Due, Shernold Edwards, Monica Eng, Joel Fields, Dan Fienberg, Tom Fitzgerald, Caroline Framke, Roxane Gay, Vlada Gelman, Sadie Gennis, Emily Gipson, Lesley Goldberg, David Graham-Caso, Ellen Grey, Michael Greyeyes, Javier Grillo-Marxuach, Brian Grubb, Kevin Guilfoyle, Roxana Hadadi, Heather Havrilesky, Joe Henderson, Libby Hill, Damian Holbrook, Melinda Hsu Taylor, Cathryn Humphris, Charlayne Hunter-Gault, Henry Jenkins, Kyra Jones, Orlando Jones, Inkoo Kang, Gloria Calderón Kellett, Katie King, John Landgraf, Martha Lauzen, Ken Levine, Michelle Lovretta, Jason Lynch, Margaret Lyons, Ira Madison III, Soraya Nadia McDonald, Caitlin McFarland, Myles McNutt, Lorenzo Marquez, Nina Metz, Natalie Morales, Jennifer Morgan, Janet Murray, Amy Nicholson, Emily Nussbaum, Sierra Teller Ornelas, Monica Owusu-Breen, Caitlin Parrish, Willa Paskin, Nichole Perkins, Harold Perrineau, Doug Perry, Anne Helen Petersen, Keith Phipps, Stacey Pinkerton, James Poniewozik, Alexia Prichard, Laura Prudom, Jennifer Kaytin Robinson, Joanna Robinson, Tasha Robinson, John Rogers, Mike Royce, Bird Runningwater, Emily St. James, Sonia Saraiya, Mike Schaub, Nell Scovell, Matt Zoller Seitz, Melissa Silverstein, Keto Shimizu, Seth Simons, David Slack, John Solberg, Zack Stentz, Rachel Talalay, Lucas Till, Scott Tobias, Rebecca Traister, Bo Travis, Kathryn VanArendonk, Elizabeth Wagmeister, Mariann Wang, Kara Warner, Evan Rachel Wood, Alice Wong, Jeff Yang, Nancy Wang Yuen, Barbie Zelizer, and Claire Zulkey. To Jamie French and Jessica Nevarez: *Texas Forever*. Eternal respect to my president, Mary McDonnell.

There are many people whose names, for various reasons, I cannot mention publicly. Just know that if we ever talked, and you ever shared your truth with me, whether or not a story emerged from those conversations, I have not forgotten you. And I never will.

To my family—Colleen, Chris, Ryan, Lauren, Tom, Christine, Lucy, Nick, Jenny, Ray, Jordan, Ming, Harry, and Jack—I love you all. Special sibling shoutout to Col (*soror mea*) and Tommy, with whom I memorized episodes of *M*A*S*H* and *Monty Python's Flying Circus*.

To my amazing son, Sean (a.k.a. @ProdGrave), I love you all the time.

To my husband, Dave: words fail. For a long time, you believed in me more than I believed in myself. I'm catching up!

Notes

Chapter 1: The Myth of Sufficient Progress

6 *"We've always talked about"*: Interview with Liz Hsiao Lan Alper, May 2022.

9 *"The Assistant faced some resistance"*: David Thomson, *A Light in the Dark: A History of Movie Directors* (New York: Knopf, 2021), 222–23 (italics in original).

10 *"In this industry, the stakes are"*: Interview with John Landgraf, January 2022.

12 *the pulse-pounding Fox drama* 24: Wayne Parry, "24 Under Fire From Muslim Groups," CBS News, January 18, 2007.

12 *"In real life the time bomb"*: James Poniewozik, *Audience of One: Donald Trump, Television, and the Fracturing of America* (New York: Liveright, 2019), 101.

12 *"character was, essentially"*: Poniewozik, *Audience of One*, 126–27.

12 *"an indictment of male aggression"*: Poniewozik, *Audience of One*, 94.

12 *the former NBC executive who later supersized*: Poniewozik, *Audience of One*, 205.

12 *"don't care. They can make"*: Kayleigh Donaldson, "Why Does Mel Gibson Keep Getting So Many Chances?," Pajiba, October 20, 2021.

13 *"It may not be good"*: Paul Bond, "Leslie Moonves on Donald Trump: 'It May Not Be Good for America, but It's Damn Good for CBS,'" *The Hollywood Reporter*, February 29, 2016.

14 *"You're not making good decisions"*: Interview with David Nevins, July 2022.

14 *"It was very thoughtful"*: Interview with David Slack, June 2022.

14 *"to prevent the complaint from becoming public"*: New York Attorney General Letitia James, "Attorney General James Secures $30.5 Million from CBS and Leslie Moonves for Insider Trading and Concealing Sexual Assault Allegations," press release, November 2, 2022, ag.ny.gov/press-release/2022/attorney-general-james-secures-305-million-cbs-and-leslie-moonves-insider-trading.

14 *"CBS and its senior leadership"*: James, "Attorney General James Secures $30.5 Million."

15 *made public November 2, 2022:* Attorney General of the State of New York and Investor Protection Bureau, *In the Matter of an Investigation by Letitia James, Attorney General of the State of New York, of CBS Corporation and Leslie Moonves*, Assurance No. 22-071, New York State Attorney General, November 2, 2022.

Chapter 2: Scott Rudin and the Myth of Necessary Monsters

17 *"He always loved movies"*: Interview with David Graham-Caso, September 2021.

17 *"dictate Greek policy for the school"*: David Graham-Caso, "Joy and Purpose: A Eulogy for Kevin Blake Graham-Caso," Medium, September 11, 2021.

18 *"was abusive, it was bullying"*: Interview with Graham-Caso.

19 *"He was something of a friend"*: Interview with Samuel Laskey, September 2021.

20 *Rudin smashed a computer monitor:* Tatiana Siegel, "Everyone Just Knows He's an Absolute Monster: Scott Rudin's Ex-Staffers Speak Out on Abusive Behavior," *The Hollywood Reporter,* April 7, 2021.

20 *involving a shattered glass bowl:* Siegel, "Everyone Just Knows."

20 *Kevin was forced by Rudin:* Anne Victoria Clark, Jackson McHenry, Lila Shapiro, Gazelle Emami, Helen Shaw, Tara Abell, Nate Jones, E. Alex Jung, and Megh Wright, "Scott Rudin, As Told by His Assistants: A Portrait of a Toxic Workplace," *Vulture,* April 22, 2021.

20 *Kevin told his brother:* Interview with Graham-Caso.

20 *A semi-admiring 2005* Wall Street Journal *profile:* Kate Kelly and Merissa Marr, "Boss-Zilla!," *Wall Street Journal,* September 24, 2005.

20 *that Rudin could be "angry":* Stephen Galloway, "The Most Feared Man in Town," *The Hollywood Reporter,* November 10, 2010.

21 *"explosive verve":* Andrew Goldman, "Hollywood's Second Oldest Story: Jon Karp Signs with Rudin, Flees," *Observer,* February 12, 2001.

21 *One* Vulture *source noted that he was "proud":* Benjamin Wallace, "Scott Rudin in the Wings," *Vulture,* August 4, 2021.

22 *"The mindset is, unfortunately":* Interview with Laskey.

23 *Huang had worked for:* Anthony Breznican, "Scott Rudin Scandal: *Swimming with Sharks* Tried to Warn Us," *Vanity Fair,* April 22, 2021.

23 Swimming with Sharks *was "required viewing":* Nina Metz, "Re-watching *Swimming with Sharks* Through the Prism of #MeToo and Time's Up," *Chicago Tribune,* May 30, 2018.

24 *"As assistants, we were treated like machines":* Interview with Liz Hsiao Lan Alper, May 2022.

24 *"You'd get told":* Interview with Wendy Mericle, March 2022.

24 *"stepping away":* Halle Kiefer, "*The Music Man* Star Sutton Foster Responds to Abuse Allegations Against Producer Scott Rudin," *Vulture,* April 18, 2021.

24 *"the surface of Scott Rudin's":* Zack Sharf, "Megan Ellison Slams Scott Rudin's 'Abusive, Racist, and Sexist Behavior' Following *THR* Exposé," *IndieWire,* April 7, 2021.

24 *"I knew enough":* Michael Chabon, "Apology of a Rudin Apologist," *Medium,* April 23, 2021.

25 *"For me to act like":* Tavi Gevinson, "Art Doesn't Need Tyrants: Scott Rudin's Downfall Is an Opportunity to Change Hollywood," *Vulture,* April 23, 2021.

25 *none of them would comment:* Michael Paulson and Cara Buckley, "Volatile and Vengeful: How Scott Rudin Wielded Power in Show Business," *New York Times,* April 24, 2021.

25 *"A-list names that Rudin has helped":* Jake Coyle, Lindsey Bahr, and Mark Kennedy, "After Scott Rudin Bullying Expose, There Are Mostly Crickets," Associated Press, April 9, 2021.

25 Vulture *piece published in June:* Zoe Haylock, "Scott Rudin Reportedly Plotting a Comeback," *Vulture,* June 23, 2021.

26 *"I think that's enough":* Mike Fleming Jr., "Frances McDormand & Joel Coen Answer All Questions on Eve of New York Film Festival Opener *The Tragedy of Macbeth*," *Deadline,* September 23, 2021.

26 *"The stories that I had heard":* Rebecca Ford, "Aaron Sorkin on Scott Rudin: 'Scott Got What He Deserves,'" *Vanity Fair,* September 30, 2021.

26 *when referring to the "cringeworthy" interview:* Josh Charles (@MrJoshCharles), "The

whole interview was cringeworthy, but this particular little nugget was especially rich for me. I don't hate the man, and actually feel kinda bad for him as being both the most insecure and egotistical must be really hard," Twitter, October 1, 2021.

27 *"flat on the mat"*: Ford, "Aaron Sorkin on Scott Rudin."

27 *"Too many are afraid to speak out"*: Scharf, "Megan Ellison Slams Scott Rudin's 'Abusive, Racist, and Sexist Behavior.'"

27 *at "nobodies"*: Interview with Laskey.

28 *"I think the quote was"*: Interview with Graham-Caso.

28 *when Kevin was told he was "nothing"*: Gene Maddaus, "Friends of Scott Rudin's Late Assistant Speak Out on Producer's Abuses: 'He Was So Terrified of That Man,'" *Variety*, April 19, 2021.

28 *"It was still very much affecting him"*: Interview with Graham-Caso.

29 *attractive men "fresh out of the Ivy League"*: Interview with Erika Herzog, October 2021.

29 *"It was kids protecting kids"*: Interview with Laskey.

29 *"I let him know"*: Interview with Graham-Caso.

30 *The A24 representative said they declined:* Email exchange with A24 PR team, June 21, 2022.

31 *"This is why I think"*: Interview with Rabbi Danya Ruttenberg, April 2022.

32 *"They all think Rudin is coming back"*: Interview with Laskey.

Chapter 3: The Myth of Value

35 *A 2020 Pay Up Hollywood study:* Pay Up Hollywood, 2020 survey, www.payup hollywood.com.

36 *"The workplace feels unsafe"*: Maureen Ryan, "*Supergirl, Arrow* Producer Suspended amid Sexual Harassment Allegations by Warner Bros.," *Variety*, November 10, 2017.

36 *a check for nearly $10 million:* Maureen Ryan, "Going Broke in Hollywood: TV's Overworked Assistants Reel from Pandemic Pay Cuts," *Vanity Fair*, June 17, 2020.

37 *"There are a lot of profits"*: Interview with Meredith Stiehm, May 2022.

37 *"People from all over"*: Interview with Liz Hsiao Lan Alper, May 2022.

38 *"in 2005, the median length"*: Ben Lindbergh and Rob Arthur, "If That British Actor Seems Familiar, They Probably Are," *The Ringer*, October 19, 2022.

38 *"Four seasons seems like a miracle"*: Maureen Ryan, "Is TV Sabotaging Itself?," *Vanity Fair*, June 4, 2020.

38 *"Quotes aren't being respected"*: Interview with Emily Silver, June 2022.

39 *"When I ask about paid development"*: Interview with David Slack, June 2022.

40 *In 2021, the total compensation:* Benjamin Mullen and Theo Francis, "Discovery CEO David Zaslav Received Walloping $246.6 Million Pay Package in 2021," *MarketWatch*, March 14, 2022.

40 *The wild-eyed socialists at* Fortune: Chris Morris and Maria Aspan, "These Are the 10 Most Overpaid CEOs in the Fortune 500," *Fortune*, May 27, 2022.

40 *"facing profound, downward pressure"*: Interview with Slack.

40 *"I feel like the chance of sustainability"*: Interview with Silver.

41 *costar David Duchovny's pay:* Mikey O'Connell, "When *The X-Files* Became A-List: An Oral History of Fox's Out-There Success Story," *The Hollywood Reporter*, January 7, 2016.

41 *"It was shocking to me"*: Katey Rich, "How Gillian Anderson Fought Inequality on *The X-Files* Twice, and Won," *Vanity Fair*, January 22, 2016.

41 *"significantly less"*: Tatiana Siegel, "Sharing Salaries: How Actresses Are Fighting Hollywood's Gender Pay Disparity with Transparency," *The Hollywood Reporter*, January 18, 2018.

42 *Natalie Portman made a third*: Alex Heigl, "'It's Not Right': 27 Actresses Who've Spoken Out About Being Paid Less Than Male Stars," *People*, November 23, 2021.

42 *$5 million less*: Karen Valby, "Jennifer Lawrence: 'I Didn't Have a Life. I Thought I Should Go Get One,'" *Vanity Fair*, November 22, 2021.

42 *Mark Wahlberg made $5 million*: Nina Metz, "Hollywood, Black Actresses and the Squishy Metrics of Who Gets Paid What," *Chicago Tribune*, March 8, 2018.

42 *"when we evaluate others"*: Metz, "Hollywood, Black Actresses and the Squishy Metrics."

42 *"the average earnings per film"*: Irene E. De Pater, Timothy A. Judge, and Brent A. Scott, "Age, Gender, and Compensation: A Study of Hollywood Movie Stars," *Journal of Management Inquiry*, January 28, 2014.

42 *"If Caucasian women are"*: Ajesh Patalay, "Strong Statements," Net-A-Porter, March 2, 2018.

42 *Taraji P. Henson wanted*: Elizabeth Wagmeister, "Taraji P. Henson Reveals She Suffers from Depression and Still Faces Pay Inequality," *Variety*, April 2, 2019.

42 *Jessica Chastain helped*: Talia Lakritz, "14 Times Celebrities Fought for Equal Pay in Their Starring Roles," *Insider*, August 17, 2022.

43 *"a history of gender segregation," and stereotyping*: #ReelEquity: The Call to End Gender Bias in the Entertainment Industry, 2018 study summary posted at www.ialocal871.org/Reel-Equity.

43 *"hundreds or even thousands of dollars"*: Working Ideal study, "Script Girls, Secretaries and Stereotypes: Gender Pay Equity on Film and Television Crews," www.ialocal871.org/Reel-Equity.

43 *cinematographer Halyna Hutchins died*: Mark Osborne, "Family of Slain *Rust* Cinematographer Halyna Hutchins Reaches Settlement with Producers," ABC News, October 5, 2022.

43 *Actors Jon-Erik Hexum and Brandon Lee both died*: CBSLA/AP, "A Timeline of Accidental Deaths on Hollywood Sets in Wake of Alec Baldwin Prop Gun Shooting," CBS Los Angeles, October 22, 2021.

43 *he died shortly after his arrival*: Ken Bensinger, "Mexico Probes Actor's On-Set Death," *Variety*, August 24, 2003.

44 *died in a helicopter incident*: Paul Feldman, "John Landis Not Guilty in 3 *Twilight Zone* Deaths, Jury Also Exonerates Four Others," *Los Angeles Times*, May 29, 1987.

44 *Sarah Jones was killed*: Scott Johnson, "A Train, a Narrow Trestle and 60 Seconds to Escape: How *Midnight Rider* Victim Sarah Jones Lost Her Life," *The Hollywood Reporter*, March 4, 2014.

44 *a stuntwoman was injured*: Brian Welk, "*Resident Evil* Stuntwoman Who Lost Arm in On Set Accident Wins Legal Battle," TheWrap, April 21, 2020.

44 *a crew member died*: Matt Donnelly, "*Resident Evil: The Final Chapter* Crew Member Crushed to Death by Prop Car," TheWrap, December 24, 2015.

44 *two pilots died*: CBSLA/AP, "A Timeline of Accidental Deaths."

44 *left him "a mess"*: Eric Hegedus, "Dylan O'Brien Was Left 'So F—king Broken' After *Maze Runner* Accident," *New York Post*, October 16, 2020.

44 *after being injured by a gun*: Etan Vlessing, "*Revenant* Actor Brendan Fletcher

Hospitalized After Firearm Injury on TV Set," *The Hollywood Reporter,* March 28, 2016.

44 *stuntman working on* The Walking Dead *died:* CBSLA/AP, "A Timeline of Accidental Deaths."

44 *Safety and Health Administration:* Meg James, "OSHA Fines *The Walking Dead* Production Company in Stuntman's Death," *Los Angeles Times,* January 5, 2018.

44 *working on* Deadpool 2 *died:* CBSLA/AP, "A Timeline of Accidental Deaths."

44 *"tore the roof and the walls off the 007 Stage":* Tom Butler, "Explosion of 007 Stage During *No Time To Die* Shoot Caused by 'Miscalculation,'" Yahoo! Movies, May 13, 2020.

44 *including "burst vertebrae":* Krutika Mallikarjuna, "*Batwoman* Crew Member Paralyzed in On-Set Accident," *TV Guide,* March 16, 2020.

44 *their departure from that program:* Marianne Garvey, "Ruby Rose Alleges Unsafe Working Conditions on *Batwoman* Set," CNN, October 21, 2021.

44 *"to escape from a straitjacket":* Drew Taylor, "Injured *AGT: Extreme* Stuntman Posts Update from Hospital," The Wrap, October 20, 2021.

44 *"Some Mexican observers":* Laura Bradley, Gilberto Santisteban, Jeremy Kryt, and Kate Briquelet, "Deadly Netflix Crash Prompts Mexico to Investigate Hiring Practices," Daily Beast, June 24, 2022.

45 *"head-to-toe pain on a daily basis":* Savannah Walsh, "Kristin Chenoweth Didn't Want to Be 'a Problem' for CBS After *Good Wife* Injury," *Vanity Fair,* March 25, 2022.

45 *210 scripted series:* Rick Porter, "Peak TV Update: Scripted Series Volume Hits All-Time High in 2021," *The Hollywood Reporter,* January 14, 2022.

45 *it was 599:* Rick Porter, "Peak TV Climbs Again in 2022, Nearly Reaches 600 Scripted Series," *The Hollywood Reporter,* January 12, 2023.

45 *"to compete for viewers":* Richard Verrier, "As Deaths Rise on Reality TV, Film Sets, Many Blame Need to Get 'Dramatic Footage,'" *Los Angeles Times,* March 11, 2015.

45 *"and 44 deaths":* Jon Schleuss, Doug Smith, and Richard Verriers, "Film Set Accidents," *Los Angeles Times,* March 11, 2015.

45 *"We're in a moment":* Interview with Slack.

45 *"widgets, they don't matter":* Interview with Alper.

46 *16,000 members in 2015:* Maureen Ryan, "Peak Inequality: Investigating the Lack of Diversity Among TV Directors," *Variety,* November 10, 2015.

46 *19,000 members in 2022:* Email from Directors Guild of America PR person, November 18, 2022.

46 *authorized a strike in 2021:* Gene Maddaus, "IATSE Members Vote to Authorize Nationwide Film and TV Production Strike," *Variety,* October 4, 2021.

46 *"Pro-union sentiment rose":* Kim Kelly, *Fight Like Hell: The Untold History of American Labor* (New York: One Signal Publishers/Atria Press, 2022), xxvii.

46 *filed for a National Labor Relations Board election:* Kelly, *Fight Like Hell,* 315.

46 *"by a wide margin":* Karen Weise and Noam Scheiber, "Amazon Workers on Staten Island Vote to Unionize in Landmark Win for Labor," *New York Times,* April 1, 2022.

47 *"We had a dept head die":* Sonia Saraiya, "These Hollywood Horror Stories Could Inspire the Biggest Industry Strike Since World War II," *Vanity Fair,* September 30, 2021.

47 *"Why do studios insist":* Jazz Tangcay, "IATSE Members Brace for Possible Strike: 'There's No Logical Reason to Work Crews to Death,'" *Variety,* September 22, 2021.

49 *"That's how people are weeded out":* Gene Maddaus, "IATSE Strike Vote Reflects Pandemic-Era Shift in Work-Life Balance," *Variety,* September 28, 2021.

49 *64 percent of female writers:* David Robb, "WGA West Survey Finds 64 Percent of Female Writers Have Been Sexually Harassed on the Job," *Deadline,* July 25, 2018.

49 *Open letters published by Latinx:* Greg Braxton, "'We Are Tired': Read the Open Letter 270 Fed-Up Latinx Writers Just Sent Hollywood," *Los Angeles Times,* October 15, 2020.

49 *Black creatives in 2020:* Anousha Sakoui, "Black Writers Call for Accountability, Revamped Hiring in Open Letter to Hollywood," *Los Angeles Times,* June 12, 2020.

Chapter 4: Some Myths of Freedom and Nonconformity

51 *"The Real Mission Impossible: Saying 'No' to Tom Cruise":* Kim Masters, "The Real Mission Impossible: Saying 'No' to Tom Cruise," *The Hollywood Reporter,* March 24, 2022.

51 *executives were afraid:* Alan Sepinwall, *The Revolution Was Televised: How "The Sopranos," "Mad Men," "Breaking Bad," "Lost," and Other Groundbreaking Dramas Changed TV Forever* (New York: Touchstone, 2015), 45.

51 *"I don't think it was":* Brett Martin, *Difficult Men: Behind the Scenes of a Creative Revolution* (New York: Penguin Press, 2013), 93.

51 *executive input made them reconsider:* Sepinwall, *The Revolution Was Televised,* 164.

52 *"I say to people all the time":* Interview with Orlando Jones, March 2022.

54 *"We appreciate you reaching out":* Email from NBC PR team, August 1, 2022.

55 *"For the young women who worked on the show":* Katie Warren, "Young Female *SNL* Staffers Say They Were Treated Like 'a Joke,' with Sexual Advances, Babysitting Requests, and an Unsolicited Nude Photo," *Business Insider,* May 23, 2022.

58 *"It's riddled with paradoxes":* Interview with Shernold Edwards, February 2022.

59 *"His abuse and lunatic behaviour":* Stuart McGurk, "Amy Adams: David O. Russell Made Me Cry Every Day on *American Hustle,*" *GQ UK,* October 7, 2016.

59 *"he was hard on me":* McGurk, "Amy Adams: David O. Russell Made Me Cry Every Day."

59 *According to a 2022* Washington Post: Sonia Rao, "David O. Russell Is Latest Face of Hollywood's Workplace Abuse Problem," *Washington Post,* October 7, 2022.

61 *"I promised to be quiet":* Interview with Edwards.

61 *"Some people are expected":* Interview with Silas Howard, June 2022.

63 *"dusky maiden" roles:* Rita Moreno in *Rita Moreno: Just a Girl Who Decided to Go For It,* directed by Mariem Pérez Riera (Los Angeles: Roadside Attractions, 2021).

63 *having her skin darkened:* Interview with Rita Moreno, February 2020.

64 *"always happy, always kind":* Donald Bogle, *Toms, Coons, Mulattoes, Mammies and Bucks: An Interpretive History of Blacks in American Films* (New York: Bloomsbury Academic, 2016), 54–57.

64 *"I've seen what power does":* Interview with Howard.

66 *who represents child actors:* David Robb, "Hollywood Child Protection Act Ignored; Here's Why It Is Important," *Deadline,* April 30, 2018.

66 *when she was fourteen:* Nardine Saad, "*iCarly* Alum Jennette McCurdy Alleges Nickelodeon Offered Her Hush Money," *Los Angeles Times,* August 5, 2022.

67 *"The Creator":* Jennette McCurdy, "'This Phony, Bizarre Sphere': Jennette McCurdy's Shocking Final Days at Nickelodeon," book excerpt, *Vanity Fair,* August 5, 2022.

67 *"not safe":* Alexandra Del Rosario, "At Burbank Protest, Former Nickelodeon Star Says Network's Child Actors 'Were Not Safe,'" *Los Angeles Times,* August 25, 2022.

67 *"over-the-top complimentary":* Saad, "*iCarly* Alum Jeannette McCurdy."

67 *stopped acting around 2018:* Corinne Heller and Charles O'Keefe, "Jennette McCurdy Reveals What Would Make Her Return to Acting," E! News, October 26, 2022.

67 *Nickelodeon ended its relationship:* Nellie Andreeva, "Nickelodeon Parts Ways with TV Series Producer Dan Schneider," *Deadline,* March 26, 2018.

67 *still owed on his contract:* Matt Stevens and Julia Jacobs, "Dan Schneider Once Reigned over Children's TV. What Happened?," *New York Times,* June 30, 2021.

67 *"temper issues":* Andreeva, "Nickelodeon Parts Ways."

67 *Schneider denied acting inappropriately:* Stevens and Jacobs, "Dan Schneider Once Reigned."

67 *atmosphere of "desperation":* Kate Taylor, "'Revealing' Teen Costumes, On-Set Massages, and a Gender-Discrimination Complaint: Inside Dan Schneider's 'Disgusting' Nickelodeon Empire," *Business Insider,* August 30, 2022.

68 *grooming an underage woman:* Ariane Lange, "The Disturbing Secret Behind an Iconic Cartoon: Underage Sexual Abuse," BuzzFeed, March 29, 2018.

68 *Ezel Ethan Channel and Jason Michael Handy:* Dawn C. Chmielewski, "Child Sexual Abuse Cases in Hollywood Attract Attention," *Los Angeles Times,* January 8, 2012.

68 *"pedophile, full blown":* Chmielewski, "Child Sexual Abuse Cases in Hollywood Attract Attention."

68 *"I never appeared in anything more revealing":* Mara Wilson, "The Lies Hollywood Tells About Little Girls," *New York Times,* February 23, 2021.

68 *"If you put your kid":* David Smith, "Alex Winter: 'I Had Extreme PTSD for Many, Many Years. That Will Wreak Havoc,'" *Guardian,* September 21, 2020.

69 *"I imagine this stuff":* Stephanie, "Jennette McCurdy in Her Own Words," Lainey Gossip, August 8, 2022.

69 *"There's this intense pressure":* Interview with Evan Rachel Wood, January 2022.

71 *"essentially raped on-camera":* Interview with Wood; also stated in documentary *Phoenix Rising,* directed by Amy Berg (New York: HBO, 2022).

71 *"not only fully coherent":* Jason Newman, "In New Doc, Evan Rachel Wood Claims Marilyn Manson 'Essentially Raped' Her On-Camera," *Rolling Stone,* January 23, 2022.

71 *"3-D technology developed by":* Chris Harris, "Marilyn Manson's Sex Scene: 'Stellar Acting' or the Real Deal?," MTV.com, May 15, 2007.

72 *"The crew was very uncomfortable":* Newman, "In New Doc, Evan Rachel Wood Claims Marilyn Manson 'Essentially Raped' Her On-Camera."

72 *"they witnessed me being given absinthe":* Interview with Wood.

72 *publicly named Manson as their abuser:* Maureen Ryan, "He 'Horrifically Abused Me for Years': Evan Rachel Wood and Other Women Make Allegations of Abuse Against Marilyn Manson," *Vanity Fair,* February 1, 2021.

72 *woman, Ashley "Illma" Gore:* Doha Madani and Diana Dasrath, "Marilyn Man-

son Files Defamation Lawsuit Against Evan Rachel Wood over Rape and Abuse Allegations," *NBC News*, March 2, 2022.

73 *"the abuse police"*: Interview with Wood.

73 *"This business is brutal"*: Heather Havrilesky, "Winona Ryder Is Still Processing," *Harper's Bazaar*, June 28, 2022.

73 *"At 19, [Christina Ricci] had breast reduction surgery"*: Thessaly La Force, "Christina Ricci's Search for Authenticity," *New York Times*, June 25, 2022.

74 *reviewed the HBO series:* Maureen Ryan, "Review: *The Vow* Follows Nxivm Down Dark, Damaging Paths," *New York Times*, August 23, 2020.

76 *"I find that the vast majority"*: Scott Johnson and Rebecca Sun, "Her Darkest Role: Actress Allison Mack's Descent from *Smallville* to Sex Cult," *The Hollywood Reporter*, May 16, 2018.

76 *"tend to pick victims"*: Kristin Neff, *Fierce Self-Compassion* (New York: Harper Wave, 2021), 99.

76 *a hardcore Raniere adherent:* Johnny Brayson and Radhika Menon, "Where Is Nicki Clyne Now? The Nxivm Member Appears in *The Vow* Part 2," *MSN*, October 17, 2022.

77 *"incredibly intimidating, cruel and punitive"*: Johnson and Sun, "Her Darkest Role."

Chapter 5: *Lost* and the Myths of a Golden Age

79 *the arrival of the half-hour show* Julia: Alice George, "Was the 1968 TV Show *Julia* a Milestone or a Millstone for Diversity?," *Smithsonian*, September 6, 2018.

79 *the first time a Black woman was the star:* Nellie Andreeva, "*Get Christie Love* Series Reboot from *Power* Creator Courtney Kemp & Vin Diesel Set at ABC with Big Commitment," *Deadline*, September 26, 2017.

79 *More than three decades passed:* Lesley Goldberg, "*Get Christie Love* Reboot in the Works at ABC," *The Hollywood Reporter*, September 26, 2017.

79 *"It was among the most thrilling"*: Alan Sepinwall, *The Revolution Was Televised: How "The Sopranos," "Mad Men," "Breaking Bad," "Lost," and Other Groundbreaking Dramas Changed TV Forever* (New York: Touchstone, 2015), 159.

79 *which cost $13 million:* Sepinwall, *The Revolution Was Televised*, 166.

80 *highest-rated debut in four years:* Joy Press, *Stealing the Show: How Women Are Revolutionizing Television* (New York: Atria Books, 2018), 114.

80 *"women remained secondary figures"*: Press, *Stealing the Show*, 76.

80 *"had pitched even mild versions"*: Sepinwall, *The Revolution Was Televised*, 29.

81 *"Harold had one of the biggest careers"*: Interview with Daniel Dae Kim, April 2022.

81 *"in the very, very beginning"*: Interview with Harold Perrineau, May 2022.

82 *"All I wanted to do"*: Interview with Monica Owusu-Breen, June 2022.

83 *"It became pretty clear"*: Interview with Perrineau.

84 *actors of color were often asked:* Interviews with Perrineau and others.

84 *"You can feel the energy"*: Interview with Perrineau.

86 *"if I'm being really candid"*: Shawna Malcom, "Harold Perrineau Dishes on His *Lost* Exit (Again)," *TVGuide.com*, May 30, 2008.

88 *"For most of television, Blackness"*: Zak Cheney-Rice, "Larry Wilmore Knows No Bounds," *Vulture*, July 6, 2022.

89 *"which was canceled in 1953"*: Margalit Fox, "Hal Kanter, a Creator of 'Julia' Series on TV, Dies at 92," *New York Times*, November 8, 2011.

89   *"I felt I was partially responsible"*: "Hal Kanter," interview by Sam Denoff, *The Interviews*, Television Academy Foundation, May 22, 1997.

89   *"I always got the phone call"*: Amy Wallace, "Viola Davis As You've Never Seen Her Before: Leading Lady!," *New York Times*, September 12, 2014.

89   *"powerful, intimidating black woman"*: Alessandra Stanley, "Wrought in Rhimes's Image," *New York Times*, September 18, 2014.

90   *"Some of it is subconscious"*: Interview with Cathryn Humphris, May 2022.

91   *After Mad Men ended*: Bryan Alexander, "*Mad Men* Creator Matthew Weiner Accused of Harassment by Former Writer Kater Gordon," *USA Today*, November 9, 2017.

91   *"[he] would say that"*: Joy Press, "Matthew Weiner in the Mirror," *Vanity Fair*, September 30, 2018.

91   *"an isolated occurrence"*: Kater Gordon (@KaterGordon), "My statement to Reuters: My memory is intact. Matthew's abuse of workplace power dynamics was rampant, and the comments he made should not be viewed as an isolated occurrence," Twitter, October 18, 2018.

91   *publicly supporting Gordon*: Marti Noxon (@MartiNoxon), "something to the effect of 'you owe it to me to show me your naked body.' I believe her. I was at work with her the day after what she described transpired. I remember clearly how shaken and subdued Kater was—and continued to be from that day on," Twitter, November 17, 2017.

91   *"emotional terrorist"*: Bryn Sandberg, "Marti Noxon Backs Matthew Weiner Harassment Accuser, Calls Him 'Emotional Terrorist,'" *The Hollywood Reporter*, November 17, 2017.

91   *Kessler later cocreated*: Brett Martin, *Difficult Men: Behind the Scenes of a Creative Revolution* (New York: Penguin Press, 2013), 166–67.

91   *"if it is an account"*: Phillip Maciak, "The Difficult Men Who Revolutionized TV Drama," Salon, August 19, 2013.

92   *"believes she was fired"*: Krystie Lee Yandoli, "Warner Bros. Keeps Citing a 'Friends' Harassment Lawsuit in HR Trainings. Former Employees Said It Felt Intimidating," BuzzFeed, June 11, 2021.

92   *"to justify inappropriate behavior"*: Email from Writers Guild of America West Board of Directors to WGA West guild members, May 22, 2018.

93   *"volatile temper and expletive-laced emails"*: Dawn C. Chmielewski and Meg James, "ABC's Biggest Mystery: Why Did Steve McPherson Leave?," *Los Angeles Times*, July 28, 2010.

93   *"sexual harassment"*: Kim Masters, "Sex Probe Led to Steve McPherson's ABC Exit," *The Hollywood Reporter*, July 28, 2010. McPherson's attorney said then that it "is not uncommon for high-level executives to be the subject of gossip and innuendo. That would include rumors of internal situations that can easily be misinterpreted or misrepresented."

93   *"The overall thing that happened"*: Interview with Humphris.

94   *where their boss was Brad Kern*: Maureen Ryan, "Veteran CBS Producer Brad Kern Fired amid Abuse Claims," *The Hollywood Reporter*, October 2, 2018.

96   *The only Asian American writer*: Interview with Monica Owusu-Breen, June 2022.

97   *"sold a white cast member"*: Interview with Javier Grillo-Marxuach, April 2022.

97   *"called me racist, so I fired his ass"*: Interviews with Owusu-Breen and others.

97   *"Everyone laughed"*: Interview with Owusu-Breen.

99   *"was a predatory ecosystem"*: Interview with Grillo-Marxuach.

99   *"Damon once said, 'I don't trust'":* Interview with Melinda Hsu Taylor, October 2021.

101   *"We finally got a female character":* Maureen Ryan, "Let's Talk *Lost*: Mother Load," *Chicago Tribune,* May 12, 2010.

102   *"We had such a talented staff":* Interview with Hsu Taylor.

103   *"I can't work for certain people":* Interview with Owusu-Breen.

104   *"It's the sort of place":* Interview with Hsu Taylor.

104   *"This sort of environment":* Interview with Grillo-Marxuach.

105   *I wrote a* Leftovers *essay:* Maureen Ryan, "*The Leftovers,* Life, Death, Einstein and Time Travel," *Variety,* May 31, 2017.

106   *a* Lost *retrospective podcast I cohosted:* Tara Bennett, "*Lost* Showrunners Reflect on George R. R. Martin Throwdowns and Collaborating Again," Syfy Wire, October 29, 2019.

106   *"My level of fundamental inexperience":* Interview with Damon Lindelof, September 2021.

106   *"Santa doesn't exist":* Interview with Owusu-Breen.

107   *"a high degree of insensitivity":* Interview with Damon Lindelof, June 2022.

108   *"I deeply regret that anyone":* Written responses from Carlton Cuse, July 25, 2022.

108   *offensive and false:* Written communication from Carlton Cuse attorney Bryan J. Freedman, October 26, 2022.

108   *"primary mission":* Written responses from Cuse.

109   *he was released from his* Lost *contract:* Interview with Harold Perrineau, October 2022.

109   *"I never, ever made that statement":* Written responses from Cuse.

110   *"The way that I conduct myself":* Interview with Lindelof, June 2022.

Chapter 6: The Myth of the Meritocracy

112   *"They were all white men":* Interview with Damon Lindelof, September 2021.

113   *"While both women":* Writers Guild of America West, "WGAW Inclusion Report 2020," June 5, 2020, www.wga.org/uploadedfiles/the-guild/inclusion-and-equity/2020_WGAW_Inclusion_Report.pdf.

113   *"I've sort of blocked a lot of it out":* Interview with Melinda Hsu Taylor, October 2021.

114   *"I was afraid for my career":* Interview with Javier Grillo-Marxuach, April 2022.

114   *"If I had a dollar for every time":* Interview with Sarah Rodman, March 2022.

114   *"started as an annual survey":* Interview with Franklin Leonard, January 2022.

115   *"I sat there with George":* Rebecca Keegan, "The 30-Year Journey to AMC's Groundbreaking Native American Drama *Dark Winds,*" *The Hollywood Reporter,* June 1, 2022.

116   *Discussing Film's Twitter account noted:* Discussing Film (@DiscussingFilm), "Hopper Penn (Sean Penn's son) and Brian D'Arcy James have been cast in 'THE RIGHTWAY' from director Destry Spielberg (Steven Spielberg's daughter) and writer Owen King (Stephen King's son). (Source: Deadline)," Twitter, July 27, 2021.

116   *"Hollywood's a meritocracy, right?":* Ethan Shanfeld, "Ben Stiller and Destry Spielberg Deny Hollywood Nepotism in Twitter Debate with Black List Founder Franklin Leonard," *Variety,* July 29, 2021.

116   *"experience, and I don't know":* Michelle Jaworski, "Ben Stiller Criticized for Re-

marks on Hollywood Nepotism After Short Film Resurfaces Debate," *Daily Dot*, July 28, 2021.

116 *"I was very surprised"*: Interview with Leonard.

117 *"it's not remotely a level playing field"*: Interview with Lindelof.

118 *"they see the business"*: Interview with Orlando Jones, March 2022.

119 *how "things were changing" for women*: Interview with Martha Lauzen, September 2021.

119 *According to a 2020 UCLA study*: Tambay Obenson, "In 2020, Hollywood Reckoned with Its Past—and Present—When It Came to Diversity," *IndieWire*, December 29, 2020.

119 *The 2022* Boxed In *study shows*: Selome Hailu, "Streaming Shows Have More Major Female Characters than Broadcast TV, Study Finds," *Variety*, October 18, 2022.

119 *in no apparent danger of rising*: Dr. Martha M. Lauzen, *Boxed In: Women on Screen and Behind the Scenes on Broadcast and Streaming Television in 2021– 22*, Center for the Study of Women in Television and Film, San Diego State University, October 19, 2022, 6.

119 *The UCLA study notes that*: Dr. Darnell Hunt and Dr. Ana-Christina Ramón, *Hollywood Diversity Report 2020, Part 2: Television*, UCLA College of Social Sciences, October 22, 2020, 14–17.

120 *Latinos are "almost half"*: David Robb, "UCLA TV Diversity Report Finds 'Progress' for Women & Minorities, But Latinos Still Lag Far Behind; White Male Show Creators Tend to Get Bigger Budgets," *Deadline*, October 27, 2022.

120 *"but that coincided with"*: Rebecca Sun, "Study: Latino Immigrant Representation on TV Decreases, Black and API Immigrants Up," *The Hollywood Reporter*, December 6, 2022.

120 *"The number of Black directors"*: Dr. Stacy L. Smith, Marc Choueiti, and Dr. Katherine Pieper, *Inequality in 1,300 Popular Films: Examining Portrayals of Gender, Race/Ethnicity, LGBTQ & Disability from 2007 to 2019*, Annenberg Inclusion Initiative, USC Annenberg, September 2020, 2–30.

120 *"stalled out"*: Jeremy Fuster, "Hollywood's Progress on Hiring of Female Directors and POC Has Stalled Out, USC Annenberg Report Says," The Wrap, January 2. 2022.

120 *according to the Directors Guild of America*: "DGA Inclusion Report Reveals Continued Incremental Gains for Directors in 2020–21 TV Season, Despite Pandemic," press release, Directors Guild of America, May 5, 2022, www.dga .org/News/PressReleases/2022/220505-Episodic-TV-Inclusion-Report.

120 *the number was half that*: "DGA Inclusion Report Reveals Continued Incremental Gains."

121 *a mere seventh of working film directors*: "Cut Out of the Picture: A Study of Gender Inequality Among Directors Within the UK Film Industry," Directors UK, May 4, 2016, directors.uk.com/news/cut-out-of-the-picture.

121 *"If you look at the numbers"*: Interview with Lauzen.

121 *"But on the other hand"*: Interview with Hsu Taylor.

122 *passed on* Dark Winds: Keegan, "The 30-Year Journey."

122 *"necessary and illuminating"*: Maureen Ryan, "Who Creates Drama At HBO? Very Few Women or People of Color: The Best Networks Have Terrible Records on Diversity," *Huffington Post*, March 6, 2014.

123 *"It boggles the mind"*: Interview with Grillo-Marxuach.

124 *to "be 'more white'":* Nancy Wang Yuen, *Reel Inequality: Hollywood Actors and Racism* (New Brunswick, NJ: Rutgers University Press, 2016), 45–46.

124 *"use pronouns":* Maureen Ryan, "*Warrior* Takes the 'Model Minority' Cliche and 'Flips It on Its Ass,'" *Vanity Fair,* September 10, 2020.

124 *"I think that meritocracy mostly":* Emily Stewart, "The Problem with America's Semi-Rich," *Vox,* October 12, 2021.

125 *"historically, Hollywood unions":* Interview with Nancy Wang Yuen, February 2022.

125 *70 percent of key on-set roles:* "DGA Inclusion Report Reveals Continued Incremental Gains."

125 *"Jim Crow laws kept":* Chi-Tsung Chang, "Hollywood and the Myth of Meritocracy" (master's thesis, Boston University, 2021), 7.

125 *"the institutionalized culture of bias":* Interview with Yuen.

126 *"Middle America," and "the assumption was that":* Interview with Yuen.

126 *"more general audience platform":* Adam Manno, "Laid-Off HBO Max Execs Reveal Warner Bros. Discovery Is Killing Off Diversity and Courting 'Middle America,'" Daily Beast, August 25, 2022.

126 *in a 2018 HBO follow-up piece:* Maureen Ryan, "HBO Hits Important Milestone in Push for Behind-the-Scenes Inclusion," *The Hollywood Reporter,* August 10, 2018.

126 *then called WarnerMedia: WarnerMedia Believes in the Power of Stories: Equity and Inclusion Report,* 2021, www.warnermedia.com/us/equity-inclusion-report.

127 *"black box":* Interview with Hsu Taylor.

127 *"I did not appreciate":* Interview with Lauzen.

127 *edition of the* Celluloid Ceiling *study:* Dr. Martha M. Lauzen, *25th Anniversary, The Celluloid Ceiling: Employment of Behind-the-Scenes Women on Top Grossing U.S. Films in 2022,* Center for the Study of Women in Television and Film, San Diego State University, January 2, 2023.

127 *"We know how fast":* Interview with Leonard.

Chapter 7: Horror Story

130 *"witnesses brought together":* Sleepy Hollow, episode 1, "Pilot," aired September 16, 2013, on Fox.

130 *"I don't know how they slipped that through":* Interview with Shernold Edwards, February 2022.

131 *If* Sleepy Hollow *came out now":* Interview with Tananarive Due, February 2022.

131 *so well regarded was her UCLA course:* Jude Dry, "Jordan Peele Lectures UCLA Film Class on *Get Out:* 'The Sunken Place Is the Silencing' of Marginalized People—Watch," *IndieWire,* February 7, 2018.

132 *ten million people:* James Hibberd, "*Sleepy Hollow* Premiere Ratings Decapitate Rivals," *Entertainment Weekly,* September 17, 2013.

132 *"was blessed with a cast":* Maureen Ryan, "*Sleepy Hollow* Finale Review: They're in a Hell of a Mess Now," *Huffington Post,* January 20, 2014.

134 *"It's part of this new cycle":* Maureen Ryan, "*Black-ish* Is the Ideal Sitcom for the Age of Black Lives Matter," *Variety,* February 23, 2016.

134 *"doing a new* Roots": Maureen Ryan, "Why TV Is Finally Embracing the Realities of Race," *Variety,* February 23, 2016.

134 *so-called "'mainstream' programming":* Ryan, "Why TV Is Finally Embracing."

134 *"CW got rid of all":* Evan Nicole Brown, "How UPN Ushered in a Golden Decade

of Black TV—and Then Was Merged Out of Existence," *The Hollywood Reporter*, February 16, 2022.

136 *Kevin Reilly departed:* Lacey Rose, "Fox's Top Executive Kevin Reilly to Depart," *The Hollywood Reporter*, May 29, 2014.

136 *took over the top jobs:* Lacey Rose, "It's Official: Dana Walden, Gary Newman to Run Fox Broadcasting," *The Hollywood Reporter*, July 14, 2014.

136 *ended in 2013:* Cynthia Littleton, "Alex Kurtzman, Roberto Orci Pact with CBS TV Studios," *Variety*, July 17, 2013.

136 *described as "amicable":* Borys Kit, "Alex Kurtzman and Roberto Orci Splitting Up as Movie Team," *The Hollywood Reporter*, April 22, 2014.

136 *"I got a master's":* Maureen Ryan, "*Sleepy Hollow* News: Head Honcho on What's Next for Ichabod, Abbie, and the Horseman," *Huffington Post*, December 9, 2013.

138 *"sudden refusals to work":* Brett Martin, *Difficult Men: Behind the Scenes of a Creative Revolution* (New York: Penguin Press, 2013), 2.

138 *"I probably could have been":* Sonaiya Kelley, "Nicole Beharie Was Called 'Problematic' and Blacklisted. *Miss Juneteenth* Brings Redemption," *Los Angeles Times*, June 19, 2020.

139 *"were both out of their depths":* Interview with Orlando Jones, March 2022.

140 *"both sick at the same time":* Kelley, "Nicole Beharie Was Called 'Problematic.'"

140 *"what you had playing out":* Interview with Jones.

142 *what she called "grueling":* Email from hairstylist, June 26, 2022.

146 *"because Black love is so rare in Hollywood":* Interview with Due.

146 *"How many more sacrifices":* Nichole Perkins, "*Sleepy Hollow*, Why Won't You Let Abbie Be Loved?," *Vulture*, March 11, 2016.

148 Atlantic *columnist Adam Serwer, "counterproductive":* Anand Giridharadas, "The News Is What You Have Forgotten," *The.Ink*, July 15, 2021.

148 *"Brunson's hopes for Quinta and Jermaine":* Mankaprr Conteh, "It's Quinta Brunson's World and We're All Just Laughing in It," *Rolling Stone*, June 28, 2022.

149 *"The needs of the white writer":* Alice George, "Was the 1968 TV Show *Julia* a Milestone or a Millstone for Diversity?," *Smithsonian*, September 6, 2018.

149 *"She was an out of work actress!":* "Diahann Carroll," interview by Henry Colman, *The Interviews*, Television Academy Foundation, March 3, 1998.

149 *"Very often I chose":* "Diahann Carroll: Julia," National Visionary Leadership Project, YouTube video, August 19, 2009.

149 *"They shut down production":* Candice Frederick, "Nicole Beharie on *Miss Juneteenth* and the Danger of Labels," *New York Times*, June 19, 2020.

149 *"I think part of what saves":* Interview with Edwards.

150 *"to protect evolving conversations":* Written answers from Clifton Campbell provided by PR person Steven Goldberg, December 29, 2022.

151 *"overly serialized":* James Hibberd, "*Sleepy Hollow*: Fox Making Changes," *Entertainment Weekly*, January 17, 2015.

152 *"I was actually disempowered":* Interview with Edwards.

158 *"The audience has seen Ichabod Crane":* Perkins, "*Sleepy Hollow*, Why Won't You Let Abbie Be Loved?"

159 *"A lot of shows pride themselves":* Maureen Ryan, "'Anyone Can Die?' TV's Recent Death Toll Says Otherwise," *Variety*, April 13, 2016.

159 *"as Nicole Beharie [has] found":* Maureen Ryan, "The Morning Show Wars, Kelly Ripa and TV's Disposable Spring," *Variety*, April 21, 2016.

161 *time for "healing":* Kelley, "Nicole Beharie Was Called 'Problematic.'"

161 *Representatives for Kadin:* Email from Heather Kadin attorney Jeff Finkelstein, June 30, 2022. Kadin's attorney wrote that "Heather's responses are that she did no such thing, nor did she cause calls to be made to the media about Beharie . . . I would caution you not to publish or disseminate false allegations about Heather. All of her rights and remedies are reserved and she will absolutely pursue them if she is defamed."

161 *and Kurtzman:* A PR representative for Kurtzman said in July 2022 that he had no involvement in *Sleepy Hollow* past the first season, that he had no recollection of ever saying anything negative about Nicole Beharie at any time, and that he had a good relationship with Beharie.

162 *"I feel like it's taken":* Kelley, "Nicole Beharie Was Called 'Problematic.'"

Chapter 8: The Myth of an Egalitarian Future

167 *"I had an interview for a coshowrunning job":* Interview with David Slack, June 2022.

171 *"plotting an expansion":* Borys Kit, "DC at a Turning Point: James Gunn Pitches Secret Movie, Dwayne Johnson Flexes His Superman Power (Exclusive)," *The Hollywood Reporter,* October 17, 2022.

171 *coheads of DC Studios:* Sarah Whitten, "James Gunn, Peter Safran Named New Heads of Warner Bros.' DC Studios," CNBC.com, October 22, 2022.

171 *Noah Hawley was handed creative control:* Anthony Breznican, "New Alien TV Series Will Be Class Warfare with Xenomorphs," *Vanity Fair,* July 1, 2021.

171 *they not only had never run a television show:* James Hibberd, "The Rings of Power Showrunners Break Silence on Backlash, Sauron and Season 2," *The Hollywood Reporter,* October 5, 2022.

172 *created by Diane Ademu-John:* Joe Otterson, "'Dune' Prequel Series at HBO Max Adds Mark Strong, Jade Anouka, Chris Mason," *Variety,* December 1, 2022.

172 *Johan Renck was set:* Peter White, "*Dune: The Sisterhood* Series Taps *Chernobyl* Director Johan Renck to Helm First Two Episodes," *Deadline,* April 27, 2022.

172 Star Trek *in the TV realm:* Cynthia Littleton, "Star Trek Captain Alex Kurtzman Extends TV Pact with CBS Studios to 2026," *Variety,* August 1, 2021.

172 *the executive creative director:* Dave Filoni bio on Lucasfilm website, www.lucasfilm.com/leadership/dave-filoni/.

172 *stepped down as coshowrunner:* Nellie Andreeva, "*Dune: The Sisterhood* Creator Diane Ademu-John Steps Down as Co-Showrunner of HBO Max Series," *Deadline,* November 23, 2022.

173 *feature film realm was entirely white:* Maureen Ryan, "Star Wars: 96 Percent of Its Film Universe Writers and Directors Are White Men," *Variety,* February 6, 2018.

173 *for a long time:* Matt Kim, "Patty Jenkins Reveals She Did Not Leave *Wonder Woman 3*, Has Returned to *Rogue Squadron*," IGN.com, December 16, 2022.

173 *see it until 2025:* Kate Erbland, "'Star Wars' Screenwriter Krysty Wilson-Cairns Can't Say 'Anything' About Her Taika Waititi Movie," *IndieWire,* October 22, 2022.

173 *production in late 2022:* StarWars.com, "The Acolyte Original Series Cast Revealed," November 7, 2022.

173 *left the project:* AFP, "New Screenwriter Recruited for the Series on Obi-Wan Kenobi with Ewan McGregor," Yahoo! News, April 3, 2020.

173 *whose father was Chinese:* Anthony Breznican, "*The Mandalorian:* Deborah

Chow Reveals the Inspiration for the Baby Yoda Rescue," *Vanity Fair,* November 22, 2019.

174 *"Lauren Ridloff's character of Connie":* Email from Alice Wong, October 22, 2022.

174 *and Native ancestry:* Rosario Dawson (@RosarioDawson), "I'm not biracial. I'm half Puerto Rican/Afro Cuban & half Irish/Native Indian. #multiracial #human #earthling," Twitter, June 13, 2013.

174 *Filoni is in charge of it:* Anthony Breznican, "*Star Wars:* Rosario Dawson Aims to Play Ahsoka Tano for Life," *Vanity Fair,* May 20, 2022.

175 *"tremendous advances":* David Robb, "UCLA TV Diversity Report Finds 'Progress' for Women & Minorities, But Latinos Still Lag Far Behind; White Male Show Creators Tend to Get Bigger Budgets," *Deadline,* October 27, 2022.

175 *"Diversity initiatives traditionally":* Marina Fang, "The Big Cuts in Hollywood Right Now Could Set Back Years of Progress on Diversity," *Huffington Post,* October 27, 2022.

175 *"Of the 7,124 books":* Richard Jean So and Gus Wezerek, "Just How White Is the Publishing Industry?," *New York Times,* December 11, 2020.

176 *"Occasionally, we would have to deal":* Interview with Naren Shankar, October 2022.

177 *"plastic representation":* Kristen J. Warner, "In the Time of Plastic Representation," *Film Quarterly,* December 4, 2017.

177 *"the surface with no effort":* Myles McNutt, "Week-to-Week: Death, Queerness, and the Discourse of the Dragon," *Episodic Medium,* September 20, 2022.

178 *I called it "puzzling":* Maureen Ryan, "*The Muppets* Returned to TV, But What Happened to Miss Piggy?," *Huffington Post,* September 21, 2015.

178 *"a constant battle":* Interview with Nell Scovell, July 2022.

179 *Creative differences were cited in trade stories:* Lesley Goldberg and Lacey Rose, "Muppets Showrunner Exits ABC Revival," *The Hollywood Reporter,* November 4, 2015.

179 *Kushell was fired from a subsequent job:* Variety Staff, "Showrunner Bob Kushell Fired from CBS Comedy *Fam* for Inappropriate Language," *Variety,* November 5, 2018.

179 *"expressed sympathy for the guy":* Interview with Scovell.

180 *"We have been doing these characters":* Ryan Parker, "Disney Says It Fired Kermit the Frog Actor over 'Unacceptable Business Conduct,'" *The Hollywood Reporter,* July 17, 2017.

181 *"the lack of joy in the first half of the season":* Lesley Goldberg, "Classic Sketches, Returning Favorites: Inside *The Muppets* Midseason Reboot," *The Hollywood Reporter,* January 10, 2016.

182 *"unacceptable business conduct":* Parker, "Disney Says It Fired Kermit the Frog Actor."

182 *"first studio album":* Disney+ press release, "Disney+ Announces *The Muppets Mayhem,*" March 7, 2022.

182 *is a Black woman:* Charlene Rhinehart, "HBCU Graduate Ayo Davis Named President of Disney Branded Television," *Black Enterprise,* September 25, 2021.

182 *"my dream job":* Written responses from Adam F. Goldberg, August 8, 2022.

182 *"the purpose of this letter":* Letter from Adam F. Goldberg's legal representatives at Glaser Weil, August 8, 2022.

183 *was just "joking":* Maureen Ryan, "'No, I Have Not Been Fired from *The Goldbergs*': Jeff Garlin Responds to Talk of Misbehavior on Set," *Vanity Fair,* December 3, 2021.

184 *"That is false and taken out of context"*: Written responses from Goldberg.

185 *"a sex crime" and a "violation"*: "Cover Exclusive: Jennifer Lawrence Calls Photo Hacking a 'Sex Crime,'" *Vanity Fair*, October 14, 2014.

188 *before production began* on Star Wars: The Force Awakens: Ben Child, "I Felt Pressured to Lose Weight for *Star Wars: The Force Awakens*," *Guardian*, December 1, 2015.

188 *"the asshole at the cinema"*: Laura Canning, "Sometimes It's Hard to Be a . . . Feminist Film Critic, or; Why I Am That Asshole at the Cinema," *Critical Media Review*, February 23, 2012.

191 *"I wanted to approach"*: Jeff Yang, Phil Yu, and Philip Wang, *Rise: A Pop History of Asian Americans from the Nineties to Now* (New York: HarperCollins, 2022), 464–65.

192 *"The executives in charge"*: Adam Serwer, "Fear of a Black Hobbit," *The Atlantic*, September 14, 2022.

192 *"Like, you guys knew what to do"*: Jimi Famurewa, "John Boyega: 'I'm the Only Cast Member Whose Experience of *Star Wars* Was Based on Their Race,'" *GQ UK*, September 2, 2020.

193 *"Our studies including over"*: Center for Work Life Law (@WorkLifeLawCtr), "Our studies including over 18,000 participants across industries consistently document that white men report lower levels of #bias than every other group," Twitter, October 19, 2021.

193 *"Chapek's 'both sides' manifesto"*: Kevin Fallon, "Disney's 'Don't Say Gay' Disaster Is Shameful and Absolutely Infuriating," Daily Beast, March 11, 2022.

194 *"nearly every moment of overtly gay"*: Adam B. Vary and Angelique Jackson, "Disney Censors Same-Sex Affection in Pixar Films, According to Letter from Employees," *Variety*, March 9, 2022.

Chapter 9: Launch Them into the Sun

195 *"I have had some great experiences"*: Interview with Harold Perrineau, May 2022.

197 *"said no multiple times"*: Savannah Walsh, "Bill Murray Misconduct Allegations, New and Old, Surface," *Vanity Fair*, October 11, 2022.

197 *pulled down the strap of her dress*: Lauren Edmonds, "Geena Davis Says a Resurfaced Interview Where Bill Murray Pulled Down Her Dress Strap Was 'So Devastating,'" *Insider*, October 22, 2022.

197 *dressing room, and cried*: Zack Scharf, "Seth Green Says Bill Murray 'Picked Me Up by My Ankles' and 'Dropped Me in the Trash' at Age 9: 'I Was Horrified and Just Cried,'" *Variety*, October 14, 2022.

197 *he hurled "insults"*: Chris Murphy, "Everyone Who Has Publicly Accused Bill Murray of Misconduct," *Vanity Fair*, October 24, 2022.

197 *his hands on Solange Knowles's hair*: Alex Gurley, "Solange Knowles Might Have Just Confirmed Another Allegation of Inappropriate Behavior Regarding Bill Murray," BuzzFeed, October 17, 2022.

197 *"couldn't move because he outweighed her"*: Walsh, "Bill Murray Misconduct Allegations."

197 *"feels like we're regressing"*: Juliana Ukiomogbe, "Issa Rae Is Not Willing to Compromise," *Elle*, October 13, 2022.

197 *filmed reshoots with them*: Julie Miller, "Ezra Miller's 'Messiah' Delusions: Inside *The Flash* Star's Dark Spiral," *Vanity Fair*, September 18, 2022.

198 *who was "toxic"*: Interview with Nancy Wang Yuen, February 2022.

198 *"He speaks almost without a filter"*: Interview with Michael Greyeyes, November 2021.

199 *"After a while, he goes"*: Interview with Sierra Teller Ornelas, November 2021.

200 *"It's absolutely freeing"*: Maureen Ryan, "Why Michael Greyeyes Was 'Low-Key Terrified' to Do Something Brand New on *Rutherford Falls*," *Vanity Fair*, January 4, 2022.

201 *"started haranguing us"*: Peter Biskind, *Easy Riders, Raging Bulls: How the Sex-Drugs-and-Rock 'N' Roll Generation Saved Hollywood* (New York: Simon & Schuster, 1998), 63.

201 *"I realized why directors"*: Biskind, *Easy Riders, Raging Bulls*, 329.

201 *"slammed on the brakes"*: Biskind, *Easy Riders, Raging Bulls*, 241.

201 *"enormous blowhard"*: Biskind, *Easy Riders, Raging Bulls*, 240.

202 *"could be a miserable prick"*: Biskind, *Easy Riders, Raging Bulls*, 88.

203 *"Almost every [woman] had a story"*: Rachel Abramowitz, *Is That a Gun in Your Pocket? Women's Experience of Power in Hollywood* (New York: Random House, 2000), xiii.

203 *screamed at by producer Scott Rudin*: Abramowitz, *Is That a Gun in Your Pocket?*, 361.

203 *"treated like a nonbeing"*: Abramowitz, *Is That a Gun in Your Pocket?*, 352.

203 *"her own ambition"*: Abramowitz, *Is That a Gun in Your Pocket?*, 347.

203 *asked to play sex workers*: Abramowitz, *Is That a Gun in Your Pocket?*, 335.

203 *"aped the testosterone-fueled antics"*: Abramowitz, *Is That a Gun in Your Pocket?*, xi.

204 *"Jared Leto was so committed"*: Mike Ryan, "*Morbius* Director Daniel Espinosa on What the Heck Happened Here," *Uproxx*, April 4, 2022.

205 *"There's a lot to unpack here"*: Brian Grubb, "The Rundown: The Good Shows Are Coming Back So Soon," *Uproxx*, April 8, 2022.

206 *Garlin told me he was "a hugger"*: Maureen Ryan, "'No, I Have Not Been Fired from *The Goldbergs*': Jeff Garlin Responds to Talk of Misbehavior on Set," *Vanity Fair*, December 3, 2021.

208 *"someone who doesn't want to be there"*: Savannah Walsh, "Wendi McLendon-Covey Breaks Her Silence on Jeff Garlin's *The Goldbergs* Exit," *Vanity Fair*, March 16, 2022.

208 *he lives with bipolar disorder*: Vanessa Etienne, "Jeff Garlin Reveals He's Living with Bipolar Disorder: 'I'm Doing the Best I Can,'" *People*, September 21, 2022.

209 *"and will return for any subsequent season"*: Email from HBO PR staff, June 27, 2022.

209 *"A story about sexual harassment"*: Glenn Kenny, "An Early, Unsuccessful, Attempt at #MeToo in Hollywood," *Columbia Journalism Review*, January 30, 2019.

209 *"why the arts and entertainment press"*: Erin Keane, *Runaway: Notes on the Myths That Made Me* (Cleveland: Belt Publishing, 2022), 14.

210 *regretted not going to the police*: James Andrew Miller, *Tinderbox: HBO's Ruthless Pursuit of New Frontiers* (New York: Henry Holt and Company, 2021), 149.

210 *"white male grabbing a white female"*: Felix Gillette and John Koblin, *It's Not TV: The Spectacular Rise, Revolution, and Future of HBO* (New York: Viking, 2022), 194.

210 *He had no issues with alcohol*: Amy Wallace, "Violence, Nudity, Adult Content: The Story of Chris Albrecht," *GQ*, November 5, 2010.

210 *"no one got hurt"*: Wallace, "Violence, Nudity, Adult Content."

210 *"loud thump"*: Gillette and Koblin, *It's Not TV*, 57.

210 *"Chris Albrecht's lies about me"*: Wallace, "Violence, Nudity, Adult Content."

210 *Albrecht made a great deal of money*: David Lieberman, "Starz CEO Chris Albrecht Made $12.9M in 2012, +132%," *Deadline*, April 26, 2013.

211 *powerful executive roles*: Tim Baysinger, "Chris Albrecht Takes Over Legendary TV as Studio Combines Domestic and International," The Wrap, February 4, 2021.

211 *"belittling—even destructive"*: Wallace, "Violence, Nudity, Adult Content."

211 *"We had nudity throughout the show"*: Miller, *Tinderbox*, 98.

211 *"it didn't have any nudity"*: Gillette and Koblin, *It's Not TV*, 50.

211 *"we have breasts in the script"*: Gillette and Koblin, *It's Not TV*, 51.

211 *Overall, there was a "frat house"*: Miller, *Tinderbox*, 117.

211 *"I was never involved with Michael"*: Miller, *Tinderbox*, 81.

211 *"there was one fucking shooting star"*: Miller, *Tinderbox*, 243.

212 *"For women, Michael was not easy"*: Miller, *Tinderbox*, 230.

212 *to an "absurd" degree*: Miller, *Tinderbox*, 316.

212 *"we would go to research meetings"*: Gillette and Koblin, *It's Not TV*, 54.

212 *"If Carolyn was a man"*: Miller, *Tinderbox*, 569.

212 *all of whom advocated*: Gillette and Koblin, *It's Not TV*, 223–25.

212 *"I was never able"*: Miller, *Tinderbox*, 715.

213 *"didn't ruin my life"*: Miller, *Tinderbox*, 402.

213 *"he wasn't Trump"*: Miller, *Tinderbox*, 525.

214 *"in an apparent fit of jealous rage"*: Gillette and Koblin, *It's Not TV*, 57. Albrecht's lawyer told the authors of *It's Not TV* that Albrecht "rejects and disagrees" with the characterization of the encounter in the book.

214 *"differences of opinion"*: Gillette and Koblin, *It's Not TV*, 58

215 *"It's almost as if the stigma"*: Gillette and Koblin, *It's Not TV*, 198–99.

215 *one of his daughters*: Chris Gardner, "Starz CEO's Daughter Skewers Dad's Former Marriage to 25-Year-Old: 'I Used to Babysit My Stepmom,'" *The Hollywood Reporter*, July 17, 2015.

215 *"boys' club"*: Miller, *Tinderbox*, 231.

215 *"were depicted on screen"*: Gillette and Koblin, *It's Not TV*, 244–45.

215 *"on leave"*: Lesley Goldberg, "Chris Albrecht Placed on Leave at Legendary," *The Hollywood Reporter*, October 10, 2022.

216 *"HBO had already helped"*: Gillette and Koblin, *It's Not TV*, 196.

216 *"CBS and its senior leadership knew"*: Meg James and Richard Winton, "CBS, LAPD Captain Led Cover-Up of Sexual Assault Report Against Moonves, AG Says," *Los Angeles Times*, November 2, 2022.

216 *"said the action constituted"*: Rebecca Robbins and Benjamin Mullin, "Les Moonves and Paramount to Pay $9.75 Million in State Case Tied to Sexual Misconduct," *New York Times*, November 2, 2022.

216 *"to fuck" her*: Maureen Ryan, "Brad Kern and the House That Moonves Built at CBS," *Vulture*, August 3, 2018. In that story, CBS denied that Moonves made the remark.

217 *professional ascent*: Gillette and Koblin, *It's Not TV*, 195.

217 *"salary to shower her with luxury gifts"*: Gillette and Koblin, *It's Not TV*, 197.

218 *Albrecht departing his Legendary job*: Scott Mendelson, "Chris Albrecht to Exit Legendary TV as President," The Wrap, December 23, 2022.

218 *"I would believe every"*: Miller, *Tinderbox*, 598.

218 *"It threw me for a loop"*: Interview with Evan Rachel Wood, January 2022.

220 *"how successful Number Ones act"*: Interview with Perrineau.

220 *"There are many different ways"*: Interview with Daniel Dae Kim, April 2022.

Chapter 10: Live from New York

221 *"My control top pantyhose"*: Interview with Jane Doe, January 2022.

221 are *"categorically false"*: Laura Bradley, "Tina Fey, Seth Meyers Among *SNL* Alums Who Allegedly Witnessed Horatio Sanz Assault Teen Fan," Daily Beast, June 10, 2022.

222 *"A Prosperous* Saturday Night *Grows Tame"*: John J. O'Connor, "Television View: A Prosperous *Saturday Night* Grows Tame," *New York Times*, March 14, 1993.

224 *"It's very hard"*: Maureen Ryan, "Live from New York: *Saturday Night Live*, Sarah Palin and Creating Those Watercooler Moments," *Chicago Tribune*, October 18, 2008.

225 *"Toronto in the 1950's was"*: Rick Marin, "The Most Entertaining Americans? Canadians," *New York Times*, June 27, 1993.

225 *"It's a one-week performance camp"*: James Andrew Miller and Tom Shales, *Live from New York: The Complete Uncensored History of "Saturday Night Live" as Told by Its Stars, Writers, and Guests* (New York: Back Bay Books, 2015), 402.

226 *"I think in exactly the same way"*: Jesse David Fox, "Live from New York Once Again: Lorne Michaels Reveals Everything About *SNL*'s 46th Season, Including the Show's New Biden," *Vulture*, September 16, 2020.

227 *"a lot of people have this mindset"*: Interview with Seth Simons, May 2022.

227 *improv mainstay The Second City*: Melena Ryzik and Jake Malooley, "Second City Is Trying Not to Be Racist. Will It Work This Time?," *New York Times*, August 12, 2020.

227 *numerous allegations of harassment*: Stephanie Marin, "Judge Authorizes Class-Action Sex Harassment Lawsuit Against Just for Laughs Former Head Gilbert Rozon," *Toronto Globe and Mail*, May 22, 2018.

227 *and sexual assault*: Stephanie Marin, "Just for Laughs Founder Gilbert Rozon's Sex-Assault Trial Begins in Montreal," *Toronto Globe and Mail*, October 13, 2020.

227 *in one case*: Canadian Press, "Just for Laughs Founder Gilbert Rozon Found Not Guilty of Rape and Indecent Assault," *Toronto Globe and Mail*, December 15, 2020.

227 *"brutally raped"*: Canadian Press, "Quebec Entertainment Mogul Gilbert Rozon Faces Civil Suit over Alleged Sexual Assault," *Toronto Globe and Mail*, April 15, 2021.

227 *comedy is "a bellwether"*: "Quotation of the Day: Political Satirist Stewart Wins the Twain Prize for Humor," *New York Times*, April 25, 2022.

228 *"how bad things are going to get"*: Interview with Simons.

228 *"comedy is a safe space for abuse"*: Seth Simons, "Comedy Is a Safe Space for Abuse," *Humorism*, August 7, 2021.

228 *inflammatory right-wing figures*: Seth Simons, "'You Can't Bury Your Head in the Sand': Why Right-Wing Comedy Matters," *Humorism*, June 10, 2022.

229 *"not an ideal situation"*: Kerry Coddett, "The Real Problem with *SNL* and Casting Black Women," *The Atlantic*, November 8, 2013.

229 *"Fuck the #MeToo movement!"*: Sara Wren (@SaraWrenComedy), "I remember when Louis CK came back to the comedy scene because I was in the green room

preparing to go on stage meanwhile the all-male line up (I was the only female on the show) was chanting, "FUCK THE #METOO MOVEMENT!!" I left to cry and quickly wash my face before performing," Twitter, April 3, 2022.

229   *"There has been zero change"*: Elizabeth Wagmeister, "Louis C.K. Sexual Harassment Accuser Slams Grammy Win: 'Nobody Cares. That's the Message This Sends,'" *Variety*, April 12, 2022.

230   *"There's no black writers on the show"*: Chris Smith, "Comedy Isn't Funny," *New York*, March 13, 1995.

230   *"My heart was racing"*: Colin Jost, *A Very Punchable Face* (New York: Crown, 2020), 107.

231   *"You've shown him your weakness"*: Miller and Shales, *Live from New York*, 719.

231   *"like an adult"*: Miller and Shales, *Live from New York*, 706.

231   *"I was a mess"*: Miller and Shales, *Live from New York*, 469.

231   *"I had no idea"*: Miller and Shales, *Live from New York*, 467.

231   *"Instantly people respect you"*: Miller and Shales, *Live from New York*, 655.

233   *"insulted everybody"*: Max Read, "He's Not Chevy, He's an Asshole: A History of Chevy Chase's Horrific Behavior," *Gawker*, April 5, 2012.

233   *"really furious"*: Miller and Shales, *Live from New York*, 297.

233   *"he made some reference like"*: Miller and Shales, *Live from New York*, 474.

233   *"There's no word for when you castrate"*: Smith, "Comedy Isn't Funny."

233   *"my last year"*: Miller and Shales, *Live from New York*, 408.

233   *"I found being a writer"*: Miller and Shales, *Live from New York*, 321.

233   *"I mean, the whole thing was weird"*: Miller and Shales, *Live from New York*, 725.

233   *"displeasure at the absence of black women"*: Miller and Shales, *Live from New York*, 680.

233   *"I got hired because"*: Miller and Shales, *Live from New York*, 378.

234   *"I don't think it's meant"*: Sam Sanders, "*SNL* Wasn't a Good Fit for Natasha Rothwell. Now on *Insecure*, She's Anything But," September 25, 2018, in *It's Been a Minute*, produced by Brent Baugham, podcast.

234   *only one of the show's twenty-three writers*: Coddett, "The Real Problem with *SNL* and Casting Black Women."

234   *"in four decades"*: Jason Zinoman, "For *SNL* Cast, Being Diverse May Be Better Than Being 'Ready,'" *New York Times*, October 29, 2013.

234   *"because she resented routinely"*: Mary Schmich, "The Short Struggle of Danitra Vance," *Chicago Tribune*, August 27, 1994.

234   *in eighteen years*: Amy B. Wang, "Awkwafina Hosted *SNL* 18 Years After Lucy Liu. Their Monologues Show How Times Have Changed," *Washington Post*, October 7, 2018.

234   *stats compiled by* IndieWire: Mark Lieberman, "*Saturday Night Live:* More than 90 Percent of Hosts Are White—Why These Numbers Need to Change," *IndieWire*, May 20, 2016.

234   *"Because it lacked Asian cast members"*: Nancy Coleman, "*SNL* Has Long Lacked Asian Players. One Just Joined the Cast," *New York Times*, September 12, 2019.

234   *"SNL doesn't have a strong record"*: Lieberman, "*Saturday Night Live.*"

235   *Vance was not out*: Will Harris, "It's Time for *SNL* Alum Danitra Vance to Get Her Due," *Vulture*, November 15, 2018.

235   *"it wasn't safe"*: Andy Hoglund, "Denny Dillon Reflects on *Saturday Night Live*'s Infamous 6th Season," *Vulture*, August 12, 2020.

235   *"We were on the show"*: Kera Bolonik, "Nora Dunn: '*SNL* Is a Traumatic Experience. It's Something You Have to Survive,'" Salon, April 7, 2015.

235 *the arrivals of Kate McKinnon:* Rachel Shatto, "A Brief History of LGBTQ+ Firsts on *Saturday Night Live*," *The Advocate* (no date given).

235 *"a traumatic experience":* Bolonik, "Nora Dunn."

235 *"Women are hard to write for":* Eve Kahn, "Women in the Locker Room at *Saturday Night Live*," *New York Times,* February 16, 1992.

235 *"subject matters can be handled":* Bolonik, "Nora Dunn."

236 *"sadly humorless":* Jeremy Gerard, "Comic Is Protested as *Saturday Night* Host," *New York Times,* May 11, 1990.

236 *"Due to the recent derogatory statements":* Cynthia Littleton, "NBC Cutting Ties to Donald Trump over 'Derogatory' Remarks About Immigrants," *Variety,* June 29, 2015.

236 *"weak, timid or predictable":* Maureen Ryan, "Donald Trump on *Saturday Night Live*: Not Hugely Entertaining," *Variety,* November 7, 2015.

237 *"Lorne would not have":* Jost, *A Very Punchable Face,* 185–90.

237 *"When Seth Meyers left":* Megh Wright, "Taran Killam Says *SNL* Became 'Less of a Happy Place' After Seth Meyers Left," *Vulture,* October 10, 2018.

238 *"What makes SNL so important":* Seth Simons, "Just A Quick Reminder That *SNL* Is Paying Its Audience to Be There," *Humorism,* February 27, 2021.

238 *"observed all safety protocols":* Seth Simons, "How Safe Is *SNL*'s Audience?," *Humorism,* October 7, 2020.

238 *"Laughs are the clear indicator":* Jesse David Fox, "Live from New York Once Again," *Vulture,* September 16, 2020.

239 *"Lorne was sick, coughing":* Heran Mamo, "Billie Eilish Recalls Horrific COVID-19 Experience: 'If I Weren't Vaccinated, I Would Have Died,'" *Billboard,* December 13, 2021.

239 *"tested positive for coronavirus":* Eric Hegedus, Eileen Reslen, Sara Nathan, and Steven Vago, "*SNL* COVID-19 Outbreak Cancels Paul Rudd Live Audience, Charli XCX Out," *New York Post,* December 18, 2021.

239 *within a "treacherous" culture:* Katie Warren, "Young Female *SNL* Staffers Say They Were Treated Like 'a Joke,' with Sexual Advances, Babysitting Requests, and an Unsolicited Nude Photo," *Business Insider,* May 23, 2022.

240 *"For someone so concerned":* Smith, "Comedy Isn't Funny."

240 *"We're a comedy show":* Dan Zak, "Lorne Michaels Still Lives for Saturday Night," *Washington Post,* November 29, 2021.

240 *"Horatio certainly is the main character":* Laura Bradley, "Horatio Sanz's Sexual-Assault Accuser Speaks Out: 'He Abused Me All over *SNL*,'" Daily Beast, February 17, 2022.

240 *"It was me and some adults":* Interview with Doe.

241 *NBC employee's email account:* Bradley, "Horatio Sanz's Sexual-Assault Accuser Speaks Out."

241 *"Jimmy Fallon introduced me to Lorne":* Interview with Doe.

241 *hosted by Tracy Morgan:* Seth Simons, "A Look Back at Tracy Morgan's *SNL* Sex Parties," *Humorism,* November 18, 2021.

241 *"on his guest list":* Supreme Court of the State of New York, County of New York, Summons, *Jane Doe v. NBCUniversal Media LLC & SNL Studios & Horatio Sanz & John & Jane Smith 1–20,* Index No. 951302/2021, Received NYSCEF August 12, 2021.

242 *saw Sanz assaulting her:* Seth Simons, "Tina Fey, Will Ferrell, and Seth Meyers Witnessed Horatio Sanz Grope Jane Doe, New Filing Alleges," *Humorism,* June 8, 2022.

242 *"did not respond"*: Laura Bradley, "Tina Fey, Seth Meyers Among *SNL* Alums Who Allegedly Witnessed Horatio Sanz Assault Teen Fan," Daily Beast, June 10, 2022.

242 *"that it's hard for the survivor"*: Interview with Doe.

243 *her allegations were "meritless"*: Bradley, "Tina Fey, Seth Meyers Among *SNL* Alums."

243 *to be dismissed:* Supreme Court of the State of New York, County of New York, Memorandum of Law in Support of Defendant NBCUniversal Media's Motion to Dismiss, *Jane Doe v. NBCUniversal Media LLC & SNL Studios & Horatio Sanz & John & Jane Smith 1–20*, Index No. 951302/2021, Received NYSCEF April 1, 2022.

243 *in news coverage of this development:* Tim Stelloh, "Lawsuit Accusing Former *SNL* Star Horatio Sanz of Grooming, Assaulting Teen Is Dismissed," NBC News, November 30, 2022.

Chapter 11: The Path Forward

251 *"people were looking for"*: Interview with Rabbi Danya Ruttenberg, April 2022.

251 *"from people who have been hurt"*: Danya Ruttenberg, *On Repentance and Repair: Making Amends in an Unapologetic World* (Boston: Beacon Press, 2022), 15.

252 *"So many people talk to me"*: Interview with Kyra Jones, April 2022.

252 *"crisp" and specific descriptions:* Interview with Ruttenberg.

252 *"we must not be too generous"*: Ruttenberg, *On Repentance and Repair,* 16.

254 *masturbating in front of multiple women:* Melena Ryzik, Cara Buckley, and Jodi Kantor, "Louis C.K. Is Accused by 5 Women of Sexual Misconduct," *New York Times,* November 9, 2017.

254 *"said they understood from their managers"*: Ryzik, Buckley, and Kantor, "Louis C.K. Is Accused by 5 Women."

254 *did not have consent:* Julia Wolov, "Counterpoint: I Didn't Consent to Louis C.K. Masturbating in Front of Me," *Canadian Jewish News,* November 19, 2019.

255 *"downplayed his own sexual misconduct"*: Elizabeth Wagmeister, "Louis C.K. Sexual Harassment Accuser Slams Grammy Win: 'Nobody Cares. That's the Message This Sends,'" *Variety,* April 12, 2022.

255 *"The feminist pretender thing"*: Interview with Ruttenberg.

257 *"They're like 'Well that person'"*: Interview with Jones.

258 *"Even though they've finished"*: Interview with Dr. Richard "Bo" Travis, June 2022.

261 *"The narcissist's need and demand"*: Kristin Neff, *Self-Compassion: The Proven Power of Being Kind to Yourself* (New York: William Morrow, 2011), 144.

261 *"All [extreme] narcissists care about"*: Barbara O'Dair, "How to Spot a Narcissist," *Health,* May 2021.

261 *experts say is rare:* O'Dair, "How to Spot a Narcissist."

261 *"They can't see it at first"*: Interview with Travis.

261 *"not play" their game:* O'Dair, "How to Spot a Narcissist."

263 *"We devolve to the individual"*: Jeremy Scahill, "Hope Is a Discipline: Mariame Kaba on Dismantling the Carceral State," *The Intercept,* March 17, 2021.

265 *"did not suddenly become less prone"*: Anne Helen Petersen, *Scandals of Classic Hollywood: Sex, Deviance, and Drama from the Golden Age of American Cinema* (New York: Plume, 2014), 2–3.

265 *starting in 2005:* Chris Francescani and Luchina Fisher, "Bill Cosby: Timeline of

His Fall from 'America's Dad' to His Release from Prison," ABC News, June 30, 2021.

265 *NBC in 2014:* Nellie Andreeva, "TCA: NBC's Bill Cosby Comedy to Be Created by Mike Sikowitz, Mike O'Malley, Who May Co-Star, Coming Summer or Fall 2015," *Deadline,* July 13, 2014.

265 *"How many decades did it take":* Interview with Jones.

266 *"1,000 sexual assaults":* "The Criminal Justice System: Statistics," Sexual Violence section, rainn.org/statistics.

267 *"compassion without boundaries":* Caroline (@Spacecrone), "i was (and am!) willing to believe that people can learn, change, and grow, and don't believe in lost causes but compassion without boundaries and accountability is a form of enabling," Twitter, September 13, 2017.

Chapter 12: A New Day for the Death Star

271 *70 percent of respondents to a Women in Film survey:* Mia Galuppo, "#MeToo, 5 Years Later: Survey Reports Employees Still Experiencing Abuse, Harassment in Hollywood," *The Hollywood Reporter,* October 5, 2022.

274 *a 2022* Rolling Stone *article:* Cheyenne Roundtree, "'He Needs to Be Stopped': Sources Say Cary Fukunaga 'Abused His Power' to Pursue Young Women on Set," *Rolling Stone,* May 31, 2022.

275 *"It has been a very complicated process":* Interview with David Nevins, July 2022.

275 *"There's more education":* Interview with Mike Royce, November 2021.

275 *"What's difficult about this":* Interview with John Landgraf, January 2022.

277 *Al Capone Theory of Sexual Harassment:* Valerie Aurora and Leigh Honeywell, "The Al Capone Theory of Sexual Harassment Can Help Silicon Valley Stop Hiring Horrible People," *Quartz,* August 2, 2017.

278 *"Any serial perpetrator":* "FAQ," Callisto, www.projectcallisto.org/faqs.

279 *"the highest revenues in the 99-year history":* Josef Adalian, "The Future of Streaming According to Jason Kilar," *Vulture,* April 12, 2022.

279 *VIA "has helped hundreds":* "About Us," Voices in Action, voicesinaction.org/learn-more-about-voices-in-action/.

279 *"to support the women assaulted":* "Show Support for the Women Assaulted by Attending Trial Dates," *Voices in Action* (blog post), October 27, 2022.

279 *"The organization was riven by disputes":* Michael Scherer, "Time's Up Group to 'Completely Rebuild' After Criticism for Its Role in Andrew M. Cuomo Sexual Harassment Accusations," *Washington Post,* November 19, 2021.

280 *"there were times in the past":* Interview with Lesli Linka Glatter, July 2022.

280 *supplies "resources and support":* "Help Line," Women in Film, womeninfilm.org/help/.

280 *"I think it depends":* Interview with Glatter.

280 *"We believe in the value of diverse":* "Values," Hollywood Commission, www.hollywoodcommission.org/values.

281 *"People feel there is a lack":* Kim Masters, "Anita Hill–Led Hollywood Commission to Launch Harassment Reporting Platform," *The Hollywood Reporter,* September 29, 2020.

282 *"prioritizing getting it right":* Written statement from the Hollywood Commission, July 21, 2022.

283 *"It's hard to think of many industries":* Interview with Landgraf.

283 *"It's not like it's rocket science":* Interview with Meredith Stiehm, May 2022.

284 *"We promote people into management":* Anne Helen Petersen, "How to Actually Build a Better Boss," *Culture Study,* October 13, 2021.

285 *began its own training program:* Lesley Goldberg, "Sony TV Launches Showrunner Training Program," *The Hollywood Reporter,* October 26, 2021.

286 *"The findings have shown":* Interview with Martha Lauzen, September 2021.

286 *with "snowcapped" structures:* Mistinguette Smith, "Nonprofit Leadership at a Crossroads," *Nonprofit Quarterly,* September 17, 2019.

286 *"In mid-century America, corporations":* Judd Legum and Tesnim Zekeria, "Starbucks versus Gen Z," *Popular Information,* June 15, 2022.

287 *Pay Up Hollywood's 2021 survey of entry-level workers:* "Surveys," Pay Up Hollywood, www.payuphollywood.com/.

287 *co-CEO Reed Hastings made $34 million:* Todd Spangler, "Netflix's Ted Sarandos to Earn $40 Million in 2022, Reed Hastings Pay to Top $34 Million," *Variety,* December 21, 2021.

287 *"A lot of showrunners":* Joy Press, "Netflix Stumbles and Hollywood Gloats: 'The Days of the Blank Check Are Over,'" *Vanity Fair,* May 12, 2022.

287 *"We took this idea":* Interview with Liz Hsiao Lan Alper, May 2022.

289 *"relentless sexual harassment":* Eliza Dushku, "I Worked at CBS. I Didn't Want to Be Sexually Harasssed. I Was Fired," *Boston Globe,* December 19, 2018.

289 *settled with CBS for $9.5 million:* Rachel Abrams and John Koblin, "CBS Paid the Actress Eliza Dushku $9.5 Million to Settle Harassment Claims," *New York Times,* December 13, 2018.

289 *noted that the "leadership coaching":* Dominic Patten, "*Bull* Star Micheal Weatherly & Showrunner in 'Leadership Training' Following Harassment Payout–TCA," *Deadline,* August 1, 2019.

289 *overall deal had been canceled:* Maureen Ryan, "CBS Drops *Bull* Showrunner Following Workplace Investigation," *The Hollywood Reporter,* May 21, 2021.

289 *turmoil at All Rise:* Nicole Sperling, "Writers Mutiny at *All Rise,* the Rare CBS Show with a Black Female Lead," *New York Times,* August 20, 2020.

289 *to bring up anything to HR:* Maureen Ryan, "'He Made Their Lives Miserable': How the Showrunner of a Popular Courtroom Drama Finally Got Fired," *Salon,* May 12, 2021.

290 *"there's no substitute":* Interview with Landgraf.

290 *"In over thirty years working":* Nell Scovell, "For Hollywood, It's Mueller Time," *Variety,* November 6, 2017.

290 *"If you're going to hide behind":* Interview with Evan Rachel Wood, January 2022.

291 *"largely frozen out":* Elizabeth Wagmeister, "After Weinstein Retaliation, Sarah Ann Masse Is Urging Hollywood to Work with Sexual Harassment Survivors," *Variety,* December 21, 2021.

291 *"afraid and intimidated":* Ronan Farrow, "From Aggressive Overtures to Sexual Assault: Harvey Weinstein's Accusers Tell Their Stories," *The New Yorker,* October 10, 2017.

291 *"Obviously, I knew that Harvey":* Julie Miller, "Mira Sorvino Is Ready for Her Next Act," *Vanity Fair,* November 9, 2021.

292 *"incidents of harassment, aggression":* Marti Noxon with Kater Gordon, "Marti Noxon: How the TV Industry Can Better Protect Writers from the Next Toxic Showrunner," *The Hollywood Reporter,* July 29, 2020.

292 *"behavior rehab":* Interview with Melinda Hsu Taylor, October 2021.

293 *"All sets are majority male":* Interview with Wood.

293 *"If you have a chemical plant"*: Interview with Landgraf.

294 *"When I was starting out"*: Lulu Wang (@thumbelulu), "When I was starting out, I worked on a major studio production where at least 250k was hidden in the budget to pay off women who might 'claim' sexual harassment against the director. I think about this a lot. You should too, whenever they tell u you're 'asking for too much,'" Twitter, June 25, 2021.

294 *"I personally was conditioned"*: Nicholas Rice, "Juliette Lewis Shares Dark Side of Acting While Supporting IATSE Strike: 'Overworked and Exhausted,'" *People*, October 16, 2021.

295 *"If you want loyal workers"*: Ed Zitron, "You Can't Beat a Bad Workplace with Therapy," *Ed Zitron's Where's Your Ed At*, April 27, 2022.

Chapter 13: The Sun King Is Dead

298 *"have a responsibility of creating safety"*: Liz Shannon Miller, "Claudia Black on Her Surprise *The Nevers* Role, the Joss Whedon Situation, and Breaking the Cycles of Trauma," *Collider*, May 22, 2021.

298 *"this industry can turn anyone"*: Interview with Noga Landau, October 2021.

299 *"aim is to assist leaders"*: "Bio: Birgit Zacher Hanson," Heads-Up Performance, headsupperformance.com/birgit-zacher-hanson/.

300 *"At thirty-one, I absolutely wouldn't"*: Interview with Samuel Laskey, September 2021.

301 *"your job is to lead and teach"*: Javier Grillo-Marxuach, "The Eleven Laws of Showrunning (The Nice Version)," January 20, 2016, okbjgm.weebly.com/essays.html.

302 *"A big takeaway for me of studying"*: Cassie Werber, "The Real Reason Toxic Leaders Keep Getting Promoted," *Quartz*, June 9, 2022.

303 *"This is a difficult task"*: Grillo-Marxuach, "Eleven Laws."

304 *"This grief people feel"*: Interview with Tananarive Due, February 2022.

304 *"That's the showrunner's job"*: Panel conversation with Judy Reyes, ATX TV Festival, Austin, Texas, June 5, 2022.

305 *"My philosophy as a showrunner is"*: Interview with Joe Henderson, January 2022.

305 *"Sometimes I think we're in danger"*: Interview with Daniel Dae Kim, April 2022.

306 *"personal touchstones"*: Email forwarded by Melinda Hsu Taylor, February 21, 2022.

308 *"born out of pain"*: Interview with Lesli Linka Glatter, July 2022.

308 *"We do it on most of my projects"*: Paul Feig (@PaulFeig), "Two words: French hours. We do it on most of my projects. 10 hour days with no lunch break but food constantly circulating on set. Hard out at the end of 10 hours. People drive home awake and see their families. I am working to let this become an option for all US productions," Twitter, March 15, 2018.

309 *"On the last project I did"*: Interview with Glatter.

309 *"paltry compared to what we should be doing"*: Interview with Aline Brosh McKenna, November 2022.

310 *"Visions of a utopian"*: Jac Schaeffer, "*WandaVision* Writer Jac Schaeffer: How I 'Created My Fantasy' Writers Room," *The Hollywood Reporter*, August 9, 2021.

310 *"You can work normal hours"*: Dan Rutstein and Noah Evslin, "Take 20: Showrunner Joe Henderson, *White Collar, Lucifer*," April 15, 2021, in *Screaming into the Hollywood Abyss*, podcast.

311   *"Nobody knows how to do my hair"*: Interview with Melinda Hsu Taylor, October 2021.

311   *"It was the most creatively fulfilling job"*: Interview with Shernold Edwards, February 2022.

313   *"What became clear to me"*: Interview with Glatter.

315   *"I have learned even"*: Interview with Kyra Jones, April 2022.

Chapter 14: Mad as Hell and Not Going to Take It Anymore

318   *"misogynistic attack"*: Eriq Gardner, "Disney Makes First Move in Scarlett Johansson's *Black Widow* Suit," *The Hollywood Reporter*, August 21, 2021.

319   *"The hope for a more equitable"*: Adam Serwer, "The Amazon Union Exposes the Emptiness of 'Woke Capital,'" *The Atlantic*, April 14, 2022.

319   *"Unpredictable hours are bad for marriages"*: Shirley Li, "The People Who Make Your Favorite Movies and Shows Are Fed Up," *The Atlantic*, October 8, 2021.

320   they *"pushed the economy"*: Kim Kelly, *Fight Like Hell: The Untold History of American Labor* (New York: One Signal Publishers/Atria Press, 2022), xxvi.

321   *"The streamers keep trying"*: Lila Byock (@LByock), "The streamers keep trying to reinstate the linear tv model without reinstating the compensation that linear tv creators used to earn," Twitter, October 13, 2022.

321   *"union critics of the DGA"*: Richard W. Hurd, Professor of Labor Studies Emeritus, Cornell University, "Reflections on Hollywood Collective Bargaining," presented at the United Association for Labor Education Annual Conference, New Orleans, Louisiana, March 24, 2011.

321   *"Nobody, as we see now"*: Joy Press, "Fran Drescher, Newly Elected President of SAG-AFTRA, Is Thinking Big," *Vanity Fair*, January 26, 2022.

321   could *"slide backwards"*: Interview with Glatter.

322   there are about 13,000 people: Email from WGA West spokesperson, December 29, 2022.

322   *"Young was widely credited"*: Dave McNary, "WGA West Exec Director David Young Signs Four-Year Extension," *Variety*, June 1, 2018.

323   *"fucking evil"*: Jordan Crucchiola, "The Hollywood Fight That's Tearing Apart Writers and Agents, Explained," *Vulture*, April 18, 2019.

323   *"The downward pressure on income"*: Gene Maddaus, "Meredith Stiehm Elected President of WGA West," *Variety*, September 21, 2021.

323   *"We're kind of working under"*: Interview with Meredith Stiehm, May 2022.

324   *"No porn at work"*: "WGAW Community Standards," www.wga.org/members/membership-information/wgaw-community-standards.

324   *"the employers are the enforcers"*: Interview with Stiehm.

324   including in a 2018 column: Maureen Ryan, "Hollywood's #MeToo Crisis Won't Subside Until the Industry Is Rebuilt," *The Hollywood Reporter*, November 30, 2018.

325   *"the huge difference in the agency"*: Interview with Stiehm.

326   *"Costume and makeup aside"*: Li, "The People Who Make Your Favorite Movies."

326   *"long been an issue for screenwriters"*: "Statement by Robert H. Wolfe," WGA West Candidates, 2022, www.wga.org/news-events/news/press/writers-guild-of-america-west-announces-final-candidates-for-2022-board-of-directors-election.

326   *"known for its horrible working conditions"*: Li, "The People Who Make Your Favorite Movies."

326   *"One of the big myths":* Interview with David Slack, June 2022.

326   *"I knew I had a decision to make":* Interview with Liz Hsiao Lan Alper, May 2022.

328   *"#OscarsSoWhite they asked to touch my hair":* April Reign (@ReignofApril), "#OscarsSoWhite they asked to touch my hair. *sad face emoji,*" Twitter, January 15, 2015.

328   *once again all white:* Rebecca Keegan and Steven Zeitchik, "Oscars 2016: Here's Why the Nominees Are So White—Again," *Los Angeles Times,* January 14, 2016.

328   *a major acting award:* Krystie Lee Yandoli, "The 2020 Oscar Nominations Are, Yet Again, So White and Barely Include People of Color," BuzzFeed, January 13, 2020.

328   *"a wider breadth of actors and filmmakers":* Imaan Yousuf, "What Is the Significance of the #OscarsSoWhite Hashtag?," Brittanica.com.

328   *"still refuse[s] to recognize":* Disney Must Pay Task Force, "Open Letter to Disney," WritersMustBePaid.org.

330   *"These are large corporations":* Interview with Sarah Rodman, March 2022.

330   *"Economically, newsrooms have been hemorrhaging":* "Survivors' Stories," moderated by Maureen Ryan, featuring Ronan Farrow, Amy Berg, Fenton Bailey, and Randy Barbato, HBO FYC site for Television Academy members, April 6, 2022.

332   *"I'm the ultimate pragmatist":* Interview with Monica Owusu-Breen, June 2022.

333   *"There's a word for this":* Justice Namaste and Sarah Scoles, "A Conversation About Race and Gender in Andy Weir's *Artemis,*" *Wired,* November 22, 2017.

334   *"There might be a special episode":* Interview with Jeff Yang, August 2020.

334   *"Why would you send out":* Interview with Orlando Jones, March 2022.

335   *"There is no hierarchy of oppression":* Tressie McMillan Cottom, "What a MacArthur Foundation 'Genius Grant' Gave Me," *New York Times,* October 12, 2022.

335   *"After being told to see things a certain way":* E. Alex Jung, "It Took Sandra Oh 30 Years to Get to *Killing Eve,*" *Vulture,* April 9, 2018.

335   *"And so typically, actors of color think":* Ayomikun Adekaiyero, "*Bridgerton* Star Adjoa Andoh Spoke Up About 'Color-Blind' Auditions: 'I Delight in My Race,'" *Insider,* November 3, 2022.

336   *"The first is the pervasive":* Email from Alice Wong, October 22, 2022.

339   *"I imagine it's satisfying":* Fonda Lee, "Twitter Is the Worst Reader," Medium, November 3, 2021.

Chapter 15: To Be Continued

344   *"he displayed egregiously misogynistic and inappropriate behavior":* Samuel Braslow and Kim Masters, "'Hiding in Plain Sight': After Being Fired from *Scrubs* for Misconduct, Alleged Rapist Eric Weinberg Kept Working," *The Hollywood Reporter,* November 14, 2022.

344   *"dozens of possible victims have contacted law enforcement":* Stella Chan, "Eric Weinberg, 'Scrubs' Producer, Charged with Multiple Counts of Sexual Assault, DA Announces," CNN, October 6, 2022.

344   *"I will never feel comfortable":* Tressie McMillan Cottom, "Through THICK and Thin," The First and 15th newsletter, January 9, 2019.

345   *"My child, the very next day":* Interview with Evan Rachel Wood, January 2022.

345   *efforts by the Consent Awareness Network:* Joyce Short, "Propelled by California's Mixed Verdict, Weinstein and Cosby Survivors Unite Behind CAN's Efforts to Make 'Consent' a Civil Right Backed by Law," PR Web, December 27, 2022.

345 *the battle to alter military law:* Joyce Short, "Driven by Consent Advocates, Andrea Constand and Joyce Short, House Passes Breakthrough Amendment to Define 'Consent' in US Military Law," PR Web, August 4, 2022.

346 *"If the Cosby survivors had not spoken out":* Interview with Stacey Pinkerton, February 2022.

347 *"By ridding a forest of dead leaves":* National Geographic Society, "Controlled Burning: Controlled Burns Are an Important Tool for Maintaining the Health and Safety of a Forest," Resource Library, National Geographic, May 20, 2022, education.nationalgeographic.org/resource/controlled-burning.

Index